Logical Form

Generative Syntax
General Editor: David Lightfoot

Recent work in generative syntax has viewed the language faculty as a system of principles and parameters, which permit children to acquire productive grammars triggered by normal childhood experiences. The books in this series serve as an introduction to particular aspects or modules of this theory. They presuppose some minimal background in generative syntax, but will meet the tutorial needs of intermediate and advanced students. Written by leading figures in the field, the books will also contain sufficient fresh material to appeal at the highest level.

Logical Form
From GB to Minimalism

Norbert Hornstein

BLACKWELL
Oxford UK & Cambridge USA

First published 1995

Reprinted 1996 (twice)

Blackwell Publishers Inc.
238 Main Street
Cambridge, Massachusetts 02142, USA

Blackwell Publishers Ltd
108 Cowley Road
Oxford OX4 1JF, UK

Library of Congress Cataloging in Publication Data
Hornstein, Norbert.
Logical form: from GB to minimalism/Norbert Hornstein.
p.   cm.–(Generative syntax)
Includes bibliographical references and index.
ISBN 0–631–17912–7 — ISBN 0–631–18942–4 (pbk)
1. Grammar, Comparative and general – Syntax. 2. Generative grammar.
I. Title. II Series.
P291.H66   1995   95–49208
415–dc20   CIP

British Library Cataloguing in Publication Data
A CIP catalogue record for this book is available from the British Library

Typeset in 10 on 12pt Palatino
by Graphicraft Typesetters Limited, Hong Kong

Contents

Acknowledgments

They say that it takes a whole village to grow a child. Books are similar. What reaches the page is the product of many minds and hands. Here is the place to thank those without whose generous (if often skeptical) efforts, this book would have remained a series of half-baked one-liners.

Portions of the book were delivered at various institutions including the Jersey Syntax Circle (Rutgers), the University of Pennsylvania, the University of Southern California, the University of Nijmegen, McGill University, Concordia University, ABRALIN (Salvador, Brazil), the Max Planck Institute (Berlin), and the University of Potsdam. I would like to thank the audiences at these various venues for all of their questions and comments.

My home base is the University of Maryland at College Park. My colleagues have been invaluable to me and the institution has been extremely supportive. The final draft was supported by a university scholarship which allowed me the time required to crank out a (more or less) final version. On a more personal level, thanks to Juan Uriagereka, David Lightfoot, Steve Anderson, Amy Weinberg, Jairo Nunes, Ellen Thompson, Cristina Schmitt, and Alan Munn.

Thanks too to my farther-flung colleagues: Joseph Aoun, Audrey Li, Barry Schein, Jean-Roger Vergnaud, Pierre Pica, Tim Stowell, Ian Roberts, Mary Kato, Mike Dillinger, Milton do Nascimento, and Paul Law.

Last of all thanks to those with the editorial know-how: David Lightfoot, Philip Carpenter, Brigitte Lee, Alan Munn, Cristina Schmitt, and Philip Tye.

Abbreviations

A-(movement)	movement to A-positions
ACC	accusative
ACD	antecedent-contained deletion
AFOP	All For One Principle
Agr	agreement
AgrO	object agreement
AgrOP	object agreement phrase
AgrS	subject agreement
AgrSP	subject agreement phrase
ASP	aspect
BP	Brazilian Portuguese
BT	Binding Theory
CED	Constraint on Extraction Domains
CI	Conceptual–Intentional (system)
CIS	clause internal scrambling
CP	complementizer phrase
d-linked	discourse-linked
DOC	double object constructions
DP	determiner phrase
DS	D-structure
ec	empty category
ECM	Exceptional Case Marking
ECP	Empty Category Principle
EE	exception ellipsis
EST	Extended Standard Theory
GB	Government-Binding
HNPS	Heavy NP Shift
IC	Island Condition
IO	indirect object
IP	inflection phrase
LCA	Linear Correspondence Axiom
LDS	long distance scrambling
LF	Logical Form
LGB	Lectures on Government and Binding
L-mark	lexically mark
MBR	Minimal Binding Requirement

MLC	Minimal Link Condition
Neg/neg	negation
NP	noun phrase
NPI	negative polarity item
PA	Perceptual–Articulatory (system)
PERF	perfective
PF	Phonetic Form
PFI	Principle of Full Interpretation
pg	parasitic gap
PG	pseudo gapping
PIO	prepositional indirect object
PP	prepositional phrase
PRED	predication
PRO	pronominal anaphor
pro	null pronoun
Q-adjunction	quantifier adjunction
QNP	quantified noun phrase
QR	quantifier raising
rc	relative clause
REL	relative
REST	Revised Extended Standard Theory
SCO	strong cross over
SP	Scope Principle
Spec	specifier
SS	S-structure
SU	subject
Tns	tense
TP	tense phrase
UG	Universal Grammar
vbl	variable
VP	verb phrase
WCO	weak cross over
WH	WH-expression
WH-R	WH-raising
XP	maximal projection of type X

1

An Introduction

1 The Grammatical Locus of Semantic Interpretation

Few points in the study of language are uncontested. One truism is that sentences are pairings of sounds with meanings. They are phonetically characterizable objects that carry a specific interpretation. Since the earliest days of generative grammar, a central concern of linguistic theory has been to elucidate how it is that a natural language sentence expresses its meaning. In earlier theories of grammar, the locus of interpretation is taken to be Deep Structure, as in (1) (see Chomsky 1965, and Katz and Postal 1964) and the transformational operations that produced Surface Structures were assumed to be meaning preserving in the sense that these operations did not contribute to the grammatical licensing of the interpretive information encoded in the Deep Structure phrase marker.

(1) Deep structure → Semantic interpretation

        Transformations

   Surface structure → Phonetic interpretation

In the 1970s, the Extended Standard Theory (EST) proposed that grammatical levels other than Deep Structure syntactically determine sentence meaning. Jackendoff (1972), for example, argued that (2) specifies how the grammar contributes to meaning. On this conception, different grammatical levels determine different features of sentential interpretation. For example, a sentence's thematic properties are a function of its Deep Structure configuration while relative quantifier scope is related to the structural properties of the Surface Structure phrase marker.

(2) Deep structure → Thematic interpretation

        Transformations → Coreference, scope

   Surface structure → Focus and presupposition

The development of trace theory in the mid 1970s made it possible to treat S-structure (SS) as the sole locus of semantic interpretation.[1] The Revised Extended Standard Theory (REST) postulates that grammatical operations do not reduce the basic grammatical information encoded in a phrase marker. For example, if a verb has an object at D-structure (DS) then it must have one throughout the course of the derivation. REST enforces this requirement by having a moved element leave behind a trace which preserves within the derived phrase marker the structural relations that obtained prior to movement. For example, whereas in EST WH-questions such as (3a) are formed from structures like (3b) yielding phrase markers like (3c), in REST the phrase marker resulting from WH-movement is the one provided in (3d) where t_i marks the position of the moved *what* while the indexing allows the content of this position to be recovered from the coindexed antecedent, i.e. the element that moved.

(3a)   What did Bill buy
(3b)   [Bill [buy what]]
(3c)   [What [Bill buy]]
(3d)   [What$_i$ [Bill [buy t$_i$]]]

Given the information-preserving quality of trace theory, semantic interpretation in REST can largely be driven by properties of the SS phrase marker. In effect, given traces, it seems possible to consolidate all the grammatical information relevant to semantic interpretation at SS. REST pictures the interaction of grammar and meaning as in (4).

(4)

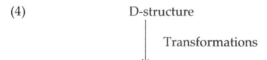

Research in the late 1970s has tended to the conclusion that REST must itself be revised. In particular, it has been argued (and we review these arguments in chapters 2 and 3) that SS cannot adequately bear the interpretive load expected of it. The locus of the grammatical conditions within contemporary Government-Binding (GB) theory is the linguistic level called "LF" (meant to suggest "Logical Form"). (5) depicts how GB conceives the grammar's contribution to semantic interpretation.

(5)

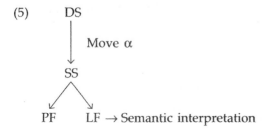

GB organizes the grammar in a "T-model."[2] D-structure phrase markers are related to SS phrase markers by applications of transformations (Move α). As in REST, movement transformations leave behind traces coindexed with their antecedents. The derivation from DS to SS is "overt syntax." It is "overt" in the sense that movement operations result in phonetic gaps at the movement sites.

At SS, the derivation splits into a track leading to PF (meant to suggest "Phonetic Form") where phonological and phonetic information is ultimately encoded and a path leading to LF where interpretive–semantic information is represented. The path from SS to LF is the domain of "covert" syntax. The derivation is syntactic because LF is derived from SS via repeated applications of Move α. However, the syntax is covert because these transformations do not have phonological consequences given the branching organization of the grammar in (5). In a sense, therefore, LF is more abstract than SS as the post SS applications of Move α that are instrumental in deriving LF do not leave phonological tracks.

This book focuses on two different views of LF. The early chapters review the properties of LF within GB theories. The later chapters consider the structure of LF within the Minimalist program. Minimalism, though distinct in many ways from its GB precursor, shares one major commitment with its predecessor. Minimalism adopts a version of the T-model and so endorses the distinction between overt syntactic operations which have phonological effects and covert syntax which does not alter the phonological form of a sentence. Broadly speaking, Minimalism differs from GB theories in not according DS and SS any grammatical significance. In effect, Minimalism postulates only two levels, PF and LF. These two levels alone are legitimate loci of grammatical well-formedness conditions on representations. The effect of this restriction is quite dramatic. It effectively requires that all output conditions (e.g. the theta criterion, subjacency, the case filter, the Binding Theory (BT)) be stated at LF as opposed to being parsed among various levels as is standardly done in GB theories (e.g. subjacency at SS, the theta criterion at DS, the binding theory at SS and LF and case theory at SS). For present purposes, however, it is enough to appreciate that Minimalist theories, like GB predecessors, assume that LF and PF do not directly "converse" and that LF derives from earlier phrase markers via repeated applications of transformations similar to those operative in overt syntax. Chapter 4 details the theoretical commitments and technological devices that drive the Minimalist LF analyses in chapters 5–9.

2   Two Ways of Identifying LF

LF can be characterized in various ways. (6) gives a "content" designation of LF. It provides a specification of LF in terms of the kind of information that the level encodes.

(6)   LF is the level of linguistic representation at which all grammatical structure relevant to semantic interpretation is provided

In terms of (6), an *Aspects* style theory identifies LF with Deep Structure, REST equates LF with SS while EST denies that LF exists, viz. that there is a single level meeting the specification in (6).

Something like (6) is standardly assumed in GB (and Minimalist) characterizations of the LF phrase marker. Thus, both approaches assume that there is a level which encodes all the information grammatically relevant to semantic interpretation. However, this does not yet say very much. To have bite, it is necessary to specify how "semantic interpretation" should be understood. If semantic interpretation is rendered via a truth definition then what LF provides is the syntactic structure appropriate for the recursive application of the clauses of the truth definition. Other views of what semantic interpretation comes to may place different structural requirements on LF. However, in practice, what this content designation amounts to is clear enough. (6) comes down to the claim that various facts that we take to be characteristic of meaning such as relative quantifier scope, scope of negation, modality, opacity, pronoun binding, variable binding, focus and presupposition structure, adverbial modification, and so forth are all "done off" the LF phrase marker. In short, LF provides the requisite compositional structure for the execution of these interpretive procedures. Thus, whatever we naively mean by "meaning" meets its grammatical or structural requirements at LF and thereby has the specific interpretive properties it enjoys.

It is possible to identify LF in various other "contentful" ways. For example, in a GB-style account, LF is the level at which the Empty Category Principle (ECP) is checked. In particular, in a theory of the *Barriers* variety, LF is the unique level at which gamma marking is checked. In many GB accounts, LF is also a level to which the BT applies.

A Minimalist theory will strongly differ from standard GB accounts when these sorts of designations are considered. The reason is that LF is the unique level with phrase marker properties. Thus, it is the *only* level at which *any* structural condition can be checked. Thus, in a Minimalist theory, the Binding theory, case theory, and every other module of the grammar that is stated in terms of structural output conditions must all apply to the LF phrase marker. Minimalist theory can pick out LF quite trivially: it is the unique grammatical level with phrase structure properties. This clearly contrasts with a GB specification of LF given that SS and DS are significant levels in this sort of theory, in addition to LF.

In sum, if one thinks about what LF does, in both GB and Minimalist theories, it inputs to semantic interpretation procedures. In Minimalist theories it is also the locus of all output conditions while in a GB theory LF is one of three levels to which conditions have been assumed to apply. As should be obvious, this second "content" designation of LF is very theory dependent.

Another way to identify LF is "formally," as in (7).

(7)   LF is the phrase marker derived from S-structure by applications of "Move α," branches with respect to PF and is input to rules of interpretation

The specification in (7) locates LF within a GB-style grammar. It is more "formal" than (6) in that it identifies LF by specifying how the LF phrase marker is derivationally related to other significant levels of linguistic representation. It goes beyond this by suggesting that the same rule that is involved in generating overt syntactic structures, Move α, is responsible for generating LF phrase markers from S-structures.

As is evident, the formal determination of LF is sensitive to grammatical detail. The formulation in (7) is tied to the specific details of the T-model (Chomsky and Lasnik 1977). The characterization of LF in (7) specifically adverts to the grammatical levels PF and SS and to the fact that LF and PF branch. Consequently, detailed changes in the rest of grammatical theory could significantly affect the formal characterization offered in (7). An illustration of the potency of background grammatical assumptions on the overall form and detail of particular analyses is provided in the contrasting approaches to interpretive phenomena within GB and Minimalist theories outlined in detail in the chapters that follow. However, even brief consideration of the leading ideas behind the Minimalist program indicates that (7) could not be used to identify the LF level in this sort of theory. The reason is that there is no SS level nor does DS exist, though there is a PF level. Nonetheless, an analogue of (7) is available within the Minimalist scheme which functionally identifies LF; it is one of two grammatical levels. It branches with respect to PF, interfaces with the conceptual–intentional system and is derived from the phrase marker that obtains at SPELL OUT (the point at which the derivation splits) via repeated applications of the available singular transformations.

3   Studying LF

What does research on LF consist in? One active empirical project has been to show that the two ways of identifying LF in (6) and (7) coincide. Research in the GB framework has been directed to show that they do, i.e. that those phenomena that we take to be characteristic of meaning are explicitly represented in a phrase marker whose structure is obtained from an SS phrase marker by the successive application of Move α.

A further research aim arises when coupled with the view that meaning is exhausted by the specification of a sentence's truth conditions. This further assumption requires that LF yields a logical syntax appropriate for recursively stating the truth conditions of a sentence. With this assumed, one can work backwards from the truth conditions of a given sentence first, to the syntax that a standard truth definition requires to yield these truth conditions, and then to operations on the SS phrase marker required to transform it into an LF phrase marker with the requisite logical syntax.

An example might help give the flavor of the enterprise. Consider the pair of sentences in (8):

(8a)   Everybody left
(8b)   John left

(8a) and (8b) are standardly treated as having distinct logical forms. *John* in (8b) is a name, a referring expression, in contrast with *everyone* in (8a) which is a quantifier. In the Frege/Russell tradition, this sentence expresses a singular proposition with a logical structure like that in (9).

(9)   Left (John) [L(j)]

This representation is meant to display the fact that *John* is a logical simple and that *left* is a one place predicate with a single argument position, filled in this instance by *John*.

In contrast, (8a) is logically more complex. *Everyone* is not a referring expression and the sentence is not of simple subject/predicate form. A variable fills the argument position of the predicate and a quantifier is appended to the whole open sentence.

(10)   (Every x: x a man) [left (x)]

The difference in logical syntax displayed in (9) and (10) reflects the purported semantic difference between names and quantified expressions. If LF is driven by the requirement of getting the truth conditions right, and we adopt the Frege/Russell distinction between names and quantified NPs, then the LF phrase markers of this pair of sentences should have structures analogous to these two logical forms. In other words, the LF phrase markers will reflect the fact that (8a) is semantically complex while (8b) is semantically simpler.

Given this, the question is how to get from the SS representation of these sentences to their respective LFs. In the case of (8b), there is hardly any problem as the SS and LF phrase markers are virtually identical, at least if we ignore orthographic conventions. (11) is an adequate LF representation of the logical form of (8b):

(11)   [John [left]]

To obtain a semantically adequate LF for (8a) we apply the rule of Move α, in the guise of quantifier raising (QR), and adjoin *everybody* to the front of the clause. QR, like other instances of Move α, leaves behind a coindexed trace that is interpreted as a variable bound by the adjoined (restrictive) quantifier.[3] (12) is the phrase marker that results from these operations and it is a plausible representation of the logical form of (8):

(12)   [Everybody$_i$ [t$_i$ left]]

This case illustrates how grammatical rules like Move α can be exploited to yield structures that deliver up the right form for the recursive specification of truth conditions. The question is not whether this can be done but if it should be. In other words, what reason is there for thinking that we should avail ourselves of these sorts of abstract rules to yield these sorts of LF phrase markers? There is nothing incoherent in denying that LF exists in the sense of a level of linguistic representation dedicated to representing the logical form of a sentence (vide Cooper 1983 for example). It is logically possible that there are not "any aspects of meaning that emerge in the course of normal maturation of the faculty for language" (Higginbotham 1985). This does not mean to say that sentences might not have the properties logicians claim for them. Rather these properties need not be *linguistic* properties, need not be represented in grammatical objects such as phrase markers nor derived via grammatical rules such as Move α. A property can be significant, interesting, and cognitive without being linguistic.[4]

To this point, we have identified several generally assumed characteristics of LF. First, it is derived via Move α from S-structure (in a GB theory). Second, it is "where all grammatically determined information that is relevant to interpretation" is consolidated (Higginbotham 1985: 549) and where certain output conditions apply. Third, it is the grammatical level that provides the correct logical syntax for the interpretive apparatus.

A fourth commonly held view is that LFs disambiguate sentences. In other words, if a sentence is *n*-ways ambiguous then it has *n* different LF phrase markers.[5]

There is a fifth additional assumption of note that is commonly held. At the level of LF, all grammars are alike. Thus, whatever surface differences disparate grammars may manifest, at the LF level, grammars are identical. This is a very powerful assumption and I would like to briefly consider the reasons adduced in its favor. The ones generally provided are of the standard poverty of stimulus variety. One version of this argument is concisely advanced in Higginbotham (1985: 550):

> the most fundamental principles of semantics are so remote from the data available to the child (situations of utterance, the behavior of other speakers etc.) that it is quite plausible to suppose that these principles vary minimally or not at all from language to language, the differences that show up being attributable to local syntactic conditions.

If one understands the first phrase – "the most fundamental principles of semantics" – as including the principles that determine LF structure then we have a poverty of stimulus argument as applied to LF. The claim above is that LF is too remote from experience to allow parametric variation across grammars. In other words, there are no data accessible to the child in terms of which s/he could directly fix different LF parameter values. Consequently, LF phrase markers must be essentially identical across speakers and languages or can only differ in ways that are dependent on differences in overt syntactic structure that the child can use in the course of specifying its grammar.

This constitutes the argument for LFs being identical across grammars. As a *form* of argumentation, the poverty of stimulus argument cannot be faulted. However, it is not clear how powerful this particular application of the argument is. There is a good sense in which SS (in a GB-style theory), the locus of "local syntactic conditions," is more remote from "experience" than LF is, at least if by experience one intends non-linguistic information. The reason is that LF is thought of as the grammatical level that interfaces with the other cognitive modules, just like PF and in contrast to SS.

To help us get a feel for the strength of the application of the poverty of stimulus argument when applied to LF, let us consider an analogy between LF and PF. PF ultimately interfaces with the modules involved with phonetic perception and muscle control systems that govern articulation. Grammarians believe that phonologies can differ across languages. If so, the reason must be that the child can fix phonological parameters by inspecting the incoming phonetic data. In other words, the relationship of PF to phonetic/motor events is transparent enough to allow a child to deduce the structure of phonological parameters from the patterns of perceptual/motor data that the child has access to.

Given the parallel between LF and PF the argument outlined by Higginbotham must amount to the claim that the relationship between the structure of LF and the information in its interface modules, say, for concreteness, a sentence's truth conditions, is more opaque than the relationship that obtains on the PF side of the grammar between phonetic data and phonological parameters. Consequently, inspecting truth conditions made manifest in a particular situation fails to be a good indicator of LF structure and so cannot be used to fix possible LF parameters. This kind of disanalogy between PF and LF is the assumption that drives the above argument. The question is why should we accept it.

Chomsky (personal communication) argues as follows:

> The basic point seems to me simple. If a child hears English, they [*sic*] pick up the phonetics pretty quickly (in fact, it now turns out that many subtle distinctions are being made, in language specific ways, as early as six months). The perceptual apparatus just tunes in. But if you observe what people are doing with language, it is subject to so many interpretations that you get only vague cues about LF.

In simpler terms, we are perceptually built for sound but not perceptually built for meaning. I do not know whether this speculation is correct. Consider recent work by Fisher et al. (1994) for example. They observe that very young children upon hearing sentences of varying adicities will reliably turn to a screen projecting the situation described by these sentences. Thus, for example, given two screens, one portraying an event described by a transitive verb and the other depicting an event expressed by a ditransitive verb, the child will reliably gaze on the one that matches the sentence broadcast to him/her. If this is correct, it appears that argument structure (the adicity of the predicates) is perceptually available in the data the child exploits in fixing his/her grammar.

For the sake of argument, consider a further possibility. Say children are able to perceptually discern quite generally which truth conditions characterize a given situation. For example, say the possible relative quantifier scopes in "a shark attacked every diver" are discernable by children in the two different sets of circumstances corresponding to the alternate truth conditions that the sentence may have: in one situation a lone shark munches on every frogman while in the other each frogman is served up to a different shark. If this occurs, then whether a given language licenses certain kinds of relative quantifier scope ambiguities can be culled directly from the linguistic context. If alternate quantifier scopes are reflected in different LF phrase markers, then LF parameters can be directly set by the primary data if this scenario obtains. I am not urging that this is indeed so, but it does not strike my pre-theoretical hunches as terribly far-fetched. What is clear is that this is an empirical judgement about an area that we know very little about. As such, it remains unclear just how powerful the poverty of stimulus argument outlined above really is. Suffice it to say that the discussions in the following chapters adhere to a principle of LF invariance in large part.

The rest of this book is divided as follows. The early chapters (2 and 3) review the canonical arguments for the existence of LF and its properties. LF in its standard version has the properties noted above. It is derived from SS via successive applications of the rule Move α. Of particular importance in these derivations is the rule of QR and WH-raising. The former Chomsky-adjoins quantified NPs to IPs and the latter moves WH-elements to complementizer positions. The various boundary conditions noted above are taken to characterize LF so that all relevant grammatical information that determines sentence interpretation is represented at LF. The kinds of arguments surveyed below include analyses of quantifier scope interactions, pronoun-binding phenomena, antecedent-contained deletion structures, and superiority effects among others. These arguments for LF are set in a GB framework of assumptions.

Later chapters (4 through 9) set these GB assumptions aside to investigate the properties of LF against the background of a Minimalist theory. Minimalism places different desiderata on grammars and one aim is to see just what these imply for the structure of LF. In addition, Minimalist grammatical technology is somewhat different from that standardly assumed for LF within GB theory. In particular, it is unclear whether WH-raising or QR obtains at LF in a Minimalist theory, at least as these operations are standardly understood. There is also far more A-movement at LF in this revised model than there is in the standard GB system. What this empirically implies for LF structures and operations in general (and for the analyses surveyed in chapters 2 and 3 in particular) is the central concern of these chapters.

2

Motivating LF

There is a series of direct syntactic arguments that bear on the form and existence of LF in a GB-style theory. They are "syntactic" in that they exploit generalizations exemplified in SS phrase markers. Interestingly, these SS conditions can be generalized and given wider empirical reach by supposing that they apply to a phrase marker similar to (but more articulated than) SS rather than to SS itself. Furthermore, this grammatical object is formally very similar to the logicians' logical form; a syntactic object sufficient for specifying the recursive interpretive structure of a sentence. This confluence of properties lurks behind the "LF" designation for this phrase marker.

In this chapter, I review some standard GB arguments supporting the conclusion that a grammatical level like LF exists. The form of these arguments is as follows. As noted in chapter 1, there is a semantic distinction between names and quantifiers, the latter being scopal elements. Suppose that scopal elements represent their scopes grammatically within LF phrase markers. Suppose as well that quantifiers assume their scope via the rule of Move α at LF, i.e. QR adjoins quantified NPs to the clauses over which they have semantic scope. If this is correct, then we expect this movement to obey the assorted grammatical restrictions that typically characterize overt movement operations. For example, we expect the movement to be constrained by principles like subjacency and the traces left by movement to be subject to the ECP (see below for the relevant definitions). Furthermore, the licit movements should result in phrase markers that reveal the semantic compositional structure of the sentence. This is what we expect if semantic information is grammatically encoded in phrase markers derived by standard grammatical processes. The data provided below support these expectations and thereby constitute evidence for the assumption that LF exists.

Before illustrating instances of this type of argument, it is worth observing that, if it can be provided, it is very powerful. What better reason can there be for postulating a new level of grammatical representation, a new kind of phrase marker (or for that matter any other kind of theoretical construct), than that it extends the domain of empirical coverage while exploiting independently motivated generalizations!

1 Interpreting LF

A range of arguments for the existence of LF arise from considering the properties of WH-elements. WH-elements are semantically akin to operators. They take scope over the propositions relevant to the interpretation of the sentence. Consider a simple case.

(1a) What did Bill buy
(1b) What does Bill know that Frank bought
(1c) John knows what Bill bought

We can think of the interpretation of a question as a function of the appropriate answers to it.[1] In (1a), for example, the answer consists of a sentence like (2) with appropriate purchases plugged into the X-position, e.g. shoes, a car, a telephone.

(2) John bought X

(1b) has a different set of appropriate responses determined by the frame (3). The set of potential answers includes statements like "Bill knows that Frank bought a hot dog," "Bill knows that Frank bought a lemon" etc. In contrast, the statement "Harry knows that Bill bought a hot dog" is not a potential answer as it exploits the wrong propositional frame.

(3) Bill knows that Frank bought X

(1c) is not a question at all though it has a question as a subpart: the embedded clause. This embedded clause determines a set of "answers" arrived at by filling in the frame (4):

(4) John knows: Frank bought X

Roughly speaking, (1c) is true just in case Bill knows if Frank bought a car, or a boat, or a stove or . . .

This very brief set of observations highlights the semantic function of the WH-operator. The moved WH has scope over the clause that it heads and this clause forms the propositional frame which helps determine the set of appropriate answers for a given question. The position from which the WH has moved further delimits the relevant propositional frame. The standard syntactic treatment of WH-questions moves the WH to sentence initial Comp(lementizer) position and leaves a trace behind. This trace functions as the variable X above, the slot that is filled to complete the set of answers. The boundary of the relevant propositional frame is determined by the position that the WH occupies; the trace functions to determine the position of the variable. The syntax of overt WH-movement in English, in effect, provides the kind of information needed to interpret a question.

Not all languages function like English. In various languages, including French and Chinese among others, WH-elements can remain *in situ* at SS. [2] Thus, at SS, these languages do not seem to render the propositional frame explicit. It is reasonable to suppose, however, that this information is somewhere provided, if not at SS then at some other level of representation. There is, in fact, considerable evidence that these WHs, despite their overt surface positions outside of the Comp slot, nonetheless act as if they were situated within it.

Consider the following type of data. (5) receives an interpretation as a simple (non-echo) question.[3] The Chinese sentence (6a) manifests the ambiguity made explicit in the English translations (6b) and (6c).

(5)   Jean a   vu   qui
      J.   *has seen who*
      "Who did Jean see"
(6a) Zhangsan zhidao [$_{CP}$ [$_{IP}$ Lisi mai-le   sheme]]
      Z.   *know*   *Lisi bought-ASP what*
(6b) What did Zhangsan know that Lisi bought
(6c) Zhangsan knows what Lisi bought

One way of accounting for the semantic parallelism between English questions, in which WH-expressions overtly move to the Comp at SS, and the French and Chinese cases, where there is no comparable SS movement, is to propose that at LF, the WH-elements *in situ* at SS in French and Chinese, move to the Comp position. Observe that if we adhere to the assumption that the interpretive (semantic) properties of grammars are uniformly represented cross-linguistically, then it is natural to assume that WH-*in-situ* elements abstractly move to Comp positions rendering languages structurally identical with regards to semantic interpretation. Note that French and Chinese thereby determine the relevant propositional frames at LF rather than SS. Assuming this, (5) has the LF phrase marker in (7) and (6a) has the ones in (8). Thus, at LF, the various French, Chinese and English sentences are formally identical and at this level, provide the relevant information for interpretation.

(7)   [Qui [Jean a vu t]]
(8a) [$_{CP}$ Sheme$_i$ [$_{IP}$ Zhangsan zhidao [$_{CP}$ t$_i$ [$_{IP}$ Lisi mai-le t$_i$]]]
(8b) Zhangsan zhidao [$_{CP}$ sheme$_i$ [$_{IP}$ Lisi mai-le t$_i$]]

WH-*in-situ* constructions are not limited to French and Chinese. English multiple interrogatives involve them as well.

(9)   Who bought what

In this case, it is supposed that the WH-*in-situ* moves at LF to the Comp containing the overtly moved WH-element (Chomsky 1973). The WH-*in-situ*, then, joins the WH in Comp at LF. This permits an absorbed interpretation for the pair of WH-operators. Thus, the appropriate interpretation for questions like

(9) involves responses of buyer–buyee pairs; John a car, Bill a boat and Cathie a motorcycle.[4] The appropriate propositional frame is something like (10) in which the pair of variables X, Y must be filled in to yield an appropriate answer.

(10)   Which X, Y [X bought Y]

An LF phrase marker like (11) makes the relevant propositional frame explicit. The traces of movement once again function like variables and the complex WH-amalgam in Comp demarcates the appropriate proposition.

(11)   [[What$_i$ [who$_j$] t$_j$ bought t$_i$]

   The examples above favor movement of WH-*in-situ* elements to pre-sentential positions on the assumption that the interpretive properties of operators have a syntactic reflex. In other words, the derivation of LF *phrase markers* to encode interpretive information is motivated on the assumption that in cases such as these, syntactic form follows interpretation. A pressing question then is whether there exist non-interpretive reasons for thinking that phrase markers such as these exist. What kind of evidence can be adduced aside from the interpretive concerns mooted above?

2   The Empty Category Principle at LF

The ECP is a condition that requires that traces be licensed to be licit. Thus, a trace in a given structure is acceptable if and only if it is properly governed (see definitions below). Thought of this way, the ECP is essentially a trace detector, a condition that makes noise when a trace fails to satisfy it. The aim of this section is to deploy this detector to hunt for possible covert traces, i.e. traces without phonological residues. The existence of such non-phonologically marked traces is implied by the existence of LF and so finding such would support the position that such a phrase marker exists. This section reviews evidence that such traces exist and trigger the ECP.
   The ECP is a condition that distinguishes the movement behavior of (i) adjuncts and arguments and (ii) subjects and objects. (12) illustrates the first contrast, (13) the second.

(12a)   (?) Which car did John wonder how to fix
(12b)   *How did John wonder which car to fix
(13a)   Which car did John say that Bill fixed
(13b)   *Which mechanic did John say that fixed the car

The ECP effects this contrast by requiring that traces formed by movement meet the locality conditions stated in (14) and (15).

(14)   *ECP:* All traces must be properly governed
(15)   A trace is properly governed iff it is governed by a head X^0 or locally bound by its antecedent[5]

Assume for the present that local binding is effected within the same clause. (14) and (15) encode the familiar head government and antecedent government options for proper government.[6] The details do not matter for the present.

The ECP distinguishes the sentences in (12) and (13) as follows. They have the structures in (16) and (17).

(16a)   [Which car$_i$ [John wonder [how$_j$ [PRO to[fix t$_i$] t$_j$]]]]
(16b)   [How$_j$ [John wonder [which car$_i$ [PRO to [fix t$_i$] t$_j$]]]]
(17a)   [Which car$_i$ [John say [that [Bill fixed t$_i$]]]]
(17b)   [Which mechanic$_i$ [John say [t$_i$ that [t$_i$ fixed the car]]]]

Consider the traces in (16a, b). The trace t_i is an argument of the verb *fix*. As such, it is sister to the verb and hence governed by it. The trace t_j is an adjunct outside the governing domain of the verb or any other lexical head. The former trace meets the ECP by being head governed by the verb. The trace of *how* can only conform to the ECP by being locally bound. In (16a), t_j is so bound by *how* from the local Comp position. However, in (16b), this fails to occur and t_j is neither head governed nor antecedent governed. An ECP violation results and the relative unacceptability of (16b) is accounted for.[7]

A similar account extends to (17a) and (17b) though the technical details differ. In the former, t_i is head-governed by *fix*. In contrast, the subject trace in (17b) has no head governor. The question is whether it is locally bound (i.e. antecedent governed) by the intermediate t_i. Assume that the Comp *that* blocks this.[8] The unacceptability of (13b) then follows from the ECP.

Consider now how the ECP interacts with non-syntactically overt WH-movement. Recall that in French it is possible to form a question without overtly moving the WH. Consider in this light the pair of sentences in (18).[9]

(18a)   Pierre a   dit que Jean a   vu qui
        P.   has said that J.   has seen who
        "Who did Pierre say that Jean saw"
(18b)   *Pierre a   dit que qui a   vu Jean[10]
        P.   has said that who has seen J.
        "Who did Pierre say that saw Jean"

The pair display a subject/object asymmetry characteristic of the ECP. Indeed, we can extend the account above to these French cases on the assumption that the *qui in situ* moves to the matrix Comp at LF and that the result of this movement is subject to the ECP. The structure of (18b) at LF is (19). The trace in subject position fails to be properly governed.[11]

(19)   [Qui$_i$ [Pierre a dit [que t$_i$ a vu Jean]]

Similar subject/object asymmetry effects are observable in English multiple interrogation constructions.[12]

(20a)   Who believes that Bill bought what
(20b)   *Who believes (that) what happened

If English multiple interrogatives involve moving the WH-*in-situ* to a Comp
containing a WH, then the LF structure of (20b) is identical to (18b) above and
results in an ECP violation (but see n. 7).

(21)   [[What$_i$ [who$_j$]] t$_j$ said [that t$_i$ happened]]]

Further evidence for LF WH-movement obtains in Chinese. Consider (22).

(22a)   Ni   xiang-zhidao Lisi zeme mai-le   sheme
         You wonder   Lisi how   buy-ASP what
(22b)   How do you wonder what Lisi bought
(22c)   What is x that do you wonder how Lisi bought x

(22a) is unambiguous in Chinese. It can be interpreted as (22c) but cannot
carry the interpretation (22b). Furthermore, the prohibition against (22b) is not
due to the inability of extracting *zeme* long distance. (23) is well formed.

(23)   Ni   renwei ta yinggai zeme lai
         You think   he should   how   come
         "How do you think that he should come"

A direct way to account for the unacceptability of (22a) with the interpretation
(22b) is via the ECP. The structure of the unacceptable sentence is (24). The
adjunct trace is neither head nor antecedent governed and hence the indicated
structure is ill-formed, in violation of the ECP.

(24)   Zeme$_i$ [ni xiang-zhidao [sheme$_j$ [Lisi t$_i$ mai-le t$_j$]]]
         How   you wonder   what   Lisi   bought

Though we have used Chinese examples to make the case, the glosses indicate that parallel facts hold for English. In effect the pair of examples in (12)
above follow the logic illustrated here. The key difference between the English
and Chinese cases is that in the former the movement is overt while in the latter
the WH-elements all move at LF. The fact that the interpretive properties of
the English sentences (which involve overt syntactic movement) and the Chinese sentences (which appear not to) are identical follows from the assumption that the ECP applies to LF phrase markers of the kind postulated.
   The ECP can also be brought to bear on another interesting set of data
involving WH-movement, superiority effects.

(25a)   I wonder who bought what
(25b)   *I wonder what who bought

Assume once again that to receive an interpretation the WH-*in-situ* moves to
the Comp containing a WH-operator and adjoins to it thereby permitting an

absorbed interpretation of the complex WH-operator. This yields (26) as the correct structure of (25).

(26a) I wonder [[what$_i$ [who$_j$]] t$_j$ bought t$_i$]
(26b) I wonder [[who$_j$ [what$_i$]] t$_i$ bought t$_i$]

Consider the traces. In (26a, b) the object trace t_i is properly governed by the verb *bought*. In (26a) the subject trace t_j is antecedent governed by *who$_j$*, or more precisely, by the complex WH of which *who$_j$* is the head. This complex WH is in the same structural proximity to the trace in subject position as a simple WH would be, e.g. as in (27).

(27) [What$_i$ [t$_j$ happened]]

This contrasts with (26b) where *who$_j$* plausibly fails to locally bind the subject trace. The intervening head of the complex WH *what$_i$* intervenes to upset the local binding relation much as *that* does in cases such as (13b) above. If we assume that this, or something like this, is correct, then superiority effects can be brought within the purview of the ECP.[13]

It is interesting to observe that we find similar superiority effects in languages in which WHs all move overtly to Comp in the syntax. Rudin (1988) observes that in Bulgarian and Romanian all WHs move to Comp by SS. These multiple questions exhibit superiority effects. (28) illustrates this using Romanian data.[14]

(28a) Cine ce   cumpara
       Who what buys
       "Who buys what"
(28b) *Ce   cine cumpara
       What who buys
       "What did who buy"

Once again, it is significant that we find overt analogues of the LF phrase markers proposed. If LF is a grammatical level, then its phrase marker properties should parallel those we find in other phrase markers. The fact that both overt movement of WHs in Romanian and covert movement of WH in English are amenable to a common analysis on the assumption that WHs-*in-situ* move at LF to Comp adds grammatical support to the hypothesis that LF exists.

Before reviewing further evidence, let us pause to consider the fine structure of the argument presented to this point. Semantically, a distinction exists between quantifiers and names.[15] The former have distinctive scopal properties which are reasonably represented grammatically by moving these expressions to positions that c-command their scopal domains. WH-operators are quantificational entities and so have scopal properties. In many languages, English being one, these scope properties are manifested overtly in the position that WH-elements occupy. It is reasonable to suppose that this movement manifests the logical structure of questions with the pre-sentential WH occupying its scope position. What we have rehearsed evidence for is a more striking proposition; that the satisfaction of semantic ends (such as assuming one's proper scope position) is accomplished by syntactic means. The line of argument above indicates that quantifiers like WH-expressions are subject to the rule of Move α and it is through a process of (grammatical) movement that WHs attain their scope positions. This movement, like overt forms of syntactic movement, leaves behind traces which are subject to conditions on trace licensing such as the ECP. This means that scope of WH is a property of phrase markers and hence that semantic content has syntactic consequences, in at least this one case. Importantly for our purposes, the phrase marker relevant to stating this confluence of semantic and syntactic fact is a phrase marker derived from SS by further application of syntactic operations. In short, LF.

Other quantified expressions conform to the ECP as well. Kayne (1981) considers some evidence from French that indicates that negative quantifiers display subject/object asymmetries with respect to abstract movement. Quantified NPs like *personne* take scope over the clause within which the negative marker *ne* appears. Typically, this is the same clause. (29a) has the LF (29b).

(29a) Jean n'aime   personne
       J.   neg likes no one
       "Jean doesn't like anyone"
(29b) Personne$_i$ [Jean n'aime t$_i$]

Interestingly, there are cases in which it is possible in some dialects to get the neg marker and the quantifier whose scope it indicates in different clauses.

(30a) Jean n'exige   que Marie a   vu   personne
       J.   neg insist that M.   has seen no one
       "Jean didn't insist that Marie saw anyone"
(30b) *Jean n'exige   que personne est venue[16]
       J.   neg insist that no one   is   come
       "Jean didn't insist that anyone came"

If *personne* moves to the clause that contains the neg marker *ne*, the LF representations of the two sentences is (31).

(31a) Personne$_i$ [Jean Neg exige [que [Marie a vu t$_i$]]]
(31b) Personne$_i$ [Jean Neg exige [que [t$_i$ est venue]]]

It is reasonable to account for the relative unacceptability of (30b) by treating (31b) as an ECP violation, on a par with (18b) above. In this instance, however, the trace is a result of a rule of quantifier raising (QR) rather than WH-raising. However, the logic is similar to the WH-case. Quantifiers are also scopal elements. On the familiar assumption that this scope is displayed at LF and effected via movement, then we expect QR to conform to the ECP.and display the asymmetry noted above.[17]

The ECP plausibly accounts for a further set of quantificational relative scope facts as well.[18]

(32a)   At least one person expects every candidate to win
(32b)   At least one person expects (that) every candidate will win

(32a) has a reading in which the universally quantified NP *every candidate* takes scope over the existential NP *at least one person*. Thus, it is compatible with the truth of (32a) that there be a different person expecting every cand- idate to get elected. This reading is unavailable for (32b). The relevant difference between this pair is that the embedded clause in (32b) is finite while the embedded clause in (32a) is infinitival. This difference is crucial. Given stand- ard assumptions, subjects of non-finite clauses under verbs like *expect* are case marked by the higher predicate. As case marking is under government, this implies that *expects* governs the subject position of the embedded clause in (32a). This, in turn, implies that this position is head-governed by *expects*. Extraction from this position should then be perfectly acceptable. This con- trasts with the subject of the embedded clause in (32b). Here case marking is via the finite inflection, which is not a proper governor. As such, extraction here should be prohibited. In effect, long QR from the embedded subject in (32a) meets the ECP while long QR in (32b) does not. The LF representations with wide scope for the universal NP are those in (33).

(33a)   [Every candidate$_i$ [at least one person$_j$ [t$_j$ expects [t$_i$ to win]]]]
(33b)   [Every candidate$_i$ [at least one person$_j$ [t$_j$ expects [t$_i$ will win]]]]

(33b) has a non-properly governed trace t_i. This accounts for the inability to give *every candidate* a wide scope reading in (32b).

Another important phenomenon displays an identical ECP effect. Consider sentences such as (34).

(34)   John likes everyone that I do

This is an example of antecedent-contained deletion (ACD).[19] The interpreta- tion of (34) is provided in (35).

(35)   Everyone that I like John likes

An appropriate LF for this interpretation is provided in (36).

(36)   [Everyone$_i$ [that [I like t$_i$]] [John likes t$_i$]]

ACDs have the following difficulty. Assume, for concreteness, that the way that we interpret a null VP is by copying the VP it is dependent on (its antecedent) into the null position. Two observations are pertinent. First, to give (34) the interpretation (35) requires interpreting the deleted VP within the relative clause. Second, copying the antecedent of the null VP cannot be effected if the quantified phrase remains *in situ*. The problem is that the null VP within the relative clause is interpretively dependent on the VP that contains it. With ACDs, this copying cannot eliminate the VP gap as copying the larger VP will result in copying the VP gap it contains. In short, copying cannot be executed without regress unless we move the whole quantified phrase out from under the VP that contains the null VP. The problem is graphically illustrated by considering the SS phrase marker of (35).

(37)   John [$_{VP1}$ likes [everyone that I do [$_{VP2}$ e]]]

It is not possible to copy VP1 into VP2 without copying the VP2 gap as well. But if we end up with a VP gap again then we still do not have a fully specified content for the clause. On the assumption that gaps must be discharged for interpretation to be well formed, the procedure outlined above is problematic, at least if stated at S-structure.[20]

Importantly, this simple procedure can proceed without a hitch if we assume that ACDs are interpreted at LF, the relevant structure being (38).

(38)   [[Everyone$_i$ that I do [$_{VP2}$ e] [John [$_{VP1}$ likes t$_i$]]]

Here VP1 can be copied into VP2 without regress as VP1 no longer contains VP2. The effect of moving the relative clause to its scope position (note that the head *everyone* is a quantificational NP) is to remove it from under VP1 and this movement circumvents the regress problem that besets SS interpretation. In effect, ACDs provide another kind of interpretive evidence for the utility of LF. We gain syntactic corroboration for the view that ACD interpretation involves LF phrase markers by considering the following contrast.

(39a)   John expected everyone that I did to win
(39b)   *John expected everyone that I did would win

The relevant interpretation of interest is the one paraphrased as "John expected everyone that I expected to win to win." It is much more difficult to give (39b) this ACD reading than (39a).[21] This follows if movement is involved and this movement is subject to the ECP. The LFs required to feed the ACD interpretation are the ones in which the relative clause moves to a position above the matrix VP. The requisite LFs for the pair of sentences in (39) are provided in (40). In both phrase markers VP2 has been moved out from under VP1.

(40a)   [Everyone [that I did [$_{VP2}$ e]] [John [$_{VP1}$ expected [t to win]]
(40b)   [Everyone [that I did [$_{VP2}$ e]] [John [$_{VP1}$ expected [t would win]]

The reason that (39b) cannot have the ACD interpretation is that (40b) violates the ECP, in contrast to (40a). In fact, (40b) has the same problem as (33b) above. The embedded trace in subject position fails to be properly governed. In both cases, the ECP prevents QR from moving the embedded subject to the next higher clause. As this is required to get the indicated interpretations, these are not available for these sentences. In the case of (39b) this prevents VP2 from moving out from under VP1 and hence we face the regress problem when interpreting the VP2 gap in (39b). In sum, ACD constructions seem subject to ECP considerations; just as expected if LF movement is involved.

Consider one more interpretive phenomenon with apparent ECP effects.[22] Sentences like (41) are ambiguous, with either *what* or *everyone* taking wide scope. The two interpretations are highlighted by the answers in (42).

(41)   What did everyone bring
(42a)   Everyone brought a bottle of wine
(42b)   John brought a bottle of wine, Fred brought beer, Cheryl, chips and Sue guacamole

(42a) corresponds to a wide scope reading for *what* while (42b) gives the universal quantifier widest scope. Call the reading in (42b) the pair–list reading.

Various ways have been proposed for representing this pair of interpretations at LF. Chapter 3 considers various analyses of these constructions. For now, let us adopt the analysis in May (1985). May (1985) assumes that the rule of QR adjoins quantified NPs to any XP. Assume here that *everyone* adjoins to IP. The LF of (41) is then (43).

(43) $[_{CP}$ What$_j$ $[_{IP}$ everyone$_i$ $[_{IP}$ t$_i$ bring t$_j$]]]

Whence the ambiguity given a solitary LF? May (1985) suggests the following definition of c-command in terms of strong domination and the following scope rule.[23]

(44)   A c-commands B iff every node that strongly dominates A strongly dominates B
(45)   A node N strongly dominates B iff every segment of N dominates B
(46)   Scope rule: If A asymmetrically c-commands B then A has scope over B

The effect of the definitions (44) and (45) as regards (43) is that in this structure *what* and *everyone* mutually c-command each other. IP does not strongly dominate *everyone* as one of the segments of IP does not dominate the adjoined universal quantifier. The only node that strongly dominates *everyone* is CP and this strongly dominates *what* as well. Given the scope rule, the effect of mutual c-command between *what* and *everyone* is to permit either to take scope over the other. In effect, May (1985) drops the requirement that sentences be disambiguated at LF. The LF phrase marker is interpretively ambiguous with either quantifier capable of bearing wide scope.

In light of this consider a sentence like (47).

(47)   Who brought everything

This sentence is unambiguous. It does not support a pair–list reading. (42b) is an inappropriate answer to (47). The ECP explains why. Consider what

LF structure would be required for the pair–list reading. *Everything* must c-command *who*, which sits in Comp. The LF structure is (48).

(48) $[_{CP}$ Who$_i$ $[_{IP}$ everything$_j$ $[_{IP}$ t$_i$ brought t$_j]]]$

However, there is a problem with this configuration. In particular, it is plausible to suppose that t_i is not properly governed given the intervening adjoined universal quantifier. If this is so, the unavailability of the pair–list reading in (47) follows. (48), the LF phrase marker required for the pair–list reading, violates the ECP.

One last issue remains. The LF of the acceptable interpretation of (47) is (49). *Everyone* is adjoined to VP. Within this configuration, *who* asymmetrically c-commands *everyone* (IP and CP strongly dominate *everyone* while only CP strongly dominates *who*) and thus is interpreted by (46) as necessarily taking scope over it.

(49) $[_{CP}$ Who$_i$ $[_{IP}$ t$_i$ $[_{VP}$ everything$_j$ $[_{VP}$ brought t$_j]]]$

The above canvassed material supports the conclusion that some semantic properties of sentences are mediated by LF phrase markers. WH-scope, quantifier scope, scope of negation, and VP ellipsis in ACD contexts all appear sensitive to whether the traces left by non-overt movement are properly governed. In short, the ECP appears to limit the effects of abstract LF operations in ways similar to the restrictions it imposes on overt SS movement. This follows if there is indeed a level of representation that mediates interpretation that is derived from SS via Move α.

3   Cross Over Effects at LF

We have been thinking of the ECP as a trace detector. There is another: cross over effects. Consider the following sentences.

(50a)   *Who$_i$ did he$_i$ give a book to t$_i$
(50b)   *Who$_i$ did his$_i$ mother give a book to t$_i$

There sentences in (50) exemplify strong and weak cross over. In (50a) the trace/variable t_i is bound by the pronoun *he* within the domain of its operator/quantifier. This is a violation of principle C (as in (51)) and yields an illicit structure.

(51)   A variable must be free in the domain of its operator[24]

The variable t_i in (50b) is coindexed with a pronoun on its left. This is illicit. A variety of principles have been proposed to rule such structures out. For current purposes it is not crucial which is adopted so I rest with a traditional favorite, the Leftness Condition.[25]

(52)   A variable cannot serve as the antecedent of a pronoun on its left

(52) bans structures with the indicated indexing in (50b) with indexation interpreted in terms of antecedence. In simple cases, if X (A-)binds Y then X is the antecedent of Y.

   (50a, b) involve SS movement. They manifest strong cross over (SCO) and weak cross over (WCO) effects respectively. (53) indicates that similar effects can be detected in sentences without any form of overt syntactic movement.

(53a)   *Who said that he$_i$ gave a book to who$_i$
(53b)   *Who said that his$_i$ mother gave a book to who$_i$

The LF structures of these sentences are provided in (54), the WH-*in-situ* having moved to the matrix Comp position.

(54a)   [[Who$_j$ [who$_j$]] [t$_j$ said [that [he$_i$ gave a book to t$_i$]]]]
(54b)   [[Who$_j$ [who$_j$]] [t$_j$ said [that [his$_i$ mother gave a book to t$_i$]]]]

The relevant interpretations here have *he* in (54a) and *his* in (54b) interpreted as bound variables. What is crucial is that they cannot have the interpretations in (55).

(55a)   For which pair of people x, y did x say that y gave a book to y (i.e. himself)
(55b)   For which pair of people x, y did x say that y's mother gave y a book

These are perfectly coherent propositions but the sentences in (53) cannot express them. More importantly, as the structures in (54) clearly demonstrate, the same principles that rule out (50) above will filter out these structures as well. Thus, once again, assuming that multiple interrogative constructions involve moving the WH-*in-situ* to the WH in Comp allows us to generalize grammatical conditions attested at SS.

   The argument carries over to non-interrogative quantifiers. (56a) cannot be interpreted as meaning "everyone gave himself a book" nor can (56b) mean "everyone's mother gave him a book."

(56a)   *He$_i$ gave everyone$_i$ a book
(56b)   *His$_i$ mother gave everyone$_i$ a book

At LF, after QR has applied, these have the structures in (57), the former induces an SCO violation and the latter displays a WCO configuration. Hence both phrase markers are ill-formed and the attendant interpretations are unavailable. Much as in the ECP cases discussed above, it appears that (51) and (52) do not discriminate between overt traces/variables or covert ones.

Neither variety may be bound or serve as an antecedent to pronouns on their left.

(57a)   [Everyone$_i$ [he$_i$ gave t$_i$ a book]]
(57b)   [Everyone$_i$ [his$_i$ mother gave t$_i$ a book]]

4   Bound Pronouns

Movement has another significant effect. It alters the c-command domain of the moved expression. Prior to movement, the WH in object position only c-commands elements within the VP in (58a). After movement, it has the entire clause as its c-command domain.

(58a)   John [$_{VP}$ bought what]
(58b)   What [$_{IP}$ John bought t]

This can be significant given principles such as (59).

(59)   If a pronoun P is c-commanded by an NP O then P can be interpreted as a variable bound by O

The movement of operators alters their c-command domains and thereby alters the pronouns that can be treated as bound variables. Consider an example.[26]

(60)   *The man [who disliked every boy$_i$] hit him$_i$

Here *every boy* does not c-command the pronoun at SS as it is embedded within the relative clause. If (59) applies at SS then *every boy*'s failure to c-command *him* accounts for the lack of a bound pronoun reading in (60). For this example, the result is the same if (59) holds at LF. QR is typically clause bound (Chomsky 1977) and at LF, (60) has a structure something like (61).[27]

(61)   The man who$_i$ [every boy$_j$ [t$_i$ disliked t$_j$]] hit him$_j$

In (61), *every boy* fails to c-command the pronoun and so the pronoun cannot be interpreted as bound. Though this instance of LF movement does not affect the pronoun-binding powers of the quantified NP, there are other cases in which it might. Consider some simple examples.

Parasitic gap constructions require that the real gap not c-command the parasitic gap. This is what differentiates the relatively acceptable (62a) from the unacceptable (62b).

(62a)   Which book did Bill read t$_i$ after Frank reviewed t$_i$
(62b)   *Which book t$_i$ was read by Bill after Frank reviewed t$_i$

In the former, the real gap is in object position. If the *after* clause is adjoined to VP, then the real gap in object position fails to c-command the trace inside the adjunct. The contrast with (62b) is attributable to the fact that subjects c-command the whole clause thereby c-commanding the adjunct and the parasitic gap within it. This c-command configuration leads to a violation of principle C and the structure is ungrammatical.[28]

Assume that this is correct. We then are confronted with a puzzle in cases such as (63).

(63a) John kissed every child$_i$ after Bill introduced him$_i$
(63b) Orson will drink no wine$_i$ before its$_i$ time

The pronouns here can be interpreted as bound variables, which should be impossible if (59) holds at SS. As we have just observed, the object NP does not c-command the adjunct at this level. This problem can be finessed, however, if we permit (59) to apply after QR. The relevant LF structures are (64) with the quantified object NP adjoined to IP via QR.[29] This LF movement suffices to place the pronoun within the c-command domain of the raised quantified NP. In short, for this case, LF movement serves to save the generalization proposed in (59).

(64a) [Every child$_i$ [John [$_{VP}$ [$_{VP}$ kissed t$_i$] after Bill introduced him$_i$]]
(64b) [No wine$_i$ [Orson will [$_{VP}$ [$_{VP}$ drink t$_i$] before its$_i$ time]]

There is some independent evidence that the trace/variable does not c-command the adjunct. Consider the distribution of epithets. It is impossible to anaphorically anchor an epithet to an NP so long as this NP c-commands the epithet.[30] (65) illustrates this.

(65) *No boy$_i$ thinks that the boy$_i$ is smart

Now consider (66).

(66) Orson will drink no wine$_i$ before the wine$_i$ is ready

It is perfectly acceptable. This follows on the assumption that the object position does not c-command the adjunct that contains the epithet, the same assumption as above. Thus, there are two kinds of data that point to the conclusion that an NP in object position at SS does not c-command a VP adjunct. The fact that pronominal binding is nonetheless possible from here supports the position that LF is the correct level for stating (59).

There are two other kinds of bound pronoun structures that support the conclusion that pronominal binding is licensed at a grammatical level different from SS. May (1977, 1985) observes that binding is possible in "inverse linking" configurations such as (67).

(67)   [$_{NP}$ Someone [$_{PP}$ from every city$_i$]] loves it$_i$

At SS, *every city* does not c-command the pronoun, as (67) indicates. By (59) the bound pronoun interpretation should be unavailable, contrary to fact. This c-command problem is solved once we assume LF movement of quantified NPs. The interpretation of (67) assigns the universally quantified NP wide scope. The LF structure is (68).

(68)   [$_{IP}$ Every city$_i$ [$_{IP}$ [someone from t$_i$]$_j$ [t$_j$ loves it$_i$]]]

Once again, there is independent evidence that *every city* does not c-command the pronoun at SS. Reinhart (1983) observes that sloppy identity constructions are subject to (59) as well. A sentence has a sloppy reading when the semantic value of the pronoun varies with that of the antecedent. The sloppy reading of (69a) is the one paraphrasable as (69b). (69c) is the strict reading.

(69a)   John loves his mother and Bill does too
(69b)   John loves John's mother and Bill loves Bill's mother
(69c)   John loves John's mother and Bill loves John's mother

That (59) applies can be seen from cases such as (70a) which only have strict readings, i.e. the readings in (70c). This is what we expect on the assumption that non-quantified NPs do not move at LF to their scope positions. Names, being scopeless, remain *in situ* even at LF and so a sloppy reading of the pronoun is not licensed.[31]

(70a)   People from Los Angles love its beaches and someone from NYC does too
(70b)   People from LA love LA's beaches and people from NYC love NYC's beaches
(70c)   People from LA love LA's beaches and people from NYC love LA's beaches

Interestingly, the sloppy reading once again becomes available in cases like (71).

(71)   Someone from every western city loves its beaches and someone from every eastern city does too

At LF, Move α derives an inverse-linked phrase marker with the pronoun c-commanded by the quantified NP. This licenses the sloppy reading.

One last point: if we replace the bound pronouns with bound epithets (or definite descriptions) the sentences remain acceptable with the same interpretations. That these anaphors are available corroborates that the SS expression does not c-command the epithet.

(72a)   People from LA love that city's beaches and people from NYC do too (strict reading only)

(72b)   People from every western city love that city's beaches and people from every eastern city do too (sloppy reading possible)

A last instance of the same effect can be found in cases like (73).

(73a)   Everyone's$_i$ mother thinks he's$_i$ handsome

(73b)   No one's$_i$ mother thinks he's$_i$ ugly

The genitive specifier is contained within the subject NP (or DP). Therefore, at SS, it fails to c-command the pronoun and hence by (59) should not be able to bind it. Nonetheless, the bound reading is available. This problem is once again solved if we assume that at LF quantifiers move and adjoin to IP. The relevant structure after movement is (74). At LF, the pronoun is c-commanded by the adjoined quantified NP and so (59) is respected.

(74a)   [$_{IP}$ Everyone's$_i$ [$_{IP}$ [$_{NP}$ t$_i$ mother] thinks he's$_i$ handsome]]

(74b)   [$_{IP}$ No one's$_i$ [$_{IP}$ [$_{NP}$ t$_i$ mother] thinks he's$_i$ ugly]]

Corroboration for the claim that at S-structure the specifier fails to c-command the pronoun comes from further consideration of principle C effects. It is possible to get a bound epithet in these configurations – (75a) – and it is possible to get backwards pronominalization – (75b). This should not be possible if the SS specifier had the IP as its c-command domain as in both cases we would have a principle C effect.[32] Contrast (75) with (76).

(75a)   No kid's$_i$ mother thinks that kid$_i$ is ugly

(75b)   His$_i$ mother gave the kid$_i$ a nickel

(76a)   *No kid$_i$ thinks that kid$_i$ is ugly

(76b)   *He$_i$ gave the kid$_i$ a nickel

Sloppy identity data add further confirmation to the claim that the SS specifier does not c-command the pronoun. In (77), the sloppy identity reading (77b) is unavailable, as expected. (77a) can be interpreted as (77c) but not (77b). The specifiers, not being quantificational, do not move to higher positions at LF. Hence *John* and *Frank* never c-command the pronouns and a bound variable interpretation remains unlicensed even at LF.

(77a)   John's mother loves him and Frank's father does too

(77b)   John's mother loves John and Frank's father loves Frank

(77c)   John's mother loves John and Frank's father loves John

Interestingly, we find sloppy readings in these configurations in cases where the specifier moves. There are two relevant cases. Reinhart (1991) has argued that bare argument ellipsis is fed by LF movement. In effect, what is elided is an LF constituent. A sentence like (78a) has the LF structure (78b) and IP1, a constituent present only at LF, is copied into the elision site IP*.

(78a) John liked your poem yesterday and your book
(78b) [$_{IP2}$ Your poem$_i$ [$_{IP1}$ John liked t$_i$ yesterday] and [$_{IP}$ your book$_i$ [$_{IP*}$ e]]

Elision, in short, involves movement of even non-quantified NPs. With this in mind consider (79).

(79) John's mother kissed him and Bill's too

In cases such as these the sloppy interpretation of the pronoun is available. (79) can carry the interpretation: "Bill's mother kissed Bill." This contrasts with the unavailability of this sloppy reading in (77a). The difference stems from the presence of elision in the latter case. Observe that the head noun has been elided, in addition to the rest of the IP. The LF structure is something like (80).

(80) [$_{IP1}$ John's$_i$ [$_{IP2}$ [NP t$_i$ mother] kissed him$_i$] and [$_{IP}$ Bill's [$_{IP*}$ e]][33]

The availability of the sloppy identity reading is expected in this sort of case if elision involves adjunction of the remnant to IP. With this LF movement, the pronoun is c-commanded and is licensed as a bound pronoun. Consequently, the sloppy reading is expected to arise.

   Confirmation of this comes from the reemergence of sloppy readings in cases without elision but with quantified determiners.

(81a) Everyone's mother kissed him but no one's father did
(81b) Every congressman's aide will support him and every senator's secretary will too

These sentences permit sloppy readings. For example, (81a) has the paraphrase: For every x, x's mother kissed x and for no y, did y's father kiss y. This is once again expected given that QR raises the quantified determiner at LF to a position from which it can c-command the pronoun. This allows it to get a bound variable interpretation in conformity with (59).

   Movement alters the c-command domain of an expression. In this section, I have surveyed arguments supporting the conclusion that the c-command domain of some NPs is larger than their SS position indicates that it should be. More interesting still, the NPs with these larger scope domains are quantificational. In this respect, they contrast with names, the scope of which are accurately reflected in their SS positions. This contrast is precisely what we expect if LF structurally reflects the semantic properties of different nominal expressions. Scopal NPs should move at LF and alter their c-command domains. Scopeless elements should not. The evidence suggests that the way things are is the way they should be.

5   Conclusion

This chapter has reviewed the standard arguments for LF. We have seen that there is considerable evidence that covert movement can alter SS c-command relations, can affect pronoun-binding conditions, can extend the reach of the WCO effect and the ECP. At the same time, we have surveyed evidence that suggests that LF phrase markers respect natural semantic distinctions such as that between names and quantifiers and also provide a grammatical basis for certain aspects of semantic interpretation, e.g. relative quantifier scope, VP anaphora in ACD structures. In sum, we have seen that there is considerable evidence that there is a grammatical level that is responsive to semantic distinctions. What is crucial is that there is a confluence of semantic and grammatical properties. The latter features implicate the presence of a phrase marker. The former makes it reasonable to call it "logical form."

Appendix   Subjacency

Some have argued for subjacency restrictions on LF movement. I review some of the arguments for this here. I take the evidence to be inconclusive. However, chapters 8 and 9 provide additional arguments to the effect that subjacency is a restriction that applies to LF phrase markers within a Minimalist theory.
    Overt instances of Move α are subject to subjacency.[34]

(82)   Movement cannot cross more than one bounding node, where IP and
       NP are bounding nodes

This condition restricts movement out of complex NPs and embedded WH-questions, among other islands. There are two ways of thinking of subjacency, as a condition on representations or derivations. The first view treats subjacency as a well-formedness condition on phrase markers that requires that links in a movement chain be locally relatable; e.g., that no two successive links be separated by more than a single bounding node. The second way of thinking of subjacency is as a condition on rule application. Here, the operative idea is that a movement operation cannot apply so as to move an expression across more than a single bounding node. In contrast with the representational view, this treats subjacency as a constraint on the operation of the rule itself rather than its output. In effect, subjacency is simply part of the *definition* of what it is to be a movement rule. Research since the early 1980s has oscillated back and forth, some results supporting the representational approach, others the derivational interpretation. For present purposes, it is the second version of subjacency that is of interest for it implies that LF instances of Move α should display subjacency effects. In this section, we review some of the evidence suggesting that this is the case. However, before beginning, it is worth considering the evidence against this position.

WH-*in-situ* constructions can appear inside islands.

(83a)   Who asked where Bill bought what
(83b)   Who likes people who live where
(83c)   Who said that pictures of what were sale
(83d)   Who denied the claim that Bill bought what

The relevant interpretation of (83a) is the one in which *what* is paired with *who*. An appropriate answer would be: John asked where Bill bought his computer and Sheila asked where Bill bought his modem. With this interpretation we appear to have a violation of the WH-island condition. Overt instances of WH-movement result in unacceptability in analogous constructions. Compare (83) and (84).

(84a)   *What did John ask where Bill bought
(84b)   *Where does John like people who live
(84c)   *What did John say that pictures of were on sale
(84d)   *What did John deny the claim that Bill bought

These data can be accommodated if we treat subjacency as a well-formedness condition on SS chains rather than a condition on movement itself.[35] However, there is some evidence that even LF movement is constrained by subjacency and that the cases in (83) are only in apparent violation of this principle.

Longobardi (1991) observes that some quantified expressions, e.g. negative quantifiers and *solo* NP ("only NP") constructions, can have scope wider than the clause that dominates them at SS but cannot scope out of islands. (85) exemplifies the first point and (86) the second.

(85)   Non credo   che lui pensi che io desideri vedere nessuno
        Neg believe-I that he thinks that I wish   to-see no one
        "I do not believe that he thinks that I wish to see anyone"
(86a)   *Non approverei la tua proposta di vedere nessuno
        Neg approve-I   the your proposal of to-see no one
        "I don't approve your proposal of seeing anyone"
(86b)   *Non ho   incontrato chi potrebbe fare niente
        Neg have meet   who might   to-do nothing
        "I did not meet (someone) who might do anything"

The examples in (86) are instances of the complex noun phrase constraint. As indicated, the negative expressions *nessuno* and *niente* cannot move to their scope marker *non* as this would involve moving out of an island.

These negative constructions also display CED (Constraint on Extraction Domains) effects. (87a) is an instance of the subject condition and (87b) the adjunct condition.

(87a)   *Chiamare nessuno sara   possibile
      to-call   no one   will-be possible
      "To call no one will be possible"
(87b)   *Non fa   il   suo dovere per aiutare nessuno
      Neg does-he the his duty   for to-help no one
      "He does not do his duty in order to help anyone"

Thus, it seems that negative scope is sensitive to island conditions and this
suggests that subjacency is involved. However, these data need not imply that
subjacency *per se* is what is involved. To establish this, it would be necessary
to show that these examples are not simply instances of antecedent government violations, a condition more restrictive than subjacency.[36] Relevant cases
are examples such as (88). These, however, are unacceptable. As such, these
data cannot support the position that subjacency is what determines the licit
distribution of *nessuno*.[37]

(88)   *Non mi chiedo dove Gianni abbia visto nessuno
     Neg self ask-I   where G.   has   seen no one
     "I don't wonder where Gianni saw anyone"

A second kind of data in support of subjacency at LF has to do with answers
to certain questions in the East Asian languages. In Chinese, for example, it
is possible to form questions while leaving the WH *in situ*, as noted above.
Furthermore, this WH can be lodged within an island. If the interpretation of
WH *in situ* requires movement of this WH to Comp at LF, then a subjacency
violation would result. The following data illustrate the problem.[38] These
examples involve apparent extraction out of WH-islands, relative clauses and
complex noun phrases.

(89a)   Ni   xiang-zhidao [shei mai-le shenme]
      You wonder   who bought what
      "What do you wonder who bought"
(89b)   Ni   zui xihuan [piping shei de   shu]
      You most like   criticize who REL book
      "Who do you like books that criticize"
(89c)   Ni   renwei [shei de hua zui   piaoliang]
      You think   whose picture most pretty
      'Who do you think that pictures of are most pretty"

Indeed, even extraction out of multiple islands is apparently possible.

(90)   Ni   zui tongqing [bei [shei xie   de   shu] piping de   ren]
     You most pity   by   who write REL book criticize REL person
     "Who is the x such that you sympathize most with the persons who are
     criticized by the books that x wrote"

However, several have argued that these violations of subjacency are only
apparent and that what occurs in cases such as these are movement of the

container of the WH rather than the WH itself.[39] They observe that the answers to the questions in (91) cannot specify the value of the WH-word alone but requires one to repeat other material in the island. In particular, (91c) is an infelicitous answer and this reflects the fact that more than the WH is in operator position at LF, as would be expected if pied piping were required to allow subjacency to be adhered to.

(91) Ni xihuan [shei xie   de   shu]
      You like   who write REL book
      "You like the book that who wrote"
(92a) Zhangsan xie de (shu)
      "The book that Z wrote"
(92b) ??Zhangsan

Fiengo et al. (1988) observe several problems with this pied piping hypothesis. First, they observe that the "minimal" answer test does not work that well. Thus in (93) we should have pied piping to avoid violation of the sentential subject condition. However, (92b) is a felicitous answer to this question nonetheless.

(93) [Shei kan zheben shu] zui   heshi
      Who read this   book most appropriate
      "That who read this book is most appropriate"

They further point out that pied piping fails to adequately account for certain observed contrasts. Consider the sentences in (94).

(94a) *Who did you get angry because I spoke to t
(94b) Who got angry because I spoke to who
(94c) *Who got angry why

The problem is as follows. If we assume that the acceptable (94b) contrasts with the unacceptable (94a) due to pied piping the whole adjunct to Spec CP at LF then we are left with no account as to why doing the same thing at LF in (94c) results in unacceptability.

   Or consider another case discussed in Aoun (1985: 62ff). Consider the pair of sentences in (95).

(95a) *Who said that what was invisible
(95b) Who said that pictures of what were invisible

(95a) can be treated as a standard ECP effect. But, if pied piping is what allows the grammar to finesse subjacency effects at LF then (95b) should be structurally identical to (95a) at LF. To avoid violating the subject condition we must pied pipe the whole embedded subject to Spec CP. But this should then leave the resultant phrase marker structurally identical to (95a). The apparent discrepancy in relative unacceptability is then left unexplained.

Fiengo et al. cite several other problems for the pied piping proposal. Consider the most serious one. As they observe, there is at best a tenuous relationship between overt pied piping and what is proposed for LF movement. As they note, acceptable pied piping varies considerably across construction types (in English). Appositive relatives seems freest while embedded questions resist most forms of pied piping. The proposal that subjacency effects are cancelled by pied piping must therefore assume very different restrictions on overt pied piping and its covert cousin. However, it is at best unclear what theoretical advantage there is to trading uniformity of Move α for non-uniformity on pied piping conditions.

In sum, there are empirical problems with the pied piping proposal and the particular data that support it are not overly compelling (the fragment answer test). It is, therefore, unclear whether much compelling evidence exists from this domain for LF movement.[40]

Reinhart (1991) examines another construction, "exception" ellipsis (EE) (96), which bears on whether subjacency holds at LF.

(96)   No one kissed his mother except for Felix

The argument is in three parts. First, Reinhart argues that in EEs the *except* remnant must be associated with another NP to be licit. In particular, one cannot interpret (96) as in (97) as the latter makes no sense. Thus, at some level, the *except* phrase and *no one* form a constituent in (96).

(97)   No one kissed his mother except Felix kissed his mother

Second, Reinhart argues that EEs are not DS units with the *except* clause moving by extraposition to its SS position. For example, (96) is not derived from (98) via extraposition.

(98)   No one except for Felix kissed his mother

The argument for this conclusion traces the differences between overt extraposition and EEs.

(99a)   *The editor agreed to publish many reviews when we pressed him [about this book]
(99b)   The editor did not agree to publish anything when we pressed him except one short review
(100a) *Jokes about everyone were told [who went to school with me]
(100b) Jokes about everyone were told except for Felix

In (99), the PP is extraposed and the result is unacceptable. The EE analogue, in contrast, is fine. In (100a), extraposition is blocked, as it usually is from a strongly quantified NP, but the EE analogue is once again acceptable.

Reinhart proposes that in EEs the *except* clause and the NP it is semantically related to form a consituent at LF. For example, in (97), QR raises *no one* and adjoins it to the remnant *except for Felix* forming a single LF operator. This sets the stage for the third leg of the argument. Reinhart argues that this instance of QR is subject to subjacency. Two facts are relevant. First, Reinhart argues that EEs can be unbounded – (101). Second, she provides evidence that islands block the construction – (102).

(101)   Lucie admitted that she stole everything, when we pressed her, except the little red book

(102)   *The fact that everyone resigned got much publicity except the defence minister

The *when* adverbial phrase is taken to mark the end of the matrix clause in (101). If so the *except* remnant is not in the same clause as its correlate *everything*. This indicates that QR can move *everything* successive cyclically so that it can adjoin to the remnant. (102) indicates that this movement is bounded and cannot take place out of complex NPs.

In sum, given that the correlate and remnant in EEs must form a constituent for interpretive reasons and given that they are unable to do so at DS then they must do so at LF. Given that this association can be unbounded but is blocked by islands, subjacency is implicated.

There are problems with the analysis, however. First, it is not clear that all islands block EEs. Consider the following WH-island violation.[41] There is a clear discrepancy between the case of overt movement in (103a) and the LF version in (103b). To my ear, the contrast is very sharp. This is unexpected given Reinhart's analysis.

(103a)   *What did you say how we might get t to Felix

(103b)   Bill told us how we might get the diamonds to Felix, when I asked him, but not the money

Second, Brody (1993) makes two important points against the analysis. He suggests that examples like (101) are misleading. *Pace* Reinhart, he proposes that the *except* remnant is associated with the embedded clause and that a stylistic reordering process allows the *when* adjunct to be interpolated. To bolster this observation Brody notes that when material that is less easily interpolated is used to mark the matrix clause boundary, unacceptability results. In (104), *to our friends* is an indirect object argument which has been extraposed from immediately after *admitted* to sentence final position. The resulting EE is considerably less felicitous than those Reinhart cites.

(104)   *John admitted that Mary stole everything to our friends except the diamonds

Brody further correctly notes that the constructed LF quantifier cannot take scope over a matrix indefinite. In (105), *everything except the car* cannot take scope over *someone*. But this too is unexpected if as Reinhart proposes it hangs so far up. The analysis requires that at LF, *everything except the car* forms a constituent hanging from the matrix IP. This should permit it to take scope over *someone*, contrary to fact.

(105)   Someone will admit that we stole everything, if you insist, except the car

One further point. If EEs are formed by LF movement we would expect them to be subject to the ECP. However, EEs do not seem to display subject/object asymmetries.

(106a)   John didn't admit that Bill saw anyone, when I pressed him, except for Frank
(106b)   John didn't admit that anyone was missing, when I pressed him, except for Frank

Taken together, these observations weaken the claim that EEs are formed via an operation like Move α subject to subjacency.

In this section, I have reviewed the standard arguments in favor of restricting LF movement by subjacency. The evidence, I believe, is inconclusive. The place of subjacency in a Minimalist theory is addressed in chapters 8 and 9.

3
More on LF

Chapter 2 reviewed the standard arguments in favor of postulating an LF level to grammatically encode the semantic properties of natural language sentences. This chapter presents more recent proposals.

The first part reviews Aoun and Li's theory of relative quantifier scope. To my knowledge, it is the only extant GB-style theory that systematically attempts to cover the intricacies of quantifier/quantifier scope interactions and WH/quantifier scope interactions in both English-type languages and East Asian languages like Chinese. The theory draws the right empirical distinctions by subtly exploiting the resources of an ECP-centered approach to the structure of LF. The aim is to review the details of this effort to better appreciate the scope and limits of GB-style, ECP-centered approaches of LF.

The second part of this chapter reviews recent work by Fiengo and May on ACD constructions. I review the rather impressive evidence that they marshal for the conclusion that VP elision sites manifest syntactic structure. In particular, the interpreted VP gaps are subject to various kinds of grammatical conditions.

1 Relative Quantifier Scope

1.1 Aoun and Li (1989)

Chapter 2 noted that QR can be used to represent the relative scope of quantified expressions. The ambiguous sentence (1a) has either of the representations (1b) or (1c), depending on whether QR applies first to the object or the subject.

(1a) Someone tried every dish
(1b) [[Every dish$_i$ someone$_j$ [t$_j$ tried t$_i$]]]
(1c) [Someone$_j$ [every dish$_i$ [t$_j$ tried t$_i$]]]

Additional evidence in favor of this QR approach to representing quantifier scope ambiguities comes from observing that certain instances of QR display apparent ECP effects in ECM (Exceptional Case Marking) constructions.

(2a) Someone expects every Republican to win reelection
(2b) Someone expects every Republican will win reelection

The examples in (2) contrast in that only the first allows the embedded universally quantified subject to have scope over the matrix indefinite. Chapter 2 shows that this follows if the ECP is assumed to limit the movement of the embedded quantified NP (QNP) in (2b). The trace left by QR-ing *every Republican* to the matrix clause so that it can enjoy semantic scope over *someone* violates the ECP in the LF structure underlying (2b) but not (2a).

Aoun and Li (1989) consider additional properties of relative quantifier scope. They concentrate on an important difference between English and Chinese as regards the ambiguity of sentences with multiple quantifiers. The facts are as follows. In English, QNPs in the same clause typically allow differential scope interpretations, as in (1). In Chinese, however, no similar ambiguity obtains. The Chinese sentence (3) only has a reading where the subject QNP takes scope over the object.[1]

(3) Yaoshi liangge ren zhaodao meige xiansuo
     If   two   men found   every clue

Observe that the English gloss is ambiguous, unlike its Chinese translation.

This contrast between English and Chinese is discussed in Huang (1982). Huang here proposes that in Chinese, in contrast to English, LF scope is isomorphic to SS c-command relations. Thus, in (3), *liangge ren*, the subject, must take scope over *meige xiansuo*, the object. Aoun and Li's theory tries to account for why this might be so in the cases that Huang discusses.[2]

In addition, Aoun and Li expand the data set considerably. They note that the data as described by Huang for Chinese are not quite right. Nor, for that matter, is the typically accepted description of English. In particular, it appears that there are constructions that permit non-SS scope order in Chinese and there are constructions that require SS scope order in English. In Chinese, passive appears to permit scope ambiguities, while in English double object constructions the relative quantifier scope reflects SS order.

(4a) Yaoshi liangge xiansuo bei meigeren zhaodao
      If   two   clues   by   everyone found
(4b) John assigned someone every problem

The Chinese (4a) is ambiguous and there can be a different two clues for every person despite the fact that *liangge xiansuo* c-commands *meigeren zhaodao* at SS. In the English (4b) *someone* must take scope over *every problem*. Thus, there are contexts in which Chinese acts like English and vice versa. The question is why.

The Aoun and Li answer has two parts. They propose a condition on LF that forbids nested quantifiers, the Minimal Binding Requirement (MBR) – (5) – and a Scope Principle (SP) to accommodate possible ambiguity – (6).

(5) MBR: Variables must be bound by the most local potential A'-binder
(6) SP: a quantifier A has scope over a quantifier B if A c-commands a member of the chain containing B

What do these two principles say? The MBR forbids phrase markers with multiple fronted quantifiers. Thus, LF cannot have structures such as (7).

(7) $Q_i Q_j [\ldots]$

Note that it is irrelevant for the MBR whether the quantifier variable structures are nested or crossed. Multiply stacked QNPs are always barred as they violate the MBR.

The MBR makes it impossible to represent the readings in which object QNPs take scope over subject QNPs in the standard way. The LF in (1b), for example, violates the MBR. Aoun and Li use the SP to accommodate these readings. SP introduces the notion of chain scope. It is not QNPs that scopally interact but their chains. In particular, if any part of a chain A is c-commanded by any part of a chain B the quantified heads of the A'-chains are in a potential scope relationship. For example, in a structure like (8), either Q_i or Q_j can be interpreted as taking scope over the other. The chain consisting of Q_i and its traces c-commands some part of the chain headed by Q_j and its traces and vice versa. Thus either Q_i or Q_j can take scope over the other.

(8) $Q_i [\ldots t_i \ldots Q_j [\ldots t_i \ldots t_j \ldots]]$

With these principles in play, LF phrase markers do not fully disambiguate relative quantifier scope (similar to May 1985). Rather, the grammar determines a family of permitted scope relations and extra grammatical factors specify a particular choice from within this group.[3] Let us consider some details.

The MBR accounts for the lack of ambiguity by forbidding quantifiers to stack. The trick is to explain why it is that ambiguity is ever possible given that relative scope cannot be represented in terms of the immediate c-command relations of QNPs after QR. What Aoun and Li (1989) suggest is that where quantificational ambiguity exists it is because there is a trace in the scope of an operator. For example, in (8) above, t_i is c-commanded by Q_j. Given the MBR, this trace t_i cannot be a variable as these must be locally A'-bound and Q_j is a more proximate potential binder than is Q_i.[4] So what must obtain in a structure like (8) is something like (9) where an NP trace (not a variable) is c-commanded by the lower Q_j.

(9) $Q_i [vbl-t_i [Q_j [NP-t_i vbl-t_j]]]$

In this configuration, Q_j can have scope over Q_i because it c-commands the NP-t. In addition, this structure does not violate the MBR because NP traces are not subject to this principle. Only variables are.

This is the mechanics. How can it be used to distinguish English from Chinese? Aoun and Li (1989) suggest that English has VP internal subjects but that this is not so in Chinese. The reason they propose for this parametric difference is that Chinese has weak Infl. This prohibits raising the subject to Spec IP. A weak Infl prevents subject raising from VP internal position to Spec IP on the (*Barriers*) assumption that V-raising (at least by LF) is required to L-mark the VP and thereby deprive it of barrierhood status. Without V-raising the VP remains a barrier and blocks A-movement from Spec VP to Spec IP.[5] English has the LF structure (10a) while Chinese has the structure (10b). The absence of a VP internal NP trace, the residue of raising the subject from VP internal position to Spec IP, prohibits Chinese from having the interpretation where the object QNP has scope over the subject.

(10a)　$[_{IP}$ QNP$_i$ $[_{IP}$ vbl-t$_i$ $[_{VP}$ QNP$_j$ $[_{VP}$ NP-t$_i$ ... vbl-t$_j$]]]]

(10b)　$[_{IP}$ QNP$_i$ $[_{IP}$ vbl-t$_i$ $[_{VP}$ QNP$_j$ $[_{VP}$ ... vbl-t$_j$]]]]

Aoun and Li claim that a structure similar to (10b) shows up in English double object constructions. They analyze these as VP small clauses. There is no NP-t in the VP small clause and hence the object cannot have scope over the indirect object. The SS of (11a) is (11b) and the LF is (11c). In the latter, no i-indexed NP-t is c-commanded by any member of the j-indexed chain. As such, the universal quantifier cannot be interpreted as taking scope over the existentially quantified indirect object.

(11a)　John gave someone every book

(11b)　[John $[_{VP1}$ gave$_i$ $[_{VP2}$ someone $[e_i$ every book]]]]

(11c)　[John $[_{VP1}$ gave$_i$ [someone$_i$ $[_{VP2}$ vbl-t$_i$ [every book$_j$ $[e_i$ vbl-t$_j$]]]]

Consider now Chinese passive constructions. They permit quantifier scope ambiguities. This is to be expected on the Aoun and Li analysis because in passive phrase markers there is an NP-t in VP object position. The structure of (12a) at LF is (12b).

(12a)　Yaoshi liangge xiansuo bei meigeren zhaodao
　　　　If　　two　　clues　　by everyone　found

(12b)　... [liangge xiansuo$_i$ [vbl-t$_i$ [meigeren$_j$ [bei vbl-t$_j$ [zhaodao NP-t$_i$]]]]

Aoun and Li observe that this analysis to relative quantifier scope also handles the ambiguity of (13). The NP-t left by subject raising affords the embedded quantifier the opportunity to take scope over the matrix indefinite.

(13a)　Someone seems to have attended every rally

(13b)　[Someone$_i$ [vbl-t$_i$ seems [every rally$_j$ [NP-t$_i$ to have attended vbl-t$_j$]]]]

It is not clear, however, whether this is a good result. The reason is that Aoun (1982) provides evidence that lowering seems to be blocked in certain configurations. For example, in (14) the higher reflexive forces the existential matrix subject to take scope over the embedded universal.

(14) Someone seems to himself to have attended every rally

These data suggest that an analysis in terms of lowering (see Aoun 1982, May 1985) is more empirically adequate. The lack of scope ambiguity in (14) follows from the Binding Theory (BT) if it holds at LF. One cannot lower because there will be an unbound anaphor left behind.

The SP cannot similarly accommodate the lack of ambiguity. The LF structure of (14) is (15). Observe that the embedded NP-t_i is still c-commanded by *every rally*$_j$. This should allow the universal QNP to take scope over the matrix subject.[6]

(15)   [Someone$_i$ [vbl-t_i seems to himself$_i$ [every rally$_j$ [NP-t_i to have attended vbl-t_j]]]]

Curiously, Aoun and Li note the absence of analogous ambiguities in Chinese raising constructions. Quantified NPs in Chinese raising constructions reflect their SS c-command relations.

(16)   Yaoshi liangge ren keneng kandao meigeren
     If   *two*   *men likely   see   everyone*

Thus, in (16) *liangge ren* must take scope over *meigeren*; this, despite the fact that after raising (16) has the structure (17a). This phrase marker supports the LF (17b) which should allow the embedded universal to take scope over the matrix existential in accord with the SP.

(17a)   [liagge ren [keneng [t_i [kandao meigeren]]]]
(17b)   [liagge ren$_i$ [vbl-t_i keneng [meigeren$_j$ NP-t_i [kandao t_j]]]]

This reading, however, is impossible in Chinese.

Aoun and Li argue that the absence of this scope reading is due to the fact that the lower NP trace is eliminated as the result of a restructuring rule that raises the embedded predicate (*kandao*) to form a single complex predicate (and thereby a single sentence) at LF. The reason for the obligatory restructuring is, once again, the absence of V to I raising in Chinese. Without it, raising the embedded subject to matrix subject position encounters barrierhood problems. Without V to I raising, the matrix VP fails to be L-marked and so is not porous. Thus, the VP dominating the subject is a barrier to A-movement. Without reanalysis to remove the offending NP-t, then, ECP problems ensue.

This solution raises another puzzle, however. If it is correct, why do barrierhood problems not hold in simple cases of passive as well? Should the barrier status of VP not block passivization or require the trace in object position to delete? Were this to obtain, it would require alteration of the above account of the quantificational ambiguity of Chinese passives. There are, no doubt, possible technical ways of differentiating the passive and raising cases. However, given that Aoun and Li pursue another more principled alternative in Aoun and Li (1993a: Chapters 2, 3), I will not suggest any.

Aoun and Li (1989) consider one more case. They observe that in contrast to the double object cases, the prepositional indirect object (PIO) constructions allow for quantifier ambiguities. Contrast the examples in (18).

(18a)   John gave someone every book
(18b)   John gave something to everyone

I provided the structure of (18a) in (11c) above. The LF structure Aoun and Li propose for (18b) is given in (19).

(19)   Something$_i$ [John [$_{VP1}$ gave$_j$ [$_{SC}$ vbl-t$_i$ [$_{VP2}$ everyone$_k$ [$_{VP2}$ e$_j$ NP-t$_i$] to vbl-t$_k$]]]]]

Observe that *everyone$_k$* has *NP-t$_i$* in its c-command domain. It is thus possible to interpret *everyone* as taking scope over *something*. Note further that Aoun and Li crucially assume (following Larson 1988) that the object in PIOs A-moves to the small clause subject position. Without this movement, there could be no scope ambiguity as the MBR prevents the A'-chains formed via QR from interleaving. The same assumptions account for the Chinese data. As in English, double object constructions (20a) do not display quantifier scope ambiguities and PIOs (20b) do.

(20a)   Wo song sange ren neiben shu
        I   gave three men every   book
(20b)   Wo song sanben shu gei meigeren
        I   gave three   books to everyone

To sum up, Aoun and Li (1989) advance a theory to handle the different relative quantifier scope facts in English and Chinese. The analysis is driven by two new principles, the MBR and the SP. In addition, various language-specific differences between English and Chinese are observed which lead to the different observed patterning of data. In particular, English, in contrast to Chinese, has VP internal subjects raising to Spec IP. In Chinese, Spec IP NPs are base generated. As expected, where raising to Spec IP is not at issue (i.e., in double object constructions) the two languages pattern identically.

Aoun and Li make use of an important ancillary hypothesis, the *Barriers* theory of A-chains and L-marking. The difference between English and Chinese is tied to the appalling weakness of Infl in Chinese. It is so weak that even LF V-raising to Infl is prohibited. This prevents the VP from being L-marked. It consequently acts as a barrier preventing A-movement across it.

As noted, this set of assumptions has some empirical problems, mainly in dealing with raising constructions. One virtue of the Aoun and Li (1993a) theory is that it does not encounter similar difficulties.

1.2   *Aoun and Li (1993a)*

Aoun and Li (1993a) present a revised theory of these quantifier scope ambiguities. They here eliminate all reference to NP-t traces in determining relative quantifier scope. The SP still determines scope via chains but only the non-NP-t links count. Thus, X takes scope over Y just in case some part of X's A'-chain c-commands some part of Y's A'-chain.[7] This reformulation of the SP helps to solve many of the problems noted above, in particular the noted discrepancy between Chinese and English raising constructions.

Aoun and Li make several key technical assumptions in revamping their account. A key one is that they adopt an adapted Generalized Binding Condition (21).[8]

(21) An A'-binder B is a potential antecedent for a variable V iff indexing B and V does not violate any grammatical principle e.g. principle C, the theta criterion, etc.

With (21) in mind, consider the basic cases. Aoun and Li adopt the *Barriers* prohibition on adjunction to expressions in theta marked positions.[9] They observe that this permits adjunction to NPs in non-theta positions. Exploiting this possibility, Aoun and Li postulate a rule of bare Q(uantifier) adjunction in which the quantifier in a QNP is adjoined to the NP that contains it. If one assumes that in English, Spec IP is a non-theta position (as it is if there is raising from a VP internal subject position) then it should be possible to adjoin a quantifier to this NP. A quantifier so adjoined has narrower scope than a quantifier adjoined to IP. (22) displays the envisioned structure at LF. Q_j has adjoined to the subject NP in this case while Q_i has adjoined to IP.

(22) $[_{IP} Q_i [_{IP} [_{NP} Q_j [_{NP} NP \ t_j \ldots] \ldots t_i \ldots]$

This gets the correct c-command relationships among QNPs. For illustration consider the example in (23a).

(23a) Some student attended every class
(23b) $[_{IP} Every_i [_{IP} [_{NP} some_j [_{NP} t_j \ student]] \ attended [_{NP} t_i \ class]]]$
(23c) $[_{IP} Some_j [_{IP} [_{NP} t_j \ student] [_{VP} every_i [_{VP} attended [_{NP} t_i \ class]]]]]$

It has as a possible LF (23b). In (23b), *every* c-commands *some*. This is interpreted as giving *every* scope over *some*. In (23c), the opposite c-command relations hold and so the opposite scope relations obtain. In effect, Q-adjunction introduces an additional option to those made available by QR. It is possible to append a Q to its immediate QNP. The appended Q does not c-command outside the NP it is appended to. So, it fails to c-command the variable t_i in (23b). This is crucial, for otherwise the structure is in jeopardy of violating the MBR. Note as well that the adjoined *some* immediately A'-binds the variable t_j. Thus, adjoining *every* to IP does not induce an MBR violation either.

For Chinese, Aoun and Li continue to assume the absence of VP internal subjects.[10] In Chinese, therefore, Q-adjunction to the NP in Spec IP is not possible as the subject is a theta position. In effect, the analogue of (23b) is illicit in Chinese as the adjunction will lead to a theta criterion violation. However, the assumption that Spec IP is a theta position in Chinese active sentences effectively prohibits scope ambiguities in these sentence types given that the only way to allow object QNPs to scope over subject QNPs is via a phrase marker like (22).

This route through the data obviates the need for invoking NP-t's to get the scope facts. This approach also implies that passive subjects in Chinese act like regular English subjects. In passives, the object is moved to Spec IP. This means that Spec IP is not a theta position in passives. As a result, Q-adjunction to the subject NP is permitted and the resulting scope ambiguities are possible.

Raising constructions are slightly more complex. Recall that in these constructions the raised quantified subject in Chinese must have scope over a lower QNP. The current approach can derive the difference between English and Chinese in a unified manner without invoking restructuring. To see this, assume that lowering can apply in either English or Chinese. The structure of a relevant raising construction prior to LF movement is (24).

(24) $[_{IP} \text{QNP}_i \dots [_{IP} t_i \dots \text{QNP}_j]]$

If lowering applies in English, then adjunction to NP is allowed by the Q because the raising position t_i is not a theta position. Consequently, (25) is a licit LF structure in English after lowering and Q-adjunction.[11]

(25) $[_{IP} t_i \dots [_{IP} Q_j [_{IP} [_{NP} Q_i [_{NP} t_i N']] \dots [_{NP} t_j N']]]]$

The structure (25) is banned in Chinese. The Q-adjunction to the NP in the embedded Spec IP position is prohibited as this is a theta position in Chinese. As a structure like (25) is necessary for getting scope ambiguities, its absence derives the Chinese scope facts in raising constructions without recourse to a restructuring process.

An additional benefit of this approach is that it allows Aoun and Li to account for the quantifier scope/binding correlation noted in (14). Lowering is prohibited from the matrix if this leaves an unbound anaphor. Thus, in cases such as (14), repeated here for convenience, the matrix subject must be interpreted as having scope over the embedded object.

(14)   Someone seemed to himself to have attended every rally

In effect, the current proposal reduces the scope possibilities within raising constructions in both Chinese and English to whatever obtains within simple clauses. This is empirically the right result. In Chinese, there is no scope ambiguity in either while in English there is.

Aoun and Li introduce one further modification to their proposal. In addition to Q-adjunction (which they regard as obligatory) they postulate a rule of NP adjunction which moves a whole QNP to an A'-position.[12] This modification is prompted by the desire to accommodate the facts concerning antecedent-contained deletion (ACD) reviewed in chapter 2 above. If ACDs are licensed by moving the whole QNP out from under the VP then simply moving the Q from an object QNP will not suffice. As such, Aoun and Li propose that whole QNPs can be moved prior to Q-adjunction. The problem is illustrated in (26). (26a) is the structure one gets without movement of the whole QNP. The problem that ACDs pose, as May (1985) observed, is that it is impossible to copy VP1 into the VP2 gap without regress. The only way to evade this problem is to move VP2 out from under VP1. QR, an operation that moves the entire QNP out, accomplishes this. Simple Q-adjunction does not. To accommodate these facts, Aoun and Li assume an analogue of QR which can adjoin an entire QNP to some A'-position prior to Q-adjunction. A structure like (26b) is thereby derivable.

(26a) $[NP [_{VP} Q_i [_{VP} V [_{NP} t_i [rc \ldots [_{VP} e] \ldots]]]]$
(26b) $[NP [_{VP} [_{NP} Q_j [_{NPi} t_j N' [rc \ldots [_{VP} e]]] [_{VP} V t_i]]]$

In contrast to Q-adjunction, NP movement is optional. It must apply prior to Q-adjunction if the NP to which the Q adjoins is in a theta position. Thus, in Chinese, the structure of a transitive clause is the one in (27a). English can have the structure (27b). The latter is prohibited in Chinese given the thematic status of Spec IP in Chinese. The possibility of Q-adjunction in English to the QNP in Spec IP is what permits the scope ambiguity in English that is prohibited in Chinese. The thematic status of Spec IP in Chinese forces the subject to adjoin to IP before Q-adjunction can take place. This, in conjunction with the MBR, restricts the object QNP from adjoining to IP and taking scope over the subject.

(27a) $[_{IP} [Q_i [t_i N']]_i [_{IP} t_i [_{VP} [Q_j [t_j N']]_j [_{VP} V t_j]]]]$
(27b) $[_{IP} [Q_j [t_j N']]_j [_{IP} [Q_i [t_i N']]_i [_{VP} t_i [_{VP} V t_j]]]]$

Observe two final points. Q-adjunction leads to a representation in which the NP acts as a restrictor on the Q. This is similar in spirit to the May QR rule and the proposal in Heim (1982) that we syntactically distinguish a quantifier's restrictive scope and its nuclear scope. However, though this is Aoun and Li's stated intent, the structure in (27b) differs from (27a) in a crucial respect which somewhat undermines this proposal. (27a) has two exposed variables bound by the quantifiers Q_i and Q_j, the ones exposed via Q-adjunction within the restrictive N's and the ones due to QNP adjunction that sit in the case-marked theta positions Spec IP and [NP, VP] respectively. In (17b), this still holds true for Q_j but not for Q_i. The latter binds only one variable, the one exposed via Q-adjunction. It is crucial to this analysis that the trace in Spec VP not be a variable. The reason is that if it were, it would have to be A'-bound. This in turn would require that Spec IP be an A'-position or that the adjoined Q_i c-command the trace in Spec VP. However, if either of these options obtained, then the postverbal variable t_j would violate the MBR. Whatever bound the variable in Spec VP, be it the QNP in Spec IP or the adjoined Q, would be a closer A'-binder for t_j than QNP$_j$ which is adjoined to IP. Therefore, it is crucial to assume that the trace in Spec VP is an NP-t not subject to the MBR. But if it is, then an important structural asymmetry obtains between Chinese and English. The latter syntactically offers fewer variables than the former for the purposes of representing the meaning of quantified sentences. This in turn suggests that the interpretation of quantification is rather different in the two types of languages. This is an unintended (and unwelcome) consequence of this version of the analysis.

Second, the semantic scope of the Q is not what it c-commands but what the NP it is adjoined to c-commands. This is important, for otherwise the relative c-command positions of the QNPs would not contribute to determining relative quantifier scope. It is also crucial to this analysis that the adjoined Q *not* c-command out of the NP it is adjoined to. In other words, it is a part of this analysis that c-command is not defined in terms of exclusion. If it were, (27b) would violate the MBR as Q_i would be a more proximate A'-binder to the variable trace in post-V position than would the QNP adjoined to IP. Curiously, then, though Q-adjunction is essential to the analysis, it does not directly contribute to the structural determination of quantifier scope. The relationship is more indirect. Q-adjunction forces QNP movement in particular circumstances and it is QNP c-command relations that determine relative quantifier scope.

Despite these caveats, the approach is very attractive in that the format eventually attained is semantically reasonable (at least most of the time). There is a rather obvious relationship between the semantics of these constructions and their logical form. Furthermore, we have eliminated use of NP-t's as part of the chain that determines scope. NP-t's are unnecessary for the representation of relative quantifier scope.

2   The Relative Scope of WHs and Quantifiers

2.1   The Problem

Aoun and Li (1993a) consider a further question: do variables play a role in relative scope or are they, like NP traces, irrelevant as well? This question relates to a comparative set of data bearing on certain subject/object asymmetries in LF that we introduced in chapter 2.

May (1985), we recall, observes the following contrast.

(28a)   What did everyone say
(28b)   Who said everything

In (28a) the subject can have scope over the WH whereas this is not possible in (28b). Why not? May's answer is that we are witnessing a typical ECP effect here similar to the ones evident in superiority cases such as (29).

(29)   *What did who say

The reasoning is as follows. May makes use of two principles. First, he assumes that the ECP holds at LF. Second, his analysis invokes a scope principle which says that elements dominated by all the same maximal projections are freely ordered with respect to each other scopally. Given this, consider the relevant structures.

The LF of (28b) (if the pair–list reading is desired) requires the scope order in (30). With the universal quantifier adjoined to IP, it is not excluded by IP and so it c-commands the WH in CP. This allows it to take scope over the WH.

(30) $[_{CP}$ Who$_i$ $[_{IP}$ every$_j$ $[_{IP}$ t$_i$ ... t$_j$]]]

However, May proposes that this structure violates the ECP and so is ill-formed. The subject is assumed not to be locally A'-bound. The only grammatically legitimate LF is (31).

(31)   Who$_i$ $[_{IP}$ t$_i$ $[_{VP}$ every$_j$ ... t$_j$ ...]]

Here *every* has adjoined to VP. However, in this structure, the universally quantified NP and the WH are not in the same scope domain as IP dominates the Q but not the WH.[13]

Contrast this with the structure of (28a).

(32)   What$_i$ $[_{IP}$ every$_j$ $[_{IP}$ t$_j$ ... $[_{VP}$ ... t$_i$]]]

Here *every* and *what* share the same projections and so can have either relative scope. Furthermore, the ECP is not relevant as the subject trace is locally A'-bound.

Aoun and Li (1993a) object to this account on two grounds. First, they observe that the ECP does not hold in Chinese, i.e. there are no subject/object asymmetries. Thus, in Chinese either a subject or an object can be extracted out of a WH-island equally well as Huang (1982) pointed out. (33a) has both the interpretation (33b) in which the WH-object has matrix scope or (33c) in which the subject does.

(33a)   Ta xiang-zhidao shei mai sheme
        He wondered   who buy what
(33b)   What did he wonder who bought
(33c)   Who did he wonder what bought

Nonetheless, the contrast observed in May (1985) for English, holds in Chinese as well. (34a) can support a pair–list reading while (34b) cannot.

(34a)   Meigeren dou maile sheme
        Everyone all buy   what
        "What did everyone buy"
(34b)   Shei maile meige dongxi
        Who buy   every thing
        "Who bought everything"

They further point out that there are problems with May's scope principle. Once again, consider the data that Aoun and Li discuss concerning relative quantifier scope. How does May's scope principle account for the fact that Chinese active sentences with two Qs are unambiguous? The only way to track these facts is to forbid QR from raising QNPs to IP in these cases. The problem, of course, is why such raising is not forbidden in passives. Thus, the Chinese facts seem to indicate that the scope principle in May (1985) is empirically inadequate.

We have seen above how Aoun and Li accommodate these data. The MBR provides the relevant restrictions if the technicalities discussed above are adopted. However, there is a problem with this solution to the relative quantifier facts when extended to the WH/quantifier interactions. In particular, how does one represent the ambiguity in (28a)? The natural suggestion is (32). But is (32) not a violation of the MBR? Aoun and Li say it is not but seeing why not requires a digression into the theory of Generalized Binding.

2.2   Generalized Binding and Variable Types

Aoun (1985, 1986) proposes an analysis of ECP effects in terms of a theory that extends notions familiar from A-binding to the A'-domain. In particular, Generalized Binding proposes two kinds of variables. In the unmarked case, variables are "anaphoric." A(naphoric) – variables must be locally A'-bound within their domains. Typical A-variables are those left by the movement of WHs such as *how, why,* and the standard QNPs such as *everyone, someone, two books,* etc.

There is a second class of variables. These are typically left by WHs such as *who, what, where,* and *when.* They are different from simple anaphoric variables in that their domains are determined more indirectly. In particular, the licensing of these variables is accomplished by considering possible coindexations and seeing whether these conform to principle C. To get a feel for the system, consider the Generalized Binding approach to superiority effects.

(35a)   Who bought what
(35b)   *What did who buy
(36a) $[[What_j [who_i]]_i [t_i Agr_i bought t_j]]$
(36b) $[[Who_i [what_j]]_j [t_j Agr_i bought t_j]]$

The central notion is that of A'-binding. The idea is that a variable must be A'-bound in its domain. The domain of a standard A-variable is the smallest one that contains a SUBJECT. SUBJECTs, following Chomsky (1981), include [NP, NP], [NP, IP], and Agr. In effect, SUBJECTs are the most prominent nominal expressions in NPs and clauses. Agr features are assimilated to other nominal expressions in just being bundles of phi-features.

In addition to A-variables, there are A/C-variables. The domain of an A/C-variable is the smallest NP or clause where it has an *accessible* SUBJECT. A

SUBJECT is accessible for an A/C-variable just in case indexing it and the A/C-variable does not violate principle C.

Assume that the variables in (36) are A/C-variables. Consider now their domains. In (36a), the domain of t_i is the matrix clause. It is indexed with the Agr node as it agrees with it. This indexing does not violate principle C or agreement would never be possible. This licit indexing leaves the matrix clause as the domain of this variable. Note that t_i is A'-bound within the matrix clause by who_i in CP.

What of t_j? It does not have t_i as an accessible SUBJECT as coindexing the two variables would violate principle C. Both are R-expressions and the subject c-commands the object. Indexation with the Agr, another (SUBJECT) is no better. The reason is that Agr is coindexed with t_i, a reflex of agreement, and so a principle C violation would ensue given the transitivity of coindexation. Hence, the object variable has no domain and so need not be A'-bound.[14] In fact, it is not A'-bound as $what_j$ does not c-command the variable. Nonetheless, t_j meets the requirements of Generalized Binding. It is A'-bound in its domain for the simple reason that t_j has no domain.

Consider now (36b). The binding domains of t_i and t_j are the same as in (36a). The difference is that t_j which need not be bound is, while t_i which must be is not. Therefore, the phrase marker is illicit and the corresponding superiority effect obtains in (35b).

To recap. Central to the theory of Generalized Binding is the postulation of at least two kinds of variable types whose domains are determined in different ways. For an A (naphoric) – variable V, D is the domain for V, iff D is the smallest constituent containing V and D has a SUBJECT. For an A/C-variable V', D is a domain for V' iff D is the smallest constituent containing V' and a SUBJECT accessible to V'. A SUBJECT is accessible to V' iff it meets (21), i.e. indexing V' and the SUBJECT do not violate principle C. With these details in mind, let us return to the problem of WH/quantifier scope interactions given the MBR.

2.3   MBR and WH/Q Structures

Consider (32) repeated here for convenience.

(32)   What$_i$ [$_{IP}$ every$_j$ [$_{IP}$ t$_j$ . . . [$_{VP}$ . . . t$_i$]]]

The problem at hand is why this structure does not violate the MBR. The reason Aoun and Li (1993a) offer is that *every* is not a potential binder for t_i as indexing the two would violate principle C. In other words, Aoun and Li invoke the theory of variable types in determining potential A'-binders. Given that *what* leaves behind an A/C-variable, its potential A'-binders are only those that are accessible under licit reindexation. With this, the reason that the universal quantifier in (32) does not trigger the MBR is that it is not a potential antecedent. Coindexing *every* and t_i violates principle C given the coindexation of *every* and t_j. Observe, further, that with the structure in (32) *every* can take scope over *what* because the two A'-chains interleave. In particular, *every*$_j$ c-commands t_j.

Observe that with these assumptions, we can account for the unacceptability of the other May (1985) cases as well. Consider (28b) again, repeated here as (37a). To have the pair–list reading it would have to have the LF structure in (37b) in which the universal quantifier is taking scope over *who* or (37c) where it takes scope over the variable in Spec IP. In either representation, the chain headed by the universal quantifier c-commands some part of the A'-chain headed by *who*.

(37a)   Who said everything

(37b)   [Everything$_i$ [t$_j$ Agr$_j$ said t$_i$]]

(37c)   [Who$_j$ [everything$_i$ [t$_j$ Agr said t$_i$]]]

Both (37b, c) must be ill-formed. (37b) is straightforward. It violates the MBR. The variable t_i is an A-variable. Consequently, its potential A'-binders are determined independently of principle C. As such, *who* is a potential A'-binder for t_i and as it is closer than *everything*, the structure violates the MBR and so is ill-formed.

(37c) should also be ill-formed to derive the relevant data. However, here things are a bit trickier. It must be the case that the structure violates the MBR. It does if *everything* is a potential antecedent for t_j. The problem is that t_j is an A/C-variable and coindexing it and *everything* does violate principle C if we assume, as we have until now, that indexing is transitive. The violation comes about from the fact that *everything* is coindexed with the variable t_i. Hence indexing *everything* and t_j will violate principle C. Thus, *everything* should not be a potential antecedent for the subject variable and the structure should be well formed.

There are other ways, however, to interpret the potential antecedent requirement to get the correct results in this case. Consider the following option. We do not relativize the notion of potential antecedent as Aoun and Li do. Instead, assume (38).

(38)   Any variable must be minimally bound in its domain

The point of (38) is that if a variable must be bound in a domain, then it must be minimally bound within it. What we have done is pack the MBR into the theory of Generalized Binding. Adopting (38), we can rule out (37c). The subject A/C-variable t_j has a domain as indexing it an Agr (a SUBJECT) does not violate principle C. But given that it has a domain, it must be minimally bound within it. This fails as *everything* intervenes between it and *who*. An MBR violation results and the structure is ill-formed, as desired.

A similar account extends to the A-variable in (37b). Here t_i is an A-variable. Its domain is the clause it is in. It is not minimally bound within this clause given the intervening *who*. In sum, given (38), all works out well for English.

Unfortunately, this account cannot extend to Chinese, where, as Aoun and Li observe, similar data hold. The reason is due to the absence of Agr in

Chinese, which in turn accounts for the absence of subject/object asymmetries in Chinese (as compared with English). The LF structures of the Chinese analogue of (37a) are (39a, b).

(39a) [Everything$_i$ [who$_j$ [t$_j$ said t$_i$]]]
(39b) [Who$_j$ [everything$_i$ [t$_j$ said t$_i$]]]

We can rule out (39a) as we did for English as an MBR violation. The problem is (39b). We cannot invoke (38) as we did in English, since in Chinese there is no Agr and so no subject/object asymmetries as regards domains. In neither case do the variables have domains. Hence in neither should they require minimal binders.

Aoun and Li suggest a remedy for this problem. They propose that not even variables play a role in assigning relative scope. *Only* the A'-links of an A'-chain are involved in determining relative quantifier scope. On this assumption, (37c) and (39b) are irrelevant. *Everything* does not c-command any A'-member of the chain headed by *who*. As such, it cannot take scope over *who*. The relevant structures are (37b) and (39a) which we saw violate the MBR.[15]

Aoun and Li provide additional empirical motivation for the proposed restriction of chain scope to A'-expressions. They point to the lack of ambiguity in cases such as (40a) and its Chinese counterpart (40b). Similarly (40c) and its Chinese counterpart (40d) are ambiguous.

(40a) What do you wonder whether everyone saw
(40b) Ni xiang-zhidao meigeren shi-bu-shi doun kandao sheme
(40c) What do you think everyone saw
(40d) Ni xiang meigeren doun kandao sheme

If this is correct then we do not wish to have variables included in the determination of relative scope as there is a WH-variable in the embedded object position in both (40a, b) and (40c, d). To distinguish these, Aoun and Li propose that in the latter cases there can be a trace of the movement of the WH-operator appended to VP (t#$_i$ in (41b)). This trace is antecedently governed from Comp. Antecedent government of a similar VP-adjoined trace is not possible in the second case. In short, in the second derivation, the relevant intermediate variable (t*$_i$ in (41a)) would have to be deleted and so there would be no A'-element of the chain headed by *what* c-commanded by any A'-member of the chain headed by the universal quantifier at LF. The relevant structures are provided in (41).

(41a) What$_i$ [you wonder [whether [everyone$_j$ [t$_j$ [$_{VP}$ t*$_i$ [$_{VP}$ saw t$_j$]]]]]]
(41b) What$_i$ [you think [t$_i$ [everyone$_j$ [t$_j$ [$_{VP}$ t#$_i$ [$_{VP}$ saw t$_j$]]]]]]

It is a further virtue of this theory that it can account for the wide scope that the *every* phrase can have over the WH in (42a) without moving the *every* phrase to matrix position, in contrast to the analysis in May (1985).

(42a) What did John say that everyone saw t

(42b) $[_{CP}$ What$_j$ $[_{IP}$ John say $[_{CP}$ t$_j$ that $[_{IP}$ everyone$_i$ $[_{IP}$ t$_j$ $[_{VP}$ t*$_j$ $[_{VP}$ saw t$_j$]]]]]]]

The LF is provided in (42b). The trace $t*_j$ adjoined to VP is an A'-link in the A'-chain headed by *what*$_j$. It is c-commanded by the IP adjoined *everyone*$_i$ (which is also in an A'-position). *Everyone* can thereby have *what* in its scope.

This is superior to the May (1985) analysis, for the sort of long movement from the finite subject position invoked there is generally unacceptable. This is demonstrated in the non-ambiguity of (43). Here, the *some* phrase must take scope over the *every* phrase. The alternative reading is not possible, as it should be if long movement from embedded finite subjects were possible.

(43) Someone believes that everyone left early

Aoun and Li note that their analysis of the data in (41) invokes a Lasnik and Saito (1984, 1992)/*Barriers* approach to the ECP. It assumes that the intermediate trace adjoined to VP must be gamma-marked to be licit. This is possible in (41b) but not (41a) as the trace $t*$ is not antecedent-governed. Aoun and Li suggest that this intermediate illicit trace could be eliminated via Generalized Binding as well. However, if so, Generalized Binding will require some further articulation. The reason is that the intermediate trace has no domain on this approach as coindexing it and any SUBJECT would result in a violation of principle C (see Aoun 1985 for details).

Note, further, that the pair–list interpretations are hard to get in structures that do not have the same antecedent government problems. Neither example in (44) supports a pair–list reading.

(44a) What don't you think everyone saw

(44b) What do you wonder whether John thinks everyone saw

These examples share a similar problem. The trace adjoined to lowest VP can be licensed from the local Comp position. As such it should allow the embedded *everyone* to take scope over the matrix *what*. However, this is not possible.

(45a) [What$_i$ [you n't think [t$_i$ [everyone$_j$ [t$_j$ $[_{VP}$ t*$_i$ $[_{VP}$ saw t$_i$]]]]]]]

(45b) [What$_i$ [you wonder [whether [John thinks [t$_i$ [everyone$_j$ [t$_j$ $[_{VP}$ t*$_i$ $[_{VP}$ saw t$_i$]]]]]]]]]

This is significant for it is not clear why the intermediate trace $t*$ in the lower VP could not remain there, being gamma marked by the trace in the local Comp. This latter trace in Comp might have to delete, but nothing in the Lasnik and Saito/*Barriers* system prevents this from gamma marking $t*$ before deleting at LF. It appears that neg elements cause problems and it is not clear that they can be finessed using the Lasnik and Saito/*Barriers* theory.

Consider how a Generalized Binding theory might account for these data. As noted above, we must more fully specify the algorithm for determining a variable/trace's domain. The technical problem can be briefly summarized as follows. It is not clear that the story that Aoun and Li tell can rule out the intermediate VP adjoined trace on Generalized Binding grounds. Consider how Generalized Binding accounts for the ambiguity of (46) on the new format.

(46)   What did everyone say

Aoun and Li would have to say there is VP adjunction by the WH-element and that the A'-trace left there is what permits the subject to have scope over the WH in Comp.

(47)   [What$_i$ [everyone$_j$ [t$_j$ [$_{VP}$ t$_i$ [$_{VP}$ say t$_i$]]]]]

Now what is it that prevents the universal QNP in subject position from being the minimal binder for the object WH-trace? It is because indexing the quantifier and the variable t_i would violate principle C. The quantifier is indexed with the subject t_j which c-commands t_i. Thus if t_i assumes *everyone*'s "j" index we arrive at a principle C violation. Observe that the adjoined VP trace had better not block principle C or this account fails here.

   Now consider the long movement cases Aoun and Li discuss. Does the adjoined trace t^* need an A'-binder? The algorithm says it does if indexing it and a SUBJECT would not violate any grammatical principle. But indexing it with any of the SUBJECTs *you* or t_j or the two Agr markers would violate principle C, just as above. The variable $t\#_i$ is coindexed with t^*_i so if the "i" indices are changed to "j", a principle C violation should ensue.

(48)   What$_i$ [you$_k$ Agr$_k$ wonder [whether [everyone$_j$ Agr$_j$ [t$_j$ [$_{VP}$ t$^*_i$ [$_{VP}$ saw t$\#_i$]]]]]]

   There is a way around this problem. Assume that reindexing the trace t^* does not lead to reindexation of the variable $t\#_i$ in embedded object position. In effect, each trace would be evaluated with respect to Generalized Binding independently of the other expressions it is in a chain relation with. Instead of changing all the "i" indices to "j" we just change the index of the element whose domain is being evaluated. If we assume this, and we assume that adjoined traces are not subject to principle C for their domain evaluations (they are not in argument positions), we can technically circumvent the current problem. The trace t^* in (48) must be bound in the lower clause. Indexing it (and it alone) with *everyone* does not lead to a principle C violation. The relevant structure for evaluating the domain of t^* is (49).

(49)   What$_i$ [you$_k$ Agr$_k$ wonder [whether [everyone$_j$ Agr$_j$ [t$_j$ [$_{VP}$ t$^*_j$ [$_{VP}$ saw t$\#_i$]]]]]]

   This elaboration of the indexing convention for domain evaluation will also work to solve the problems (45) raised. The principles of Generalized Binding apply to LF phrase markers. Hence they apply after deletion. This prevents intermediate traces from licensing their bindees (i.e. gamma marking them) and then deleting. This effectively forces the gamma marker of an intermediate trace to remain at LF and itself become licensed. In (45), this means that the intermediate trace in Comp must be bound. We assume that Neg blocks this in a manner analogous to a WH in Comp, then the unacceptability of these cases follows. The relevant structures are provided in (50). To license t^* we require that $t\#$ locally bind it. But then $t\#$ must in turn be locally licensed. It cannot be. Hence it must be deleted. However, if it deletes, then t^* must delete as well as it cannot be locally licensed.

(50a) [What$_i$ [you n't think [t#$_i$ [everyone$_j$ [t$_j$ [$_{VP}$ t*$_i$ [$_{VP}$ saw t$_i$]]]]]]]

(50b) [What$_i$ [you wonder [whether [John thinks [t#$_i$ [everyone$_j$ [t$_j$ [$_{VP}$ t*$_i$ [$_{VP}$ saw t$_i$]]]]]]]]]

In sum, we can derive the correct relative scope configurations in these cases given a revised version of Generalized Binding. Crucial to the result is that the principles of Generalized Binding apply at LF, that the MBR restricts LF phrase markers and that only A'-elements are relevant for computing relative quantifier scope.[16]

Before moving on, it is worth observing that there is currently no other theory that attempts to cover such a rich and complex empirical domain. The fact that the theory required to cover these data is intricate is in and of itself no ground for rejecting it. Furthermore, it is important to observe that many of the complications stem from elaborations of an A'-movement/ECP approach to issues of scope and quantification. Within GB-style theories, there are not many ways of reining in A'-movement operations except in terms of the ECP. Thus, if one represents quantification in terms of A'-movement there is little theoretical choice beyond elaborating the conditions on antecedent government, be this through the traces it applies to (e.g. to adjunct traces in one way, argument traces another), the domains it is effective in (e.g. domains defined in terms of barriers or SUBJECTs) or the mechanics of its applicability (e.g. gamma marking, binding at SS and LF or just at LF).

I mention this because there is a general perception that Generalized Binding is too baroque to be plausible. It is not clear to me that Generalized Binding is any more involved than theories of the *Barriers* variety, which also have their share of rococo definitions to allow blocking categories and barriers to function adequately. This said, it is not hard to agree that all ECP-centered theories including those in Aoun (1985, 1986), Aoun et al. (1987), Aoun and Li (1993a), Chomsky (1986a), Cinque (1990), Lasnik and Saito (1984, 1992), and Rizzi (1990) are technically very complex and often lack intuitive appeal. The relevant question is whether there are any empirically viable alternatives that do not suffer from overdue complexity. If the diagnosis above is correct, viz. that the complexity stems from treating scope in terms of A'-operations and the consequent elaboration of the ECP, then only rethinking these aspects of the problem is likely to lead to more elegant theoretical approaches. Starting in chapter 4, I elaborate a possible alternative approach to these LF problems cast within a Minimalist framework that dispenses with the A'/ECP approach to issues of scope.

3 Antecedent-contained Deletion (ACD)

Chapter 2 outlined the May (1985) analysis of ACDs and the implications for LF. May (1985) observes that if VP deletion is actually a copying rule of some kind then it requires a rule of LF for the correct target for copying to be produced. Fiengo and May (1990) detail the properties of the copied expression and consider what this tells us about LF. Let us review their proposal.

As noted in May (1985), if the ACD construction is an instance of VP deletion, then it is responsible to a level more abstract than SS.[17] Fiengo and May provide evidence for another interesting result. They observe that the interpreted elided material in ACDs conforms to principles of the Binding Theory (BT). For example, we observe something very much like principle C. Consider the contrast in (51).

(51a) *Mary introduced John$_i$ to everyone that he$_i$ did
(51b) Mary introduced John$_i$ to everyone that his$_i$ mother did

Fiengo and May note two things about this pair of sentences. First, the contrast is unexpected if SS is taken as the relevant level for satisfying the BT. In neither example would any principle of BT be contravened if *John* were antecedent of *his/he*. Second, they show that the contrast is straightforwardly accounted for once the elided material is copied into the VP gap. The structure of the sentences at LF prior to copying is (52).[18]

(52a) [[Everyone that he did [$_{VP*}$ e]]$_i$ [Mary [$_{VP1}$ introduced John to t$_i$]]]
(52b) [[Everyone that his mother did [$_{VP*}$ e]]$_i$ [Mary [$_{VP1}$ introduced John to t$_i$]]]

If VP1 is copied into VP* in the two LFs, we end up with the following relevant structure.

(53a) ... that he introduced John to ...
(53b) ... that his mother introduced John to ...

Now it is clear why the contrast obtains. Principle C of the BT prevents *he* in (53a) from being coindexed with *John* because *he* c-commands *John*. Nothing prevents this coindexing in (53b). Hence, if elided material in ACDs must respect BT we derive the correct results.

This is a very interesting result for it argues to three very strong conclusions. First, that VP ellipsis actually involves copying of syntactic structure. Second, that the BT must apply at LF, i.e. after ACDs are interpreted. Third, that the BT cannot apply at SS. It should be clear how the second conclusion is supported by these data. The third simply reiterates the point that if binding conditions are optionally satisfiable at SS then there should be no difference between the two sentences. Both would allow *John* to be coindexed with the pronoun, contrary to fact. The first conclusion follows on the assumption that the BT applies to phrase markers. If this is so, then elision must copy syntactic configurations.[19]

Fiengo and May also argue that there are bleeding relations with respect to principle C in ACDs. However, here the issues are less clear. Consider the examples in (54) that Fiengo and May cite.

(54a)   Mary always buys him whatever John's other friends do
(54b)   Mary gave him for his birthday the same thing that John's mother did

In (54a) we appear to have a principle C violation if the indirect object pronoun c-commands the direct object. Fiengo and May argue that this is just an apparent violation as at LF, after QR, the whole QNP is no longer c-commanded by the indirect object. The same argument applies to (54b). If QR moves the definite description out of the VP at LF, then no principle C violation should ensue. The proposed structures for the two sentences are given in (55).

(55a)   [[Whatever John's other friends do [e]]$_i$ [Mary always buys him t$_i$]]
(55b)   [[The same thing that John's mother did]$_i$ [Mary gave him for his birthday t$_i$]]

There are problems with this argument, however. First, if QR appends QNPs to IP, then we should be able to evade the principle C effects in (56) as well. However, the sentences are clearly unacceptable.

(56)   He$_i$ likes every picture that Bill$_i$ does

To get around this problem, they suggest that QR is adjunction to VP in the unmarked case. It is not clear, however, what constitutes the marked case. With unstressed *he* the indicated coreference is never available so far as I can judge. Or consider a more complex case. The sentences in (57) seem to be tolerably acceptable multiple interrogative constructions one of whose WHs is also an ACD.

(57a)   Which book did John give to which person that Bill did
(57b)   To whom did John give how many books that Bill did

These sentences, though complex, seem acceptable. An answer to the first might be "John and Bill each gave *Moby Dick* to Sharon." An answer to the second would be "John and Bill each gave six books apiece to Sue, Mary, and Helen." However, if we substitute *he* for *John* in these examples, it cannot be interpreted as coreferential with *Bill*. This despite the fact that the WH-*in-situ* moves to Comp to join the other WH at LF. The structure of (58) should permit a violation of principle C. However, the coreference is impossible.

(58)   [[[Which person that Bill$_i$ did]$_j$ [which book]$_k$] [he$_i$ gave t$_k$ to t$_j$]]

Second, it is not clear that QR should be able to evade principle C even in the cases cited in (54). If we change the phrase that is moved and forget about the ACD aspect, we find principle C effects once again. In (59), it should be possible to move the indirect object phrase containing Bill outside the c-command domain of the *him*.

(59a) *Mary always buys him$_i$ every portrait of Bill$_i$
(59b) *Mary gave him$_i$ Bill's$_i$ book
(59c) *Mary showed him$_i$ every plan to kill Bill$_i$

Indeed, there are well-known cases in which overt SS movement fails to obviate principle C. This despite the fact that the WH-phrase is in a position in which Fiengo and May suggest the principle should be obviated.

(60) *Whose claim that Bill$_i$ shot Sam did he$_i$ deny

These remarks do not account for why the examples in (54) seem to violate principle C. However, they cast doubt on the claim that the attenuation of this effect has much to do with QR.

Fiengo and May point out that the elided VP also meets other binding conditions. Principle B also holds.

(61) *Mary introduced him$_i$ to everyone that he$_i$ did

This contrasts nicely with (62) where this effect is not evident.

(62) Mary introduced him$_i$ to everyone his$_i$ mother did

The LF structure of the pair is provided in (63).

(63a) [Everyone that he$_i$ did [$_{VP}$ e = introduced him$_i$ to t]] [Mary introduced him$_i$ to t]
(63b) [Everyone that his$_i$ mother did [$_{VP}$ e = introduced him$_i$ to t]] [Mary introduced him$_i$ to t]

The binding in (63a) between *he* and *him* violates principle B in that *him* is not free in its domain. In (63b), in contrast, *his* does not c-command *him* so there is no principle B violation.

Fiengo and May further observe specified subject effects in ACD contexts.

(64a) Mary introduced him$_i$ to everyone John$_i$ wanted her to
(64b) *Mary introduced him$_i$ to everyone that she wanted John$_i$ to

The LF representations of these sentences are given in (65). It is clear from these that indexing *John* and *him* in (65a) should be fine. The intervening subject *her* functions to license the binding. In (65b), in contrast, the binding violates principle B. *John* and *him* are in the same domain and so binding is illicit.[20]

(65a) [Everyone that John$_i$ wanted her to [e = introduce him$_i$ to t]] Mary introduced him$_i$ to t]

(65b) [Everyone that she wanted John$_i$ to [e = introduce him$_i$ to t]] Mary introduced him$_i$ to t]

Fiengo and May observe that things are not as neat as this and they require an additional assumption to make the BT work out right in some relevant cases. Consider the following case of VP ellipsis and its LF representation after ellipsis interpretation.

(66a) Mary loves John$_i$ and he$_i$/John thinks that Sally does too

(66b) ... and he$_i$/John thinks that Sally does [love John$_i$] too

The LF structure in (66b) should lead to a principle B violation. However, the second conjunct in (66a) is quite acceptable under the indicated interpretation.

To accommodate such cases, Fiengo and May introduce a notion of *vehicle change*. If two elements A, B are semantically coextensive except for their pronominal features, then they can be substituted for each other. For example, a pronoun can go surrogate for a name if the two are coreferential. The effect of vehicle change is to eliminate principle C effects in ellipsis. More specifically, only violations of principle C that are also violations of principle B will lead to ungrammaticality. To see an example of vehicle change consider (66b) once again. With vehicle change we can substitute a pronoun for *John* in the elided constituent. The LF structure is then (67). Observe that this LF configuration, with the indicated binding, is perfectly licit.

(67) ... and he$_i$/John$_i$ thinks that Sally does [love him$_i$] too

Consider now a case of ACD and vehicle change. The sentence (68a) without vehicle change is expected to be unacceptable as it violates principle C (68b). With vehicle change it is well formed (68c). Contrast this with (69a–c) in which the sentence is ungrammatical even after vehicle change. (69c) violates principle B with the indicated coindexing.

(68a) Mary introduced John$_i$ to everyone he$_i$ wanted her to [e]

(68b) Everyone he$_i$ wanted her to [introduce John$_i$ to t] ...

(68c) Everyone he$_i$ wanted her to [introduce him$_i$ to t] ...

(69a) Mary introduced John$_i$ to everyone she wanted him to [e]

(69b) Everyone she wanted him$_i$ to [introduce John$_i$ to t]

(69c) Everyone she wanted him$_i$ to [introduce him$_i$ to t]

Vehicle change also leads to the elimination of WCO effects in ACD ellipsis:

(70a) Mary introduced every boy to someone his mother did

(70b) [Every boy$_i$ [someone$_j$ [his$_i$ mother did [introduce t$_i$ to t$_j$] [Mary introduced t$_i$ to t$_j$]]

In (70b), t_i and *his*$_i$ are in a configuration in which WCO is typically violated. However, if the variable t_i is subject to vehicle change and rewritten as a pronoun, WCO effects should disappear.

Fiengo and May (n. 9) observe, however, that there is more to WCO than this. In (70b), even under vehicle change, we have a WCO configuration. The structure after vehicle change is (71).

(71) [Every boy$_i$ [someone$_j$ [his$_i$ mother did [introduce pronoun$_i$ to t_j] [Mary introduced t*$_i$ to t_j]]

Here too the original pronoun *his* and *pronoun*, the output of vehicle change, are in a WCO configuration with t^*_i. Nonetheless, no effect is evident.

Fiengo and May also provide evidence of subjacency effects in ellipsis sites.[21] They observe the contrasts in (72). The relevant structure of (72a) is provided in (73).

(72a) *Dulles suspected everyone who Angleton wondered why Philby did
(72b) Dulles suspected everyone that Angleton believed that Philby did
(72c) ?Who did Angleton wonder whether Philby suspected
(73) Everyone$_i$ [who$_i$ [Angleton wondered [why [Philby suspected t_i]]]

(73) plausibly violates subjacency. The trace t_i is related to *who*$_i$ across a WH-island. They further note that the enhanced status of (72c) is also expected given that *whether* induces weaker subjacency violations than *why*.

However, as Fiengo and May observe, given vehicle change, it is not clear that we should find a subjacency effect at all. If the trace t_i is changed to a pronoun under vehicle change there should be no effect of subjacency. To prevent this, they suggest that in a language like English, without resumptive pronouns, traces cannot rewrite as pronouns or we would expect no bounding effects at all. They cite the following English example in support of the ban against resumptive pronouns in English.

(74) *Who did Angleton wonder why Philby suspected him

However, a more relevant contrast would have been the relative clause version of this, which is considerably better than the WH-question.

(75) The man who Angleton wondered why Philby suspected him

The relative acceptability of (75) suggests that the problem with (72a) is not the lack of resumptive pronouns in English. Rather, it would seem to indicate that these pronouns cannot be bound, i.e. have quantificational antecedents. Thus, note that the following is also not very felicitous.[22]

(76) ??Everyone who Angleton wondered why Philby suspected him[23]

The Fiengo and May analysis is rich in its implications concerning the properties of LF. They provide very interesting arguments that VP elision sites have the structure of phrase markers. They also supply evidence that the BT must apply after VP interpretation has taken place. This seems to suggest that it must apply at LF and cannot apply at SS. Chomsky (1993) has recently argued for a similar conclusion. We start to address these issues in chapter 4.

4   Conclusion

Chapters 2 and 3 present the following portrait of LF. LF is a level of derivation essentially concerned with representing relative quantifier scope and pronoun-binding properties of sentences. Quantifiers effect their scope properties by moving to A'-positions either overtly prior to SS or covertly at LF. The principal grammatical condition that constrains these operations is the ECP (in one of its myriad formulations). In effect, LF is essentially the province of A'-syntax. The operations that provide the relevant phrase markers target A'-positions as landing sites and the principal condition that reins in this movement is the "antecedent government" part of the ECP, a condition principally interested in A'-relations. This picture of LF is reconsidered in the following chapters. The aim will be to cover the same ground reviewed here but using notions derived from the Minimalist program.

4

Some Minimalist Background

1 Where We Are

The last two chapters sketched an approach to LF based on GB assumptions first advanced in Chomsky (1981). Several key ideas are at the center of the proposals surveyed.

First, there is a distinction between A and A'-bound empty categories. The latter are identified as variables. Variables are A'-bound by operators and are generally case-marked. The two relevant kinds of A'-positions are Spec CP, in which WH-operators reside, and adjunct positions (i.e. adjunction to any XP), to which non-WH quantified expressions move. The syntactic c-command relations between operators at LF mirrors the relative semantic scope these expressions enjoy. So, for example, if operator A c-commands operator B at LF then A has scope over B semantically. The discussion above reviewed variations on this basic theme. We observed that alternate versions of c-command yielded different scope options. May (1985), for example, allows operators all adjoined to the same XP to freely have scope over one another by providing a definition of c-command in terms of exclusion. Similarly, by calculating c-command in terms of chains headed by operators rather than the individual operators themselves, Aoun and Li (1989, 1993a) permit an operator A c-commanded by an operator B to still enjoy scope over B if a part of A's chain c-commands a part of B's.

These variations are motivated by the extended empirical coverage that they underwrite. However, despite the important empirical differences we have observed, the set of theories canvassed start from the common intuition that grammars distinguish operators (quantified noun phrases (QNP)) in A'-positions) and variables (A'-bound traces in A-positions) and that the syntactic distribution of these elements at LF is what underlies the semantic scope properties that QNPs enjoy. These proposals further adhere to the view that the syntax of LF intimately reflects the semantic powers of quantifiers. Semantically, quantifiers take propositions as arguments. Syntactically, QNPs are adjoined to, and thereby govern, the sentences that express these propositions at LF just as predicates govern the arguments they take. In effect, LF consists of various movements that adjust phrase markers so that a recursive truth definition (or its surrogate) can efficiently compute a semantic interpretation. The GB legacy is that these LF movements are largely adjunctions and that scope and quantification are grammatically the domain of A'-syntax. In other words, given the broad distinction between A-chains and A'-chains (the former derived via operations like NP movement and the latter via operations like WH-movement) scope and quantification are expressed grammatically via A'-movement operations and are defined over A'-chains.

A second core idea is that the distribution of variables and operators is largely traceable to the operations of the ECP. Using the ECP to constrain the grammar of quantification is natural once the latter is treated as a by-product of A'-operations. In fact, within the confines of a GB-style theory, few other options are available. The grammar can constrain the distribution of variables via conditions like the ECP or Generalized Binding and the distribution of operators via principles like the Minimal Binding Requirement (MBR) or Relativized Minimality. If scope is a matter of A'-relations, there are no other grammatical options available. Thus, through the workings of the ECP some form of (antecedent) government comes to play an essential role in the grammar of scope and quantification in GB-style theories. In non-standard approaches to the ECP, like Generalized Binding, analogues of the locality notions "barrier" and "antecedent governor" occupy a central position in the theory. For example, in Generalized Binding, SUBJECT is a core primitive and functions to specify binding domains for variables similar to the way that blocking categories and barriers function to specify adequate antecedent government configurations for variables in *Barriers*-style theories.

The survey in chapters 2 and 3 repeatedly noted that the versions of the ECP or Generalized Binding at work in deriving the various empirical results involved elaborations of the core ECP principles rather than their direct application. For example, to derive the subject/object asymmetries observed in the *ne . . . personne* cases, it was crucial to disallow movement of *personne* via Spec CP successive cyclically. Were such movement countenanced, the ECP could not account for the observed data. In (1b), with a trace in Spec CP, the subject t_i is antecedent governed (and meets principle A of Generalized Binding).

(1a)   *Je n'exige   que personne soit arrêtée
       I   neg-require that no one   be   arrested
(1b)   Personne$_i$ [je n'exige [t_i que [t_i soit arrêtée]]]

A similar assumption is required to account for the distribution of WH-*in-situ* constructions in French. Recall the contrast between (2a) and (2b), the latter only being usable as an echo question.

(2a)   Jean a   dit que Pierre a   vu   qui
      Jean has said that Pierre has seen who
(2b)   *Jean a   dit que qui est venu
      Jean has said that who is   come
(2c)   Qui$_i$ [Jean a dit [t_i que [t_i est venu]]]

The unacceptability of (2b) can be traced to the ECP but only on the assumption that *qui* cannot move through Spec CP at LF, as in (2c). There are various ways to force this result (see Aoun et al. 1981 for some proposals). However, it is worth observing that extra assumptions are required to make an ECP account work. The ECP alone does not yield the desired empirical differentiation.

The same problem occurs in English multiple interrogation constructions. The difference between (3a) and (3b) can be traced to the ECP but only if the WH-*in-situ* at SS cannot move through the local Spec CP, as in (3c). This prohibited movement would allow the embedded trace to be antecedent-governed and gamma-marked by the lower trace in Spec CP, thereby eliminating any subject/object asymmetry.

(3a)   Who said Bill bought what
(3b)   *Who said what was bought
(3c)   [[What$_j$ [who$_i$]] [t$_i$ said [t$_j$ [t$_j$ was bought]]]]

In fact, the pattern illustrated in the three examples above is quite general. The typical LF analysis that exploits the ECP as the prime explanatory construct generally requires ancillary assumptions to allow the ECP to make the necessary distinctions. Consider a few more examples.

Reducing superiority effects to the ECP requires saying something special about cases such as (4). The WHs-*in-situ* are not subjects and so ECP considerations should not apply.

(4a)   *What did John persuade who to buy
(4b)   *What does John expect who to say

Getting WH/quantifier interactions to fall under the ECP requires the assumption that quantifiers adjoined to IP block antecedent government of a subject trace. Thus, we need to assume that in (5b) the adjoined *everything* prevents t_i from being antecedent-governed. This forces (5a) into the phrase marker (5c), where the only available interpretation has *who* taking scope over *everything*.

(5a)   Who bought everything
(5b)   [Who$_i$ [everything$_j$ [t$_i$ [bought t$_j$]]]]
(5c)   [Who$_i$ [t$_i$ [everything$_j$ [bought t$_j$]]]]

Furthermore, for this account to work, we must also countenance apparent violations of the ECP. In cases such as (6), a pair–list reading is available. Given the May (1985) theory, this requires that the universal quantifier be adjoined to the matrix IP so that it can take scope over the WH in matrix Spec CP.

(6a)   What did John say that everyone saw
(6b)   [What$_i$ [everyone$_j$ [John say [that [t$_j$ saw t$_i$]]]]]

There are problems with this claim, however. Theoretically, it is quite unclear why t_j in (6b) does not violate the ECP. Recall that such an ECP violation was invoked in accounting for why it is that the universal quantifier in (7) cannot take scope over the matrix existential. In effect, a full account of the lack of WH/quantifier ambiguities requires a rather subtle elaboration of the ECP and its application.

(7)   Someone thinks (that) everyone saw you at the rally

Non-standard ECP theories have similar rough edges. In chapter 3, we reviewed the details of the delicate algorithm required to get Generalized Binding plus the MBR to handle the cases above. Moreover, the entire Generalized Binding system only works if one adopts the theory of variable types outlined in chapter 3. It is fair to say that this elaborate classification has little semantic support. There is little semantic reason for differentiating variables left by *who* and those left by *someone/everyone*. Nonetheless, empirically the accounts above depend on treating the former as A/C-variables and the latter as simply A-variables. Similarly, there is little intuitive support for the elaborate gamma-marking, ordering and deletion operations that serve the same functions within *Barriers*-style theories of the same phenomena.

This said, the above catalogue of difficulties should not be taken as indicating that there is anything inherently inappropriate with these additions, emendations and elaborations of the ECP or Generalized Binding. Rather, these inelegancies suggest that it is worth considering alternative theoretical routes through these interpretive data. The remaining chapters outline a non-GB style theory, one based on the Minimalist program outlined in Chomsky (1993). A key feature of this theory is that it eliminates government as a core grammatical relation. As a result, all ECP-centered accounts of LF phenomena become suspect. In addition, under one interpretation, the one that I will be elaborating, a Minimalist theory leaves QR like A'-movement adjunction rules without a theoretical place. This eliminates most applications of the rules of QR and WH-raising from the grammar. As the application of these two rules form the bulk of LF operations, Minimalism suggests that most LF phenomena will have to be reanalyzed.

The remainder of this chapter lays out the Minimalist concepts and assumptions I assume later on. In the chapters following, I elaborate alternatives to the standard approaches to multiple questions, superiority, ACD and relative quantifier scope that fit with these assumptions.

2   Where We Are Going: Outlines of a Minimalist Theory

Chomsky (1993) offers a wholesale revision of the principles of Universal Grammar (UG). The general aim is to develop a theory of grammar based exclusively on natural concepts, ones required by "virtual conceptual necessity" (Chomsky 1993: 2). The idea is to develop as conceptually economical a theory as possible that is based on notions that no theory of grammar can do without. Among such concepts, the following are of particular relevance for what follows.

2.1 LF and PF as the Sole Grammatical Levels

Chomsky (1993) proposes that UG has only two grammatical levels, LF and PF. The Minimalist motivation for limiting UG to just two levels is that this is the minimum required by virtually any theory of grammar. It is indisputable that natural language sentences are pairings of sound and meaning. PF and LF are the theoretical reflexes of this obvious fact.[1] It is in this sense that any theory of grammar must postulate PF and LF levels, grammatical levels that interface with those modules responsible for the sound and meaning features of language. Chomsky (1993) assumes that PF interfaces with the Perceptual–Articulatory (PA) system and LF interfaces with the Conceptual–Intentional (CI) system.

The two-level Minimalist proposal contrasts with earlier GB-style theories in which four significant grammatical levels are identified. In addition to the conceptually necessary levels PF and LF, GB theories include two further levels, DS and SS. A central aim of the Minimalist program is to show that the grammatical levels DS and SS do not exist. What this is taken to mean is that the theory of grammar need not, and should not, distinguish DS and SS phrase markers from other levels of derivation. Practically, this requires showing how to refashion the principles of grammar that apply to DS or SS phrase markers so that they can cover the same empirical ground and yet apply exclusively to LF or PF. As Chomsky (1993) assumes that only LF has the structure of a phrase marker, the reallocation of principles from DS and SS is to LF exclusively. For our purposes, LF is the main focus of concern.

The elimination of DS and SS as levels over which grammatical principles can be defined has serious implications. Here are several.

(1) The question of whether LF "exists" becomes largely moot. With the elimination of DS and SS the *only* level at which principles of grammar can be stated is LF. In earlier LGB-style theories it was interesting to ask whether LF was needed *in addition* to SS or could all grammatical structure relevant to meaning just be read off the SS phrase marker.[2] This is what was meant by the question of whether LF existed. With the elimination of SS from UG this question loses its footing. Within the context of Minimalism, the claim that LF exists becomes the trivial one that principles of grammar "exist."

(2) Case theory does not apply at SS as standardly assumed in GB-style theories. Rather case is an LF phenomenon. Technically, this has two implications. First, that case is not assigned but is checked. Lexical elements are inserted with case features. Second, at LF the grammar "checks" to see that this is so. The case filter or its analogue applies to LF phrase markers.

(3) Locality conditions on movement such as subjacency and parasitic gap licensing conditions cannot be stated as conditions on SS representations as there are no S-structure conditions permitted within a Minimalist theory. This

requires reanalyzing such cases in terms of conditions on derivations, (rather than representations), showing that these principles actually apply at LF and/ or eliminating large classes of movement rules. For example, as noted in chapter 2, the LF movement of WHs-*in-situ* can violate island conditions. In Huang (1982), this is theoretically accommodated by treating subjacency as a condition on SS phrase markers. However, this option is not minimalistically kosher. Subjacency, for example, can still be treated as part of the definition of "Move α", i.e. derivationally. But, this in turn implies that WH-raising at LF is not a movement rule, i.e. an instance of "Move α" as it fails to obey island conditions. In short, the elimination of SS suggests that WHs-*in-situ* are not subject to movement at LF. This is a conclusion that Chomsky (1993) embraces. Adopting this conclusion, however, requires reanalyzing the various WH-*in-situ* constructions surveyed above. An analysis of these constructions compatible with Minimalist concerns is provided in chapter 7. The reassignment of subjacency and parasitic gap licensing to LF is addressed in chapters 8 and 9.

(4)   The Binding Theory (BT) must apply exclusively at LF. In contrast to several suggestions within the LGB framework, it cannot optionally apply at DS, SS, or LF.[3] This means that the binding-theoretic data that crucially exploit the optional application of the BT throughout the derivation must be reanalyzed. Chomsky (1993) in fact spends a considerable amount of time reanalyzing some of the reconstruction data that have motivated these alternative approaches to the BT. I review Chomsky's basic argument here for it is presupposed in later chapters.

Chomsky (1993) makes the following methodological observation. All things being equal, a theory in which only LF application of the BT is permitted is preferable to one in which it can apply at several levels. Exclusive application of the BT at LF also comports with Minimalist assumptions which, Chomsky argues, are the optimal ones. Suffice it to say that a theory with only two significant grammatical levels, LF and PF, is *ceteris paribus* better than one with two additional levels, SS and DS. As such, a Minimalist theory that can empirically match the results of one that allows multiple binding levels is preferred. Non-Minimalist accounts must shoulder the argumentative burden for postulating more levels of representation.

To derive the correct empirical results, Chomsky makes the following assumptions. First, movement is actually copying and deletion. Thus, a full copy of a moved constituent is left at the launching site. Second, at LF all copies but one must be deleted. Third, in cases of A'-movement, there is a preference principle which requires that as much of the redundant material as possible be deleted from the head of the A'-chain.[4] For example, given a two-membered A'-chain of lexically identical material, delete as much material from the first member of the chain as possible. Or, to put it another way, all things being equal, reconstruct! Now consider the following data.

(8a)   Which picture of himself$_i$ did Bill$_i$ buy

(8b)   *Which picture of John$_i$ did he$_i$ buy

These examples can be accounted for if principle C must apply at DS (ruling out (8b)) and principle A optionally applies there (allowing the reflexive in (8a) to receive an antecedent). However, each also follows given the Minimalist technology provided above. The following configurations obtain prior to deletion at LF.

(9a)   Which picture of himself [John buy which picture of himself]
(9b)   Which picture of John [he buy which picture of John]

Consider now the deletions required to obtain a well-formed LF. Assume that *which* remains in Spec CP to match the +WH feature in C^0.[5] Given the Preference Principle, we prefer to delete all the rest from the WH-phrase in Spec CP. Thus, after deletion is completed, the LF phrase markers look like (10).[6]

(10a)   [Which$_i$ [John buy [t$_i$ picture of himself]]]
(10b)   [Which$_i$ [he buy [t$_i$ picture of John]]]

With these LF phrase markers, we can easily account for the data in (8) while assuming that the BT applies exclusively at LF. Given (10a), it is not surprising that *John* can be the antecedent of the reflexive. If we assume that reflexivization is mediated by movement of the reflexive to I^0, the LF structure looks like (11).

(11)   [Which$_i$ [John [himself$_j$ I^0] [buy [t$_i$ picture of t$_j$]]]]

In (10b), principle C will prevent *John* from being interpreted as the antecedent of *he* given that *he* c-commands *John*. Once again, given this phrase marker, principle C of the BT can be taken as exclusively applying to LF without adverse empirical consequences.

   The above illustrates how treating movement as copying and deletion, in conjunction with a preference for deleting from the head rather than the tail of an A'-chain, allows us to dispense with the assumption that the BT applies to any level other than LF. Chomsky (1993) provides a stronger argument still for the exclusive application of the BT to LF. First, consider the following data and their implications for the Preference Principle. (12a) has the LF structure (12b) before deletion.

(12a)   John wonders which picture of himself Bill saw
(12b)   John wonders which picture of himself[a] Bill saw which picture of himself[b]

If reflexivization is executed via movement we have two possibilities. Either *himself*[a] or *himself*[b] moves. The two possibilities are provided in (13).

(13a)   John [himself$_i$ [wonders [which picture of t$_i$ [Bill saw which picture of himself]]]
(13b)   John wonders [which picture of himself [John himself$_i$ saw which picture of t$_i$]]

In (13a) only deletion of the lower copy will yield a well-formed structure. Deletion of the higher elements will result in a theta criterion violation as the chain headed by the cliticized *himself*[a] will not include a theta position.[7] In (13b) the upper copy must delete for the same reason.[8] With this in mind, consider (14).

(14)   John wonders which picture of himself Bill took

Chomsky observes two things about (14). First, the embedded clause can be idiomatically or non-idiomatically interpreted depending on whether *take* is interpreted as part of the idiom *take a picture of* (i.e. photograph) or is interpreted as an independent predicate with the picture NP as complement (i.e. pick up and walk away with). Second, on the idiomatic interpretation, *Bill* must be the antecedent of the reflexive, while on the non-idiomatic reading of *take* the sentence is ambiguous. Chomsky further shows that this is what we would expect on a Minimalist theory without DS and in which the BT applies exclusively at LF. Consider the details.

   In GB theories, idioms are characterized as DS units. With the elimination of DS, the representation of idioms as units must be relegated to LF. Assume, then, that at LF idioms must form a unit. Consider now the two alternative derivations of (14).

(15a)   John [himself$_i$ [wonders [which picture of t$_i$ [Bill took which picture of himself]]]
(15b)   John wonders [which picture of himself [John himself$_i$ took which picture of t$_i$]]

The theta criterion requires the deletion of the lower copy in (15a). But with this deletion, the idiomatic interpretation becomes unavailable as *take* cannot be treated as part of the idiom *take a picture of* since it is separated from the picture NP in Spec CP.[9] If option (15b) is taken, the verb can be interpreted idiomatically as the reconstructed NP and the *take* can be treated as a unit. Thus, if we assume that idioms must form units, then the only option in a Minimalist theory is that this restriction be stated at LF. Similarly, the BT must apply exclusively at LF. With this, the data in (14) are accounted for.[10] Importantly, if we assume that binding can apply throughout the derivation, these facts cannot be explained. We should be able to bind the reflexive at SS after movement and prior to LF idiom interpretation (or at SS after DS idiom interpretation).[11] In short, Chomsky here provides an argument to the effect that the methodologically superior option is also empirically more adequate.[12]

   To recap, Chomsky shows that it is both possible and desirable to limit the BT to LF as prescribed by a Minimalist theory of grammar. The prerequisites for this are to treat movement as copying and deletion and to adopt the Preference Principle for deletion in A'-chains.[13] In later chapters, we adopt this technology. The point of the above discussion is to see how the technology relates to larger Minimalist assumptions. The point of this brief review has been to show that the aim of applying the binding principles exclusively at LF is unrealizable without these technical assumptions concerning movement, deletion, and the A'-preference principle.

2.2   Basic Grammatical Relations are X'-theoretic

A motivating intuition of the Minimalist program is that the fundamental notions of grammar are couched in X'-terms. The main motivation for this is the inevitability of X'-notions in the grammar. It is hard to see how any theory of grammar can do without the concepts "head," "specifier," and "complement" and the relations that come along with them. The Minimalist ethos suggests that we should try to do with only these.

There are two important consequences of this commitment. First, this removes the notion of (head) government from the inventory of basic grammatical relations, at least insofar as this notion extends beyond what obtains between a head and its complement. As a result, case theory, part of the ECP, and parts of the theory of L-marking must be recast, given their reliance on the notion.

An example should make this clearer. The canonical head-government configuration is what obtains between a head and its theta-marked complement, e.g. a V and its direct object. However, this notion is not sufficiently broad to accommodate all that is required from the government relation. Accusative case marking, for example, occurs in configurations in which the case-marked NP is not sister to the case-marking verb or preposition.

(16a)   John believes [$_{IP}$ him to be insane]
(16b)   I want very much [$_{CP}$ for [$_{IP}$ him to leave]]

In both (16a and b) *him* is case-marked by a head that does not govern *him* the way that a verb governs its internal argument. Similarly, the +finite Infl does not govern the subject the way that a verb governs its object, though this too is considered an instance of the government relation. Note that in (17) the configuration is definable in X'-terms as the Spec–head relation. However, it is different from the relation instantiated by verbs and their internal arguments as well as the cases noted in (16).

(17)   [$_{IP}$ He [$_{I'}$ + finite [like books]]]

As these examples show, though it is possible to define the head–complement relation in pure X'-terms, the extended notion of government required to undergird case theory cannot be stated in a unified manner in purely X'-terms. Standard objects are complements of the heads that case-mark them, standard subjects are specifiers of their case markers and *him* in (16) is neither a specifier nor a complement of the head that case-marks it. Head government was intended to cover all three cases and there is no unitary way of doing this using only primitive X'-relations.

Similar remarks hold for other core relations. For example, proper head government is assumed to hold in subject-to-subject raising constructions such as (18). In particular, *seems* head-governs the trace left by raising.

(18)   John$_i$ seems [t$_i$ to like books]

However, the relation between *seems* and t_i does not fall under standard X'-relations any more than the case-marking configurations in (16) do.[14] In sum, if one only allows relations statable in X'-terms into one's basic inventory of grammatical relations, then head government as it has been used in GB theory loses its legitimacy.

Chomsky (1993) proposes recasting case theory in terms of a Spec–head agreement relation. This has a theoretical advantage beyond just being minimalistically acceptable. In GB theories of case, as noted, there is a fundamental asymmetry between nominative case assignment and all the other structural cases. Nominative is assigned by a tensed inflection to the NP in Spec IP. Accusative and dative cases are assigned by Vs and Ps to the NPs they govern (though, as noted above, not all instances of government are structurally identical). The Minimalist program eliminates the asymmetry by treating all case assignment as an instance of the Spec–head relation. Given the elimination of government as a fundamental grammatical relation, there is no other alternative if case is to be treated in a unified manner. The principal consequence of this analysis of case is the assumption that NP objects of verbs and prepositions move to Spec positions of higher AGR nodes in order to fulfill case requirements. Accusative case is discharged in Spec AgrO. The V+AgrO complex checks the case of the NP in Spec AgrO position after the verb has raised to AgrO (see (19a)). I assume that structural prepositional case is assigned in a similar fashion (see (19b)).

(19a)   [. . . [$_{AgrOP}$ NP$_{obji}$ V$_j$ + AgrO [$_{VP}$ e$_j$ t$_i$]]]
(19b)   [. . . [$_{AgrP}$ NP$_i$ [P$_j$ + Agr [e$_j$ t$_i$]]]]

A second consequence of the elimination of non-X'-notions is that the ECP becomes a suspect principle. Clearly, head government is no longer a viable well-formedness condition as it is defined in terms of the notion government. However, even antecedent government is suspect as it is unclear that the proper conditions for antecedent government are statable in X'-terms. To redeem these notions, it is necessary to define "blocking category," "barrier," "L-marking," "direct theta marking," "indirect theta marking," and "minimality" in X'-terms. One thing is certain, these notions are not simple instances of the Spec–head or head–complement relations. For example, Chomsky (1986a) defines a blocking category as follows: for Z to be a blocking category for Y, Z cannot be L-marked and Z must dominate Y. Thus, whatever else is true, the blocking relation (i.e. the relation "Z is a blocking category for Y") is not reducible to a statement about Z and Y in X'-terms. However, this then means that the *Barriers* theory requires notions not reducible to X'-primitives and relations. Given that without the blocking relation, the barrier relation cannot be defined, and without the barrier relation the antecedent government relation cannot be defined, we are left with the tentative conclusion that antecedent government falls outside the theoretical grasp of Minimalist assumptions. In short, the Minimalist program must do without the ECP.[15]

The most likely place for barrier-like notions within Minimalism is in stating locality conditions for overt movement.[16] Since Ross (1967), there is considerable empirical evidence that syntactic extraction from islands is ungrammatical. How to express island conditions in minimalistically acceptable terms is something that I put to one side here (but see chapters 8 and 9). Given the focus in the following chapters on LF phenomena and the elimination of WH-raising at LF, this should not hamper us a great deal. I simply assume that islands can be defined in minimalistically acceptable terms and that extraction from islands is generally illicit. See chapter 6 for some discussion of islands and their semantic effects.

2.3 Elements Move to Satisfy Morphological Requirements

A final characteristic of Minimalist theories is that movement is the means for serving morphological ends. The core idea is that lexical elements are extracted from the lexicon and packaged into phrase markers already laden with their morphological features. These features must be "checked" in the course of the derivation for the output to be licit. Checking takes place by moving to the appropriate functional projections. Morphological features are then checked within these functional categories. For example, a DP/NP is drawn from the lexicon bearing accusative case morphology. This morphology must be checked in all languages. In some languages, however, these features must be checked prior to the point where the LF and PF paths split, i.e. prior to SPELL OUT. In English, checking is done at LF. The object raises to Spec AgrO where the accusative case feature is checked under Spec–head agreement with the V+AgrO. This same operation also checks a feature on the verb. In many languages, verbs agree with their objects. These agreement features are checked in the Spec–head configuration that monitors accusative case. Other features are checked in similar fashion. Unless all features are checked by LF the derivation is illicit and "crashes." I rehearse this litany here to highlight that movement in the grammar, be it V-raising to some Infl projections, DP/NP movement to a case position, or WH-movement to Spec CP, is driven by the requirement that morphological features are checked.

Importantly, this movement is semantically myopic. Minimalism assumes that only morphological requirements drive movement. The fact that lack of movement might lead to unintelligibility does not suffice to license movement. Furthermore, movement is selfish. An element only moves to satisfy its own morphological requirements. It does not move so as to be able to satisfy another expression's morphological needs.

Chomsky discusses existential constructions as an illustration of these points (Chomsky 1993: 32ff). Consider the contrast in (20a and b).

(20a)   There is a man in the garden
(20b)   *There seems to a man that Bill left

Following his earlier analysis in Chomsky (1991), Chomsky (1993) argues that
a man is not in a case-checking position in overt syntax. To have its case
features checked, it must raise and adjoin to *there* at LF. The LF structure is
provided in (21).

(21)   [$_{IP}$ [a man$_i$ [there]] is [t$_i$ in the garden]]

Chomsky assumes that this adjunction results in *there* being internal to a
complex word that results from the adjunction. This renders *there* "invisible"
at the LF interface. This is a good result given Chomsky's assumption that
there has no semantic interpretation, for unless *there* is removed from the LF
structure, its lack of interpretability will result in semantic deviance.

With this in mind, consider the analysis of (20b). Chomsky argues that
sentences such as (20b) are perfectly grammatical though semantically deviant. They are grammatical in that all the features of the various elements can
be checked. For example, the case of *a man* is checked by the preposition *to*.
As its morphological requirements are met, its movement is no longer forced.
As it is not required, it cannot take place. As a result, *there* cannot be removed
and remains uninterpretable at the LF interface. Thus, (20) is perfectly grammatical despite the fact that it carries no intelligible interpretation. Note that
were *a man* to raise and adjoin to *there*, burying it within the complex word
thereby derived the sentence would be fully interpretable, just as (20a) is.
However, it is myopic morphological concerns that drive movement not global
requirements on intelligibility. The fact that *a man* meets all of its requirements
without adjoining to *there* means that it cannot so adjoin. The fact that *there* is
left stranded and that gibberish results is of no grammatical consequence.[17]

The contention that movement is driven by morphology has several interesting potential consequences. It requires that we postulate some morphological
feature that is checked whenever we assume movement. For WH-movement,
Focus movement or even Topicalization, this requirement is not particularly
onerous. It is reasonable to believe that WH-features, Focus features and Topic
features exist as they appear to be present overtly in a variety of languages.
When it comes to standard quantifier movement, however, things are much
less clear. There is no obvious analogue of WH-features for quantifiers in
general. We could always postulate Q-features that quantified expressions
must have checked (via LF movement in English) analogous to case or WH-
features. However, such Q-features are not terribly well motivated.

Another (perhaps more interesting) possibility is that QR and Minimalism
simply do not mix well. We have noted that Chomsky (1993) eschews LF WH-
raising. It is worth investigating whether LF A'-movement exists at all.[18] A flat-
footed reading of the morphological requirement on movement suggests that
Minimalism should dispense with QR altogether. I investigate this possibility in chapters 5 and 8 and suggest a non-QR approach to ACD and relative
quantifier scope.

3 Conclusion

The aim of this chapter has been to outline the Minimalist assumptions adopted in the next several chapters. The rest of the book is divided as follows.

Chapter 5 concentrates on ACD constructions. I reanalyze the standard QR treatment proposed in May (1985) and the Baltin (1987) proposal. The chapter also investigates antecedent contained ellipsis cross-linguistically and proposes an interaction between the viability of this sort of deletion and V-movement.

Chapter 6 addresses WH/quantifier interactions. Here I examine Chierchia's (1992) analysis which reduces these cases to instances of WCO. I further examine the Lasnik and Stowell (1991) account of WCO and suggest an alternative. The alternative lends further support for Chierchia's approach.

Chapter 7 reanalyzes superiority effects. The chapter generalizes the account in chapter 6 and reduces superiority effects to WCO violations. The problems that ECP approaches to superiority encounter are largely eliminated by this reduction. I also discuss some cross-linguistic data on superiority including the data first broached in Rudin (1988) on superiority effects in languages where WHs all move to CP, anti-superiority effects in Japanese and the attenuation of superiority effects in certain English, Hebrew, Italian, Japanese, and Spanish constructions.

Chapter 8 focuses on the grammatical representation of relative quantifier scope. I argue that it is possible to provide an empirically adequate theory of quantifier scope without employing any form of A'-movement. I also reanalyze in Minimalist terms the Aoun and Li (1993a) cross-linguistic material on quantifier scope reviewed in chapter 3. In addition, I discuss negative polarity licensing, quantifier/negation dependencies and quantifier scope/binding interactions.

Chapter 9 shows how to derive the properties of some principles required in earlier chapters from more basic Minimalist assumptions. I also show that Minimalist theories are irreducibly derivational in that the sorts of accounts advanced in earlier chapters cannot be sustained simply by placing structural conditions on the LF phrase marker which is the output of these operations. Lastly, the chapter points out that it is possible to relocate several problematic SS conditions to LF if the analyses developed in the earlier chapters are essentially correct.

5

Antecedent-contained Deletion[1]

As noted in chapters 2 and 3, one of the strongest arguments for the level of LF and its distinctive properties and operations comes from the antecedent-contained deletion (ACD) construction. The argument, recall, goes as follows. Consider sentences with deleted VPs such as (1). The VP gap is interpreted as identical in meaning to the indicated VP. Assume that this is accommodated by copying the non-elided VP into the gapped VP position to yield (2).[2]

(1) John *kissed John's mother* and Sally did [$_{VP}$ e] too
(2) John kissed Bill's mother and Sally did [$_{VP}$ kiss Bill's mother]

ACD sentences like (3) show that SS cannot be the relevant linguistic level for the copying operation.

(3) John kissed everyone that Sally did [$_{VP}$ e]

To generalize the copying procedure we must alter the S-structure form of the sentence containing the empty VP so as to remove it from under the VP that gets copied there. The reason is that if the only VP around that we can copy dominates the empty VP that must be filled, then copying the first VP into the second leads to a regress with yet another empty VP that must be filled. For example, in (3), *kissed everyone that Sally did [$_{VP}$ e]*, is the VP we must copy but copying it leads to yet another null VP in the resultant structure: *kissed everyone that Sally did kiss everyone that Sally did [$_{VP}$ e]*. The presence of the null VP leaves the sentence as a whole without a determinate content. Call this the "regress problem."[3]

What ACDs show then, is that a null VP cannot be interpreted unless we can somehow remove it out from under the VP that it is anaphorically related to. May (1985) observed that if we assume that QNPs are moved to adjoined positions at LF then we can avoid regress. In particular, if we assume that the grammar contains a rule like QR that moves a QNP at LF and adjoins it to IP then we can solve the regress problem posed by (3).[4] At LF the relevant structure is (4).

(4) [$_{IP}$ [Everyone [that [Sally did [$_{VP}$ e]]]]$_i$ [$_{IP}$ Bill kissed t$_i$]]

If we copy *kissed t_i* into the null VP we obtain (5), which also provides an accurate representation of the meaning of (3): "everyone such that Sally kissed that person is such that Bill kissed that person."

(5) $[_{IP}$ [Everyone [that [Sally did $[_{VP}$ kissed $t_i]]]]_i$ $[_{IP}$ Bill kissed $t_i]]$

Thus, if we assume that deleted elements get content via copying or some analogous process, then we can circumvent the regress problem in ACD structures by assuming that QR applies at LF and thereby alters the domination relations among the participating VPs. This is a very elegant argument both for LF and for the particular rule of QR. In fact, ACDs appear to provide an argument both for the necessity of LF and for its format. The aim of this chapter is to review this argument in the context of the Minimalist assumptions outlined in chapter 4.

1   Baltin (1987) on ACD

Baltin points out a series of difficulties for a theory of ACDs that relies on a rule like QR. In particular, he argues that pied piping the relative clause at LF along with the quantified head leads to empirical difficulties in multiple question constructions. The argument is as follows. Assume that multiple WH-questions such as (6a) involve moving the WH-*in-situ* to the WH in Spec CP at LF to yield a structure like (6b). Observe that the operation moving the WH-*in-situ* conforms to the format of QR in that the whole quantified NP is moved. This is required as these sorts of constructions license ACDs as shown in (6c).

(6a)   Who reviewed how many books that Bill bought
(6b) $[_{CP}$ Who$_i$ [how many books that Bill bought]$_j$ $[_{IP}$ t_i bought $t_j]]$
(6c)   Who reviewed how many books that Bill did

The problem, Baltin argues, is that this predicts that sentences such as (7a) should be ambiguous with the null VP being interpreted as either VP1 or VP2. However, this is empirically incorrect. (7a) can be read as (7d) but not (7c). Call this fact the Boundedness Restriction on ACDs.

(7a)   Who thought that Fred read how many of the books that Bill did
(7b) $[_{CP}$ Who$_i$ [how many books that Bill did $[_{VP}$ e]]$_j$ $[_{IP}$ t_i $[_{VP1}$ thought $[_{CP}$ that $[_{IP}$ Fred $[_{VP2}$ read $t_j]]]]]]$
(7c)   Who thought that Fred read how many of the books that Bill thought that he had read
(7d)   Who thought that Fred read how many of the books that Bill read

Baltin argues that boundedness restrictions in ACDs is incompatible with the May (1985) analysis of ACDs. To accommodate ACD structures, he suggests that the regress problem is solved by extraposing the relative clause at SS. This moves the null VP out from under the VP that immediately dominates it and hence allows the regress problem to be circumvented. Furthermore, by invoking the Right Roof Constraint, Baltin accommodates the boundedness facts. The relative clause can be extraposed across at most one VP due to the Right Roof Constraint. Thus, the higher of two VPs is not a potential antecedent for the null VP. If extraposition does not take place, we are left with a violation of the i-within-i condition, a principle that Baltin claims to hold at SS. A consequence of these assumptions is that extraposition cannot be allowed to leave behind a trace on pain of violating the i-within-i condition. Baltin takes this to be an acceptable consequence and assumes that extraposition is not required to leave behind traces.

Baltin provides some independent evidence for the extraposition approach to ACDs. The following unacceptable sentences are cited as independent evidence for the analysis.[5]

(8a)   *John will find everyone that Bill does easy to work with
(8b)   *John will make every student that Bill does take an extra exam
(8c)   *I believe everyone that you do to be polite

In (8), there has been no SS extraposition so the sentences are predicted to be unacceptable. Furthermore, they are predicted to contrast sharply with (9) where multiple instances of extraposition can render ACD possible (cf. Baltin 1987: 587, ex. 33).

(9)   John persuaded everyone that you did to be polite

We return to these data in the next section. However, it is worth noting that the data in (8) are not uniformly judged to be unacceptable, and that the contrast with (9) is quite subtle. Moreover, for those that find the contrast, the sentences in (8) are hardly word salad. Thus, (8c) is taken to mean that John finds everyone that you believe to be polite to be polite. However, it is unclear how speakers are able to interpret these sentences at all if Baltin (1987) is correct. After all, without extraposition the regress problem looms. But regress implies that there is no possible well-formed LF or SS. But this implies that the sentences are simply uninterpretable as given the ensuing infinite regress their LFs specify no determinate propositional content. In other words, if Baltin (1987) is right here, then the sentences in (8) should not just be unacceptable, they should be uninterpretable. But this is clearly not the case.[6]

2   Larson and May's Reply

Larson and May (1990) present strong arguments against Baltin's positive proposal. They make the following points. First, it is unlikely that the generation of ACDs is actually related to extraposition given that one can find ACDs even when extraposition is disallowed. For example, as they point out (p. 105, ex. 6), extraposition and Comp deletion do not co-occur (cf. Stowell 1981, Aoun et al. 1987).

(10)   I visited a man recently who/that/*ø Mary asked about

Nonetheless, ACD is permitted whether or not the Comp is present (p. 106, ex. 8, 9).

(11a)   I visited everyone who/that/ø you did
(11b)   John would reject any suggestion which/that/ø Mary would

   Second, Larson and May observe that there are many sentences structurally analogous to (8) above in not having an extraposed structure which are nonetheless quite acceptable.

(12a)   I gave everyone that you did two dollars
(12b)   Tommy put everything he could into his mouth

Furthermore, they observe that even the cases that Baltin describes are not terribly bad. In fact, they observe the following contrasts.

(13a)   *I expect (that) everyone you do will visit Mary
(13b)   ?I expect everyone you do to visit Mary
(13c)   *John believed (that) everyone you did was a genius
(13d)   ?John believed everyone you did to be a genius

Larson and May point out, and I concur, that whereas (13a, c) are completely unacceptable, (13b, d) are "merely awkward at worst" (p. 107). Furthermore, they observe that an extraposition analysis cannot account for the observed contrasts in (13) given that neither involve extraposition. This seems correct. They further suggest that the contrast supports the May (1985) analysis as QR cannot extract a quantified NP from a tensed clause. Thus, (14a) cannot be interpreted with the universal quantifier having scope over the existential NP, though this is marginally possible in (14b) (cf. Aoun and Hornstein 1985).[7]

(14a)   At least one person expected every Republican would win
(14b)   At least one person expected every Republican to win

The contrast in (14) follows if QR cannot raise the embedded quantified subject from a finite clause. However, things are not likely to be this simple. It is not quite correct to say that all non-finite clauses allow QR to extract an embedded subject to the next highest clause. Consider the sentences in (15). It appears that the universal QNP in (15a) can have scope over the existential NP but this is virtually impossible in (15b).[8]

(15a) At least one person considers every senator to be smart
(15b) At least one person considers every senator smart[9]
(15c) At least one person considers every senator to be out to lunch
(15d) At least one person considers every senator out to lunch

However, if Larson and May's suggestion were correct, we would expect sentences such as (16) to be rather unacceptable, though, as they observe, this is not so.

(16) I consider everyone you do smart/out to lunch

Thus, though, Larson and May provide a good argument against Baltin (1987), it is less clear that the contrast that they cite speaks strongly in favor of the May (1985) analysis.

A third problem for the extraposition analysis lies with the requirement that extraposition does not leave behind a trace. Larson and May point out that there is a class of comparative and comparative-like constructions in which the clausal complement is selected and so presumably must leave a trace under extraposition if the Projection Principle is to be respected (p. 119, ex. 46, 47).

(17a) Alice will find as many marbles as Felix will
(17b) Brian couldn't possibly take a different train than you do

In (17a) *as Felix will* is semantically a selected complement of the degree morpheme *as* while in (17b) the clausal complement headed by *than* is complement to *different*. Larson and May observe that this selection is morphologically signalled in that the choice of Comp (i.e. *as* versus *than*), is tied to the head morpheme that it is related to semantically. If this is correct, then the strategy behind the extraposition analysis cannot be generalized.[10]

In fact, there are additional problems to generalizing the extraposition account. Consider one more. As Larson and May observe, to get things to work out right, Baltin (1987) must assume a whole slew of vacuous movement rules. For example, it must be assumed that in the case of headless relatives, vacuous Heavy NP Shift (HNPS) can apply given the acceptability of (18).

(18) I said whatever you did

However, it appears that one can get ACDs with headless relatives even where HNPS is prohibited.

(19a) John gave the man from France this book
(19b) *John gave this book the man from France
(19c) John gave whoever he could two dollars

We have seen that there are strong arguments against the extraposition approach to ACDs. What do Larson and May say concerning Baltin's boundedness effects? They provide examples suggesting that it is a spurious generalization. They cite the following example.

(20a) Which student wants to visit which city that you do
(20b) Which student wants to visit which city that you visit
(20c) Which student wants to visit which city that you want to visit

(20a) is ambiguous. The reading available in (20c) violates the Boundedness Restriction. Hence, Larson and May suggest the purported restriction is actually a spurious generalization.

There are, however, problems with this reply. First, the original examples illustrating the restriction involved finite clauses (see (7)). Infinitives are well known to be more porous than finite clauses. Second, and more importantly, the data that Larson and May note rely heavily on the particular matrix verb. Thus, if one substitutes *expect/hope/intends* for *want* the reading analogous to (20c) fades away.

(21a) Which student expects/hopes/intends to visit which city that you do
(21b) Which student expects/hopes/intends to visit which book that you visit
(21c) Which student expects/hopes/intends Bill to visit which city that you expect to visit

(21) only has the reading in which the VP gap obeys the Boundedness Restriction, (21b) not (21c).

In fact, *want* constructions without a PRO embedded subject also display boundedness effects. The non-bounded reading in (22b) is quite marginal.

(22a) Which student wants Bill to read which book that you do
(22b) Which student wants Bill to read which book that you want Bill to read

These considerations suggest that the example Larson and May provide say more about verbs like *want* than about boundedness effects. In fact, it is reasonable to suppose that *want* is not a typical embedding verb. In many languages it is a restructuring verb. If we assume that this is so in English as well, then the apparent violations of the Boundedness Restriction fall into place.[11] The boundedness effects disappear just in case restructuring can apply. This process cannot apply unless the embedded clause is PRO, hence the data in (22). Nor can it apply unless the matrix verb is a restructuring verb, hence the data in (21). Furthermore, we expect that other typical restructuring verbs will license the same ambiguities witnessed with *want*. This seems to be correct.

(23a) Which man has to read which book that you do
(23b) Which man started to sing which song that you did

There is interesting evidence that this analysis is on the right track. First, in contrast to most embedding verbs, quantifiers embedded in clauses under *want* can have matrix scope. Consider the contrast in (24).

(24a)   Someone expects to dance with every woman
(24b)   Someone wants to dance with every woman

It has long been observed that sentences like (24a) do not allow the embedded QNP to take scope over the matrix subject (cf. Burzio 1986: 201ff.). This can be traced to the general clause boundedness of QR.[12] What is curious is that this restriction is not apparent in (24b). Here the embedded universally quantified NP can take scope over the matrix existential. The distinction noted here is plausibly tied to a restructuring which alters the biclausal structure of (24b).

Roberts (1992) offers a second piece of evidence that *want* is a restructuring verb from *wanna* contraction. He observes that the class of contraction verbs in English is a subset of the restructuring verbs in the Romance languages.

(25)   I wanna/hafta/useta/beganna go

If contraction is just a surface manifestation of restructuring, this is what we would expect. I will consider the details of Roberts' theory in a later section when we return to consider these constructions within a Minimalist framework.

3   ACDs and Minimalism

Here is where the discussion has led. There are empirical problems with both Baltin's (1987) approach to ACDs and May's (1985) theory. The biggest problem with the latter is that it has no account of boundedness effects. The problems with the former involve technical difficulties in getting extraposition to generalize appropriately to handle the full range of ACD cases, in making distinctions between the relative acceptability of non-clause final ACDs in the subject position of finite and non-finite clauses, in accounting for violations of the Boundedness Restriction with the class of "restructuring" verbs and in squaring with other well-known facts concerning extraposition such as its incompatibility with Comp deletion. Thus, empirically, there are reasons to search for an alternative account to both approaches.

Furthermore, neither approach above comports with Minimalist assumptions. Interestingly, the Minimalist theory contains the outlines of an alternative approach that appears to meet all of the empirical points in sections 1–3. The aim of this section is to look at the QR and extraposition approaches to ACDs through Minimalist spectacles. In the next section, I outline a positive solution consistent with this perspective.

From a Minimalist point of view, there are two problems with a QR solution to ACDs. First, a Minimalist theory eschews LF pied piping (Chomsky 1993: 26). As such, a rule like QR cannot be invoked to move the relative clause along with the rest of the QNP. If QR exists at all, it only moves the quantifier, leaving the restrictor in place. Unfortunately, this less expansive LF movement leaves the resultant LF structure subject to regress problems as the dependent

VP remains dominated by its antecedent. In short, the quantifier scoping operations proposed in Chomsky (1993) cannot serve to move the anaphoric VP in ACDs out from under its dominating antecedent and thus cannot serve to eliminate regress.

Furthermore, even if pied piping were permitted in these sorts of cases, recall that Minimalism assumes (in the guise of the Preference Principle) that reconstruction applies when it can. This serves to "minimize the restriction in the operator position" (Chomsky 1993: 41). This Preference Principle is crucial for allowing the BT to apply exclusively at LF. This, we noted in chapter 4, is a centerpiece of any Minimalist theory. However, the Preference Principle also leads to regress problems.

In sum, the type of pied piping built into the standard rule of QR is at odds with some central assumptions of Minimalism. Insofar as a rule like QR exists given these assumptions, it does not have the capacity to circumvent regress problems. Thus, Minimalist assumptions are incompatible with the May (1985) approach to ACDs.

The same is true for the Baltin (1987) theory. Baltin's theory treats ACDs as essentially an SS phenomenon. This is sufficient to put it at odds with Minimalist assumptions. Technically, it requires adopting substantive SS restrictions (the i-within-i condition) in terms of which acceptable ACDs are licensed. Furthermore, the theory requires quite a bit of string vacuous movement, movement that is not driven by any apparent morphological, phonological, or focus considerations. On the assumption that movement prior to LF is forced by PF considerations, i.e. that procrastination obtains, it is hard to see how *string vacuous* movement could ever be motivated. By assumption, it leaves the apparent surface form entirely intact. In contrast to standard forms of extraposition, which plausibly alter focus relations and intonation structure, it is hard to fit an all but invisible string vacuous SS process with Minimalist inclinations.

It thus appears that, from a Minimalist viewpoint, neither approach is particularly attractive. I turn next to a Minimalist alternative.

4   A Minimalist Theory of ACDs

The theoretical outlines of a Minimalist theory of ACDs is fairly clear. The operation that removes a VP inside a relative clause out of the antecedent that dominates it at SS must be a form of A-movement. The reason is that in contrast to A'-operations, A-movement is not subject to the Preference Principle (Chomsky 1993: 36–7), i.e. reconstruction is not a preferred option in A-chains.[13] Given that reconstruction induces regress problems, it follows on Minimalist assumptions that it must be A-movement that feeds licit ACD formation. Second, this movement must be obligatory, must apply at LF, and must serve to move the relative clause out of the dominating VP. As it turns out, a core Minimalist operation serves all three functions. Recall that a central tenet of the program is that structural case marking is a Spec–head phenom-enon. Accusative case is assigned when the object moves out of VP into Spec AgrO. In English, this operation takes place at LF. Furthermore, the movement is obligatory given the postulated relation between case marking and feature checking. The structure of a transitive clause is (26) (Chomsky 1993: 7, ex. 2).

(26) $[_{CP}$ Spec $[_{C'}$ C $[_{AgrSP}$ Spec $[_{AgrS'}$ AgrS $[_{TP}$ T $[_{AgrOP}$ Spec $[_{AgrO'}$ AgrO $[_{VP}$ NP$_S$ V NP$_O$]]]

At LF, NP$_{O(bject)}$ moves out of its SS position and raises to Spec AgrO where it is case marked. This is a standard case of A-movement, is obligatory, and applies at LF. Furthermore, as should be clear, this operation moves NP$_O$ out of the VP and so enables the LF structure of an ACD construction to evade any regress problems. Consider an example, with the relevant structure displayed.

(27a) John bought everything that you did [e]
(27b) John$_j$ [T $[_{AgrOP}$ [everything that you did [e]]$_i$ [AgrO $[_{VP}$ t$_j$ $[_{VP1}$ buy t$_i$]]]]

If we interpret [e] in (27a) as the VP1 in (27b) we get the desired ACD con-figuration.[14]

Furthermore, we are able to account for virtually all of the data noted above. Observe that by making ACDs dependent on A-movement, we derive the boundedness condition noted by Baltin. A-movement is quite a bit more local than A'-movement. In particular, in a multiply embedded structure, we cannot A-move successive cyclically to higher and higher Spec AgrOs in the standard case. Recall that economy is what drives movement in a Minimalist theory. An expression only moves to check its features. Once these are checked, the expression does not move any further. Therefore, once in Spec AgrO an NP object will typically cease its peregrinations. What is important is that this implies that the interpretation of a null VP in ACDs is upwardly bounded. Consider Baltin's original example, once again.

(28) Who thought that Fred read how many of the books that Bill did

The NP$_O$ is *how many books that Bill did*. This is moved to the Spec AgrO of the embedded clause. Any further A-movement is blocked by the economy con-siderations that block long A-movement. Thus, the only VP that this NP has been moved out from under is the most embedded one. Thus only this one can be copied without running into the regress problem. Observe that subsequent A'-movement will not provide more expansive copying possibilities for the Minimalist reasons canvassed above. Importantly, VP2 is not a candidate for copying into the null VP position as it dominates the null VP. This leaves VP1 as the only source of the ACD interpretation.[15]

(29) Who $[_{VP2}$ thought $[_{CP}$ that $[_{IP}$ Fred$_j$ $[_{AgrOP}$ [how many of the books that Bill did]$_i$ [AgrO $[_{VP}$ t$_j$ $[_{VP1}$ read t$_i$]]]]]]]]

This approach to ACDs also accounts for the data noted in Larson and May. Recall that the latter observed the following contrast and noted that an extraposition approach to ACDs could not really account for the data.

(30a) *I expect everyone you do will visit Mary
(30b) ?I expect everyone you do to visit Mary

The Minimalist story outlined above implies this contrast. (30b) is an ECM structure where the embedded subject is case-marked by the higher predicate. In Minimalist terms, this means that *everyone that you do* raises to the matrix Spec AgrO position at LF and so out of the matrix VP that dominates it at SS. But this then licenses copying of this VP into the empty VP in the relative clause. This same operation, however, is barred in (30) as it is not an ECM structure and raising to the matrix Spec AgrO violates a slew of conditions, e.g. it will not be an instance of last resort movement. As such, there is no VP that can be copied into the gap without inducing regress problems.

Note that this account for the contrast in (30) does not run into the same problems that the QR theory faced. Recall that Larson and May tied the contrast to the clause boundedness of QR. However, it is not clear that this account is general enough, as the discussion of the contrast in (15) suggested. We observed that, whereas the universal quantifier in (15a) could take scope over the matrix existential, this was not so for (15b), which indicated that in these cases QR was clause bounded. However, as Larson and May observe, ACDs are licit nonetheless. The relevant data are repeated here.

(15a) At least one person considers every senator to be smart
(15b) At least one person considers every senator smart
(16)   I consider everyone you do smart

In the Minimalist story above, it is not QR that licenses ACDs but A-movement to Spec AgrO. As these are ECM constructions, movement to Spec AgrO must apply and so we expect (16) to be acceptable. In short, QR and ACDs are decoupled and so we do not require that they swing together as they must on the QR approach.[16]

Consider now the fact that verbs like *want, used to, have to,* etc. do not display boundedness effects. I have suggested that the reason is that these are restructuring verbs. Roberts (1992) has argued that the distinctive feature of restructuring verbs is that they unify the domains of the embedded and restructuring verb into one complex. This licenses local A-movement across sentential boundaries in the form of clitic climbing and scrambling in languages such as Italian, Old French, and Dutch. In restructuring contexts, the object moves to the higher Spec AgrO, the one associated with the restructuring verb. This movement is overt in languages such as Italian, Dutch, and Old French (cf. Roberts 1992 for discussion).[17]

(31) . . . [$_{AgrOP}$ . . . [$_{VP}$ want . . . [$_{IP}$ . . . [$_{VP}$ . . . NP$_O$ . . .]]]]

If we assume that this same process is available at LF in languages like English then we can account for the Larson and May observations. In restructuring contexts, the embedded object moves out from under both the lowest VP and the higher one. This then allows either VP to be copied into the VP gap within the relative clause without regress problems. Thus, this sort of long A-movement at LF accounts for the ambiguity that Larson and May noted. Furthermore, this accounts for why it is that boundedness effects reappear when restructuring is blocked (cf. (21) and (22)). It also accounts for the scope facts discussed in (24) above. In short, if restructuring licenses A-movement to the higher Spec AgrO by merging the biclausal structure into one domain, the Minimalist analysis of ACDs accounts for the ambiguities Larson and May observed without deriving the observed unacceptable sentences.

The present analysis also handles ACDs in a unified manner. Thus, unlike the treatment in Baltin (1987) which required the proliferation of string vacuous movement operations, virtually all of the cases cited in Larson and May follow. For example, the cases in (17) above involving comparatives and *different* NPs can be handled in the same manner as other ACDs.

One last point in favor of this approach. May (1985) observed that names were not subject to QR and claimed that this accounted for the lack of ACDs with appositive relative clauses.

(32)   *Dulles suspected Philby, who Angleton did

Baltin's approach also accounts for these data given the lack of extraposition of appositive relative clauses. Data such as this, however, constitute a puzzle for the approach pursued here, as we would have A-movement for case reasons regardless of the quantificational status of the head of the relative clause. However, what appears to be a problem, is, I believe, really a virtue. There are many cases of ACDs with appositive relatives which are perfectly acceptable.[18]

(33)   Dulles suspected Angleton, who, incidentally, Philby did as well

It thus appears that the indicated judgement in (32) has little to do with ACDs *per se*. The relative unacceptability of (32) is more likely related to the peculiar intonational properties of appositives. As is well known, they are intonationally set off from the head in ways restrictive relatives are not. Furthermore, it appears that standard cross-sentential VP ellipsis requires these sorts of particles as well.[19]

(34a)   John left and Bill did *(too/as well)
(34b)   John is tall and Mary is *(too/as well)

Given that appositives are standardly interpreted as simple conjuncts with the relative pronoun coreferential with the head (cf. Jackendoff 1977) it seems likely that the unacceptability of (32) can be grouped with that in (34). If this is so, then (32) ceases to be a problem for this analysis. However, the acceptability of (33) becomes an argument against either a QR treatment of ACDs or an extraposition approach given that appositive relatives are not subject to QR nor do they support extraposition.

There is a way of accommodating the data in (33) within an approach that still treats names as distinct from QNPs in only having the latter subject to QR.[20] There is a well-known parallelism between appositive relative clauses and conjuncts. Perhaps licit ACDs in appositives are tied to this. Thus, (33) is interpreted at LF as (35) and this is what accounts for the acceptability of ACDs.

(35)   Dulles suspected Angleton, and, incidentally, Philby did as well

This assimilation of appositives to LF conjuncts gains support when certain pronominal binding facts are considered. There is a sharp difference in acceptability in binding into restrictive versus appositive relative clauses.

(36a)   Everyone/no one$_i$ likes the man who just kissed his$_i$ mother
(36b)   *Everyone/no one$_i$ likes John, who, incidentally, just kissed his$_i$ mother

This can be accounted for if (36b) is interpreted as a matrix conjunct, like the appositive in (35). It patterns, as expected, with (37) in which the bound pronoun is outside the scope of its quantificational antecedent.[21]

(37)   Everyone/no one$_i$ likes John$_j$ and he$_j$, incidentally, just kissed his$_i$ mother

With this diagnostic in mind, consider the data in (38).

(38a)   *Everyone/no one$_i$ expected John, who, incidentally, kicked his$_i$ mother to leave
(38b)   *Everyone/no one$_i$ expected John, who, incidentally, kicked his$_i$ mother would leave

Both sentences in (38) are unacceptable with the indicated binding. This follows if in both cases the appositive relative is treated as a matrix conjunct, paraphrasable as (39).

(39a)   *Everyone/no one$_i$ expected John$_j$ to leave and he$_j$, incidentally, kicked his$_i$ mother
(39b)   *Everyone/no one$_i$ expected John$_j$ would leave and he$_j$, incidentally, kicked his$_i$ mother

However, if this is correct then we expect that appositive relatives should freely license ACDs in (40). In other words, if appositives are matrix conjuncts at LF as the data in (38) suggest, then whether they are raised at LF to Spec AgrO should be irrelevant. This is incorrect, as the contrast in (40) indicates.

(40a)   Dulles believes Philby, who Angleton does as well, to be a spy
(40b)   *Dulles believes Philby, who Angleton does as well, is a spy

Observe that the acceptability of (40a) in contrast to (40b) follows if raising to Spec AgrO is required to feed ACDs in appositive relative clauses to avert regress.[22] However, the contrast is difficult to account for simply by assuming that appositive relative clauses are LF conjuncts.

I have argued that a Minimalist theory of ACDs has considerable empirical support. Given that ACDs are tied to A-movement, the boundedness effects observed in Baltin (1987) follow directly. Indeed, even the counterexamples to boundedness noted by Larson and May can be accounted for. Furthermore, given that this A-movement takes place at LF, the problems noted for Baltin's analysis by Larson and May do not beset this approach. At least for the standard cases, a Minimalist treatment is empirically well founded.

5   Adjunct ACDs

One set of cases remains to be discussed. To this point, I have shown how a Minimalist theory could accommodate cases of ACD in which the elided VP is contained within an object relative. The account ties the acceptability of ACD structures to the fact that internal arguments A-move out of the VP shell at LF for case reasons. However, there is an apparent problem for this sort of account. By tying ACD licensing to case theory how are cases such as (41) and (42) handled?

(41a)   John talked to everyone that Bill did
(41b)   John gave his address to everyone that Bill did
(42a)   John worded the letter as quickly as Bill did
(42b)   John recited his lines in the same way that Bill did

These cases are parallel but not identical. In (41) we find ACDs in objects of prepositions which are plausibly indirect objects of the verb. In (42) we find ACDs in manner adverbs, either obligatory manner adverbs as in (42a) or optional ones as in (42b). The problem in all of these cases is that we appear to have a licit elided VP inside a constituent contained within the antecedent VP but where case theory appears to be irrelevant. The Minimalist analysis above might appear to imply that these ACDs should be illicit, contrary to fact.

Minimalism permits two options for such cases. There is some evidence that both are exercised; one by indirect object constructions like (41), the other by XPs that are not indirect objects such as (42). The two options are as follows.

First, we can finesse the regress problem by generating expressions outside of VP; either adjoined to VP or higher. In the cases at hand, if the adverbs in (42) are generated outside (or adjoined to) the VP shell, then no problem of regress arises. In the case of (42a) this implies that *as quickly as Bill did* is an adjunct not an argument and that it is possible to adjoin it to VP (or some higher projection) and still meet its selection requirements. This could be done by leaving selection to the semantics and removing it entirely from the syntax, as was argued in Jackendoff (1972: 18–19).[23] Given that Minimalism dispenses with DS, the traditional locus of selection, this proposal is the natural way of treating selection restrictions. In Minimalist terms, this implies that sentences such as (43) are grammatically impeccable but fail to meet a lexical *semantic* restriction that the verb *word* has, viz. that it be modified by some manner expression. This restriction exercises its influence at whatever point a complete semantic reading is obtained.

(43)   ?John worded the letter[24]

Given these assumptions, the sentences in (42) have the structures in (44).[25] Here, the elided VP* can be interpreted as VP2 without inducing a regress.

(44a)   John [$_{VP1}$ [$_{VP2}$ worded the letter] as quickly as Bill did [$_{VP*}$ e]]
(44b)   John [$_{VP1}$ [$_{VP2}$ recited his lines] in the same way that Bill did [$_{VP*}$ e]]

The second option consistent with Minimalist assumptions is that some PPs are subject to case checking at LF and that they raise out of the VP at LF to Spec positions. This plausibly takes place in cases such as (41). This treats the preposition *to* as a realization of dative case in English, as suggested in Larson (1988). Given this assumption, the relevant LF structure of (41) is (45).[26]

(45a)   John [$_{AgrIO}$ [to everyone that Bill did [$_{VP*}$ e]]$_i$ [$_{VP}$ talked t$_i$]]
(45b)   John [$_{AgrO}$ [his address]$_i$ [$_{AgrIO}$ [to everyone that Bill did [$_{VP*}$ e]]$_j$ [$_{VP}$ gave t$_i$ t$_j$]]]

In sum, we have two logically possible ways of evading the regress problem with non-objects. Either they are case-marked expressions and raise (like direct objects do) to some VP external Agr position. Or these XPs are adjuncts that can be adjoined onto or outside of VP. Both options enable elided VPs within such expressions to evade the regress problem.

Evidence exists indicating that both these logical options are realized.[27] Recall that restructuring verbs like *want* have the property of letting an argument from an embedded complement raise to the Spec AgrO of the restructuring verb to get case, as in (46). In English this occurs at LF, while in some of the Romance languages this occurs overtly.

(46)   NP . . . [$_{Agr}$ Object$_i$ [want [PRO to [$_{VP}$ V t$_i$]]]]

Consider how such verbs would interact with the two options considered above. Indirect objects would raise to Spec Agr positions above the restructuring verbs, just as direct objects do. Adjuncts, on the other hand, would not so raise. We could thus find that elided VPs contained in IOs under restructuring verbs might optionally get interpreted as including the restructuring verb. In contrast, if the elided VP is inside an adjunct, the restructuring verb would not be part of the interpretation of the null VP. Consider some examples.

(47a)   John wanted to talk to everyone that Bill did
(47b)   John wanted to give his address to everyone that Bill did
(48a)   John wanted to word every question as I did
(48b)   I want to dance just the way Bill does
(48c)   John needs to phrase his letters as elegantly Bill does

The pair of examples in (47) are ambiguous. The VP gap in (47a) can be interpreted either as including or excluding the matrix restructuring verb *want*. Similarly, (47b) can have either interpretation in (49). On the assumption that in this case the *to* PP is an indirect object that raises to a Spec Agr position at LF for case checking, we can account for this ambiguity. The IO raises to a Spec Agr position above the matrix restructuring verb and can thus take either the embedded or the matrix VP as its antecedent.

(49a)   John wanted to give his address to everyone that Bill gave his address
        to
(49b)   John wanted to give his address to everyone that Bill wanted to give
        his address to

   In contrast, the elided VP gap in (48) does not include the matrix restructuring verb. (48a) is interpreted as (50a).

(50a)   John wanted to word every question as I worded it
(50b)   John wanted to word every question as I wanted to word it

The same holds true for (48b). Here the manner adverbial is most naturally interpreted as modifying the lower VP. Thus, it hangs within the embedded clause. This prevents it from having the interpretation (51b) if we assume that such expressions, in contrast to IOs, do not raise to Spec Agr positions at LF.

(51a)   I want to dance just the way Bill dances
(51b)   I want to dance just the way that Bill wants to dance

Similar remarks apply to (48c). The elided VP is interpreted as meaning that John needs to phrase his letters as elegantly as Bill phrases his letters rather than as elegantly as Bill needs to phrase his letters.[28]
   The contrast in ACD interpretation between these different XPs provides evidence for the pair of possibilities canvassed above. It is worth observing that PP raising to Spec Agr positions is limited to IOs, at least if we follow the ACD test. Instrumental PPs and *about* PPs do not seem to license the same ambiguities that *to* PPs do.

(52a)   John started to talk to every student that I did about Bill
(52b)   John started to talk to Bill about every student that I did

To my ear, it is hard to get the elided reading that includes *start* in (52b), in contrast to (52a).

(53a) John started to talk to every student that I (started to talk to about Bill) about Bill

(53b) John started to talk to Bill about every student that I (started to talk to Bill about)

Similar considerations hold for cases such as (54a). These do not have readings parallel to (54b).

(54a) John wants to draw a picture with every pen that I did

(54b) John wants to draw a picture with every pen that I want to draw a picture with

If this is correct, then only true IOs raise at LF to Spec Agr positions, all other PPs being adjunct-like.[29, 30]

To sum up, Minimalism allows ACD structures to evade the regress problem either by moving out from under a dominating VP at LF via A-movement for case reasons or by being adjoined outside the relevant VP to begin with. We have considered how these options apply to indirect objects (with *to*) and adverbials and have provided evidence that each option is realized.

6   Further Implications

There are several technical loose ends that a Minimalist theory must grapple with. I would like to review a number of these here.

First, I have been assuming that the gap in ACD constructions is a VP. This is possibly incorrect (but see chapter 9, n. 9). Even on non-Minimalist accounts it is unclear whether the gap is a VP or a V'. Assuming a Minimalist account, the option of it being an AgrO' comes into play. It all depends what the LF structure from which copying takes place looks like. I have been assuming that V has not raised to AgrO at the point at which copying takes place. However, it is consistent with the above account that V raises to AgrO first and then the copying proceeds. However, it also appears that *further* movement is not compatible with the current story. The problem is that a Minimalist theory assumes LF V-movement to T^0 and then to AgrS in languages like English. After all movement has taken place, an LF phrase marker has the following form.

(55) $[_{AgrSP}$ NP$_S$ $[_{AgrS'}$ $[[[V_k + AgrO_j] + T]]_i$ AgrS$]$ $[_{TP}$ t_i $[_{AgrOP}$ NP$_O$ $[t_j$ $[_{VP*}$ t_S $[_{VP}$ t_k $t_O]]]]]]]]$

Here is the problem. If NP$_O$ contains an elided predicate we cannot interpret it by copying AgrS' into it. Assume it has the structure (56).

(56) $[_{NP}$ Q $[_{N'}$ N $[_{CP}$ WH-$_i$ $[_{IP}$ NP$_j$ did $[e]$ . . . $]]]]$

To get a well-formed LF we need to "complete" the A'-chain headed by the relative WH-operator in CP and the A-chain related to the subject NP$_j$. This is necessary on empirical as well as theoretical grounds given that in (57) *Bill* has a clear theta role, in fact the same theta role that *John* has. Copying the VP* into [e] allows us to accommodate this fact.

(57)   John ate everything that Bill did

But, if we copy AgrS' from (55) into [e] we will end up with NP$_S$ coindexed with NP$_j$. To complete NP$_j$'s A-chain we copy AgrS' into [e]. For NP$_j$'s A-chain to be licit, NP$_j$ and the trace in the subject of VP* have to be coindexed; S = j. But this leads to a principle C violation at LF and so this indexing should be illicit.

There are several ways around this problem. First, we might assume that indices are not copied. This is consistent with Minimalist assumptions (Chomsky 1993: 43 and n. 52). If they are not "real" entities but simply annotate structural relations among elements in a tree then we should expect not to "copy" them. If we allow "free" indexing, then the interpretive properties of these structures, in conjunction with one of the standard well-formedness conditions on chains, will yield the right results. For example, unless NP$_j$ becomes "tied" to a trace in Spec VP, its chain receives no theta role and so the LF structure "crashes." Similarly, unless the WH in CP in (56) becomes linked to a well-formed A-chain with a theta position and a case-marked position it will be a vacuous operator and this will suffice to crash the derivation. So it appears that not copying indices is a way consistent with Minimalist assumptions that will solve this problem.[31]

There are other solutions as well. It is consistent with Minimalist principles to base generate subjects directly in Spec AgrS and not move them there from VP, as assumed here. Generating VP internal subjects is empirically motivated. It is not minimalistically required. If VP internal subjects go, the problem above disappears.[32]

A third way around the difficulty is to assume that it is not the output of LF, the interface LF phrase marker, that feeds the copying procedure but some earlier LF phrase marker, say the one that obtains prior to V-raising to AgrO. If we assume this then we can generate the phrase marker in (56) with traces in the Spec Agr case positions. Only the last bit of the VP shell would remain to be copied. Concretely, at LF prior to copying, we would have the phrase markers (58) and (59), the latter being a detailed version of the internal structure of NP$_O$. The trace of WH-movement inside the relative (59) sits in Spec AgrO and has been generated prior to LF. We then copy VP1 in (58) into [$_{VP}$ e] in (59). This completes the A-chain required for interpretation. Note, that NP$_O$ in (58) and t_i in (59) will bear the same index given that the relative clause is predicated of the head and thereby the indices are identified.[33]

(58)   [$_{AgrSP}$ NP$_S$ [$_{AgrS'}$ AgrS [$_{TP}$ T$_i$ [$_{AgrOP}$ NP$_O$ [AgrO$_j$ [$_{VP}$ t$_S$ [$_{VP1}$ V$_k$ t$_O$]]]]]]]
(59)   [$_{NP}$ Q [$_{N'}$ N [$_{CP}$ WH-$_i$ [$_{IP}$ NP$_j$ did [$_{AgrOP}$ t$_i$ [AgrO [$_{VP}$ t$_j$ [$_{VP}$ e]]]]]]]]

Each of these solutions suffices to circumvent the principle C problem noted above. However, there are some reasons for thinking that the first alternative will not suffice as it stands. The main reason is the following: if we must copy the verbal content into the elided predicate or fail full interpretation, then we must copy AgrS'. However, this will result in several problems. First, we will have too many tenses inside the relative clause, the one provided by the relative itself (i.e. the one supported by *do*) and the one copied into the relative. Thus, if we are not to get too many tenses into the ACD structure and we are to get the verbal content into the ACD by copying the verb itself then the source of the copying must be an LF phrase marker where the V is dissociated from the tense. This means something like what we outlined in (58) and (59). Second, even if we could finesse the issue of too many tenses, copying AgrS' is not possible as this would induce regress. Note that the object is in Spec AgrO which is dominated by AgrS'. Thus there is no way to copy the latter into the former without running afoul of the regress problem.

This suggests one of two options: either that it is not the output of LF operations that are relevant but some prior derivational level or one need not copy the verb itself into the VP gap; a trace of the verb suffices. Consider each option in turn.

In and of itself, it is consistent with Minimalist assumptions to interpret ACD structures via a level of representation other than LF. However, it is more in the spirit of Minimalism to limit copying so that it only has access to interface levels as input. Something like this is hinted at in Chomsky (1993: 35). If we assumed that only LF feeds ACD interpretation, we could copy the verb into the VP gap by assuming that V-movement need not apply in English at all or that it only moves the V to AgrO rather than all the way up to T. Assuming this, AgrO' in (58) has determinate verbal content and suffices to interpret the VP gap.[34] However, it is also contrary to the analysis in Chomsky (1993).

Now, it is unclear to me how serious an alteration of the Minimalist program this is. It is certainly central to the content of Chomsky (1993) that V-movement take place at LF in English. However, this is driven by rather abstract learnability considerations dealing with the identity of LFs across languages (see chapter 1). The idea is that if something happens in one language overtly then it happens in all languages covertly. The reason given is that LF is too remote from experience to differ across languages and that different LFs imply different interpretations. As far as I can tell, neither reason is particularly compelling. Strictly speaking, if what one means by experience is interface with another cognitive system (and what else could it mean in the present context given that the language faculty is not itself a perceptual system?) then the interface level LF is not terribly remote from experience. As for the second point, it is quite unclear what interpretive effects V-raising has so that raising it or not will have an effect on the meaning of the sentence. It is quite consistent with all that we know that phrase markers that differ syntactically at LF with respect to verbal position might not differ in any way that affects their interpretation. What is required is some account of how the hierarchical position of a V at LF affects the interpretation of the clause. This has not yet been provided.[35]

Consider now the second alternative. If the verb raises to AgrS then we cannot copy the verb into the gap. All that is available is a trace of the verb

e_k and the verb+AgrO complex e_j as in (60). Recall that we cannot copy more than AgrO' into NP$_O$ on pain of regress. The problem is how to get determinate content here, on the assumption that the traces of verbs are not themselves contentful but derive whatever interpretation they have in virtue of being in the chain headed by the raised V.

(60) $[_{AgrSP}$ NP$_S$ $[_{AgrS'}$ $[[[V_k$ $[AgrO_j]]$ $T_i]$ AgrS$]$ $[_{TP}$ e_i $[_{AgrOP}$ NP$_O$ $[_{AgrO'}$ e_j $[_{VP}$ t_S $[_{VP1}$ e_k $t_o]]]]]]]]$

Consider the following solution. Assume that the structure of the raised NP object is as in (61) prior to VP interpretation and that what is copied into e is AgrO' from (60). This yields (62).

(61) $[_{NP}$ Q $[_{N'}$ N $[_{CP}$ WH-$_i$ $[_{IP}$ NP$_j$ did $[_{AgrOP}$ t_i $[e]]]]]]$
(62) $[_{NP}$ Q $[_{N'}$ N $[_{CP}$ WH-$_i$ $[_{IP}$ NP$_j$ did $[_{AgrOP}$ t_i $[_{AgrO'}$ e_j $[_{VP}$ t_S $[_{VP1}$ e_k $t_o]]]]]]]]$

To get a well-formed structure, we must assume that *NP$_j$* in (62) and t_i are related to theta positions so as to receive interpretations. However, on pain of not violating principle C, we must assume that the indices from (60) have not been copied and that NP$_j$ and t_i can bind t_S and t_O in (62). Assume, then, that the copying here can dispense with the indices on the indicated NP traces inside VP in (62). We then get (63).

(63) $[_{NP}$ Q $[_{N'}$ N $[_{CP}$ WH-$_i$ $[_{IP}$ NP$_j$ did $[_{AgrOP}$ t_i $[_{AgrO'}$ e_j $[_{VP}$ t_j $[_{VP1}$ e_k $t_i]]]]]]]]$

This is still not enough. We must still bind e_k *and make sure that it is interpreted as the same verb V_k as in (60)*. If *did* binds this verbal trace, then it must have the same index, viz. *did$_k$*. But then it is also coindexed with the matrix verb V_k in (60) and can thereby inherit its content. Observe that this guarantees that in an ACD structure, the elided verb must be interpreted as identical to the matrix verb. (64a) is only interpretable as (64b) not (64c).

(64a)   John kissed everyone that Bill did
(64b)   John kissed everyone that Bill kissed
(64c)   John kissed everyone that Bill saw

So we have derived the correct interpretive results and still allowed verb movement to AgrS. However, there is a cost. We have had to assume that indices on some traces are copied, viz. those of verbs. Without this assumption, we would not have derived the required coindexation between *did* and V_k and the interpretive facts exemplified in (64). It appears then that verbal traces have indices that can get copied but that traces of argument NPs do not. With this assumption, and the assumption that *do* can be anaphorically dependent on another verb and thereby inherit its content (cf. Pollock 1989), we can interpret ACDs at LF and still allow V-raising all the way to AgrS.

Consider one more possible consequence of this analysis of ACDs. It is well known that VP deletion as it appears in English is somewhat idiosyncratic. For example, Spanish has an elliptical analogue but not one that leaves an auxiliary remnant.

(65a) Juan vio un coche y   Pedro también
      Juan saw a   car   and Pedro too
(65b) Juan llego, y   creo   que Pedro también
      Juan arrived and I think that Pedro too

However, what does not occur in Spanish is the equivalent of English ACDs.

(66) Juan ne vio nada   que Pedro *(vio)
     Juan   saw nothing that Pedro (saw)

Why not? Observe that in Spanish, there is syntactic raising of V to AgrS. As such, at LF we are faced with a structure like (55) and (56) above in ACD configurations. But as we noted, this confronts the regress problem and so there is no way to derive a well-formed LF for this sentence. In other words, in the elliptical constructions in (66) we must copy an AgrS' or TP as this is the constituent that is missing.[36] However, given that objects only raise to Spec AgrO, this copying cannot proceed without regress. This accounts for the lack of ACD structures in languages like Spanish that do not have VP deletion.

   If this account for the absence of ACDs in Spanish is correct, it supports the first alternative noted above in which V is not raised beyond AgrO at LF in English. If it were raised higher, then the only way to account for the difference between English and Spanish would be to link it somehow to specific properties of *do*. We could say that *do* can be anaphoric to another verb but there is no null counterpart of this in Spanish. However, as shown below, data similar to the Spanish facts hold in languages like Brazilian Portuguese and the East Asian languages where copies of the elided verb are present. Assuming then that the possibility of ACDs in English is not due to the specific properties of *do*, we have evidence that Vs need not raise all the way to AgrS at LF.

   Note that the May (1985) analysis in terms of QR cannot similarly account for the lack of ACDs with these forms of ellipsis in Spanish. The reason is that QR can append the QNP object containing the deletion site to a position higher than AgrOP. In fact, there is nothing to prevent appending the quantifier phrase to AgrSP/IP. However, from this position, copying will not confront the regress problem and we should have a well-formed ACD structure.[37]

7 ACDs and LF V-raising: Some Cross-linguistic Considerations

The last section explored a possible correlation between verb raising and the presence of ACD constructions. The gist of the claim is that object ACDs in English are licensed via movement to Spec AgrO at LF. This enables the elided

VP to be interpreted without regress as it has been removed from under the VP that serves as its antecedent. To work best, this proposal requires the verb in ACD constructions not to move higher than AgrO.

More abstractly, like May's (1985) proposal, the current analysis ties together the presence of ACDs with LF movement operations that get the constituent containing the elided gap out from under the constituent that is copied into the gap. However, in contrast to earlier approaches, Minimalism requires a specific kind of movement. If a gap is dominated by its filler then the only way of avoiding the regress problem is to A-move the constituent containing the gap out from under the filler. In short, ACDs rest on two requirements, (i) the position of the verb and (ii) the grammatical ability to A-move beyond it.

These requirements suggest that how high a verb sits and what kind of A-movement processes a language has can affect its capacity to sustain ACDs. In this section, I provide further support for this analysis by considering the properties of ACD constructions in the East Asian languages.

Otani and Whitman (1991) argue that null object constructions in the East Asian languages involve verb raising. The proposal centers on the proper analysis of sloppy identity in null object constructions such as (67).[38]

(67a)   John-wa   [zibun-no tegami-o]   sute-ta
        John-NOM self-GEN   letter-ACC discard-PERF
        "John$_i$ threw out self$_i$'s letters"

(67b)   Mary-mo [e] sute-ta
        Mary-also   discard-PERF
        = "Mary$_i$ also threw out self$_i$'s letters" (i)
        = "Mary also threw out John's letters" (ii)

As indicated, a null pronoun in sentences such as (67b) can license either a sloppy (i) or a strict (ii) reading. Otani and Whitman argue that the correct analysis of the sloppy identity reading (67b (ii)) involves an operation that raises the V^0 out of VP to yield a representation identical to VP ellipsis constructions in English. The derivation of (67a) is provided in (68).

(68a)   John-wa [[zibun-no tegami-o]$_{NP}$ [sute-]$_V$]$_{VP}$ -ta
(68b)   John-wa [[zibun-no tegami-o]$_{NP}$ [t$_v$]$_V$]$_{VP}$ [sute]$_v$-ta
(68c)   John-wa [λx [x [x-no tegami-o]$_{NP}$ [t$_v$]$_V$]$_{VP}$] [sute]$_v$-ta

(68b) represents the V-raising operation. Otani and Whitman assume that it applies prior to SPELL OUT.[39] (68c) displays the application of the derived VP rule and the reflexive rule, both of which apply at LF. The derivation of (67b) parallels that of (68). At LF we have the structure in (69).

(69)   Mary-mo [e]$_{VP}$ [sute]$_v$-ta

The structure permits copying of the VP in (68c) into the null VP in (69) to yield the final LF (70) which underlies the sloppy reading.

(70)   Mary-mo [λx [x [x-no tegami-o]$_{NP}$ t$_v$]]$_{VP}$ sute$_v$-ta

Takahashi (1993b) extends the Otani and Whitman analysis to ACD structures in Japanese. Following Otani and Whitman, he takes the presence of sloppy identity to signal the presence of VP ellipsis. Takahashi observes two important facts. First, in standard sentences, object ACDs are not permitted. (71) does not permit the sloppy interpretation. It cannot be interpreted as saying "John sent John's mother every book that Mary sent to Mary's mother."

(71) John-ga/mo   [zibun-no hahaoya]-ni [[Mary-ga [e] okkutta] dono
      John-NOM/also self-GEN   mother-to   Mary-NOM   sent   every
      hon] -mo okutta
      book   sent
      "John sent his mother every book that Mary did"

The sentence in (71) is an ACD configuration. It has the structure in (72) with the elliptical VP* contained within the matrix VP.

(72) [IP John-ga [I' [VP zibun-no hahoaya] -ni [V' [NP [IP Mary-ga [I' [VP* e] [I
      okutta]]] dono hon] -mo tv [okutta]]]

Takahashi points out that these data are problematic for a QR analysis of ACDs. The NP containing the elided VP is quantificational. QR should enable it to evade regress problems at LF. The fact that this construction is illicit with the sloppy/ACD reading speaks against the QR treatment of ACDs.

Takahashi's second important observation is that if we scramble the NP containing the VP gap out of the containing VP, the sentence is acceptable with a sloppy reading: "Mary sent her mother every book that John sent his mother."

(73) [IP [NP Mary-ga [VP* e] okutta] dono hon]i-mo [IP John-gamo [VP zibun-no
      hahoaya]-ni ti okutta]]
      "Every book that Mary did, John sent his mother, too"

Takahashi, following Saito (1985), assumes that scrambling adjoins the scrambled NP to IP. This movement moves the elided VP out from under the matrix VP and allows the sloppy/ACD interpretation.

This array of data perfectly fits the abstract characterization of ACD constructions above. Two points are noteworthy, in addition to Takahashi's observation that a QR-based account of ACDs cannot adequately account for the Japanese data. First, in Japanese, non-scrambled objects do not license ACDs. This is as what we expect given the Otani and Whitman/Takahashi analysis of VP ellipsis. Recall that in this analysis the verb raises to a prominent inflection projection prior to SPELL OUT. As such, even after raising to Spec AgrO, the object NP will still be dominated by the verb. In effect, because of verb raising, movement of an object to Spec AgrO does not suffice to neutralize the regress problem. Just as in the Spanish cases discussed above, verb movement prevents any copying of the constituent containing the raised verb into the VP deletion site without regress. The relevant abstract structure is (74) after the object has raised to Spec AgrO.[40]

(74)   [NP$_{subj i}$ [$_{AgrOP}$ [$_{VP}$ t$_i$ t$_v$ t$_j$] t$_v$ NP$_{obj}$] Verb-ta]

The second important point is that short distance scrambling permits the sloppy / ACD interpretation to emerge. This is expected on a Minimalist analysis on the assumption that scrambling is a species of A-movement whose landing site is a projection higher than Spec AgrO. Both provisos are empirically well founded.

Takahashi observes that there is good evidence that clause internal scrambling (CIS) patterns like A-movement. Saito (1992) notes that CIS can alleviate WCO effects and can license anaphor binding.[41] These are two signature properties of A-movement. The relevant contrasts are provided in (75) and (76): (75a) and (76a) record the acceptability judgements without CIS, and (75b) and (76b) indicate that CIS allows for the indicated readings.

(75a)   ?*[Masao-wa [Hanako-ga pro$_i$ yomu mae-ni] dono hon$_i$-o
        Masao-TOP   Hanako-NOM   read   before   which book-ACC
        yonda]] no
        read   Q
        "Masao read which book before Hanako read"

(75b)   Dono hon-o$_i$ [Masao-wa [Hanako-ga e$_i$ yomu mae-ni] [t$_i$
        Which book-ACC M-TOP   H-NOM   read   before
        yonda]] no
        read   Q
        "Which book did Masao read before Hanako read it"

(76a)   ?*[Masao-ga [[otagai$_i$-no   sensei]-ni [karera$_i$-o syookaisita]]] (koto)
        -NOM   each other-GEN teacher to they-ACC introduced   fact
        "Masao introduced them to each other's teachers"

(76b)   [Karera-o$_i$ [Masao-ga [[otagai$_i$-no   sensei]-ni [t$_i$ syookaisita]]]] (koto)
        They-ACC M-NOM   each other-GEN teacher to   introduced   (fact)
        "Them, Masao introduced to each other's teachers"

From the present perspective, what CIS does is A-move the scrambled NP above the raised V. Saito assumes that CIS is A-movement to a prominent Spec IP position (Saito 1992: 77). It is reasonable to suppose that this A-position is higher than the position of the raised verb. As such, we expect CIS to license the sloppy / ACD interpretation, as in fact occurs.[42]

Consider one more wrinkle. Saito (1992) provides evidence that clause external "long distance" scrambling (LDS) is a species of A'-movement. In contrast to CIS, for example, LDS cannot bind an anaphor.

(77)   *[Karera-o$_i$ [Masao-ga [otagai$_i$-no   sensei]-ni [$_{CP}$ [$_{IP}$ Hanako-ga t$_i$
        Them-ACC M-NOM   each other-GEN teacher to   H-NOM
        hihansita] to]   itaa]] (koto)
        criticized   COMP said   (fact)
        "Them$_i$, Masao said to each other's teachers that Hanako criticized t$_i$"

If this is correct then LDS should not be able to license ACDs, if, as argued above, only A-movement can evade the regress problem. Consider the following data, assuming the underlined constituent is scrambled to matrix initial position.

(78) [Sam-ga [Bill-ga zibun-no haha-ni [[John-ga pro okutta] dono
       S-NOM B-NOM self-GEN mother-to J-NOM   sent   every
       hon]-mo okutta to]   itta (koto)
       book   sent   COMP said (fact)
       "Sam said that Bill sent to his mother every book that John sent"

It is possible to get the sloppy reading in these constructions with the indicated NP scrambled to the matrix. Importantly, the reading that one gets is the one paraphrasable as "Sam said that Bill sent to Bill's mother every book that John sent to John's mother." In other words, the antecedent of the elided VP is the embedded VP.

Now consider another reading, one that is *not* available. We change the verb in the relative clause so that we force the reading in which the matrix VP is antecedent of the elided VP, i.e. we substitute *itta* (said) for *okutta* (sent).

(79) [Sam-ga [Bill-ga zibun-no haha-ni [[John-ga pro itta] dono hon]-mo
       S-NOM B-NOM self-GEN mother-to J-NOM   said every book
       okutta to]   itta (koto)
       sent   COMP said (fact)

(79) cannot be read as saying "Sam said that Bill sent to Sam's mother every book that John said that Bill sent John's mother." This is the reading that would obtain were the higher VP the filler of the deleted VP. Two points are relevant here. First, the absence of this reading is what we would predict if LDS involves A'-movement. Recall that A'-movement requires that the relative clause restrictor be reconstructed to the tail of the A'-chain. Thus at LF, the structure that we have will resemble one that obtains prior to scrambling, i.e. what is present in (79). Given this representation, the matrix VP is not a possible antecedent of the VP gap due to the regress problem. LDS, then, acts as predicted.[43]

A second interesting point. These cases indicate that even overt syntactic movement of a VP gap out from under its antecedent does not license ACDs. This is very interesting for it argues that ACD licensing cannot be stated at SS (or SPELL OUT). This is precisely what a Minimalist theory would predict. All interpretive rules must work off of the LF phrase marker in a Minimalist theory. The data in (78) and (79) indicate that SS, *even when it meets the apparent requirements*, cannot be used to feed ACD interpretation. In short, ACDs provide evidence that not only can interpretation be "done off" LF exclusively, it must be.

The Japanese data have English analogues. Consider the following English case of WH-movement.

(80) How many books that I should have did you tell Bill that Frank reviewed

(80) carries the interpretation (81a). It cannot be interpreted as (81b).

(81a)   How many books that I should have reviewed did you tell Bill that
       Frank reviewed

(81b)   How many books that I should have told Bill that Frank reviewed did
       you tell Bill that Frank reviewed

This fact parallels the Japanese one above. Despite the fact that overt WH-
movement removes the VP gap out of the matrix VP, the matrix VP is not a
potential filler for this gap. If ACDs are interpreted at LF exclusively and we
assume the Preference Principle for A′-chains then this follows. At LF, the
relative clause is reconstructed into the embedded one. This, on pain of regress,
prevents the matrix VP from serving as antecedent of the VP gap.[44]

Consider one more piece of cross-linguistic data in favor of the above analysis. Otani and Whitman observe that in certain dialects of Portuguese that
permit object drop (Brazilian Portuguese (BP) is one such), it is possible to find
VP ellipsis facts identical to those observed in Japanese. Otani and Whitman
(1991: 357, ex. 31) cite the following VP ellipsis data. (82b) shows sloppy identity in VP ellipsis constructions.

(82a)   O   João$_i$ encontrou o   seu$_i$ mestre de elementário
       The João met   the his   teacher of elementary
       "João met his elementary school teacher"

(82b)   A   Maria também encontrou [e]
       The Maria also   met
       = "Also Maria met João's teacher"
       = "Also Maria met Maria's teacher"

What of ACD constructions in these dialects of Portuguese? As is well known,
Portuguese, like the other Romance languages, overtly raises verbs to prominent inflectional projections prior to SPELL OUT. As such, we should not find
sloppy/ACD constructions in BP. This seems to be the case.[45]

(83)   O   João disse pra mãe   dele   tudo   que o   Pedro disse
       The J.   said for mother of him everything that the Pedro said
       "John said to his mother everything that Pedro said"

(83) cannot have a sloppy interpretation in BP. This is expected if the sloppy
readings are only possible in licit ACD constructions. In BP, raising the object to Spec AgrO will not suffice to license ACDs given the fact that verbs
raise above AgrO overtly prior to SPELL OUT. Thus, BP provides further
evidence for the hypothesis linking NP movement, verb raising, and ACD
constructions.[46]

8   Conclusion

I have argued that Minimalism requires reworking the analysis of ACDs. I
have shown that each of the two current contending analyses suffer from

empirical drawbacks and that these are resolved within a Minimalist framework. Several issues concerning verb movement have been broached. We return to these in chapter 9. Further implications of this approach to ACDs and its interaction with quantifier scope are reviewed in chapter 8 section 2.

Appendix 1   Nominative Objects

Consider one last piece of Japanese data. As discussed in Tada (1992), there is a class of Japanese verbs whose objects can be either accusative or nominative. These verbs have one of three kinds of affixes; *-rare* ("can"), *-ta* ("want") and *tough* predicates like *-yasu* ("easy") and *-niku* ("difficult").[47] These verbs allow either accusative or nominative case marking on the thematic object.

(84) John-ga   nihonogo-o/-ga   hanas-e-ru   (koto)
      John-NOM Japanese-ACC/NOM speak-POT-PRES (fact)
      "John can speak Japanese"

Tada accounts for this by assuming that in these constructions a kind of restructuring can occur in which the embedded verb and the matrix form a monoclausal predicate. Assume that this is correct. The question that arises is how nominative and accusative case are assigned. Tada assumes that accusative case is assigned when restructuring does not apply and we have a biclausal structure. Nominative case is assigned when restructuring applies. Nominative, Tada proposes, is checked in an AgrO projection in the higher clause. There is another possibility. Though accusative case is checked in Spec AgrO, nominative is checked in a projection higher than AgrO. There is some evidence in favor of this latter hypothesis.
     Consider the following data from Takahashi (1993b).

(85a) John-ga/mo   zibun-no kodomo-ni [[Mary-ga [$_{VP}$ e] yometa]
       John-NOM/also self-GEN child-to   Mary-NOM   could read
       muzukasii hon]-<u>o</u>   yometa
       difficult   book-ACC/NOM could read
       "John could read the difficult book that Mary could read to his child"
(85b) John-ga/mo   zibun-no kodomo-ni [[Mary-ga [$_{VP}$ e] yometa]
       John-NOM/also self-GEN child-to   Mary-NOM   could read
       muzukasii hon]-<u>ga</u>   yometa
       difficult   book-NOM could read

The difference between the two cases involves the case on the relative clause containing the deleted VP. According to Takahashi, the latter is far better than the former on the ACD interpretation.[48] This can be accounted for given the assumptions above if the nominative case-marked relative clause raises to a Spec position above AgrO at LF. Note that movement to Spec AgrO will not suffice given the fact that the Japanese verb raises beyond AgrO.

Appendix 2   Just Where is LF?

I have assumed that LF feeds VP ellipsis interpretation. Concretely, some portion of the LF phrase marker is copied into the gap site. What is the object that is the output of this copying operation? There are various answers to this in the literature. Sag (1976) assumed that what was copied was not a syntactic structure but a logical structure. If so, then the output of this process is not a phrase marker but some non-linguistic object of the CI interface components.

There are other views of this interpretive process, however. Chapter 3 reviewed arguments by Fiengo and May (1990, 1994) that the gap site displays syntactic properties. If this is so, it implies that the output of the gap site interpretation procedure is itself the LF phrase marker. However, if so, how can LF be both input and output to the operation of ellipsis interpretation?[49]

The Minimalist account outlined above aimed to have LF constrain the interpretation process. We can meet this aim, however, and finesse the problem noted here. Assume that the phrase marker that is the output of the copying operation constrains the copying process in the following way: except for filling in the gap site, the phrase marker cannot be altered in any way. In effect, we require that the output of the operation and the input be isomorphic up to the elided material. Thus, the LF phrase marker, the output of the copying procedure, determines what structure of the input phrase marker can be copied into the gap site. In this sense, the LF phrase marker drives ellipsis interpretation.

With this view of ellipsis interpretation, we can keep to the Minimalist spirit of things in having LF determine interpretation while still allowing that the output of the ellipsis interpretation procedure be the LF phrase marker. This is important, for it is this object that is subject to grammatical principles such as the BT and subjacency, as Fiengo and May have argued. In sum, there is a way to reconcile the approach outlined here with the findings in Fiengo and May on the structure of ACDs in chapter 3.

6

Linking, Binding, and Weak Cross Over

1 Introduction

This chapter provides a linking theoretic treatment of weak cross over (WCO) effects. It has two aims. The narrower aim is to show that the supposition that a pronoun cannot be linked to a variable on its left accounts for standard WCO effects and provides a superior explanation for the lack of such effects in certain recently studied cases, so-called "weakest cross over" (Lasnik and Stowell 1991). In addition, the chapter argues that one can and should reformulate the WCO prohibition in more structural terms and, further, that this formulation provides evidence for the Minimalist project.

The broader aim is to outline a reanalysis of WH/quantifier interpretations in terms of WCO. This kind of analysis is proposed in Chierchia (1991) and a slightly modified version is presented here. The basic facts of interest are provided in (1), in particular, the absence of a reading for (2) in which the universal quantifier takes scope over the WH. This interpretive gap has been standardly accounted for in terms of the ECP, as outlined in chapter 2. Chierchia (1991) proposes generalizing some observations by Engdahl (1985) pertaining to the interpretation of WH-questions to allow these facts to be assimilated to WCO configurations. The details are provided below.

(1) What did everybody say
(2) Who said everything

A reanalysis of the phenomena illustrated in (1) and (2) in terms of WCO furthers the Minimalist program by removing these phenomena from the purview of the ECP. Chapter 4 observed that ECP-centered accounts of LF phenomena have certain drawbacks. First, they require ancillary assumptions of dubious standing to be empirically adequate. Second, theoretically, ECP principles do not fit well with Minimalist inclinations. As such, it is an interesting exercise to see whether these phenomena can be reanalyzed in terms more congenial to the Minimalist program. The WCO approach to these constructions fits nicely with Minimalist assumptions. The present chapter addresses WH/quantifier interactions. The analysis is extended in the next chapter to accommodate superiority effects.

2   Linked Pronouns

It is well known that pronouns cannot be treated as bound variables in WCO configurations such as (3) where neither the pronoun nor the variable c-commands the other.

(3) $Q_i \ldots pronoun_i \ldots vbl_i \ldots$

The earliest proposals for dealing with these WCO effects was to prohibit a variable from being the antecedent of a pronoun on its left (Chomsky 1976: 201, ex. 105)

(4)   *Weak Cross Over Principle (WCOP):* A variable cannot be the antecedent of a pronoun on its left

Given the standard assumption that an NP can be the antecedent of a pronoun if and only if the two are coindexed, we can restate (4) as (5).

(5)   A variable cannot be coindexed with a pronoun on its left

More recently, the left / right character of (4) and (5) has been replaced by more structural restrictions stated in c-command terms (cf. Koopman and Sportiche 1983).[1]

(6)   In configurations such as (3), vbl_i must c-command *pronoun_i*

However, the grammatical rendering of antecedence in terms of coindexation has remained, i.e. A is an antecedent of B iff A and B are coindexed.
     Higginbotham (1983, 1985) develops a different view of the grammatical nature of antecedence.[2] This approach starts from the observation that the semantic notion of antecedence is fundamentally asymmetric and that this asymmetry is not reflected in the grammatical mechanism of coindexing. To syntactically reflect the inherent asymmetry of the semantic relation, Higginbotham proposes removing coindexation from the grammar and replacing it with *linking*. This latter is an asymmetric relation able to grammatically model the asymmetry of the antecedence relation in a way that indexing cannot.
     If we replace indexation with linking, (7) replaces (5) as the correct formalization of (4).[3]

(7)   A pronoun cannot be linked to a variable on its right *Q . . .
      pronoun . . . vbl . . .

If we replaced indexing with linking, (6) could be stated as (8).

(8)   If a pronoun P is linked to a variable V, then V must c-command P

In what follows, I adopt (7). I return, in section 6, to a discussion of how to state a linked version of WCO in more structural terms by revising the definition of c-command.

Observe that for the standard cases, (7) is empirically equivalent to (5). Consider an example. In (9) *his* can only be linked to the variable on its right, there being no other suitable linker. This, however, violates (7) and so we witness a WCO effect.[4]

(9a)   His mother kissed everyone
(9b)   Everyone$_i$ [his mother kissed t$_i$]^5

What then is the advantage of a linking reformulation of the WCOP? Its virtues become apparent in more complex cases where WCO effects are alleviated. A slew of apparent counterexamples to the WCO effect are discussed in Lasnik and Stowell (1991). They observe that WCO effects are alleviated in a variety of constructions despite the fact that a pronoun and variable are in the standard WCO configuration (3).

(10a)   Who$_i$ will be easy for us to get his$_i$ mother to talk to t$_i$
(10b)   Who$_i$ did you stay with t$_i$ before his$_i$ wife had spoken to t$_i$
(10c)   This book$_i$, I expect its$_i$ author to buy t$_i$
(10d)   Gerald$_i$, who$_i$ his$_i$ mother loves t$_i$

The examples in (10) appear to have a variable coindexed with a pronoun on its left and so should be unacceptable. However, they are dramatically better than standard WCO sentences such as (11).

(11a)   *Who$_i$ did his$_i$ mother kiss t$_i$
(11b)   *His$_i$ mother told everyone$_i$ about Santa Claus

To accommodate these data, Lasnik and Stowell suggest that the traces in (10) are not really variables. Rather, they are null epithets, null analogues of *the SOB* in (12).

(12)   John told every senator$_i$ that the SOB$_i$ was incompetent

As Lasnik and Stowell note (p. 709), epithets are like pronouns in that they can be interpreted as bound variables but differ in that they do not induce WCO effects. In contrast to pronouns, furthermore, they are subject to principle C and so should grammatically look like variables with respect to the standard principles of the BT.

(13)   Some tenant in every apartment building$_i$ has asked its$_i$ owner to paint the place$_i$

Note that *the place* is interpreted as a bound variable and it is coindexed with a pronoun to its left. If the empty categories in (10) are null epithets rather than variables, the amelioration of WCO effects is to be expected.

To make this account empirically adequate, however, it is necessary to limit the distribution of null epithets. For example, if the empty categories in (11) could be such, then we would never expect to observe WCO effects at all. To meet this problem, Lasnik and Stowell propose that only empty categories that are bound by non-quantificational operators can be null epithets. The relative pronoun in appositives is non-quantificational as is the 0-operator in *tough* constructions, parasitic gaps, and topicalization structures. These contrast with standard quantificational NPs such as *everyone* and *no one*, the relative pronoun in restrictive relatives, and the WH in questions. Only the traces of elements in the former group can be null epithets and thus only constructions where they are involved can cancel WCO effects.

There is another analysis of the data in (10) that a linking approach makes available. Observe that the examples in (10) share a common structure, exemplified in (14).

(14)   r-expression$_i$ . . . pronoun$_i$ . . . r-expression$_i$ . . .

In all the examples, the rightmost r-expression is a trace/variable on standard assumptions. In (10a, b) the left most r-expression is also a variable while in (10c, d) it is a name. Thus, (10a, b) have the structure (15a) while (10c, d) have the structure (15b).

(15a)   vbl^1 . . . pronoun . . . vbl^2 . . .
(15b)   name . . . pronoun . . . vbl^2 . . .

Assume now that pronouns cannot be linked to variables on their right. It is possible to get a well-formed linking in (15) so that all three elements are linked and (7) is respected. All one does is link the pronoun to *vbl*^{1} to its left in (15a) and to *name* in (15b). Note that the remaining variables will be linked to the vbl/name on the left in the usual way, presumably via the 0-operator. What is crucial here is that the "extra" r-expression provides another linker for the pronoun, one that is to the left rather than the right.

(16a)   vbl^1 . . . pronoun . . . vbl^2 . . .

(16b)   name . . . pronoun . . . vbl . . .

In short, linking enables us to account for these weakest crossover data without the use of null epithets. Moreover, the reason that we can do this is that linking has replaced coindexation as the formal realization of antecedence. Coindexation is an inherently transitive relation. Given coindexing as the grammatical reflection of antecedence, there is no way of coindexing *vbl*^{1} with the pronoun without also having *vbl*^{2} coindexed with the pronoun. The first coindexing is necessary to represent antecedence. But then this automatically induces a WCO effect given the transitivity of indexation. The only way to avoid this problem is to do as Lasnik and Stowell have proposed, which is to allow the indexing but deny that *vbl²* is actually a type of variable governed by the WCOP. This lies behind their suggestion that *vbl²* is a null epithet. If we represent antecedence via linking, on the other hand, no similar problem arises. Given the non-symmetric nature of linking we do not induce the unwanted transitivities and need not block the unwanted result by postulating a new type of empty category. This further eliminates the responsibility of determining the distributional properties of this novel category.

This last fact is not without its own rewards. The null epithet theory must take it as a brute fact that only non-quantificational operators can bind null epithets. This does not follow from an independent property of epithets interpreted as variables. Hornstein and Weinberg (1990) show that actual epithets can be locally A'-bound at LF by a real quantified expression. Lasnik and Stowell (p. 709, ex. 66) provide further relevant examples.

(17)   Some tenant in every apartment building$_i$ has asked its$_i$ owner to repaint the place$_i$

Thus, the restriction invoked by Lasnik and Stowell prohibiting real quantifiers from binding null epithets does not follow independently. As this stipulation drives the proposed analysis, methodological advantage accrues to an account that can do without it, all things being equal.

There are other reasons for preferring a linking version of the WCOP. The logic of (16) extends to cases that are beyond the empirical reach of the null epithet account. Consider the structure (18).

(18)   ... pronoun^1 ... vbl ... pronoun^2 ...

Assume that the pronouns in (18) have bound variable interpretations, i.e. the variable semantically anchors the two pronouns. On a standard indexing approach to antecedence this implies that all three expressions are coindexed. Consequently, a WCO effect should arise given that *vbl* is coindexed with *pronoun¹* on its left. In contrast, a linking theory can finesse this WCO effect with the linking relations indicated in (19).

(19)   ... pronoun^1 ... vbl ... pronoun^2 ...

In light of this, consider the data in (20).

(20a)   *His$_i$ mother gave his$_i$ picture to every student$_i$
(20b)   His$_i$ mother gave every student$_i$ his$_i$ picture
(20c)   *His$_i$ mother packed his$_i$ sandwiches for every boy$_i$
(20d)   His$_i$ mother packed every boy$_i$ his$_i$ sandwiches
(20e)   *His$_i$ mother introduced every boy$_i$ to Mary
(20f)   His$_i$ mother introduced every boy$_i$ to his$_i$ teacher

A decisive weakening of WCO effects occurs in the second sentence of every pair. In (20a, c) we have a structure like (21) at LF.

(21)   pronoun^1 ... pronoun^2 ... vbl

Here there is no way of linking either pronoun to the variable without inducing a WCO violation. The variable is to the right of both potential linked pronouns and so (7) will be violated. (20b, d, f) manifest the structure in (18) at LF. WCO effects are attenuated. This follows from a linking approach to WCO. The null epithets account is inert here. Note that the variables in these cases are "real" variables. The operators are true quantifiers and so the empty category formed by LF movement must be a variable and cannot be a null epithet. Consequently, a null epithets approach cannot extend to these cases.

Observe that the element to the right of the variable need not be a pronoun. Any anaphoric expression will do; PRO, reflexives, epithets all suffice as all can instantiate the linking configuration in (19) and all induce weakest cross over effects.[6]

(22a)   *His$_i$ mother persuaded every boy$_i$ that Mary should participate
(22b)   His$_i$ mother persuaded every boy$_i$ PRO to participate
(22c)   His$_i$ mother persuaded every boy$_i$ that he$_i$ should participate
(22d)   *Who$_i$ did his$_i$ mother tell t$_i$ about John
(22e)   Who$_i$ did his$_i$ mother tell t$_i$ about himself$_i$
(22f)   *His$_i$ mother gave every first grader's$_i$ picture to someone
(22g)   His$_i$ mother gave every first grader's$_i$ picture to the cutie pie's$_i$ dad

Another piece of evidence for a linking approach to WCO effects comes from considering an odd property of languages with clitic doubling. Clitic doubling eliminates WCO effects. Consider some examples in Spanish (23a) and Modern Greek (23b,c).[7]

(23a)   A   quien$_i$ (*lo$_i$) sorprende su$_i$ actitud t$_i$
        To whom him   surprises   his attitude
        "Who does his attitude surprise"
(23b)   Kathe pedi$_i$ i   mitera tou$_i$ (*ton$_i$) agapes t$_i$
        Every child the mother his (him) loves
        "Every child, his mother loves"
(23c)   Pjon (*ton$_i$) agapa i   mitera tou$_i$ t$_i$
        Who him   loves   the mother his
        "Who does his mother love"

At LF the following linking holds at LF on the assumption that clitic doubling involves a linking relation between the doubled expression and the clitic.[8] The relevant linking structure of (23a) is provided in (24). As indicated, the linking does not violate (7) and the structure is well formed. Note that when the clitic *lo* is dropped, the bound pronoun can only be linked to the variable on its right. This induces a WCO violation and accounts for the unacceptability of these sentences without the clitic. The Greek examples have a similar analysis with *ton* being the clitic.

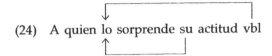

(24)   A quien lo sorprende su actitud vbl

A non-linking theory does not have a parallel account for the elimination of WCO effects when doubled clitics are present. Under an indexing theory the variable to the right of the pronoun and the pronoun are coindexed. As such, WCO effects should ensue. For example, the structure of (23a) under an indexing theory is (25). Observe, furthermore, that in (25) the trace has a quantificational WH-antecedent and so it cannot be a null epithet.[9]

(25)   A quien lo_i sorprende su_i actitud t-vbl_i

For completeness, we must examine one more set of cases discussed by Lasnik and Stowell (695, ex. 26). They provide a pair of examples that the proposed linking theory rules ungrammatical.

(26a)   Which man_i is everyone who asks his_i wife to talk about t_i usually interested in t_i .
(26b) Who_i did his_i mother's stories about t_i annoy t_i

The structure of these sentences is (27).

(27)   ... pronoun ... vbl^1 ... vbl^2

The only permissible linkings contravene (7); *pronoun* is to the left of both vbl^1 and vbl^2. Lasnik and Stowell judge these sentences acceptable with the WCO reading.

There are various things an advocate of the linking theory could say in reply to these examples. First, (26a, b) are not on a par with regard to their acceptability. (26b) is superior to (26a). Indeed, most find (26a) at least as unacceptable as a standard WCO effect. There is little doubt that (26a) is quite a bit less acceptable than (27), a subject parasitic gap construction without a hint of WCO. This is expected if (26a) involves a violation of the WCOP.

(28)   Which man is everyone who asks Bill to talk about t usually interested in t

What of (26b)? It is uniformly judged better than (26a). However, observe that this involves a psych verb and it is plausible that this is what ameliorates its unacceptability. This is confirmed by the fact that similar constructions without psych verbs degrade considerably in acceptability.[10] The sentences in (29) are quite a bit worse than (26b).

(29a)　Who$_i$ did John give his$_i$ mother's picture of t$_i$ to t$_i$

(29b)　Who$_i$ did his$_i$ mother's picture of t$_i$ resemble t$_i$

This said, why should the psych verb cases be more acceptable? One plausible reason is that they conform to (7) at LF. On one widely accepted theory, the SS object in psych verb constructions moves to a position that c-commands the SS subject at LF.[11] If correct, then at LF the relevant structure of (26b) is the one in (30), which allows a linking that adheres to (7) (link the pronoun to *vbl^1*).

(30)　vbl^1 . . . pronoun . . . vbl^2

As the sentences in (29) do not involve psych verbs, a similar LF movement will not take place and their observed relative unacceptability with respect to (26b) can be traced their violating (7). This construal of the data is inconsistent with a theory that (i) adopts a 0-operator analysis of subject parasitic gaps and (ii) assumes the theory of null epithets in Lasnik and Stowell.[12]

The theoretical problem posed by the null operator in parasitic gap constructions is actually the tip of a much larger difficulty. What unites the constructions that Lasnik and Stowell discuss is the presence of a 0-operator. However, it is not clear that the 0-operators in the structures discussed are all of a piece. It is plausible that the 0-operator in *tough* constructions, topicalization structures, and relative clauses are semantically akin to lambda operators. This makes them quite different from the 0-operator in parasitic gap constructions, which is essentially invisible at LF (see Browning 1987). However, the Lasnik and Stowell theory requires treating the 0-operator in restrictive relatives as truly quantificational while treating the others as parallel to the 0-operator in parasitic gaps. This is not a very natural semantic categorization. Thus, it is only by downplaying the interpretive differences among these construction types that theoretical unity has been achieved. Once one divorces WCO effects from 0-operators, as a linking theory does, these problems can be avoided. Furthermore, we predict that sentences like (26a) and (29) should exhibit WCO effects. At the very least, these predictions are no less accurate than those made by the null epithets theory.[13]

3　Stating the Weak Cross Over Principle

To this point, I have considered a linear version of the WCOP but have restated it in terms of linking rather than binding. In this section, I elaborate a structural version of the linking approach to WCO.

The most prominent structural accounts of WCO invoke a biuniqueness condition between operators and elements that they bind. For example, the Koopman and Sportiche (1983) theory makes (8) a consequence of the prohibition against an operator's locally binding more than one "variable." The data surveyed in (20) and (22) suggest that this approach is faced with empirical problems. It is hard to see how *adding* another pronoun should improve matters if the problem is establishing a biuniqueness between operators and variables. Why, after all, should binding two expressions be worse than binding three if the problem is to avoid non-biunique relations of operators to variables? Note that the various participating expressions need not be in a c-command or local binding configuration in ameliorated WCO configurations.[14]

(31a)   *His$_i$ teacher gave his$_i$ report card to every student$_i$'s mother
(31b)   His$_i$ teacher gave every student's$_i$ mother his$_i$ report card
(31c)   Q$_i$ [[pronoun$_i$ ...] ... [pronoun$_i$ ...] ... [vbl$_i$ ...]]
(31d)   Q$_i$ [[pronoun$_i$ ...] ... [vbl$_i$ ...] ... [pronoun$_i$ ...]]

None of the semantically bound expressions in (31) c-commands the other. Nonetheless, we observe amelioration of WCO effects simply by changing the linear order of the elements. (31a) has the structure (31c) while (31b) has the structure (31d).[15] So it appears that violations of local binding do not fully account for WCO effects.

   This conclusion is not very surprising given the acceptability of binding from the determiner position of NPs/DPs, the acceptability of binding into adjuncts from postverbal positions and the acceptability of inversely linked binding structures.

(32a)   No one's$_i$ mother kissed him$_i$
(32b)   John read every book$_i$ before reviewing it$_i$
(32c)   Someone from every small town$_i$ hates it$_i$

Examples such as those in (32) also constitute the best evidence against an SS approach to pronoun binding. In fact, the success of bijection theories is intimately tied to that of SS approaches to binding. Both LF and SS theories of pronominal binding license licit binding in terms of the c-command relations between variables and the pronouns that they bind. For most of the relevant data, this licensing condition can be stated at SS or LF without prejudice. However, when LF movement alters binding configurations that hold at SS, as in (32), SS binding theories and bijection run into trouble. This said, there is something right about the intuitions behind the local binding versions of WCO advocated by bijection. In what follows I consider ways of redeeming the intuitions behind this approach to WCO. Consider, first, the contrast between (32a, c) and the examples in (33).

(33a)   *At least one picture of every senator$_i$ graced/adorned his$_i$ desk.
(33b)   *The AG's investigation of every senator$_i$ threatened his$_i$ career.
(33c)   *A small part of every article$_i$ undermined it$_i$
(33d)   *The election of no one$_i$ to the Hall of Fame hindered his$_i$ career
(33e)   *The accreditation of no college$_i$ regulates its$_i$ quality

In each of these examples, it is possible for the indicated QNP to have scope over the entire clause, as (34) indicates.

(34a)   At least one picture of every senator was on the desk
(34b)   The AG's investigation of every senator lasted on average a week
(34c)   A small part of every article was republished in our collection
(34d)   The election of no one to the Hall of Fame was recorded
(34e)   The accreditation of no college is a laughing matter

Further evidence that a quantifier within an NP can take sentential scope comes from considering negative polarity items. In (35a), *ever* is licensed, presumably by the negative quantifier *no one* that can take *ever* in its scope. Witness the contrast with the unacceptable (35b) where no negative element exists to license *ever*.

(35a)   The accreditation of no college ever takes longer than three years
(35b)   *The accreditation of every college ever takes longer than three years

The data in (34) and (35) suggest that what is difficult in (33) is licensing the bound pronoun, not scoping the quantifier out of the NP. As noted, these cases contrast with (32a, c). In fact, if the postnominal QNP is moved to pre-nominal genitive position, the binding becomes readily acceptable once again.

(36a)   Every senator's$_i$ portrait was on his$_i$ desk
(36b)   No one's$_i$ election to the Hall of Fame hinders his$_i$ career
(36c)   No college's$_i$ disaccreditation leads it$_i$ to improve

Why these contrasts? The distinction seems to be that whereas binding is possible without c-command from "adjunct" positions, it is not possible from internal argument positions. In the unacceptable cases in (33) the quantifier originates from a postnominal internal argument position. In the acceptable cases of inverse linking (32c) and the cases in (32a) and (36) the QNP origin-ates outside the immediate projection of the head, i.e. from a non-internal argument position. If this is the correct cut, we can assimilate the unacceptable sentences to WCO effects in terms of the following revised WCO principle.

(37)   A pronoun P may be linked to a variable V iff V almost c-commands P[16]
(38)   A almost c-commands B $=_{def}$ A c-commands B or the projection C that dominates A c-commands B

In addition, I assume that domination is defined in terms of exclusion – (39).

(39)   A dominates B iff every segment of A dominates B

What is crucial is that if B is adjoined to A then A does not exclude B and so does not dominate it.

Consider the data above given these definitions. Their net effect is to allow expressions in the specifiers of NPs/DPs and in PPs adjoined to NPs to almost c-command whatever the NP itself c-commands. This then makes the variables in these positions potential linkers. The LF structures of (32a, c) and (33a) are provided in (40).

(40a) No one's$_i$ [$_{IP}$ [$_{DP}$ t_i [$_{NP}$ mother]] loves him$_i$]
(40b) Every small town$_i$ [$_{IP}$ [$_{NP/DPj}$ [$_{NP/DP}$ someone] [$_{PP}$ from t_i]] [$_{IP}$ t_j hates it$_i$]]
(40c) Every senator$_i$ [$_{IP}$ [$_{DP}$ at least one [$_{NP}$ picture of t_i]] adorned/graced his$_i$ desk

In (40a) the variable t_i almost c-commands the bound pronoun. Though the variable itself does not c-command the pronoun, the DP that immediately contains it does. This allows the pronoun to licitly link to the variable given (37). (40b) is analogous. The variable t_i is contained within the PP adjunct adjoined to the subject. As an adjoined expression, the PP is not dominated by the subject DP/NP. Consequently, it c-commands the indicated pronoun. Thus, t_i almost c-commands this pronoun and hence can be a viable linker. In (40c), t_i fails to almost c-command the pronoun. The first category that dominates it, i.e. NP, does not c-command the pronoun. This prevents t_i from being a licit linker and the unacceptability of the indicated binding can be assimilated to standard WCO effects.

Observe, first, that the problem in cases such as (40c) is that the variable is not a potential linker. The quantifier can have scope over its containing DP/ NP. Thus, the examples in (34) should be acceptable with the inversely linked readings. Furthermore, we expect the contrast between (33) and (36) as moving to prenominal position is moving to a position that almost c-commands the pronoun and thereby licenses linking the pronoun to the variable. Third, it seems phenomenologically accurate to assimilate the unacceptable bindings in (33) to instances of WCO as they seem about as unacceptable as more standard cases of this effect. But, if this is so, then WCO cannot be stated in linear terms. In other words, (7) cannot be accurate for it fails to apply to cases such as (33).

This is of some importance. One very positive feature of the bijection approach to WCO effects is that it eliminates the only known exclusively linear condition on binding from the grammar.[17] The WCOP (37) stated in terms of almost c-command has a similar virtue.

One last point. The WCOP stated in (37) also handles the standard WCO cases. In such constructions, the variable is typically in postverbal position at SS and the pronoun is to the left higher up the tree, e.g. (41).

(41) [$_{IP}$ Q$_i$ [$_{IP}$ [$_{NP}$ pronoun$_i$ ...] ... [$_{VP}$ ... t_i]]]

Here t_i does not almost c-command the pronoun and so linking will be illicit. In (41), the variable t_i is within VP and VP does not c-command the pronoun in subject position.[18]

In sum, (37) handles all of the cases subsumed under (7) and extends the empirical coverage of the system. (37) differs from (7) in incorporating a hierarchical condition on pronominal linking. It differs from more standard hierarchical conditions by replacing linking with binding and proposing "almost c-command" as the correct structural notion. Conceptually, it differs from bijection-like theories in tracing the problem with WCO configurations not to the local relations of the quantifier to its variables but in the structural relationship between anaphoric pronouns and the variables that they are linked to.[19] However, it still requires the rather unnatural condition of "almost c-command." This infelicity is addressed in section 6.

4   The WCOP and Minimalism

The last section proposed that only pronouns linked to variables that almost c-command them can avoid WCO effects. This assumption confronts an apparent problem in (32b), however, repeated here for convenience.

(32b)   John read every book$_i$ before reading it$_i$

The LF structure of this is (42).

(42)   Every book$_i$ [John [$_{VP}$ [$_{VP}$ read t$_i$] [without PRO reviewing
        it$_i$]]

The problem is that here the variable t_i does not almost c-command the pronoun that is linked to it and yet a bound variable interpretation for the pronoun is readily available. The *without* phrase is adjoined to the VP and so is not dominated by it. The V' that contains the trace is the first branching category that dominates it and it does not c-command the adjunct. Thus, the variable t_i does not almost c-command the indicated pronoun.[20] Put another way, the trace is a complement to the verb and, as noted above, complements do not almost c-command outside the immediate projection that contains them. Given this, it is unclear why pronominal binding is possible in this case.

There is a Minimalist way out of this problem. As in chapter 5, we can assume with Chomsky (1993) that objects move out of the VP to Spec AgrO for case-checking reasons at LF. If this happens, the object NP moves to a position high enough to almost c-command the adjunct at LF and from here linking is licit. Given standard assumptions, this Spec AgrO position is the variable position as it is case-marked. The LF-linking configuration is provided in (43).

(43)   Every book$_i$ [John$_j$ [$_{AgrOP}$ t$_i$ [$_{VP*}$ [$_{VP*}$ t$_j$ [$_{VP}$ read t$_i$]] [without PRO reviewing
        it$_i$]]

There is independent evidence favoring this analysis. I have argued that a variable must be high in the tree with respect to the pronoun whose antecedent it is in order to be a licit linker for that pronoun. There is also evidence that in parasitic gap constructions the real gap cannot c-command the parasitic gap (Chomsky 1982). This means that the adjunct must be higher in the tree than the real gap at LF. This pair of facts together imply that if an adjunct contains both a parasitic gap and a bound pronoun that there might be trouble appropriately placing the adjunct so that it can be high enough to be out of the c-command domain of the variable that licenses the parasitic gap, but low enough to be almost c-commanded by the variable that serves as the linker for the bound pronoun. With this in mind consider the following pair of sentences.

(44a) Which song$_j$ did John tell everyone$_i$ about t$_j$ (without/before) recording t$_j$ for him$_i$

(44b) *Which man$_i$ did John tell t$_i$ about every song$_j$ (without/before) recording it$_j$ for t$_i$

Why is (44b) so much less acceptable than (44a)? Recall the pair of requirements that such structures must meet. In (44a) the adjunct must hang high enough so as not to be c-commanded by the variable t$_j$ and low enough to be almost c-commanded by the variable left in Spec of AgrO after movement of *everyone* to this position at LF. This is readily doable, if, for example, we append the adjunct to VP (as we did in (43)).

(45) [Which song$_i$ [everyone$_j$ [John [$_{AgrOP}$ t$_j$ [$_{VP}$ [$_{VP}$ tell t$_j$ about t$_i$] [without/before PRO recording t$_i$ for him$_j$]]]]]]^{21}

Consider now how to meet these two requirements in (44b). The LF structure without the adjunct (*Without/before PRO recording it for t*) is given in (46).^{22}

(46) Which man$_i$ [every song$_k$ [John [$_{AgrOP}$ t$_i$ [$_{VP}$ tell t$_i$ about t$_k$]]]]]

The "real" parasitic gap variable is the one in Spec AgrO. The potential linker for the adjunct pronoun is t_k. The crucial question is whether the adjunct can be adjoined anywhere in this tree and be both outside the c-command domain of t_i in AgrO and inside the almost c-command domain of t_k. The answer is clearly no. To meet the anti-c-command requirement on parasitic gaps, it must hang higher than AgrOP. But to meet the almost c-command condition on linked pronouns, it must hang below AgrOP. As this is clearly impossible, (44b) is unacceptable with the indicated interpretation.^{23}

In sum, the sort of NP movement that Minimalism proposes is required if the condition in (37) is to be empirically adequate. The data in (44) provide independent motivation for the adequacy of both (37) and the Minimalist proposal that accusative case is checked at LF in English in a Spec Agr position outside the VP.

5 A Further Consequence: Linking and Quantifier/ WH Interactions

The analysis outlined above bears on one further question of current interest. Consider the sentences in (47).

(47a)   What did everyone say
(47b)   Who said everything

Chapter 2 observed that (47a) is ambiguous in that *what* can be interpreted as having scope outside or inside *everyone*. Thus, both a pair–list and standard WH-reading is available for (47a). (47b), in contrast, does not felicitously support a pair–list reading. May (1985) analyzed the lack of the pair–list reading in (47b) as due to the ECP.[24] Very briefly, the ambiguity in (47a) is due to two different scoping possibilities for the two quantifiers *what* and *everyone*. The lack of the reading where *everyone* takes scope over *who* in (47b) is traced to the ill-formedness of structures such as (48) in which the subject trace is not properly governed.

(48)   Who$_i$ [everyone$_j$ [t$_i$ said t$_j$]]

Let us consider an alternative analysis of these constructions less beholden to the ECP, more semantically restricted and more consonant with the basic thrust of the Minimalist program.

Chierchia (1991) notes that quantifying into questions involves complicating the standard semantics of quantification. He argues against so complicating the semantics. If this suggestion is adopted, it prevents the ambiguity of (47a) from being traced to *everyone* having scope over *what*. Furthermore, the absence of this reading in (47b) cannot be traced to an inability to quantify into the question for *syntactic* reasons, which is what an ECP-style account does.[25] How then are these data to be analyzed?

Chierchia suggests another source for the asymmetry in cases such as (47). He ties the interpretive asymmetry observed in (47a, b) to the one that obtains in WCO structures. Recall that a pronoun in an NP in object position can be bound by a quantifier in subject position but the reverse is not the case. The core idea in Chierchia's approach is to tie the interpretive gap in (47b) to this fact. Consider the details.

The proposal begins with the observation (going back to Engdahl 1985) that questions can be answered in at least two ways:

(49a)   Who does everyone love
(49b)   Mary
(49c)   His mother

(49b) gives an "individual" (i-)answer to the question and (49c) gives a "functional" (f-)answer. The functional answer in (49c) maps one individual (which is a value for the variable bound by *everyone*) to a second individual (that person's mother). The mapping is mediated by the pronoun, *his*, bound to its antecedent, *Bill*.[26] It is important to differentiate the answers in (49c) and (49b). Consider a few more complex cases:

(50a)   Who does every linguist admire?
(50b)   His advisor
(50c)   Lasnik admires Chomsky, Barss admires Higginbotham and Santorini admires Kroch

(50b) is not simply a shorter version of (50c). The two sentences provide different information. More importantly, some questions that allow the functional answer have no pair–list answers at all.

(51a)   Who does no linguist admire?
(51b)   His mother
(51c)   Who do most linguists admire?
(51d)   Their mothers

Chierchia asks why there is not a pair–list answer for questions like (51a, c). He proposes that the absence of such an answer suggests that complicating semantic theory to allow quantifying into questions is empirically unwise. Chierchia considers the semantics of questions to see why (51) resists pair–list readings.

A standard approach to the semantics of questions identifies their meanings with the set of their true answers. So the meaning of (49a) is (52).[27]

(52)   ?{P: P is true and for some x: P = everyone admires x}

The full answer to this will be a set of propositions that we get by truly filling in the "x"-position. Observe that this provides the individual reading of the WH-expression. There is another possible "functional" answer whose interpretation is provided in (53).

(53)   ?{P: P is true and for some f, P = (every$_x$ (X loves F(X)}

What LF phrase marker corresponds to the functional reading? Chierchia proposes a structure that involves a bound expression at LF.

(54)   Who$_i$ [John loves [$_{NP}$ e$_j$ t$_i$]]

The "i" is the f(unction)-index while "j" is the a(rgument) index. The idea is that the a-index can act as a bound pronoun while the f-index is bound by the WH in Comp. An intuitive way of thinking of this is that what we have in the a-index is a bindable pronoun analogous to the one that arises in the overt functional answer. Assume that this is *literally* the case. Then, the LF of a sentence like *who does every man love* with the pair–list reading has roughly the LF structure given in (55) in which the a-indexed pronoun is bound by the quantifier.

(55)   Who$_i$ [every man$_j$ [t$_j$ [love [pro$_j$ t$_i$]$_i$]]]

A way of interpreting this LF in Minimalist terms is that the copy left by moving the WH to Spec CP can be interpreted as having the structure with an implicit (bindable) pronoun. At LF, prior to interpretation at the CI interface, the copies must delete, leaving all but one (see Chomsky 1993 and chapters 8 and 9). If the copy in Spec CP is deleted then the object copy has the f(unctional) interpretation. If the object copy is deleted, then the structure is interpreted as having the i(ndividual) interpretation. The two relevant LF phrase markers are provided in (56) (parentheses indicate deletion).[28]

(56a)   [(Who) [every man$_j$ [t$_j$ [love who]]]

(56b)   [Who [every man$_j$ [t$_j$ [love (who)]]]]

In effect, then, the current proposal assumes that the functional and individual readings noted by Chierchia are structurally disambiguated at LF and that which copy of the WH-chain is deleted determines the semantic contribution of the WH-expression.

   If (55) underlies the pair–list reading, the subject/object asymmetry observed in (47b) can be reduced to the WCO effect. In particular, a sentence like (47b) on the pair–list reading will involve binding a pronoun to the left of the variable, in violation of WCO, as in (57).[29]

(57)   Who$_i$ [everything$_j$ [[pro$_j$ t$_i$] bought t$_j$]]

   Chierchia notes that having a functional interpretation is a necessary but not sufficient condition for supporting a pair–list reading. The function supplies a way of mapping a given domain of entities to a range of values, i.e. a pair–list relating an element in the domain with an element in the range. Chierchia suggests that only some expressions can "provide" a domain, the generators. Consider, for example, universal quantifiers which easily support pair–list readings. Universal quantifiers denote all the supersets of a given set. For example, *every man* is the set of sets that have the set of men as a subpart. The set of men "generates" the set of supersets. Universal quantifiers allow one to "retrieve a domain" immediately. And retrieving a domain, Chierchia proposes, is crucial for generating a list.

   Assume that this is right. The theoretical upshot is a two-part proposal. WH/quantifier structures generate pair–list readings (i) when WHs have functional interpretations in which there is an implicit pronoun bound to the quantifier and (ii) the quantifier is of a type that can generate a domain. This binding, like all pronoun binding, is subject to WCO restrictions and it is this that induces the subject/object asymmetry we find in WH/quantifier interactions.

   Chierchia provides interesting empirical evidence for the proposal. As noted, it easily accommodates the standard subject/object asymmetries. In addition, the approach accounts for the following kinds of cases in which subjects are not involved.

(58a)   Tell me where$_i$ John put every book t$_i$

(58b)   Tell me what$_i$ John put t$_i$ onto every table

(58a) supports a pair–list answer but (58b) does not. This follows on a WCO account. The pair–list reading requires LF structures like (59). (59b) involves a WCO violation.

(59a)   Tell me [where$_i$ [every book$_j$ [John put t$_j$ [pro$_j$ t] $_i$]]]
(59b)   Tell me [what$_i$ [every table$_j$ [John put [pro$_j$ t] $_i$ on t$_i$]]]

The account also extends to English double object constructions. (60a, b) are fine with a pair–list reading.[30] The sentences in (61) do not felicitously support this interpretation. Relevant LF phrase markers are provided in (62). The LF phrase marker (62a) obeys the cross over condition. Thus, the pronoun is licitly bound and a pair–list reading is available. In contrast, the structure in (62b) violates WCO and thus a pair–list reading is not available.

(60a)   What did you give everyone for Xmas
(60b)   What did you assign everyone
(61a)   Who did you give everything
(61b)   Who did you assign everything
(62a)   [What$_i$ [everyone$_j$ [you give t$_j$ [pro$_j$ t] $_i$ for Xmas]]]
(62b)   [Who$_i$ [everyone$_j$ [you assign [pro$_j$ t] $_i$ t$_i$]]]

Consider one more minimal pair.

(63a)   I know what you gave everyone for Xmas
(63b)   I know what you gave to everyone for Xmas

Of the pair, only (63a) felicitously supports a pair–list reading. The LFs required for a pair–list interpretation are provided in (64). (64a) is well formed. (64b) displays a WCO configuration.

(64a)   I know [what$_i$ [everyone$_j$ [you gave t$_j$ [pro$_j$ t] $_i$]]]
(64b)   I know [what$_i$ [everyone$_j$ [you gave [pro$_j$ t] $_i$ to t$_i$]]]

An interesting feature of these sentences is that the availability of pair–list readings *inversely* correlates with the possibility of quantifier scope ambiguities.[31]

(65a)   John sent someone everything
(65b)   John sent something to everyone

(65b) allows a reading in which the universal *everyone* takes scope over the existential *something*. This is not possible in (65a).[32] *Someone* must take scope over *everything*. This strongly suggests that the availability of pair–list readings is not just another manifestation of scope ambiguities.[33]

The present theory also accommodates the data in (66a) without assuming that the embedded universal quantifier must raise to the matrix. As noted in chapter 4, this sort of quantifier raising is a problem given the sentence-bound nature of quantifiers in general.

(66a)   Who do you think that everyone invited t
(66b)   Who do you think t invited everyone

The LF structures required to support the pair–list reading are provided in (67). (67b) violates WCO and this blocks the pair–list reading for (66b).

(67a)   Who$_i$ [you think [everyone$_j$ [t$_j$ invited [pro$_j$ t] $_i$]]]
(67b)   Who$_i$ [you think [everyone$_j$ [[pro$_j$ t] $_i$ invited t$_j$]]]

There exists a second gap in the interpretive paradigm of WH/quantifier interactions. Aoun and Li (1993a) point out that extraction out of WH-islands eliminates pair–list readings.

(68a)   ?What did you wonder whether everyone brought t
(68b)   What did everyone know how to fix

(68a) displays the standard WH-island effect, presumably due to a subjacency violation. Aoun and Li observe that the same interpretive gap appears in Chinese.

(69)   Ni   xiang-zhidao meigeren shi-bu-shi dou kandao shenme
       You wonder   everyone be-not-be all saw   what
       "What do you wonder whether everyone saw?"

(68b) reinforces the point made by (69) that the pair–list readings disappear even when overt subjacency violations do not lead to apparent unacceptability.[34] (68b) is perfectly acceptable, clearly better than (68a). Nonetheless, it does not support a pair–list reading.

We can explain these by modifying a suggestion in Aoun (1985), Aoun et al. (1987), Cinque (1990), and Rizzi (1990). They propose a distinction between variables that are referential and those that are not. This distinction aims to distinguish operators like *who* and *what* versus those like *why* and *how*. Only the former appear to be able to extract out islands. Szabolcsi and Zwarts (1992–3) recast this distinction as one between operators whose variables range over individuals and those whose variables do not range over individuals, but whose elements exhibit partial orderings. Let us accept this distinction between individual and non-individual-denoting variables and assume that only operators ranging over individuals freely extract from islands.[35]

(70)   *Island Condition (IC)*: A WH-operator outside a given island can licitly bind a trace[36] within that island iff the trace is interpreted as a variable ranging over individuals

The IC distinguishes individual from pair–list answers in a useful manner. Only i-answers will be permitted for WHs extracted from islands as only in i-answers do the WH-traces denote individuals. In structural terms, for WH-elements like *what* or *who* this means that a WH-t inside an island must have a structure like (71a). Structures like (71b) are prohibited by IC.

(71a)   WH$_i$ . . . [island . . . t$_i$ . . .]
(71b)   WH$_i$ . . . [island . . . [pro t] $_i$ . . .]

With the IC, the data in (68) and (69) can be accounted for. In order to get a pair–list reading for these examples we need the trace of WH-movement to be functionally interpreted. However, as this trace is within an island, the IC prohibits this. As such, the pair–list reading is unavailable. To illustrate, consider (68a). To have a pair–list reading, it must have a structure like (72a). However, this violates the IC. The only available licit structure is (72b) in which the variable trace is interpreted as ranging over individuals.

(72a)   What$_i$ did you wonder [whether [everyone$_j$ [t$_j$ fixed [pro$_j$ t] $_i$]]]
(72b)   What$_i$ did you wonder [whether [everyone$_j$ [t$_j$ fixed t$_i$]]]

If the IC governs extraction out of islands in general, then we can also account for the absence of pair–list readings in the following cases.[37] (73a, b) are cases of "inner" neg-islands. (73c, d) involve extraction out of a noun–complement structure. (73e) extracts out of an adjunct.

(73a)   What did you say that everyone didn't buy t
(73b)   What didn't you say that everyone bought t
(73c)   What did everyone make a plan to say t[38]
(73d)   What did you make the claim that everyone said t
(73e)   Who did everyone go to Rome without visiting t

Consider one final wrinkle of this approach to WH/quantifier interactions. If the absence of pair–list readings in examples like *Who said everything* are due to WCO, then we should be able to ameliorate these sentences by the addition of more bound pronouns (given the linking version of the WCOP). In other words, structures such as (74) should make pair–list readings available.

(74)   Who$_i$ [everything$_j$ [[pro$_j$ t$_i$] V t$_j$ . . . pronoun$_j$ . . .]]

Contrast the sentences in (75).

(75a)   Who packed every boy sandwiches
(75b)   Who packed every boy$_i$ his$_i$ sandwiches
(75c)   Who told everyone that Bill must shut up
(75d)   Who told everyone$_i$ PRO$_i$ to shut up
(75e)   Who escorted every boy to Sheila's bus
(75f)   Who escorted every boy$_i$ to his$_i$ bus

In (75a, c, e) a pair–list reading is unavailable. In (75b, d, f) such a reading exists. So, for example, one can felicitously answer (75d) with (76).

(76)   John told Frank to shut up, Harry told Susan to shut up and Mary told Howard to shut up

The reason that this contrast obtains is that in (75a, c, e) there is a WCO violation as the pair–list readings of these sentences have structures analogous to (57). The reason that these readings reappear with the addition of the pronouns in (75b, d, f) is that they instantiate the structures in (74).

Note that the amelioration of these sentences with the addition of an extra pronoun cannot be accounted for by an ECP analysis of these constructions. The required scoping of the universally quantified object to IP would continue to induce an ECP violation. As such, it should remain impossible to get the WH-operator in the scope of the universal quantifier and a pair–list reading should remain unacceptable, contrary to fact.[39]

6   A Loose End: Reanalyzing "almost c-command"

In the previous section, I provided evidence in favor of a structural reformulation of WCO in terms of the notion "almost c-command." As noted, this is not a very attractive theoretical primitive and the world would be a better place if it could be replaced with a more natural notion. This section aims to do just that. I propose to replace (37) with (8) above repeated here.

(8)   If a pronoun P links to a variable V then V c-commands P

As Koopman and Sportiche (1983) observed, (8) is a very natural condition and is quite desirable should it be defensible. In the present context, what could be more natural than that the semantically asymmetrical relation of linking should be mirrored by the grammatically asymmetrical condition of c-command! However, to get (8) to work requires adjusting some other grammatical definitions so as to allow c-command to operate. This section explores two approaches, both of which fit with (8).[40]

Before getting into technical details, let us briefly recapitulate what is required of an adequate proposal. It was observed that pronoun binding is licit just in case the variable to which a pronoun is linked is "prominent" enough. Evidence has been provided that a pronoun can link to a variable in the specifier position of a nominal expression (e.g. *everyone's$_i$ mother kissed him$_i$*) or if contained within an adjunct PP (e.g. *a person on every panel$_i$ praised it$_i$*). Binding from the complement position, however, leads to relative unacceptability (e.g. **a participant in every group$_i$ left it$_i$*). Schematically, the linking in (77a, b) are fine while that in (77c) is not.

(77a)   Q$_i$'s [t$_i$ N] . . . pronoun

(77b)   Q$_i$'s [[NP] [P t$_i$]] . . . pronoun

(77c)   *Q$_i$'s [Det [N' P t$_i$]] . . . pronoun$_i$

Given these facts, consider two possible approaches.

One avenue follows suggestions in Kayne (1993). Kayne proposes treating specifiers as adjuncts. This proposal partially relates the structural configurations in (77a, b). If we adopt this, and a definition of c-command in terms of exclusion, then a specifier c-commands out of the phrase it specifies. In particular, with this assumption, t_i in (77a) c-commands the pronoun that is linked to it.

Things are still not quite right, however. Note that in (77b) the prepositional object does not c-command the pronoun that links to it. But, the whole PP does, as it is not dominated by the phrase that it is adjoined to, though the complement of the preposition itself does not. We can remedy this by once again pursuing Minimalist principles. Recall that structural case relations in the Minimalist program are species of Spec–head relations. If so, the correct configuration for case checking within PPs involves moving the prepositional object to some higher Spec position. Assume for concreteness that this movement is to some higher Agr position. This has empirical motivation given the instances of agreement attested within PPs in postpositional languages.[41] The proposed LF structure of a PP is provided in (78). The object of the preposition has moved to the Spec Agr position to get case-checked and the P, like a V, has adjoined to the Agr head to check the case.

(78) $[_{Agr} NP_i [Agr+P_j [_{PP} e_j t_i]]]$

Given (78), the c-command difficulty noted in (77b) disappears. The relevant LF structure is (79). The variable t'_i c-commands the pronoun that is linked to it. The variable is in a Spec position of an agreement phrase, i.e. it is an adjunct to an adjunct. Therefore, it c-commands whatever the adjunct it is adjoined to c-commands.

(79) Q_i's $[[NP] [_{Agr} t'_i [Agr+P_j [_{PP} e_j t_i]]]] \ldots$ pronoun

Thus, Kayne's proposal of treating specifiers as adjuncts, combined with the Minimalist assumption that case is checked in Spec–head configurations, and a definition of c-command in terms of exclusion, reduces the licit configurations in (77a, b) to simple instances of c-command. Note, in addition, that the variable does not c-command the pronoun that is linked to it in the LF of (77c).

(80)   *Q_i's $[[Det [N' [_{Agr} t_i [Agr+P_j [_{PP} e_j t_i]]]]] \ldots$ pronoun$_i]$

Nor does the variable c-command the pronoun that is linked to it at LF in standard WCO configurations such as (81).

(81a)   His$_i$ mother kissed everyone$_i$
(81b)   Everyone$_i$ $[_{AgrS}$ [his mother]$_j$ $[_{TP}$ past $[_{AgrO} t_i$ kiss$_k$ $[_{VP} t_j e_k t_i]]]]$

In sum, if the proposals above are adopted, we can restate (37) as (8) and retain the empirical adequacy of earlier approaches to WCO.[42]

Kayne (1993) provides some interesting independent evidence in favor of his assimilation of specifiers to adjuncts. He observes that anaphor binding is marginally possible from Spec positions in certain cases.

(82a)   ?Every girl$_i$'s room contains a picture of herself$_i$
(82b)   ?Every candidate$_i$'s platform was presented by himself$_i$
(82c)   ?Everyone$_i$'s room suited himself$_i$

These sentences contrast with those in (83), which are considerably less acceptable.

(83a)   *Every girl$_i$'s father admires (pictures of) herself$_i$
(83b)   *Every candidate$_i$'s mother was introduced by himself$_i$
(83c)   *Everyone$_i$'s escort suited himself$_i$

In addition, they contrast with the examples in (84) which are also quite poor.

(84a)   ?*Mary's room contains a picture of herself
(84b)   *John$_i$'s platform was introduced by himself$_i$
(84c)   *John's room suited himself

Kayne (1993) accounts for the contrast between (82) and (83) by observing that, for example, *every girl's father* is a closer potential antecedent for the anaphor in (83a) than is *every girl's*.[43] Kayne assumes that this more local antecedent interferes with the specifier's binding of the anaphor. In (82), *every girl's room* is not a potential antecedent for *herself* and so its potential interference is weaker.[44]

What of the contrast with (84)?[45] One possibility is that quantified expressions do not occupy the same positions, at least at LF, as other non-quantificational NPs. Let us assume that at LF quantified arguments are in Spec DP while non-quantificational ones remain in Spec NP. This suffices to undergird the contrast between (82) and (84).

There is further suggestive evidence in support of this proposal. First, it would help account for some sloppy identity data reviewed in chapters 2 and 3. Recall that quantified specifiers are able to license sloppy identity readings in cases where names could not. (85a) only has a strict reading, in contrast to (85b) in which a sloppy reading is available.

(85a)   John's mother loves him but Bill's father doesn't
(85b)   Everyone's mother loves him but no one's father does

If we assume that genitive quantifiers are in Spec DP at LF but non-quantificational expressions remain in Spec NP, then only in cases such as (85b) does the specifier c-command the pronoun and hence license its interpretation as a bound variable.[46]

(86a)   [$_{DP}$ [$_{NP}$ John's mother]] loves him
(86b)   [$_{DP}$ Everyone$_i$'s [$_{NP}$ t$_i$ mother]] loves him

Thus, on the assumption that a pronoun can be interpreted as a variable only if c-commanded by that variable (i.e. if we adopt (8)) the proposed structures make the right empirical cut.

Second, the proposed structural differences save the standard account for principle C effects. As is well known, an r-expression cannot be the antecedent of a pronoun that c-commands it. Standardly, the difference between the examples in (87) is attributed to the fact that the pronoun in the specifier does not c-command the r-expression it is indexed with in (87a) in contrast to (87b).

(87a) His$_i$ mother said that John$_i$ was tall
(87b) *He$_i$ said that John$_i$ was tall

However, this account is in jeopardy if we assume that the pronoun in the specifier of the subject c-commands the clause in (87a). The assumption that non-quantificational expressions do not reside in Spec DP at LF blocks this unwanted conclusion. *His*, not being quantificational, stays in Spec NP rather than moving to Spec DP. As such, it does not c-command the entire clause. The relevant structure is provided in (88).[47]

(88) [$_{DP}$ [$_{NP}$ His mother]] said that John was tall

In sum, the assumption that quantified nominal specifiers reside in Spec DP at LF while others remain in Spec NP has some empirical justification. Its theoretical justification is that it enables us to retain principle (8).

There is a second theoretical route to (8), one that does not require the assumption that specifiers are adjuncts. We can adopt a definition of c-command that distinguishes functional from lexical XPs. Consider (89).

(89) A c-commands B iff every lexical category that dominates A dominates B

This effectively eliminates Agr phrases and DPs as relevant in computing c-command.[48] If we continue to define domination in terms of exclusion, assume that prepositional objects move to a higher Spec Agr position for case checking, and assume that quantificational specifiers are in Spec DP at LF, then (89) will correctly distinguish the structures in (77). At LF, they have the structures in (90). In all the structures, the variable *t'* c-commands the pronoun that is linked to it given the definition in (89).

(90a) Q$_i$'s [[$_{DP}$ t$'_i$ [$_{NP}$ t$_i$ N]] ... pronoun ...]

(90b) Q$_i$'s [[[NP] [$_{Agr}$ t$'_i$ [Agr+P$_j$ [$_{PP}$ e$_j$ t$_i$]]]] ... pronoun ...]

(90c) *Q$_i$'s [[[Det [N' [$_{Agr}$ t$'_i$ [Agr+P$_j$ [$_{PP}$ e$_j$ t$_i$]]]]] ... pronoun$_i$ ...]]

(89) can also correctly account for standard cases of WCO, if we assume that TP is a lexical rather than a functional category. Consider the examples in (81) once again.

(81a)   His$_i$ mother kissed everyone$_i$
(81b)   Everyone$_i$ [$_{AgrSP}$ [$_{DP}$ [$_{NP}$ his mother]]$_j$ [$_{TP}$ PAST [$_{AgrOP}$ t$_i$ kiss$_k$ [$_{VP}$ t$_j$ e$_k$ t$_i$]]]]

Note that TP dominates the variable t_i but does not dominate the linked pronoun. As such, the variable does not c-command the pronoun using the definition in (89). Consequently, linking violates (8) and a WCO effect ensues.

The main difference between these two alternate approaches to rationalizing (37) rests on whether it is useful to distinguish specifiers from adjuncts. As nothing here directly relates to this question, it suffices for present purposes to adopt either of the two approaches. In sum, it seems both possible and desirable to replace (37) with (8) and thereby eliminate the theoretically awkward notion of "almost c-command."[49]

7   Conclusion

I have argued that WCO effects are best analyzed in terms of a structural principle that incorporates linking rather than binding and is stated in hierarchical rather than linear terms. The latter conclusion is not very novel, though the particular proposal differs from earlier suggestions in requiring some new definitions to allow c-command to operate successfully. I have also argued, following a proposal in Chierchia (1991), that certain WH/quantifier interactions which have been previously analyzed in terms of the ECP are actually more closely related to cross over constructions. This reanalysis allows these cases to be removed from the purview of the ECP, a position more in keeping with Minimalist concerns. In addition to this theoretical desideratum, analyzing these constructions in WCO terms allows us to account for cases in which pair–list readings disappear. In the next chapter, I extend this sort of analysis to cover superiority effects.

7

Superiority Effects

1 Introduction

Chapter 6 reanalyzed some influential LF data whose previous grammatical analysis relied on some version of the ECP. The proposal traced the interpretive asymmetries in quantifier/WH interactions to WCO rather than the ECP. This chapter presents a non-ECP based theory of superiority effects. Here too the aim is to reduce the subject/object asymmetries characteristic of superiority effects to conditions on WCO.

To focus discussion, consider an example. (1) displays a typical instance of the superiority effect.

(1) I wonder
    (a)   who bought what
    (b)   *what who bought

The contrast in (1) has various potential explanations. Chomsky (1973) accounts for it in terms of a condition on rule application that explicitly forbids applying a given rule R to an expression Y if there is a "superior" expression Z to which it equally applies.

(2) *Superiority Condition*: No rule can involve X, Y in the structure

    $\ldots X \ldots [_a \ldots Z \ldots -WYV \ldots] \ldots$

    where the rule applies ambiguously to Z and Y and Z is superior to Y

A category A is superior to a category B if every major category that dominates A dominates B, with N, V, A the major categories. In the case at hand, the rule of WH-movement can apply to raise either *who* or *what* to Spec CP. As subjects are superior to objects, (2) requires that the former be moved.

Chapters 2 and 3 reviewed approaches to superiority which attempt to reduce the contrast in (1) to some version of the ECP. The structures of (1a, b) at LF are those in (3), with the SS WH-*in-situ* adjoined to the SS WH-expression in Spec CP. If the adjoined expression cannot bind or antecedent govern its trace then the contrast in (1) can be reduced to the standard subject/object asymmetry characteristic of ECP effects.[1]

(3a)   [[Who$_i$] what$_j$] [t$_i$ bought t$_j$]]
(3b)   [[What$_j$] who$_j$] [t$_i$ bought t$_j$]]

This chapter considers yet another approach to superiority effects, one that builds on the analysis in Chierchia (1991) outlined in chapter 6. The proposal here is that superiority effects are actually manifestations of WCO and that the unacceptability of (1b) reflects an illicit pronoun-binding configuration at LF.

There are various reasons for pursuing this option. First, as noted in chapter 4, from a Minimalist viewpoint, there is sufficient theoretical motivation to dispense with ECP-style accounts of LF phenomena.[2] Given that the dominant approach to superiority effects is in terms of the ECP, they are ripe for reanalysis. Furthermore, the standard ECP-style accounts only succeed when supplemented with considerable ancillary hypotheses and technical devices of the sort reviewed in chapter 4. For example, elaborate Comp indexing algorithms are required to get the details to work out correctly.[3]

Second, neither of the above-mentioned options is above reproach. The Superiority Condition suffers from being much too descriptive. It does not apply to much beyond multiple questions and this sort of construction specificity robs (2) of the generality needed for true theoretical appeal. In addition, it is empirically inadequate. Examples such as (4) violate (2) and hence should be unacceptable, contrary to fact.[4]

(4)   Which book did which person read

ECP approaches suffer a different fate. They are empirically broad-based in that they apply to myriad construction types besides multiple questions. Unlike the approaches based on the Superiority Condition, ECP analyses of superiority effects reduce them to the argument/"adjunct" asymmetries the ECP was originally designed for. For example, the effects noted in (1c) are handled as an instance of the standard subject/object asymmetry. However, there are well-known empirical puzzles that this sort of analysis inadequately addresses. For example, Hendrick and Rochemont (1982) note that sentences like (5b) display superiority effects without either of the WHs being in subject position. The Superiority Condition can account for these cases straightforwardly as *who* is superior to *what*. However, an ECP-style analysis has to postulate that *who* in such cases is actually a kind of subject or adjunct and that this is what prevents its LF movement. Though it is possible to elaborate such an ECP-style theory, it lacks naturalness.[5]

(5a)   Who did you persuade to buy what
(5b)   *What did you persuade who to buy

A third reason for reanalyzing superiority effects is that it comports nicely with certain aspects of the Minimalist program. Chomsky (1993) suggests that the properties of multiple question constructions should follow from their interpretations: ". . . the LF rule that associates the in-situ *wh*-phrase with the *wh*-phrase in [Spec, CP] need not be construed as an instance of move-α" and that it "need satisfy none of the conditions on movement" (Chomsky 1993: 26).

As Chomsky further observes, this has empirical appeal given that conditions on movement do not fully hold for multiple questions. Specifically, LF WH-movement seems to violate economy considerations (i.e. the Minimal Link Condition (MLC) (Chomsky 1994)) in cases such as (6a) where *what* moves across a more proximate landing site (*who* in the embedded Spec-CP) in moving to the matrix Spec CP. This is not possible if the movement of *what* is overt. The challenge that (6a) presents is removed if the interpretation of *WH-in-situ* does not involve movement at all.[6]

(6a) Who remembers who bought what
(6b) *What did Bill remember who bought

The WCO approach outlined below has the property of interpreting multiple questions without invoking WH-movement at LF.[7]

2 Superiority and Functional WHs

Let us quickly recap the WCO account of quantifier/WH interactions from chapter 6. Pair–list readings of sentences like (7a) are mediated by the functional interpretation of the WH-expression. Thus, at LF (7a) has a structure like (8).

(7a) What did everyone say
(7b) Who said everything
(8) $[_{CP}$ What$_i$ $[_{IP}$ everyone$_j$ $[_{IP}$ t$_j$ say [pro$_j$ t$_i$]]]]

In (8) *pro* is an implicit pronoun that is bound by the quantifier *everyone$_j$*. This bound structure can generate a list if the quantifier is of the appropriate type, i.e. a generator. Thus, pair–list readings are a function of two specific properties. First, certain WHs can have functional readings that involve implicit bound pronouns. Second, pronouns bound by quantifiers that are generators can produce pair–list readings.

These assumptions prohibit pair–list readings in (7b) as follows. To have a pair–list interpretation requires that (7b) have an LF such as (9). However, this is a canonical WCO configuration; a pronoun is coindexed with a variable on its right. Thus, the structure is illicit and the pair–list reading is unavailable.

(9) [(Who) [everything$_j$ [[(who=) pro$_j$ t] say t$_j$]]]

This approach to quantifier/WH scope interactions straightforwardly extends to cover superiority effects. Configurations that display superiority effects are parallel to those that forbid pair–list readings. Consider the sentences in (10).

(10a) Who bought what
(10b) *What did who buy

(10a) has a pair–list reading. The appropriate answer to (10a) consists of exhaustively listing the buyer/buyee pairs (compare (10a) with the pair–list interpretation of *What did everyone buy*). In fact, all multiple question constructions obligatorily receive pair–list readings.

Let us assume that the pair–list interpretation in multiple questions stems from the same ingredients that generate this reading in (7a). This requires a quantifier of the right sort, viz. a generator, and a functionally interpreted WH-element containing a pronoun which is bound by that quantifier. Assume that the WH in Spec CP functions like *everyone* in (7a) on the pair–list reading. *Who*, then, is the quantifier that generates the list.[8] For the pair–list reading to emerge we still need a functionally interpreted WH with a bound pronoun. Take the WH-*in-situ* as the functionally interpreted expression. (10a), then, is the LF structure of the multiple interrogative.

(11)   [Who$_i$ [t$_i$ bought [pro$_i$ N]]][9]

Observe that a parallel structure for (10b) induces a WCO effect, making the same assumptions as we did in (11), viz. the WH in Spec CP is the quantifier and the WH-*in-situ* is interpreted functionally.

(12)   [What$_i$ [[pro$_i$ N] bought t$_i$]]

The *pro$_i$* in (12) is coindexed with a variable t$_i$ on its right. This results in a WCO violation. This accounts for the unacceptability of (10b).

This treatment of superiority effects extends to all of the standard acceptable cases. Observe that the same analysis accounts for the facts in (13).

(13a)   Who saw Aida where
(13b)   Who saw Aida when
(13c)   When did you see Aida where[10]
(13d)   Where did you see Aida when

For example, (13c) has the LF in (14).

(14)   [When$_i$ [you see Aida t$_i$ [pro$_i$ N]]]

It also extends without further complication to the Hendrick–Rochemont cases mentioned above.

(15a)   *What did you expect who to buy
(15b)   *What did you persuade who to buy

In both these examples a WCO violation arises, as the LFs in (16) make clear. Both phrase markers have *pro* coindexed with a variable to its right.

(16a)   [What$_i$ [you expect [[pro$_i$ N] to buy t$_i$]]]
(16b)   [What$_i$ [you persuade [pro$_i$ N]$_j$ [PRO$_j$ to buy t$_i$]]]

Other cases of superiority are accounted for as well. Indirect object constructions, in both the double object NP version and the PP version, display superiority effects (see Larson 1988: 136–8).

(17a)   Who did you give what/which check
(17b)   *What/which check did you give who
(18a)   What/which check did you send to who
(18b)   *Who(m) did you send what/which check to

The LF structures of these sentence is provided in (19) and (20).

(19a)   [Who$_i$ [you give t$_i$ [pro$_i$ N]]]
(19b)   [What$_i$ [you give [pro$_i$ N] t$_i$]]
(20a)   [What$_i$ [you send t$_i$ to [pro$_i$ N]]]
(20b)   [Who$_i$ [you send [pro$_i$ N] to t$_i$]]

Both (19a) and (20a) are well-formed phrase markers. In contrast, both (19b) and (20b) violate WCO as the *pro* is coindexed in each case with a variable on its right.

The binding account of superiority elaborated here makes a prediction that is well illustrated by indirect object constructions. It ties superiority effects together with WCO and the ability to manifest pair–list readings in constructions involving WHs and *every N* phrases. The WCO account of the cases in (17) and (18) implies the following pattern of data in indirect object constructions.[11]

(21a)   I gave everyone$_i$ his$_i$ paycheck
(21b)   *I gave its$_i$ owner every paycheck$_i$
(21c)   Which man$_i$ did you send his$_i$ paycheck
(21d)   *Whose$_i$ pay did you send his$_i$ mother
(22a)   I sent every book$_i$ to its$_i$ author
(22b)   *I sent his$_i$ book to every author$_i$
(22c)   Which book$_i$ did you send to its$_i$ author
(22d)   *Which author$_i$ did you send his$_i$ book to
(23a)   What did you give everyone
(23b)   Who did you give everything
(24a)   What did you assign to every student
(24b)   Who did you assign every problem to

(21) and (22) illustrate WCO effects. The current account implies that WCO violations should occur overtly in cases parallel to (17b) and (18b). This is what we find in (21b, d) and (22b, d).

We also expect the pair–list readings in (23) and (24) to be possible in sentences parallel to the acceptable multiple question cases in (17) and (18). In particular we expect that (23a) and (24b) should allow for a pair–list interpretation while (23b) and (24a) should not tolerate this. This appears to be the case. Note that only in the former pair is binding of the implicit *pro* possible without inducing WCO, just as in (17a) and (18a).

In sum, this account ties the properties of three different construction types very closely together: WCO structures, pair–list readings of WH/universal quantifier constructions, and multiple questions. In just those cases where pronoun binding is licit and pair–list interpretations are available we expect multiple questions to be well formed. The cases in (21) through (24) nicely confirm this feature of the analysis.

A similar prediction holds for the pronoun binding and pair–list analogues of the Hendrick–Rochemont sentences.

(25a)   *What$_i$ do you expect its$_i$ author to rewrite

(25b)   *What$_i$ did you persuade its$_i$ author to rewrite

(26a)   Who did you expect to say everything

(26b)   What did you expect everyone to say

(26c)   Who did you persuade to say everything

(26d)   What did you persuade everyone to say

In (25) we witness a pair of WCO effects that parallel the superiority effects in (15). The absence of pair–list interpretations in (26a, c) and their presence in (26b, d) are also expected on the assumption that this reading is mediated by the kind of binding that licenses multiple questions and bound pronoun interpretation. So here too the three sets of phenomena swing together as the WCO analysis implies they should.

Before exploring additional empirical consequences of this approach, let us pause to consider its costs. There are two basic ingredients to the present proposal. First, we must assume that WH-expressions can be functionally interpreted. In particular, the present proposal treats WHs not in Spec CP at LF as functionally interpreted. These WHs are to be distinguished from those in Spec CP. The latter WHs form operator variable structures at LF.[12] This is clearly a benign assumption given the substantial empirical justification provided in Engdahl (1985) and Chierchia (1991). What is less benign, perhaps, has been the current implementation of this assumption. I have suggested that this be cashed out at LF in terms of a "[pro N]" structure. This configuration is an LF analogue of the overt forms that functional answers typically have. That functional answers should be grammatically distinguished at LF does not trivially follow from Engdahl's original observations. However, I do not see that it raises any serious problems either. Furthermore, were the phenomena removed from the syntax entirely (including LF) and relocated in the semantics, this would suit the purposes here just fine. The core empirical claim is that the same sort of pronoun binding that is implicated in pair–list readings and pronoun binding is also at work in multiple questions. And, most importantly, that just as WCO limits the interpretation of bound pronouns and restricts pair–list interpretations in certain WH/quantifier configurations, so too it underlies superiority effects. In short, all that this analysis requires is that wherever WCO is stated, be it at LF or in the semantics, it applies to all three types of structures. I confess that I find it likely that WCO is an LF phenomenon given that it is structurally governed and has no reasonable semantic motivation. However, were this belief proven untenable, the key idea explored here would survive translation into a more semantic idiom.[13]

The second key assumption is that a WH-element such as *who, what*, etc. can act as a quantificational generator for a pair–list reading. This is crucial, for as Chierchia (1991) showed, not all quantifiers can do this. For example, (27) only has the individual interpretation in which the thing brought does not vary from person to person.

(27)   What did many/most/no people bring

The problem is that questions are generally treated as involving existential quantification and so should not be able to generate the pair–list readings, as I have assumed that they do. However, I do not think that this is a serious problem for the account. The reason is that, in fact, there is a requirement of universality on multiple interrogatives Consider (28).

(28)   Who sang what at the Met last night

(28) requires that a full list of singers and their parts be provided. It does not suffice to offer up the partial answer "Domingo sang Cavaradosi." We also need to know who sang the other (major) roles for the answer to be felicitous (e.g. Millo as Tosca, Diaz as Scarpia). I submit that this requirement of exhaustiveness suffices to generate the PR reading in these cases. In other words, whatever it is that constrains multiple questions to be full and complete in the way indicated suffices to allow the WH to generate the required interpretation.

Let me put this another way. Chierchia (1991: 84) suggests that the distinctive property that universal quantifiers have is that they enable us to identify the domain of the function f (the one that the binding of *pro* in [*pro N*] sets up) in terms of which we generate the list in a pair–list reading. He notes that only certain quantifiers "determine" a domain, viz. the ones that have a generator set, the universal ones. However, what drives this part of the analysis is that we have some way of identifying the domain of the function f so that we can generate the list. If in multiple interrogatives we already have an identified domain then this should suffice to generate the list. What seems required in multiple interrogatives is that the domains that the WH-element in Spec CP singles out be discourse familiar. For example, in (28) we know the relevant set of persons and we are asking for the mapping to their roles. This comes out clearly in considering the pair of sentences in (29). It is perfectly felicitous to use (29a) in the absence of any knowledge of the potential invitees. However, this same ignorance renders (29b) very odd. It seems that to ask the latter there must at least be a discourse specification of who's coming.[14]

(29a)   Who's coming to the party tomorrow
(29b)   Who's bringing what to the party tomorrow

3   Further Facts: Multiple *Which* Questions

The WCO theory of superiority can account for the disappearance of superiority effects in certain contexts. Consider a sentence like (30) one more time.

(30)   Who bought what

As noted, the felicity of (30) presupposes a given set of people of which the speaker is asking what things each purchased. Further, the answer should be exhaustive, saying of each individual what s/he bought. In contrast to the given set, over which the *who* ranges, there need not be a given object set, over which *what* ranges. Furthermore, if there is one, it need not be that every element therein be paired with some element of the subject set (see n. 14). This contrasts, I believe, with a sentence like (31) where it is presupposed that each reviewer is paired with a book and vice versa.

(31)   Which man reviewed which book

What, then, distinguishes the WHs in (30) from those in (31)? In a multiple interrogative, a simple WH like *who*, *what*, etc. must be in an A'-position, i.e. Spec CP, in order to be d(iscourse)-linked. Elements like *which N*, in contrast, are inherently d-linked.[15] Consider what this means for superiority assuming the WCO analysis.

Making the Minimalist assumption that a moved element leaves a full copy behind, the structure of the phrase marker underlying (32a) right after SPELL OUT is (32b).

(32a)   What did who buy
(32b)   [What$_i$ [who buy what$_i$]]

Note that we have not yet applied deletion at LF. To get the correct interpretation we must find an individual level quantifier that generates a pair list and a pronoun for it to bind. Assume, as we did in chapter 6, that WHs interpreted as ranging over individuals bind syntactic variables (i.e. case-marked traces, i.e. categories whose contents have been deleted). Full copies, in contrast, are interpreted functionally. If we read *who* functionally and treat *what* as the individual level quantifier we end up with the LF in (33). This phrase marker violates WCO.

(33)   [What$_i$ [[pro$_i$ N] buy t$_i$]]

Why can we not do the opposite in (32b): interpret *who* as the individual quantifier and the copy of *what* as the functional expression? Note this is exactly what we do in cases such as (34) where there is another individual level quantifier that can generate the set, viz. *everyone*.[16]

(34a)   What does everyone like t
(34b)   [What [everyone like what]
(34c)   [(What) [everyone$_i$ likes [pro$_i$ N]]

Note that in terms of economy, as regards (34b), it is equally costly to interpret the *what* copy (the one interpreted as the functional expression) and "delete" the *what* in Spec CP as it is to retain the one in Spec CP and delete the copy (and thereby get an individual variable reading). Crucially, this is not so in (32b). Recall a vital assumption. To give either *who* or *what* a d-linked interpretation, as is necessary for the pair–list reading, one of the two WHs must be in Spec CP. This means that in (32b), aside from deleting the *what* in Spec CP we must also raise *who* to Spec CP and then delete its copy in Spec IP so that *who* receives an individual level interpretation. In other words, we must go through the following series of steps.[17]

(35a)   [What [who bought what]]
(35b)   [[who bought what]]
(35c)   [Who [who bought what]]
(35d)   [Who [t bought what]]
(35e)   Who$_i$ [t$_i$ bought [pro$_i$ N]]]

(35d) can receive the intended interpretation (35e) as now we have all the required ingredients in positions where they are permitted. There is a quantifier that has a given set of individuals associated with it, the *who* in Spec CP. There is a full WH that can be functionally interpreted, *what*. In addition, the pronoun is bound correctly.

Why is this derivation not permitted? Two possible explanations come to mind. Consider them in turn.

First, we could propose that the derivation in (35) is less economical than the one that underlies (32b). The latter merely requires deletion of one of the two WHs to yield a well-formed LF. The derivation in (35) involves deletion of the lower WH, raising of the WH-*in-situ* and subsequent deletion of the copy. This is a more involved derivation and given that economy, rather than expressibility, drives grammaticality in a Minimalist theory, the existence of a more economical derivation, (32b), blocks the alternative derivation (35).

This economy account assumes that WH-raising does not normally apply to a WH-*in-situ* raising it either to Spec CP or adjoining it to IP. If WHs in non-A'-positions at LF had to raise via a QR-like operation then the full derivation of (32b) would not make the required economy distinctions. The full derivation assuming obligatory A'-movement of WHs *in situ* would go as follows.[18]

(36a)   [What [who likes what]
(36b)   [What [who [who likes what]
(36c)   [[Who [who likes what]]]
(36d)   [[Who [t likes what]]]
(36e)   [[Who$_i$ [t$_i$ likes [pro$_i$ N]]]]

In short, if we count the QR-like steps in (36c, d) then the two derivations underlying (32b) are equally costly. I take this to imply that a QR-like operation should not apply to WHs-*in-situ*.[19] Without QR, economy makes the desired distinctions.

A second alternative is to prevent step (35c) above. In Chomsky (1993: 32) it is assumed that WH-movement is driven by "morphological necessity."

> Certain features must be checked in the domain of a head, or the derivation will crash. Therefore, raising of an operator to [Spec, CP] must be driven by such a requirement. The natural assumption is that C may have an operator feature . . . and that this feature is a morphological property of such operators as *wh*-. . . . If the operator feature of C is strong, the movement must be overt . . . the *wh*-operator feature is universally strong.

That features disappear when they are checked (p. 28ff) implies that there is no WH-raising to Spec CP at LF. WH-features, being universally strong, must be checked and eliminated by SPELL OUT. But this suffices to prevent step (35c).[20] The additional assumption made above, viz. that simple WHs in multiple interrogatives can only be d-linked if in Spec CP, leads to the conclusion that the alternative derivation for (32a) in (35) fails to provide a generator (a d-linked WH) necessary for the pair–list reading. Observe that on this alternative, nothing prevents moving quantified expressions (including WH-quantifiers) via QR. What is prevented is movement to Spec CP. So, in (34) *everyone* can undergo QR. Similarly for *who* in (35a). However, this will not suffice to make *who* d-linked if we assume that being in Spec CP is required to obtain this interpretation. As this is necessary for generating the pair–list reading in multiple interrogatives we correctly account for the data.

Of these two explanations, the economy account of (32b) is clearly preferable as it makes fewer *ad hoc* assumptions. For example, given the economy approach we need not theoretically distinguish A'-positions, only permitting WHs in Spec CPs to function as generators. All we need assume is what we have already assumed, viz. pair–list readings require generators, generators are individual level operators, and being in A'-position is what is required of a non-inherently d-linked operator like *who* if its variable is to have an individual level interpretation. This, plus economy, makes the desired empirical distinctions. This said, either of the two approaches above suffices for what follows.

Now consider a case like (37).

(37)   Which book did which man review

This case is theoretically more like (34) than (32b). By assumption, *which N*s are inherently d-linked, i.e. they need not be in an A'-position like Spec CP to receive a d-linked interpretation.[21] If so, then all we need do is delete the WH in Spec CP and functionally interpret its copy *in situ* to get the right interpretation. This is no less economical than deleting the copy and thereby getting the individual level interpretation. So, what we cannot do with *who* and *what* we can do with *which N*s. The reason is directly traced to the fact that the latter are inherently d-linked (and so can be generators without moving to Spec CP) while the former only so function when in Spec CP.[22] The two derivations are provided in (38) (the individual reading) and (39) (the functional reading).

(38a) [Which book [which man reviewed which book]]
(38b) [Which book [which man reviewed t]]
(38c) [Which$_i$ [[pro$_i$ man] reviewed t$_i$]]
(39a) [Which book [which man reviewed which book]]
(39b) [[which man reviewed which book]]
(39c) [[which man$_i$ reviewed [pro$_i$ book]]]

As with (34), the only computational option is whether to delete the upper or lower WH. In (39), we delete the WH in Spec CP and interpret its copy functionally. The pronoun binding is licit. *Which man*, by assumption, is a generator. It binds the implicit pronoun in the functionally interpreted WH.

(38) illustrates a second option. The WH-copy in the trace position is deleted and the WH in Spec CP is retained. *Which man* in Spec IP is interpreted functionally. This structure is illicit as it violates WCO.

There is a third option worth considering. We interpret both WHs as ranging over individuals. The relevant LF after deletion is (40).

(40) [Which book$_i$ [which man$_j$ reviewed t$_i$]]

I would like to suggest that this structure cannot be interpreted, though it is perfectly grammatical. Two points are noteworthy. First, given the present analysis that pair–list readings are mediated by the functional interpretation of a WH, there is no need for a process of absorption that combines a pair of WH-operators to form a single binary quantifier. Simplicity therefore dictates that this superfluous process be dropped. Second, recall that one of Chierchia's (1991) initial motivations for the WCO analysis is a desire to simplify the semantics of questions by prohibiting quantification into questions. If we follow this logic, a structure like (40) should be impossible as it involves quantification into a question, in this case by another question operator. In other words, on the assumption that quantification into questions is prohibited, then all but one of the WHs must be interpreted functionally in multiple WH-constructions. This effectively renders (40) uninterpretable. In the next section, I provide some cross-linguistic data in support of this conclusion.[23]

To recap. A full WH-*in-situ* can be functionally interpreted. A WH in Spec CP that is binding an empty category (i.e. what one gets after the copy is deleted) is interpreted as an individual level quantifier. In multiple WH-constructions, a simple WH like *who* or *what* is interpreted as d-linked when in this configuration. In fact, to be d-linked such a WH must be in this configuration. In contrast, *which N* WHs are inherently interpreted as d-linked. This means that for these expressions, moving to Spec CP is not required for them to act as generators for pair–list readings. I have argued that these facts suffice to make (32a) unacceptable by reasons of economy or lack of a generator. In contrast, (37) can find a grammatical LF that is minimalistically impeccable.

In short, combined with the present hypothesis, the Minimalist framework in Chomsky (1993) permits an account of the contrast in cases like (32b) and (37).[24]

This account has one further noteworthy consequence. Recall that chapter 6 observed that WH-extraction out of WH-islands does not support the functional interpretation of a WH-trace, though an individual level interpretation of a WH-trace is acceptable. This observation was elevated into a principle prohibiting WH-traces inside islands from ranging over non-individuals. For example, (41) requires the reading in which everyone heard the same thing.

(41)   What did you wonder whether everyone heard

The same fact holds for movement across negation.

(42)   Who don't you believe that everyone kissed

This too fails to felicitously support a functional answer or a pair–list reading.
    With this in mind, consider the following sentences.

(43)   Which man didn't sing which song
(44)   *Which song didn't which man sing

(44) is unacceptable. Its unacceptability is on a par with a standard superiority effect. This is surprising given that *which* Ns do not induce superiority effects, as we have just seen in (37). The present approach, in combination with the prohibition against non-individual construals of WH-traces inside islands, implies that (44) should display a superiority effect. Consider the details.

Recall that to account for the absence of superiority effects in cases such as (45) requires deletion of the WH in Spec CP and a functional interpretation of the copy. This permits *which man* to bind the pronoun of the functionally interpreted WH.

(45a)   Which song did which man sing
(45b)   [[which man$_i$ sing [pro$_i$ song]]

However, if functionally interpreted expressions cannot cross (inner neg) islands, then this option is not available in (44) given the intervening *Neg*. The only option that remains for the interpretation of the multiple interrogatives in (44) is to interpret *which man* functionally and delete the copy of *which song* so that it can receive an individual level interpretation.[25] But this structure then induces a WCO violation. So (46a) is out by the prohibition against interpreting WH-traces inside islands non-individually and (46b) is out by WCO. In short, we derive the unacceptability of (44).

(46a)   [[which man$_i$ Neg sing [pro$_j$ N]$_i$]
(46b)   [Which song$_i$ [[pro$_i$ N] Neg sing t$_i$]

Observe that (43) should be fully acceptable, in contrast to (44). It has the well-formed structure in (47).[26]

(47)   [Which man$_i$ [t$_i$ Neg sing [pro$_i$ N]]]

Similar superiority effects appear when there is extraction from other kinds of islands.

(48a)   Which person didn't believe that Bill reviewed which book
(48b)   Which book didn't Mary/*which person believe that Bill reviewed
(48c)   Which person believes Bill didn't review which book
(48d)   Which book does Mary/*which person believe Bill didn't review
(48e)   Which person knows where to review which book
(48f)   Which book does Mary/*which person know where to review
(48g)   I can't recall which person had plans to read which book
(48h)   I can't recall which book Mary/*which person had plans to read
(48i)   Which man left Rome before reading which book
(48j)   Which book did John/*which man leave Rome before reading

The data roughly act as expected. Thus, (48b) with *which person* in place of *Mary* is less acceptable than (48a) without extraction out of the neg island as well as the case in which superiority is not implicated, i.e. with Mary in place of *which person*. The same holds for the four other pairs of sentences.

4   Some Comparative Superiority Data

4.1   *Languages with Multiply Fronted WHs*

English multiple interrogatives involve a WH in Spec CP and one or more WHs-*in-situ*. Rudin (1988) describes languages in which all the WH-operators move to the front in a multiple question.[27] These languages divide into at least two distinct types. On the one hand there are languages like Polish (P), Czech, and Serbo-Croatian, and on the other languages like Romanian and Bulgarian (B).[28] Rudin describes the following differences between P-type and B-type languages.

  1   The P-group resists multiple WH-extraction from an indicative clause while the B-group allows this.

    (49a)   Koj$_i$ kude$_j$ mislis   [ce t$_i$ e   otisul t$_j$] (B)
             Who where think-2SG Comp has gone
             "Who do you think went where"
             (Rudin ex. 6a)
    (49b)   *Co   komu   Maria chce, zeby Janek kupil (P)
             What to whom Maria wants that Janek buy
             "What does Maria want Janek to buy for whom"
             (Rudin ex. 12b)

2 The B-group freely permits WH-island violations. The P-group does not.

(50a) Vidjah   edna kniga, kojato; se cudja   [koj znae [koj
       Saw-1SG a   book   which wonder-1SG who knows who
       prodava t;]] (B)
       sells
       "I saw a book which I wonder who sells (it)"
       (Rudin ex. 19)

(50b) *... maszyna ktora; on zapytal [kto wynalazl t;] ... (P)
       Machine   which he asked   who invented ...
       "The machine which he asked who invented"
       (Rudin ex. 25b)

3 In the P-group, but not the B-group, clitics, adverbs, parentheticals, and particles follow the first WH-word. (51a) illustrates this for Bulgarian. The words *ti* and *e* are clitics and cannot break up the WH-cluster. In Polish, *sie* is a clitic and it can intervene between the first and second clause initial WH.

(51a) *Koj ti   e   kakvo kazal? (B)
       Who you has what   told
       (Rudin ex. 28b)

(51b) Kto sie komu   podoba? (P)
       Who refl to whom likes
       "Who likes who"
       (Rudin ex. 37a)

4 P-languages, but not B-languages, allow free nominative/accusative WH-word order. Rudin analyzes there word order restrictions as superiority effects. Her conclusion is that B-languages manifest superiority effects while P-languages do not.

(52a) Koj kogo vizda? (B)
       Who whom sees

(52b) *Kogo koj vizda (B)
       (Rudin ex. 54a, b)

(52c) Kto co   robil (P)
       Who what did

(52d) Co kto robil (P)
       (Rudin ex. 60a, b)

To account for these differences between Bulgarian and Polish, Rudin proposes that WH-elements move to different positions in the two language groups. In Bulgarian Spec CP may contain several WH-words (at SPELL OUT). In Polish, in contrast, Spec CP contains only a single WH with the other WH-operators either adjoined to IP or arrayed in lower Comps. Rudin assumes that in B-languages a WH can adjoin to a WH in Spec CP while in P-languages all but the most prominent WHs are adjoined to IP. With these assumptions, (53a) shows the structure of multiple WH-constructions in B-languages and (53b) of P-languages.

(53a) $[_{CP} [_{wh1} WH_2 [_{wh1} WH_1]] [C^0 [_{IP} \ldots]]$
(53b) $[_{CP} WH_1 [C^0 [_{IP} WH_2 [_{IP} \ldots]]$

Two questions arise given Rudin's observations. Why do B-languages show superiority effects and why do P-languages not display them? In what follows, I outline two possible analyses which assume Rudin's structures and the theory outlined in sections 2 and 3. Consider first the question why P-languages do not display superiority effects.

Given the analysis above, there are two ways that superiority effects can be finessed. First, there can be a form of movement which cancels WCO effects. As superiority on the present analysis is a species of WCO, any movement that cancels WCO should also eliminate superiority. A second way of cancelling superiority effects would be to have multiple generators. If a language treated all WHs as potential generators, then we would expect multiple WHs in such a language to show the same insensitivity to superiority that English multiple interrogatives like (54) show.

(54) Which book did which person read

Consider each possibility in turn.

It is well known that A-movement can cancel WCO effects, as shown by examples such as (55).

(55a) *It seems to his$_i$ mother that everyone$_i$ is handsome
(55b) Everyone$_i$ seems to his$_i$ mother t$_i$ to be handsome

Not surprisingly, they also alleviate superiority effects.

(56a) *What did it seem to whom fell off the shelf
(56b) What seemed to whom to fall off the shelf

With this in mind consider the following analysis of Japanese in Takahashi (1993a). Nishigauchi (1990) notes that multiple WH-constructions in simple clauses do not display superiority effects.

(57a) Dare-ga   nani-o   tabeta no?
       Who-NOM what-ACC ate Q
       "Who ate what"
(57b) Nani-o dare-ga tabeta no?

Takahashi observes that this follows given the presence of both A and A'-scrambling in Japanese.[29] Intraclausal scrambling can be either A or A'-movement. Interclausal scrambling must be A'-movement. In the case of multiple WH-sentences like (57), this leaves the following possibility. Before moving to Spec CP, a WH A-moves to IP. This allows the sentences in (57) to have the LFs in (58).

(58a) $[_{CP}$ Dare-ga$_i$ $[_{IP}$ dare-ga$_i$ nani-o tabeta no]]
(58b) $[_{CP}$ Dare-ga$_i$ $[_{IP}$ t$_i$ [pro$_i$ thing] tabeta no]]
(58c) $[_{CP}$ Nani-o $[_{IP}$ nani-o $[_{IP}$ dare-ga nani-o tabeta no]]]
(58d) $[_{CP}$ Nani-o$_i$ $[_{IP}$ vbl-t$_i$ $[_{IP}$ [pro$_i$ person] NP-t$_i$ tabeta no]]]

Observe that given the present analysis neither phrase marker violates WCO and so superiority effects should not be evident. Takahashi further observes that if one of the WHs is scrambled out of its clause, WCO effects appear.

(59)   ??Nani-o$_i$ John-ga   dare-ni   [Mary-ga t$_i$ tabeta to]   itta no?
       What-ACC John-NOM who-DAT Mary-NOM ate   Comp said Q
       "What did John tell who that Mary ate"

This too is expected on the assumption made by Takahashi, following Mahajan (1990) and Saito (1992), that long scrambling is a species of A'-movement and that a long scrambled WH acts as if it were in a +WH Spec CP. The structure of (59) on these assumptions is (60). The long scrambled WH is the generator, and the WH *in situ* is functionally interpreted. This set of requirements leads to WCO violation as indicated in (60b).

(60a) $[_{CP}$ Nani-o $[_{IP}$ John-ga dare-ni $[_{CP}$ $[_{IP}$ Mary-ga nani-o$_i$ tabeta] to] itta] no]]
(60b) $[_{CP}$ Nani-o $[_{IP}$ John-ga [pro$_i$ person] $[_{CP}$ $[_{IP}$ Mary-ga t$_i$ tabeta] to] itta] no]]

   Takahashi's analysis of Japanese suggests the following approach to P-languages. Assume that the adjunction of WH to IP suggested by Rudin is an instance of A-movement. As Rudin observes, this adjunction is intraclausal. The main difference between Polish and Japanese, then, is the absence of long scrambling in Polish. If this is tenable, we have a straightforward account of the absence of superiority effects in P-languages.[30] The structure of the problematic Polish example (52d) is (61) at LF. Observe that binding of the implicit pronoun made available on the functional interpretation of the WH-operator after reconstruction obeys WCO.

(61a) $[_{CP}$ Co$_i$ $[C^0$ $[_{IP}$ co$_i$ $[_{IP}$ kto$_j$ $[_{IP}$ kto$_j$ rubil co$_i$]]]]]]
(61b) $[_{CP}$ Co$_i$ $[C^0$ $[_{IP}$ vbl-t$_i$ $[_{IP}$ $[_{IP}$ [pro$_i$ person] rubil NP-t$_i$]]]]]]

   Consider a second possible analysis of the Polish data assuming this time that the adjunction to IP postulated by Rudin is actually a species of A'-movement. Section 3 makes two proposals which can be put to service here. First, d-linked operators can act as generators. Second, non-inherently d-linked operators must be in A'-position to get a d-linked reading. These two assumptions plus the assumptions that IP adjunction is A'-movement and that WCO underlies superiority together imply that P-languages should not manifest superiority effects. More specifically, these assumptions imply that P-languages should manifest the behavior of the English examples (37) above, repeated here.

(37) Which book did which man review

How so? Overtly moving all WHs to A'-positions before SPELL OUT permits all the WHs in Polish to be interpreted as d-linked and so act as generators. Consider the derivation of (52c, d). At SPELL OUT they have the following structures.

(62a) $[_{CP}$ Kto$_i$ $[_{IP}$ co$_j$ $[_{IP}$ kto$_i$ robil co$_j]]]$
       Who   what   did
(62b) $[_{CP}$ Co$_j$ $[_{IP}$ kto$_i$ $[_{IP}$ kto$_i$ robil co$_j]]]$

Observe that both WHs are in A'-positions, on the assumption that the adjoining to IP is a species of A'-movement. Hence both are potential generators. To get a well-formed LF adopting our prior assumptions, we must delete one of the WHs and interpret its trace functionally. Deletion of either WH will suffice. Assume, then, that we decide to reconstruct *co* and interpret it functionally and we delete the copy of *kto* and interpret it as ranging over individuals. The structures we get are those in (63).

(63a) $[_{CP}$ Kto$_i$ $[_{IP}$ $[_{IP}$ t$_i$ robil $[$pro$_i$ thing$]]]]$
(63b) $[_{CP}$ $[_{IP}$ Kto$_i$ $[_{IP}$ t$_i$ robil $[$pro$_i$ thing$]]]]$

Both structures obey the WCO Condition, both have a generator. Therefore, neither should display superiority effects, and, as Rudin nodes, P-languages do not in fact display such effects. In sum, the fact that P-languages have their WHs overtly moved to A'-positions makes each WH a potential generator, in contrast to English. This allows P-languages to finesse superiority.[31]
    Now consider the Bulgarian sentences (52a, b), repeated here.

(64a) Koj kogo vizda? (B)
      Who whom sees
(64b) *Kogo koj vizda (B)
      (Rudin ex. 54a, b)

After SPELL OUT they have the structures in (65).

(65a) [[Koj [kogo]] [C^0 [koj vizda kogo]]]
(65b) *[[Kogo [koj]] [C^0 [koj vizda kogo]]]

Observe that both WHs are in Spec CP. This follows Rudin's analysis of B-group languages. However, this structure is different than Rudin's in one respect, it adheres to the principle that adjunction is to the left, as Baker (1988) originally proposed.[32] Rudin assumes that the complex WH in Spec CP is right branching.

This aside, why does Bulgarian display superiority effects? In particular, what is it about the structure of B-type languages that prevents them from finessing superiority effects just like P-type languages do?

Note that given Rudin's proposal, the movement of WHs in B-languages is to Spec CP. Thus, given Takahashi's typology, it must be a species of A'-movement. In other words, we do not expect this kind of movement to pattern like the sort of A-movement plausibly occurring in Polish and Japanese. Given this, consider the options available at LF for the structures in (65). We can delete either WH and interpret either WH copy functionally. If we interpret *kogo* functionally and treat *koj* as the generator in (65a) we end up with the well-formed structure in (66).

(66) $[[Koj_i [[C^0 t_i vizda [pro_i thing]]]]]$

What of (65b)? If *kogo* is the generator and *koj* the functionally interpreted WH we end up with a WCO violation.

(67) $[Kogo_i [[pro_i person] vizda t_i]]$

There is a further option, however. What prevents treating *koj* as the generator and *kogo* functionally as in (66)? One possibility is that this violates the Island Condition (IC) proposed in chapter 6. Recall that we prohibited WH-traces from receiving anything but an individual interpretation within WH-islands. In short, WH-traces within +WH CPs cannot be interpreted functionally. It is plausible that we are violating this in the Bulgarian example if *kogo* is interpreted functionally. *Koj*, by hypothesis, is the first WH in Spec CP. It agrees with the +WH feature in C^0. Therefore, the leftmost WH is related to a trace inside a +WH-headed CP. This is parallel to relating a WH to its trace within a WH-island. On the assumption that this is permitted here, just as it is in English, only if the WH is interpreted individually, i.e. not functionally, the option canvassed here is blocked. In short, there is no legitimate way of treating *koj* as the generator in the LF of (65b). As such, there is no well-formed LF for this sentence.[33]

There is another possible explanation that leans less heavily on the IC. Consider once again the structure of (65b) if *kogo* reconstructs and is functionally interpreted, while *koj* acts as the generator, i.e. the copy *in situ* deletes so that the empty category can be interpreted as a variable ranging over individuals.

(68) $[[[Koj_i]] [C^0 [t_i vizda [pro_i thing]]]$

Here is the question: in (68) is *koj* a licit operator? If it is not, then this structure will not generate the requisite pair–list reading. In fact, it will generate no reading at all. This is the desired result. The question is can we find a reason for doubting that *koj* can play the role required of it. One possibility is that it is too "encumbered" to function adequately. Concretely, assume that elements to which other elements have adjoined are semantically inert.[34] We can implement this suggestion by assuming either that "reconstruction" does not erase brackets, or that reconstruction does not involve deletion at all in the sense of eliminating an expression but rather it is a sort of bracketing process, the bracketed element being "ignored" by the interpretive mechanisms at the interface. On this second proposal the structure of (68) is more adequately represented as (69).[35]

(69) $[[(\text{Kogo}) [\text{koj}_i]] [C^0 [t_i \text{ vizda } [\text{pro}_i \text{ thing}]]]$

What happens if we choose to "reconstruct" *koj* instead and have *kogo* act as the generator? In that case the structure we get is (70). This structure is ill-formed as it violates WCO. The pronoun within the functional WH is to the left of the variable that it links to.

(70) $[[\text{Kogo}_i [(\text{koj})]] [C^0 [[\text{pro}_i \text{ person}] \text{ vizda } t_i]]$

In sum, (64b) has no well-formed LF capable of meeting the interpretive requirements. Hence we witness superiority effects.

Note that the LF of (64a) does not suffer the same fate. The following is a perfectly adequate structure.

(71) $[[\text{Koj}_i [(\text{kogo})]] [C^0 [t_i \text{ vizda } [\text{pro}_i \text{ thing}]]]]$

To sum up, the assumptions from the previous sections combine with Rudin's analysis to provide two possible accounts for the lack of superiority effects in languages like Polish as well as for the presence of such effects in languages like Bulgarian. The fact that B-languages adjoin WHs to one another in Spec CP restricts their powers in ways that adjoining each WH to IP does not.

4.2   Subject Postposing and Superiority

Consider a second set of cases in which superiority effects appear to fade away.[36] Jaeggli (1981) observed that superiority effects do not hold in simple multiple interrogatives in Spanish.

(72a)   Quién dijo qué?
         Who   said what
(72b)   Qué dijo quién?

However, Boscovic (1993: ex. 9, 10) shows that superiority is respected in more complex cases.

(73a)　?*Qué$_i$ le　　ha pedido a quién qué compre t$_i$
　　　　What him-DAT has asked whom that buy-subj
　　　　"What has she asked whom to buy"

(73b)　?*Qué$_i$ dijo quién qué Juan compra t$_i$
　　　　What said who that Juan bought
　　　　"What did who say that Juan bought"

We can account for these data given a standard approach to subject WH-extraction in Romance. Rizzi (1982) observed that Italian does not display Comp–trace effects. To account for this, he proposed that WH-extraction in Italian proceeds from postverbal position after a process of subject inversion has applied. This analysis has been extended to Spanish by Jaeggli (1981) among others.[37] Let us assume that the option of having subjects in postverbal position is available in Spanish. And let us assume that these subjects are adjoined to VP.[38] This accounts for the lack of superiority effects in (72b). The structure at LF is (74a). After deletion, the structure is (74b), with *qué* acting as the generator and *quién* as the functionally interpreted WH.

(74a)　[$_{CP}$ Qué$_i$ [$_{IP}$ pro dijo$_j$ [$_{Tns}$ dijo$_j$ [$_{AgrO}$ qué$_i$ [dijo$_j$ [$_{VP}$ [dijo$_j$ qué$_i$] quién]]]]]]

(74b)　[$_{CP}$ Qué$_i$ [$_{IP}$ pro dijo$_j$ [$_{Tns}$ t$_j$ [$_{AgrO}$ t$_i$ [t$_j$ [$_{VP}$ [t$_j$ t$_i$] [pro$_i$ person]]]]]]]

Observe that (74b) obeys WCO and so is free of superiority effects.

There is independent empirical support for this analysis. The present proposal reduces superiority to WCO. The implication is that binding into postverbal subjects should ameliorate overt cases of WCO and that WH/quantifier interactions should not show any subject/object asymmetries. This seems to be correct.[39] There is a clear contrast between (75c) and (75d), with the former showing attenuation of WCO effects. Furthermore, both (75a) and (75b) support pair–list readings. These data follow on the assumption that WH-movement to Spec CP can proceed from the postverbal position. For example, the LF representation after deletion of (75b) is (76), a structure that supports a pair–list reading.

(75a)　Qué compro todo　　dios
　　　　What bought everybody

(75b)　Quién compro todo esto
　　　　Who bought everything

(75c)　?Telefonéo a todo el mundo$_i$ su$_i$ madre
　　　　Telephoned to everyone　　his mother

(75d)　?*Su$_i$ madre telefonéo a todo el mundo

(76)　　[$_{CP}$ +WH [$_{IP}$ pro dijo$_j$ [$_{Tns}$ t$_j$ [$_{AgrO}$ todo esto$_i$ [t$_j$ [$_{VP}$ [t$_j$ t$_i$] [(quién=) pro$_i$ person]]]]]]]

Consider now the LF structure of the examples in (73) that display superiority effects. Subject inversion does not alleviate WCO difficulties and so superiority effects are expected to appear. The LF structure (after deletion) of (73b) is provided as illustration. The inversion of the matrix subject does not place it in the c-command domain of the embedded object trace. Consequently, linking between the functional *pro* and the variable-trace t_i is illicit.

(77) $[_{CP}$ Qué$_i$ $[$dijo$_j$ $[_{IP}$ pro $[_{VP}$ t$_j$ $[$(quién=) pro$_i$ person$]]$ $[_{CP}$ qué Juan compra t$_i]]]]]$

One further fact follows on the present analysis. Should subject inversion not take place in simple clauses, we expect to find the reemergence of superiority effects. Boscovic (1993: ex. 14) points out that this indeed occurs.

(78) *Qué quién dijo
What who said

However, Boscovic also observes that the Spanish cases are not that interesting as verb inversion is always required with WH-movement. Thus, *Qué Juan dijo* is also unacceptable. However, the Hebrew data that he cites are subject to the same analysis as provided for the Spanish data but do not require V to C-movement in questions. The relevant data are provided in (79).

(79a) Ma kana mi
What bought who
(79b) *Ma mi kana
(79c) Ma Ur kana
What Ur bought

Incidentally, Boscovic, citing Shlonsky (1987), observes that postverbal subjects in Hebrew are possible and they attenuate WCO effects, as the current analysis would lead us to expect.

(80a) Mi$_i$ ohev et hor-av$_i$ yoter mi-kulam
who loves ACC parents-his more than everybody
"Who loves his parents more than everybody else"
(80b) ?*Et me$_i$ hor-av$_i$ ohavim yoter mi-kulam
ACC who parents-his love more than everybody
(80c) ?Et mi$_i$ ohavim hor-av$_i$ yoter mi-kulam

4.3 Superiority in Clauses with Three WHs

The combination of the present analysis of multiple questions and a linking version of WCO effects has one further interesting empirical consequence. It provides an explanation of certain contrasts first noted in Kayne (1984).

Kayne observed that superiority effects are mitigated with the addition of an extra WH. (81a) is worse than (81b).

(81a) *What did who buy there
(81b) (?) What did who buy where

Given the assumptions above, in these constructions the WH in Spec CP acts as the generator for the pair–list interpretation. Furthermore, the WHs-*in-situ* are interpreted functionally, i.e. they involve implicit pronouns linked to the generator's variable. In this case, (81a) has the structure (82), which violates WCO.

(82)   What$_i$ [(who=) [pro$_j$ person] bought t$_i$ there]]

Now consider (81b). The second WH in (81b) is also interpreted functionally. The LF structure is (83). Adopting the linking version of WCO outlined in chapter 6 implies that the presence of a second functionally interpreted WH will mitigate the effects of WCO. The structure is well formed with the indicated linking.[40]

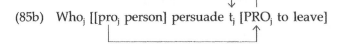

(83)   What$_i$ [(who=)pro$_j$ person] bought t$_i$ [(where=) pro$_j$ place]]

Note that we mitigate superiority effects in analogous cases with overt pronominals licensing a linking similar to the one in (111).

(84a)   *Who did who persuade that Bill should leave
(84b)   Who did who persuade PRO to leave
(84c)   *What did who reveal about Paul
(84d)   What did who reveal about his mother

The relevant structures of (84a, b) are given in (85).

(85a)   Who$_j$ [[pro$_j$ person] persuade t$_j$ [that Bill left]]

(85b)   Who$_j$ [[pro$_j$ person] persuade t$_j$ [PRO$_j$ to leave]

(85a) is ill-formed as it violates WCO given that the variable does not c-command the indicated pronoun. In (85b), however, a licit linking is possible and we get amelioration of the sentence as expected.

4.4   Anti-superiority Effects in Japanese[41]

S. Watanabe (1994) shows that the present set of ideas also accounts for anti-superiority effects in Japanese. The crux of his proposal is that *naze* ("why") in multiple interrogatives is interpreted functionally and so cannot act as a generator. More specifically, Watanabe assumes that generators must range over individuals. He assumes that expressions like *naze* range over non-individuals (properties in Aoun (1985) and Cinque's (1990) sense). Thus they can never function as generators. This implies that when *naze* is in a sentence with another WH, the other WH must function as the generator.[42] If so, it is predicted that in a double question, *naze* must occur within the scope of this other generator. The data are provided in (86).

(86a) John-ga nani-o   naze katta no?
      -NOM *what-ACC why bought Q*
      "Why did John buy what?"
(86b) *John-ga naze nani-o katta no?
(87a) Dare-ga   naze soko-ni itta no?
      Who-NOM why there-to went Q
      "Why did who go there?"
(87b) *Naze dare-ga soko-ni itta no?
(88a) Mary-wa naze [John-ga nani-o   katta ka] shiri- tagatteiru no?
      M-TOP why J-NOM   what-ACC bought Q know want   Q
      "Why does Mary want to know what John bought?"
(88b) *Mary-wa naze [John-ga nani-o   katta to] itta no?
      M-TOP   why J-NOM   what-ACC bought Q said Q
      "Why did Mary say that John bought what?"

(86) and (87) indicate that when *naze* is in a simple clause with another WH-operator, it must be to the right and in the scope of this operator. (88) shows that *naze* can be to the left of another WH but only if that WH does not have the same scope as *naze*. In (88a) *nani-o* takes embedded scope and the sentence is acceptable. In (88b) it must take matrix scope and the sentence is unacceptable. Once again, *naze* is not to the right of the operator.

Watanabe's proposal can be illustrated using the following assumptions. Following Aoun and Li (1993b) and A. Watanabe (1991) assume that before SPELL OUT a WH-expression comes to be in each +WH CP and that at'LF this expression binds a WH *in situ* endowing it with whatever quantificational force it enjoys.[43] The expression so bound at LF is the generator in a multiple WH-construction. The other WH must be functionally interpreted. If generators must range over individuals, this requires that in an acceptable multiple WH-construction with *naze* (one of) the other WH is the generator. Schematically, then, (89a) is required. (89b) violates WCO.

(89a) [[. . . WH$_i$. [(pro$_i$ N') =naze] . . .] Q$_i$]
(89b) [[. . . [(pro$_i$ N') =naze] . . . WH$_i$ . . .] Q$_i$]

The unacceptable examples above all have the structure (89b) and hence are instances of WCO.[44] The acceptable examples realize the schema in (89a). In sum, because *naze* cannot be a generator (it does not range over individuals), anti-superiority effects are simply another instance of WCO.

A. Li (personal communication) informs me that the same pattern of data obtains in Chinese multiple interrogatives. *Weishenme* cannot be to the left of the other WH in a double question.

(90a)   Shei weishenme da ta[45]
      Who why   hit him
(90b)   *Weishenme shei da ta
(90c)   *Lisi weishenme mai-le sheme
      Lisi why   buy   what

   These data are amenable to the same analysis Watanabe proposes for Japanese. Pair–list constructions involving *weishenme* in Chinese provide further empirical support for the analysis.[46] Aoun and Li (1993a: 165) report the following data.

(91a)   Meigeren dou weishenme da ta (ambiguous)
      Everyone all why   hit him
      "Why did everyone hit him"
(91b)   Ta weishenme da meigeren (unambiguous)
      He why   hit everyone
(91c)   Weishenme meigeren dou da ta (unambiguous)
      Why   everyone all hit him

   These data pattern like those in (90). In particular, the multiple interrogative is unacceptable just when the pair–list reading is unavailable. This is what the present theory predicts. Watanabe's proposal amounts to saying that in a licit multiple interrogative, the implicit pronoun of the functionally interpreted element *weishenme* must be properly bound. This binding is prohibited in (90b, c) by WCO. But as we saw in chapter 6, the same sort of binding is required to get a pair–list reading. Thus, only (91a) can have one. In (91b, c) the pair–list reading is blocked by WCO. In short, both pair–list constructions and multiple interrogatives require that *weishenme* be functionally interpreted and its implicit pronoun properly bound. This makes both subject to WCO effects. This accounts for the data above.
   Consider a last piece of evidence in favor of this treatment of anti-superiority effects. Watanabe observes that anti-superiority effects are attenuated in triple interrogatives. This is similar to the data noted by Kayne for English and discussed in the previous section. The Japanese data are subject to the same analysis. Schematically the Japanese data are as follows. If there are three WHs in a clause then the anti-superiority effects disappear. There are two relevant cases.

(92a) $[[\ldots \text{Naze} \ldots \text{WH}^1 \ldots \text{WH}^2 \ldots] \text{Q}]$
(92b) $[[\ldots \text{WH}^1 \ldots \text{naze} \ldots \text{WH}^2 \ldots] \text{Q}]$

These structures are realized in (93).[47]

(93a)   Naze dare-ga (doko-ni/*soko-ni) itta no?
      Why who   where   there   went Q
      "Why did who go (where/there)"
(93b)   (*John-wa/dare-ga) naze nani-o tabeta no?
      John/who   why what ate   Q
      "What did (John/who) eat why"

The cancellation of anti-superiority effects observed here follows from the linking approach to WCO advocated in chapter 6 and illustrated in the Kayne cases discusses just above. The structures in (92) are grammatical with the following linking.

(94a)   [. . . [(Naze) = pro N'] WH$_i^1$ [(WH^2 = pro N')] Q$_i$]

(94b)   [WH$_i^1$ . . . [(naze) = pro N'] . . . [(WH^2) = pro N'] Q$_i$]

4.5   *Multiple Interrogatives with "Why"*

It is well known that *why* resists being left *in situ* in multiple interrogation constructions.

(95a)   *What did Bill buy why
(95b)   Why did Bill buy what

An early account of the unacceptability of (95a) tied it to the *why* and *what* being different kinds of WH-operators and this prevented them from forming an absorption structure.[48] It was unclear, however, why this did not also render (95b) equally unacceptable.

A second approach to the distinction in (95) relates it to the ECP in some form. Being an adjunct, *why* must be antecedent governed at LF. To become antecedent governed, it must be in Spec CP at SS (at least in English). However, this solution also has its problems. Most particularly, it theoretically relies quite heavily on the ECP, a condition on grammars that a Minimalist theory might better do without.

This section tries to rehabilitate a version of the first approach. In particular, we can come very close to accounting for the distribution of *why* in multiple interrogatives on the assumption that it can only be generated in Spec CP, if we couple this assumption with the restriction that only elements that range over individuals can function as generators.[49] Consider some examples.[50]

(96a)   I wonder who bought what
(96b)   *I wonder why who came
(96c)   *I wonder why Bill left when
(96d)   *I wonder why Bill lives where

Let (96a) establish the acceptability baseline. This is a perfectly acceptable embedded double question. In contrast, none of the three other sentences in (96) are particularly felicitous. (96b) is a typical instance of an ECP effect. The other two examples, however, are equally odd but neither involves a

WH-subject. All three unacceptable sentences can be accounted for if we assume that *why* cannot function as a generator and is generated in Spec CP. At LF, for example, (96b) has the LF structure (97).

(97) I wonder [$_{CP}$ why [$_{IP}$ Bill left (when=[pro time])]]

To derive an interpretation for this general question, the *when in situ* must be provided with an interpretation. For this to occur the implicit pronoun that drives the functional reading must be bound and a pair list must be generated. However, *why* in Spec CP, by assumption, cannot function as a generator and thus the whole sentence remains uninterpreted. Observe that in contrast to the Japanese cases discussed above, there is no way to treat *when* as the generator. The reason is that it is not in Spec CP and, as shown above, being in Spec CP is a necessary condition for simple WHs to act as generators. However, even if it could function as a generator, we could still not derive a grammatical outcome. To see why, consider (98).

(98a) *I wonder why which person came
(98b) *I wonder why Bill lives in which city

In contrast with standard "simple" WHs, *which* phrases can function as generators without moving to Spec CP. Still the sentences remain unacceptable. (98a) is particularly interesting in this regard for *which* Ns in subject positions do not generally show superiority effects, as noted in section 2 above.[51] This is expected on the assumption that *why* is base generated in Spec CP. To get a well-formed multiple question, the generator must bind the implicit pronoun inside the functional WH. At LF, then, we need a structure like (99) for (98b).

(99) I wonder [(why=[pro reason]) [Bill lives in which city]]

Note, however, that the variable associated with *which city* cannot licitly bind *pro* as linking *pro* to this position violates WCO. Thus, even with an appropriate generator available, the *why* in Spec CP cannot enter into a licit binding relation.

There is one problem, however. What of (95b)? Why is it acceptable?

(95b) Why did Bill buy what

The only answer available is that contrary to appearances, it is not grammatical. I suggest that the illusion of acceptability comes from the ease with which (95b) can be heard as a sort of echo or focus question (see n. 52). To back this conclusion up, observe that the sentence substantially degrades in acceptability when embedded under *I wonder*.

(100) *I wonder why you bought what

It is very hard to understand this sentence as a multiple embedded question akin to (101).

(101)   I wonder who bought what

Note, moreover, that many other *why* matrix multiple interrogatives are quite unacceptable, even though they are structurally similar to (95b).

(102a)   ??Why did John throw who the ball
(102b)   *Why does John expect who to win
(102c)   ??Why did John give what to Bill

These are particularly degraded when placed under *I wonder*.

(103a)   *I wonder why John threw who the ball
(103b)   *I wonder why John expected who to win
(103c)   *I wonder why John gave what to Bill

Given that these are structurally quite similar to (95b), i.e. an accusative WH is paired with a *why in situ*, but are quite unacceptable nonetheless, suggests that (95b) itself is ungrammatical despite appearances.[52]

Note two last points that support the conclusion that *why* does not function as a generator. First, consider the interpretation of (95b). The sentence means roughly the following: I know what Bill bought, tell me why he bought each thing. In other words, the set of purchased items is given and a reason for each purchase is being requested. It cannot be interpreted as saying that I have a bunch of reasons, tell me which thing was purchased for that reason. In other words, whatever the grammatical status of (95b) it is interpreted as if *what* were the generator. Second, with the addition of another (appropriate) WH, it seems that we can improve the acceptability of multiple *why* interrogatives. Compare the sentences in (104).

(104a)   *I wonder why which man danced
(104b)   ?I wonder why which man danced with which woman

These data are reminiscent of the Japanese data in (93). Note that the same analysis is possible here. At LF, the implicit pronoun within the functionally interpreted *why* can be linked to the pronoun in the other functionally interpreted WH. (105) is a licit linking structure and *which man* is a licit generator.

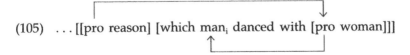

(105)   ... [[pro reason] [which man$_i$ danced with [pro woman]]]

Without the additional WH, the *why* pronoun cannot be properly linked.

The analysis proposed here leads to the conclusion that multiple *why* questions in English are generally illicit. The WCO analysis of multiple interrogatives proposed here combined with the analysis of anti-superiority effects in the East Asian languages leaves little theoretical room for any other conclusion. It is possible to accommodate the bulk of the English data by assuming that *why* is base generated in Spec CP (in contrast with East Asian analogues) and that it cannot function as a generator as it is not an individual level operator.[53] This leads to the conclusion that sentences such as (95b) are most likely ungrammatical, contrary to the standard judgements. If this is correct, it suggests that earlier treatments of absorption were more correct than their later descendants.[54]

4.6   Yes/No Questions

To end, consider one more case. Not all WH-forms can participate in multiple interrogative constructions. Thus, one cannot combine a yes/no (Y/N) question operator like *whether*, *if*, or *did* and another WH-form to yield a well-formed general question.

(106a)   *Did John eat what
(106b)   *I wonder whether/if Bill bought what

In earlier literature, this was handled by citing the inability of these operators to form absorbed operators with WH-elements like *what*. The question, however, is why is absorption not permitted. It would seem that (106b) is a reasonable kind of indirect question. It would indirectly ask for an explicit exhaustive partition of the acquired merchandise.

(107)   I wonder which of these things are such that Bill did or didn't buy them

Similarly, one might imagine (106a) asking of every food group whether or not John partook of it. (108) would then be a good answer.

(108)   He ate the salad and the meat but not the pie or soup

(106a) is unacceptable and does not have (108) as a possible answer. Why not?

Note that if we say that the Y/N question operator lacks the power to act as a generator (like *why* it does not range over individuals) or that it cannot bind an implicit pronoun, then we can account for these data. No multiple interrogatives of this variety are derivable as there is no way of generating a pair–list reading.

The assumption that the Y/N operator cannot bind implicit pronouns comports rather well with the earliest analysis of questions in the generative literature. Katz and Postal (1964: 96) analyze Y/N questions as involving a WH-form like (109). If this is correct, it is quite understandable why the Y/N WH cannot bind a pronoun. It is of the wrong categorial type.

(109)   [$_{adv}$ WH-either/or]

Interestingly, if we follow the Katz and Postal analysis, Y/N WH-forms are exactly parallel in form to other WH-questions. In particular, the WH binds a trace which is a sentential adverb. (110a) has a structure like (110b) (Katz and Postal 1964: 104).

(110a)   Did John sleep (or not)
(110b)   [[$_{adv}$ WH-either/or]$_i$ [[John sleep] t$_i$]]

Can Y/N variables have functional interpretations? Consider (111).

(111a)   Did everyone have a good time?
(111b)   Did John attend every seminar?

I personally find pair–list readings for these sentences quite felicitous. Thus, the answers in (112) seem acceptable.[55]

(112a)   John, Bill, and Mary did but Frank and Sue didn't.
(112b)   He attended Frank's seminar and Sue's but not Bill's

These are analogues to more standard *WH/every* sentences like those in (101).[56] If these answers are indeed available and felicitous, how can this be? Taking a flat-footed approach like the one above would suggest that the trace of the Y/N WH can have functional structure.[57]

(113)   [[$_{adv}$ WH-either/or]$_i$ [[everyone$_j$ [t$_i$ sleep] [pro$_j$ t$_i$]]

In (113), the *pro* is bound by the quantified subject and so a pair–list reading should be possible. Thus, in Y/N questions, if these data are correct, the semantic interpretation that cannot be achieved via a well-formed multiple interrogative can be gained via sentences like (111). We can account for these data on the assumption that the quantifier in Y/N questions can not serve to bind a pronoun while the trace of this operator can get a functional structure.

A last point. If the Y/N variable is at the right periphery as in (110b) and (113) then we can drop the assumption that the Y/N operator cannot bind pronouns. Even if it could, it would induce a WCO violation.[58] The LF structure of (106a) is provided in (114).

(114)   [[$_{adv}$ WH-either/or]$_i$ [[John eat [pro$_i$ N'] t$_i$]

4.7   Concluding Remarks

The analyses in the last several sections tacitly presuppose that absorption does not obtain in UG. To be specific, there is no grammatical operation analogous to the one proposed in Higginbotham and May (1981) that takes a series of one place WH-operators and combines them to form a single *n*-ary WH-operator. The absence of absorption as a grammatical option is what forces all but one WH in a multiple interrogative to be functionally interpreted. This, recall, is in turn the reflex of the prohibition Chierchia (1991) proposes against quantifying into questions. The problem with absorption, then, from this point of view, is that it changes a structure like (115a) into one like (115b), i.e. a structure in which there is quantification into a question into one in which there is not.[59]

(115a) $[WH_1 [WH_2 [\dots t_1 \dots t_2 \dots]]]$
(115b) $[WH_{1,2} [\dots t_1 \dots t_2 \dots]]$

The absorption operation has been replaced with a theory that licenses WHs-*in-situ* if they can be functionally interpreted. Technically, this account ties the acceptability of multiple interrogation structures to the grammatical legitimacy of a certain kind of pronoun binding. This implies that such constructions will be illicit if either this binding cannot occur or if the pronominal binder does not have the semantic powers to generate a list. This section has tried to show that there are considerable empirical benefits to viewing things in this way, especially in a cross-linguistic context. The payoff for Minimalism is that this is accomplished without resorting to the antecedent government or any of its GB surrogates.[60]

5   Conclusion

This chapter has provided an analysis of superiority effects that ties their distribution rather tightly to structures with bound pronouns. Modifying a suggestion by Chierchia (1991) I have proposed that multiple interrogative constructions are subject to standard WCO conditions and that this is what underlies superiority effects. The analysis presupposes that WHs can be functionally, as well as individually, interpreted. Functionally interpreted WHs involve a bound pronoun that is interpreted much like E-type pronouns in Chierchia (1992). Binding this pronoun requires that WCO be respected. Given this apparatus, superiority effects can be assimilated to WCO. As noted, this treatment fits rather nicely with the Minimalist program, in particular with the assumption that WHs-*in-situ* are not moved at LF but are interpreted in some other fashion. The aim in this chapter has been to outline what this "other fashion" might look like.

8

Quantifier Scope

1 Introduction: Basic Assumptions

The last three chapters have concentrated on reanalyzing LF phenomena which GB theories account for via A'-movement and the ECP. The upshot of these efforts (if successful) is to significantly reduce the empirical underpinnings for LF adjunction processes in general and QR-like A'-movement rules in particular. It appears that anything that QR or WH-raising can do can be done as well, indeed better, using standard substitution operations and independently motivated processes of reconstruction. Bluntly put, empirically, the phenomena that most strongly motivate the A'-syntax characteristic of LF are reanalyzable without recourse to QR-like rules.

This is an intriguing theoretical result. For, as noted in chapter 4, it is hard to see how to motivate QR-like processes given Minimalist concerns.

QR-like rules are odd from this perspective for several reasons. First, QR is typically treated as an adjunction process. In most elaborated treatments (e.g. Aoun and Li 1993a, May 1985) QR adjoins a quantified phrase to any maximal projection. It is not at all clear, however, that "core" syntactic processes involve adjunction. For instance, the paradigmatic A'-operation is WH-movement. However, it is standardly assumed that WH-movement is a substitution rather than an adjunction operation though it is acknowledged that WHs have A'-landing sites. Chomsky (1993) has put the distinction between A and A'-positions central to various grammatical processes on a new theoretical footing. A-positions are characterized as L-related while A'-positions are not (Chomsky 1993: 28).[1] Spec CP is the primary non-L-related position. Thus, even though WH-movement is a substitution operation, WHs move to A'-positions. In effect, then, the A/A' distinction has been cleanly separated from the adjunction/substitution distinction. This leaves the obvious question of whether it is not just simpler (and hence desirable) to dispense with adjunction operations altogether, including QR.

There is a second problem with QR. It as unlikely that QR adjunction operations are morphologically driven. This is tacitly acknowledged theoretically. For example, both May (1985) and Aoun and Li (1993a) crucially allow QR to adjoin a quantified phrase to any XP. This lack of a specific target for the movement is what is expected if QR lacks a morphological trigger. It is useful to contrast QR in this regard with WH-movement. The latter is typically treated as morphologically driven and WHs are seen as having very specific landing sites; not just any adjoined position will do.[2] All of this does not mean to say that abstract morphological Q-features cannot be specifically invented for the purpose of accommodating QR. However, methodologically speaking, such features are too easy to postulate and go against the grain of Minimalist concerns. Thus, they should only be adopted if they can be given strong independent empirical motivation. This chapter argues that theories embodying QR to Spec Q positions are empirically inadequate if movement to Spec Q yields A'-chains. The aim is to eliminate all forms of LF A'-movement from UG. I argue that this is both theoretically desirable inasmuch as A'-operations are rather suspect given Minimalist assumptions and empirically desirable as well.

This is the agenda. The first item of business is to reanalyze quantifier scope phenomena in Minimalist terms without invoking any form of adjunction or A'-movement. QR effects comprise a major type of phenomenon standardly treated in terms of adjunction or A'-movement still left to be reanalyzed.[3] This chapter sets out an approach that treats relative quantifier scope as largely a property of A-chains. Several assumptions are required if this proposal is to work. The assumptions are intended to be compatible with Minimalist theory. Two are old hat. Three are freshly minted for present concerns.

First, and most importantly, I assume that only a single link in an A-chain is interpreted at the Conceptual–Intentional (CI) interface. Consequently, if an A-chain is multimembered, as most will be, it is necessary to delete all but one member. Further, A-chain deletion is not subject to the sort of Preference Principle Chomsky (1993) motivated for A'-chains. Rather, any member of an A-chain can be deleted and all but one must be.[4] This is reflected in (1).

(1)   At the CI interface an A-chain has at most one and at least one lexical link[5]

(1) plausibly derives from the Principle of Full Interpretation (PFI). The requirement that A-chains have at least one member is not problematic and must be part of any conceivable theory. The restriction that A-chains have one visible link at the CI interface is reducible to the PFI as follows. If all visible elements at an interface must be interpreted, then multimembered chains create problems for PFI unless it is assumed that the individual links of chains are not subject to CI interpretation. One way of assuring this is to simply stipulate that chains rather than their members are the proper objects of CI interpretation. A second (less stipulative) way of finessing the PFI is to adopt (1) which, for interpretive purposes, wipes out the distinction between a chain and the links that comprise it. This way, (1) can be seen as a way of operationalizing PFI in a world of extended chains.

The second required assumption is that relative quantifier scope is grammatically reflected at LF (after the requisite deletion) in terms of (asymmetric) c-command as in (2).

(2)   A quantified argument Q_1 takes scope over a quantified argument Q_2 iff Q_1 c-commands Q_2 (and Q_2 does not c-command Q_1).[6]

Third, I assume that something like Diesing's Mapping Principle holds of LF representations (Diesing 1992: 9, ex. 13). In particular, I assume that definites (d-linked presupposed DP/NPs) sit in positions outside the VP shell. In effect, I assume, with Diesing, that VP defines the nuclear scope of the proposition and that elements interpreted as definite or specific in her sense must be outside VP.[7] The practical effect of this is to force A-chains headed by "definites" to delete links inside the VP shell.[8]

(3)   A definite argument must be outside the VP shell at the CI interface

In addition, the following two standard Minimalist assumptions are required. (i) NPs in English begin in VP internal positions and move out of the VP shell to Spec Agr positions for case checking. In particular, objects move to Spec AgrO at LF and subjects to Spec AgrS before SPELL OUT. (ii) Movement is copying and deletion. Hence chains contain copies of the moved expression all but one of which is deleted due to (1).

With these assumptions, it is possible to provide a theory of quantifier scope without invoking QR, or so I argue.

2   Subject and Object Quantified NPs

Consider the following ambiguous sentences.[9]

(4)   Someone attended every seminar

After case checking has applied, (5) is the LF phrase marker for (4).[10]

(5)   [$_{AgrS}$ Someone [$_{TP}$ Tns [$_{AgrO}$ every seminar [$_{VP}$ someone [$_{VP}$ attended every seminar]]]]]

Deletion must now apply as there is a pair of two membered chains in this phrase marker. Given (1), we must delete one member of each chain. This results in the following possibilities.[11]

(6a)   [$_{AgrS}$ Someone [$_{TP}$ Tns [$_{AgrO}$ every seminar [$_{VP}$ (someone) [$_{VP}$ attended (every seminar)]]]]]
(6b)   [$_{AgrS}$ Someone [$_{TP}$ Tns [$_{AgrO}$ (every seminar) [$_{VP}$ (someone) [$_{VP}$ attended every seminar]]]]]
(6c)   [$_{AgrS}$ (Someone) [$_{TP}$ Tns [$_{AgrO}$ (every seminar) [$_{VP}$ someone [$_{VP}$ attended every seminar]]]]]
(6d)   [$_{AgrS}$ (Someone) [$_{TP}$ Tns [$_{AgrO}$ every seminar [$_{VP}$ someone [$_{VP}$ attended (every seminar)]]]]]

(6d) results in the interpretation in which the universally quantified *every seminar* has scope over the existential *someone*. In all the other structures, it has scope under the existential. (6b, c) cannot be interpreted at the CI interface if we adopt Diesing's Mapping Principle. Strong quantifiers like *every* are definite and so must be outside the VP shell after deletion, given (3). In short, (6a) and (6d) are the phrase markers underlying the two possible readings of (4).[12]

The present account has quantifier scope grammatically piggy backing on abstract A-movement required for case checking. The same logic should extend to overt A-movement which serves the same function. In fact, the same apparatus accounts for the ambiguities found in raising constructions in English. In (7) the sentence can be interpreted with either the universally or existentially quantified NP having wide scope.

(7)   Someone seemed to attend every class

The structure of the raising construction prior to LF deletion is (8a). The reading in which *someone* has scope within *every class* is provided in (8b).[13]

(8a)   [Someone seemed [someone to [every class [someone attend every class]]]]
(8b)   [(Someone) seemed [(someone) to [every class [someone attend (every class)]]]]

The non-ambiguity of the sentences in (9) also follows.[14]

(9a)   Someone persuaded John (PRO to attend every class]
(9b)   Someone hoped [PRO to recite every poem]
(9c)   Someone believes John to be attending every class

In each case, *someone* starts off from the internal position of the matrix VP and the universal quantifier begins from a position within the embedded VP. As such, no amount of deletion of A-chain links can get the matrix indefinite within the scope of the embedded universal. Hence these sentences are unambiguous with *someone* always enjoying scope over the *every* phrase.

Certain ECP data follow as well. Aoun and Hornstein (1985) observe the contrast between (10a) and (10b). The former can be interpreted with *someone* as inside the scope of *every Republican*. This interpretation is unavailable in (10b). It only has the reading in which *someone* has wide scope.

(10a)   Someone expected every Republican to win
(10b)   Someone expected every Republican would win

These facts follow from the fact that exceptional case marking involves movement of the embedded subject to the matrix Spec AgrO position. In embedded finite clauses, the embedded subject moves only as high as the embedded Spec AgrS. Prior to deletion the phrase markers are as follows.

(11a)   [$_{\text{AgrS}}$ Someone [$_{\text{AgrO}}$ every Republican [$_{\text{VP}}$ someone [expected [$_{\text{AgrS}}$ every Republican [$_{\text{VP}}$ every Republican to win]]]]]]
(11b)   [$_{\text{AgrS}}$ Someone [$_{\text{VP}}$ someone [expected [$_{\text{AgrS}}$ every Republican would [$_{\text{VP}}$ every Republican win]]]]]]

In (11a), the subject must move to the matrix Spec AgrO to get its case checked because the embedded clause is infinitival. This allows it to.take scope over the matrix VP. If the copy of *someone* is then deleted and all copies of *every Republican* but the highest are deleted, we get a phrase marker in which latter has scope over the former.

(12) [$_{AgrS}$ (Someone) [$_{AgrO}$ every Republican [$_{VP}$ someone [expected [$_{AgrS}$ (every Republican) [$_{VP}$ (every Republican) to win]]]]]]

An analogous structure cannot be obtained with (11) as the embedded subject never raises to the matrix Spec AgrO. It can have its case checked in the embedded case active Spec AgrS. Consequently, least effort prohibits it from raising any further. Thus, all the A-chain positions of *every Republican* are lower than those of *someone*. Hence the latter must scope over the former. In effect, we derive ECP effects without invoking the ECP. The Minimalist assumptions that movement is greedy and economical and that accusative case marking in ECM constructions involve raising to matrix Spec AgrO suffice to account for the data.[15]

Recall that a Generalized Binding theory accounts for the data in (9) and (10) by treating variables left by QR as anaphors (see chapter 2). Thus, the locality effects displayed are assimilated to those characteristic of anaphors and their restrictions under principle A of the BT. The present approach achieves the same result in a less encumbered way.[16] Scope is essentially a function of A-movement. Thus, it is not surprising that scope effects track principle A given that A-chains are known to respect this same locality restriction. In Minimalism, however, the restriction is recast in least effort terms with movement being a last resort requirement. This has the effect of lengthening the chain of the embedded subject in ECM structures and thereby allowing it the option of taking scope over the matrix subject.

There is a further very nice feature of this assimilation of quantifier scope to properties of A-chains; it explains why quantifier scope is largely clause-bounded.[17] May (1977) tried to derive this fact from subjacency. Aoun and Hornstein (1985) (and Hornstein 1984) argued that May's account was empirically inadequate. They replaced the subjacency account with a Generalized Binding approach which postulated that variables left by standard quantifiers were A'-anaphors. The clause-bounded scope of these quantifiers followed from a generalization of principle A of the BT. However, to derive this result, Aoun and Hornstein had to make some *ad hoc* assumptions, e.g. allowing Agr to be a SUBJECT for QNPs adjoined to IP. There is little independent evidence for this assumption. Nor did Aoun and Hornstein have a theoretical reason for classifying variables left by QR as A'-anaphors, i.e. similar to the variables left by *how* and *why* rather than those left by *who* and *what*. Semantically, it is more natural to think that *everyone* and *someone* should pattern with *who* and *what* as they all range over individuals. However, empirically, it is necessary to assume the other classification. The present analysis sets these difficulties aside. The clause boundedness of quantification is straightforwardly derived. Quantifier scope is clause-bounded in natural language because it is a function of

A-chains. As demonstrated above, this assumption suffices to derive all the locality effects that quantification is subject to.

3 Scope Restrictions

There exist interactions between binding and relative quantifier scope that can be accounted for in terms of the present approach. Consider some classic examples.[18]

(13a)   Someone played every piece of music you know
(13b)   Someone$_i$ played every piece of music he$_i$ knew

(13a) is ambiguous with either the existential or universal quantifier taking wide scope. In particular, there can be a different player per piece. This contrasts with (13b). Here there is at least one musician who played his entire repertoire. In particular, we cannot have a different musician per piece even if the entire repertoire is thereby played. In effect, *someone* must have wide scope if it binds a pronoun within the universally quantified phrase. This restriction on scope follows on the Minimalist theory sketched above. Consider the details.

Minimalism requires that all binding conditions be met at LF (recall: it is the only level with phrase-marker-like structure). In particular, a bound pronoun (i.e. a pronoun interpreted as a bound variable) must be c-commanded by the quantifier that determines its semantic value at LF. Quantifier scope too must be settled at LF. In sum, the LF phrase marker that interfaces with the CI system settles both which pronouns can be interpreted as bound and what scopes quantifiers enjoy. With this in mind consider the LF of (13b) prior to the deletion of "extraneous" chain members.

(14)   [$_{AgrS}$ Someone [$_{Tns}$ [$_{AgrO}$ [every piece of music he knew] [$_{VP}$ someone [$_{VP}$ played every piece of music he knew]]]]]

The deletion necessary to get the existential in the scope of the universal quantifier involves deleting *someone* in Spec AgrS and the universally quantified argument inside the VP shell. However, this prevents the pronoun inside the *every* relative clause from being interpreted as a pronoun bound by *someone* as *someone* does not c-command *his* after this deletion. For *he* to be interpreted as a bound pronoun, *someone* must be higher than the *every* phrase after deletion of copies. For example, we can delete the existential within the VP shell and retain the one in Spec AgrS. The LF phrase marker we get is (15).[19] Given (2), *someone* must be interpreted as taking scope over the *every* phrase, as desired.

(15)   [$_{AgrS}$ Someone$_i$ [$_{Tns}$ [$_{AgrO}$ [every piece of music he$_i$ knew] [$_{VP}$ (someone) [$_{VP}$ played (every piece of music he knew)]]]]][20]

Raising constructions offer another instance of this phenomenon.

(16) Every picture seemed to someone to be out of focus

(16) has a reading in which different people consider different pictures out of focus, i.e. *someone* is in the scope of *every picture*. Now consider the interpretation of (17).

(17) Every picture of his$_i$ dog seemed to someone$_i$ to be out of focus

There are two noteworthy facts. First, WCO effects are attenuated in this case. This is typical of raising constructions. (18) provides one more illustration of this fact.

(18) [His$_i$ mother]$_j$ is believed by every boy$_i$ t$_j$ to be a saint

The felicity of leftward pronoun binding follows if we assume that the LF of (18) after deletion is (19). In this structure the pronoun is in the scope of *every boy*.[21]

(19) [$_{AgrS}$ ([His$_i$ mother]) ($_{Tns}$ is [$_{AgrO}$ ([his mother]) believed by every boy$_i$ [$_{AgrS}$ [his mother] to be a saint]]]]

This allows for an explanation of the second interesting property of (17). As in the case of (14) the indefinite must be interpreted as having wide scope. The LF structure of (17) must have the bound pronoun lower in the tree than its antecedent. The only way of achieving this is to delete all copies of the A-chain headed by *every picture of his dog* higher than *someone*. This implies, however, that the universal quantifier will be in the scope of the existential phrase. A plausible LF representation is (20). The pronoun can be bound by *someone* and the universal phrase is within the scope of the existential one.

(20) [$_{AgrS}$ (Every picture of his$_i$ dog) [$_{VP}$ seemed to someone$_i$ [$_{AgrS}$ every picture of his dog to be out of focus]]]

The correlation observed here between binding and quantifier scope requires that the scope of quantification be determined via A-chains, at least in a Minimalist theory. The reason is the Minimalist Preference Principle for A'-expressions. It requires reconstruction of the "restrictor" to an A-position, all things being equal. Thus, if we assumed that quantifier scope were a function of an A'-movement rule like QR, then at LF (21) would be a perfectly well-formed structure in the standard theory (irrelevant structure and movements omitted).

(21) [$_{IP}$ Every$_i$ [$_{IP}$ some$_j$ [$_{IP}$ t$_j$ [$_{VP}$ [t$_j$ one] played [t$_i$ piece of music he knew]]]]]

In (21) *some* is in the scope of *every* and *he* is in the scope of *some*. In short, the correlation noted above is no longer accounted for. Thus, given Minimalist assumptions, the position that an A'-movement process like QR grammatically determines quantifier scope is empirically inadequate.[22]

A second feature of these examples is that they correlate quantifier scope with binding but divorce these effects from overt surface order. The correlation makes it difficult for any version of the BT that permits the binding principles to apply at several levels to handle these data. The fact that the correlation is not mirrored in overt syntax argues that it must be accounted for at a level more abstract than SS. Thus, the evidence points to a monostratal theory of binding with LF being the relevant level. We return to both these points more fully below.

There are other data that support an intimate relation between binding and quantifier scope. Aoun (1982) observed that in contrast to examples such as (22a) in which the *someone* can be interpreted as within the scope of the embedded universal quantifier, the same is not true for examples (22b, c).

(22a)   Someone seemed (to Bill) to be reviewing every report
(22b)   Someone$_i$ seemed to his$_i$ boss to be reviewing every report
(22c)   Someone$_i$ seemed to himself$_i$ to be reviewing every report

The lack of a narrow scope reading for *someone* in (17b, c) follows on the present account. Recall that binding principles in a Minimalist theory only hold at LF. To meet the indicated binding of (22b, c) requires a structure at LF such as (23a, b). In these cases, the lower copies of the A-chain headed by *someone* are deleted so that the LF phrase marker meets the indicated binding conditions. But given (2), this prevents a reading in which *someone* is in the scope of *every report*.

(23a)   [Someone$_i$ seemed to his$_i$ boss [(someone) to be [every report [(someone) reviewing (every report)]]]]
(23b)   [Someone$_i$ seemed to himself$_i$ [(someone) to be [every report [(someone) reviewing (every report)]]]]

These data support the Minimalist contention that LF is the only level at which grammatical conditions can be met. If binding conditions could be met indifferently at LF or SS (at SPELL OUT) or could be met throughout the history of the derivation (as proposed, for example, in Belletti and Rizzi 1981 and Lebeaux 1988, 1990) then the fact that binding restricts quantifier scope would not follow. In effect, these data provide a very direct argument for the assumption that binding conditions apply wherever quantifier scope is determined, i.e. at LF. This is precisely what the Minimalist program requires.[23]

The argument presented by the data in (22) can in fact be generalized to "simple" clauses. Consider the data in (24).

(24a)   Someone danced with every woman
(24b)   Someone reviewed every brief
(24c)   Someone$_i$ danced with every woman before he$_i$ left the party
(24d)   I got someone$_i$ to review every brief without PRO$_i$ leaving the office

(24a, b) are ambiguous. In particular, *someone* can have scope inside the universal quantifier. This is not the case with (24c, d). We can account for this on the standard assumption that adjuncts are adjoined to VP or higher.[24] Consider their structures at LF prior to deletion of extraneous A-chain links.

(25a) [$_{AgrS}$ Someone [$_{Tns}$ [$_{VP}$ [$_{VP}$ someone danced with every woman] [before he left the party]]]]

(25b) [$_{AgrS}$ Someone [$_{Tns}$ [$_{AgrO}$ every brief [$_{VP}$ [$_{VP}$ someone to review every brief] [without PRO leaving the office]]]]]

In order for the pronoun in (25a) and the PRO in (25b) to be properly bound at LF, they must be c-commanded by their antecedents. Thus, the only well-formed structures require deleting all copies of *someone* except the one in Spec AgrS.

(26a) [$_{AgrS}$ Someone$_i$ [$_{Tns}$ [$_{VP}$ [$_{VP}$ (someone) danced with every woman] [before he$_i$ left the party]]]]

(26b) [$_{AgrS}$ Someone$_i$ [$_{Tns}$ to [$_{AgrO}$ every brief [$_{VP}$ [$_{VP}$ (someone) reviewed (every brief)] [without PRO$_i$ leaving the office]]]]]

The phrase markers in (26) do not allow the universal quantified phrase to take scope over *someone*, as desired.

Note, in addition, that if an object binds a pronoun there is no effect on scope interactions.

(27) Someone questioned every suspect$_i$ before he$_i$ left

Someone can have either wide or narrow scope with respect to *every suspect* in (27). This is expected given that the object's binding a pronoun is licit in either of the LF structures in (28).[25]

(28a) [$_{AgrS}$ (Someone) [$_{AgrO}$ every suspect$_i$ [$_{VP}$ [$_{VP}$ someone questioned (every suspect$_i$) [before he$_i$ left]]]]]

(28b) [$_{AgrS}$ Someone [$_{AgrO}$ every suspect$_i$ [$_{VP}$ [$_{VP}$ (someone) questioned (every suspect$_i$) [before he$_i$ left]]]]]

Two points are of interest. First, if this is correct, then relative quantifier scope is a function of A-chains even in simple clauses. This eliminates SS theories of quantifier scope in which quantifiers in the same clause are treated as freely able to scope over one another. The most prominent and persuasive version of this approach is in Williams (1986). These data indicate that such a position cannot be maintained since binding and quantifier scope interact in complex ways even in simple clauses. Second, this account requires abandoning the Larson (1988) view of adjuncts as VP internal syntactic complements. The account above crucially hinges on treating adjuncts as adjoined to VP or higher. In fact, the account requires structurally distinguishing adjuncts from complements in a pre-Larsonian way. The reason is that the interaction between binding and quantifier scope recedes in the case of true complements. Consider (29).

(29a)   Someone$_i$ asked every attendant if he$_i$ could park near the gate
(29b)   John got someone/at least one patron$_i$ to tell every critic that he$_i$ hated the play

These sentences are able to support interpretations in which the existential phrase has scope inside the universal, in contrast to those in (24c, d). Their LF phrase markers are provided in (30).

(30a)   [$_{AgrS}$ (Someone) [$_{AgrO}$ every attendant [$_{VP}$ someone$_i$ asked (every attendant) if he$_i$ could park near the gate]]]
(30b)   John got [$_{AgrS}$ (someone/at least one patron) to [$_{AgrO}$ every critic [$_{VP}$ someone/at least one patron$_i$ tell (every critic) that he$_i$ hated the play]]]

In sum, if a target pronoun is in a complement rather than an adjunct, binding can properly occur from VP internal position. As such, the narrow scope reading for the existential remains a licit possibility.

The above accounts rely on the Minimalist claim that all grammatical conditions hold exclusively at LF. The data in (22) show that binding and quantifier scope must be determined at the same level. The data in (24) and (29) indicate that this level cannot be SS for at SS (actually at SPELL OUT) quantified subjects are invariably in Spec AgrS and so should always enjoy widest scope, contrary to fact. Therefore, the only empirically viable level at which conditions can be stated is LF. As this is the only alternative a Minimalist theory allows, these cases provide support for the program as a whole.[26]

The examples above display interactions between quantifier scope and binding. Abstractly, the argument can be characterized as follows: certain instances of binding require the antecedent to be in Spec AgrS at LF and being in this position endows the antecedent with wide scope. The general moral is that any requirement that prohibits an expression in Spec AgrS from "reconstructing" to VP internal position also requires that the subject be interpreted as having scope over all other quantified phrases. Let us consider ACD constructions once again for another illustration of this generalization; one that does not involve pronominal or anaphoric binding.

(31)   John ate everything that Bill did

In (31), *Bill* has the same theta role that *John* does. This follows if we assume the theory in chapter 5. We end up with the structure in (32) at LF.

(32)   John$_i$ [$_{AgrO}$ [everything that Bill did [e]]$_j$ [$_{VP}$ t$_i$ ate t$_j$]]

With the VP copied into *[e]*, the relative clause has the structure in (33). This allows *Bill* to link to t$_i$ and thereby get its proper theta role.[27]

(33)   Everything that Bill$_i$ did [$_{VP}$ t$_i$ ate t$_j$]]

Now, if the interpretation of elided VPs is determined at LF as all other interpretive processes are (and as assumed in chapter 5), then, strictly speaking, (32) is the structure at LF *after* deletion of A-links has taken place. In other words, a more correct way of describing what is required in ACD structures is that the VP internal subject of the matrix clause must be outside the VP shell or the subject in the relative clause will not receive a theta role. As this is in violation of the theta criterion, the ACD structure as a whole will be ungrammatical. However, this implies that in ACD structures, the phrase in Spec AgrS cannot reconstruct. Thus, we expect the following: in ACD structures, the subject must have wide scope. Consider the following contrast.

(34a)   I got someone/at least one other person to interview every candidate that I interviewed

(34b)   I got someone/at least one other person to interview every candidate that I did

(34a) has a reading in which the existentially quantified subject is interpreted as within the scope of the universal object. This option disappears in (34b). The subject here must be interpreted as having wide scope.

The reason for this contrast should now be evident. In (34b) the matrix subject must be outside the VP shell after deletion for otherwise the copied VP could not provide the subject of the relative clause with a theta role. In (34a), in contrast, the relative clause subject does not get its theta role from a copied verb but from the actual verb present in the structure. Put another way, the structure of the matrix VP in ACD structures determines that of the embedded VP as the latter is a copy of the former. This is not so when there is not an elided VP to interpret. The LF structure of (34b) prior to deletion and VP copying is provided in (35a). (35b), which deletes *someone*^{2}, provides a VP with all the powers necessary for a well-formed LF structure after interpreting the elided VP. Deleting *someone*^{2} fails to provide *I* with a theta role after the elided VP is filled in.

(35a)   I got [$_{AgrS}$ someone^1 [$_{Tns}$ to [$_{AgrO}$ [every candidate that I did e] [$_{VP}$ someone^2 interview [every candidate that I did e]]]]]

(35b)   I got [$_{AgrS}$ someone^1 [$_{Tns}$ to [$_{AgrO}$ [every candidate that I did e] [$_{VP}$ (someone^2) interview ([every candidate that I did e])]]]]

(35c)   I got [$_{AgrS}$ (someone^1) [$_{Tns}$ to [$_{AgrO}$ [every candidate that I did e] [$_{VP}$ someone^2 interview ([every candidate that I did e])]]]]

Observe one important point about the above account. It cannot be replicated if scope is a function of QR. The difficulty is that there is no way of preventing the relative clause from QRing over the subject.[28] A QR approach to quantifier scope is mute concerning the correlation observed here because this correlation crucially hinges on taking quantifier scope to be a function of A-movement. To put this another way, on the present analysis, any grammatical condition that forces subjects to be outside the VP shell at LF will force them to have wide scope. ACD structures are just another instance of this generalization. However, as movement out of the VP shell is not what determines scope on a QR theory, it fails to address why subjects have wide scope in ACD constructions.[29]

4 Chinese Quantifiers

The quantifier scope facts characteristic of English in which SS objects can take scope over SS subjects fails to be attested in the East Asian languages. In chapter 2, I reviewed Aoun and Li's (1993a) Generalized Binding approach to this parametric difference. This section shows how to account for the noted differences between English and Chinese assuming the present theory and the parametric difference exploited by Aoun and Li to differentiate the two types of languages. In particular, I assume, as they do, that English subjects begin in VP internal position and are A-moved to Spec AgrS while Chinese subjects are not moved to Spec AgrS from VP internal position. Elements in Spec AgrS are directly generated there. For the purposes at hand it is irrelevant why this difference obtains. All that is required is that English subjects head A-chains with feet inside the VP while this is not so in Chinese (see Aoun and Li 1993a: 22ff).

Before getting theoretical, let us recap the basic empirical facts as reviewed in chapter 3. First, in active Chinese sentences SS subjects have scope over SS non-subjects. This contrasts with English, in which scope ambiguities obtain. Second, in Chinese passive sentences, scope ambiguities reappear. In particular, SS subjects can be interpreted as having scope within SS non-subjects. Third of all, raising constructions do not display the ambiguities attested in English sentences like (22a), repeated here.

(22a)   Someone seemed (to Bill) to be reviewing every report

Consider now how to derive these results given the above theory of quantifier scope and the proviso that English subjects begin within the VP and A-move to Spec AgrS while Chinese subjects are directly generated in Spec AgrS. The LF structure of a simple clause in the two languages before deletion is provided in (36) and (37).

(36)   [$_{AgrS}$ Subject [$_{Tns}$ [$_{AgrO}$ object [$_{VP}$ subject V object]]]]
(37)   [$_{AgrS}$ Subject [$_{Tns}$ [$_{AgrO}$ object [$_{VP}$ V object]]]]

The way that subjects come to be interpreted as in the scope of objects in English is by deleting the expression in Spec AgrS and retaining the expression in Spec AgrO.

(38)   [$_{AgrS}$ (Subject) [$_{Tns}$ [$_{AgrO}$ object [$_{VP}$ subject V (object)]]]]

However, this option is not available in Chinese because there is no copy of the subject in VP internal position, as (37) makes clear. The only issue is which link in the object A-chain is deleted. Whichever option is exercised, however, the subject continues to c-command the remnant and so is interpreted as having wider scope. This explains why sentences such as (39) are unambiguous (Aoun and Li 1989: 146, n. 8 ex. (v)).

(39) Yaoshi liangge nuren du guo meiben shu...
      If   two   women read ASP every   book
      "If two women read every book..."

Chinese passives differ in an important respect. They necessarily have traces in VP internal position. (40) is the structure of a Chinese passive.[30] (41) is a possible structure after deletion.[31]

(40) [$_{AgrS}$ Object [$_{AgrO}$ object [$_{VP}$ bei-subject [$_{VP}$ V object]]]]
(41) [$_{AgrS}$ (Object) [$_{AgrO}$ (object) [$_{VP}$ bei-subject [$_{VP}$ V object]]]]

In (41), the SS passivized object has reconstructed into VP internal position from whence it moved. This allows *subject* to c-command *object* and thereby take scope over it. This allows (42) to be scopally ambiguous.

(42) Yaoshi liangge xiansuo bei meigeren zhaodao
      If   two   clues   by everyone found
      "If two clues were found by everyone..."

Raising constructions essentially reduce to simple active sentences on this account. They are expected to be unambiguous. Aoun and Li (1993a: 27) report that they are. At LF a raising sentence has the structure (43). There is no set of deletions which will allow a copy of the subject to be within the scope of a copy of the object because the subject is generated outside the embedded VP in Chinese.[32]

(43) [$_{AgrS}$ Subject [$_{AgrO}$ [$_{VP}$ V [$_{AgrS}$ subject [$_{AgrO}$ object [$_{VP}$ V object]]]]]]

5 Weak Cross Over, Superiority, and Polarity

The previous sections have tied quantifier scope together with the structure of A-chains. As noted in chapters 6 and 7, A-movement also attenuates WCO effects. Thus, it should be possible to attenuate WCO effects even in "standard" cases under the right conditions. In particular, if there is a pronoun within an indefinite subject, it should be possible for an "SS" quantifier in object position to bind this pronoun. With this in mind, consider the contrast in (44).

(44a)   A picture of his$_i$ mother adorned/graced everybody$_i$'s desk
(44b)   *The/every picture of his$_i$ mother adorned/graced everybody$_i$'s desk

At LF (44a) has the structure (45) prior to deletion.

(45)   [$_{AgrS}$ [A picture of his mother] [$_{AgrO}$ everybody's desk [$_{VP}$ [a picture of his mother] graced everybody's desk]]]

If we delete the copy in Spec AgrS and the VP internal copy of the object, we meet the conditions for pronoun binding.[33]

(46)   [$_{AgrS}$ ([A picture of his mother]) [$_{AgrO}$ everybody's desk [$_{VP}$ [a picture of his mother] graced (everybody's desk)]]]

In (46), *everybody* is in a position to bind *his* without violating WCO.
   This contrasts with (44b) because in the latter case, we must delete the copy of the subject in Spec VP given principle (3) above. Recall that definites must be outside the VP shell at LF. Thus, the only acceptable representation of (44b) is (47).

(47)   [$_{AgrS}$ [The picture of his mother] [$_{AgrO}$ everybody's desk [$_{VP}$ ([the picture of his mother]) graced (everybody's desk)]]]

With the copy of the subject inside the VP obligatorily deleted, it is impossible for the object to bind the pronoun inside the subject without violating WCO. This accounts for the unacceptability of (44b).[34,35]
   Corroboration for this analysis comes from considering the following data.[36] Superiority contrasts exist in sentences like (48).

(48a)   What did a friend of who say to Bill
(48b)   *What did each/the/every friend of who say to Bill

At LF, (48a) can have the structure (49) after deletion.

(49)   [What$_i$ +WH [(a friend of who) [(what) [a friend of who say (what) to Bill]]]]

This LF can be interpreted as (50).

(50)   [What$_i$ +WH [(a friend of who) [vbl$_i$ [[a friend of [pro$_i$ N']] say t$_i$ to Bill]]]]

Thus, the implicit pronoun in the functionally interpreted *who* is licitly bound by the variable in Spec AgrO.[37]
   (48b) does not have an analogous structure. Because the functionally interpreted WH is within a definite NP, at LF the copy of this expression must be in Spec AgrS. This forbids the implicit pronoun from being bound as it is to the left of the indicated variable and the binding would lead to a WCO violation.[38]

(51) [What$_i$ +WH [the friend of [pro$_i$ N'] [vbl$_i$ [(the friend of who) say t$_i$ to Bill]]]]]

The account of these data rely on assumption (3) above which allows definites and indefinites to occupy different positions with respect to the VP. Consider another consequence of this assumption.

Linebarger (1980, 1987) argues that negative polarity items (NPIs) have to be in the immediate scope of negation at LF to be licit.

(52) No "logical" expression can intervene between an NPI and the negation that licenses it at LF[39]

What counts as a "logical" expression is somewhat unclear, but it suffices for our purposes if quantifiers such as *every, some, many, several*, etc. count as such. Assume that "logical" expressions are just expressions that have scope semantically. In light of this consider the following contrasts.

(53a) I don't believe that John bought anything
(53b) *I don't believe that everyone bought anything
(53c) I don't believe that many people bought anything

The acceptability of (53a) follows from (52) on the reading of "logical" in which names are scopeless. The LF of (53a) after deletion is (54) and nothing of the relevant type intervenes between *anything* and the matrix neg.[40]

(54) I Neg believe [that [$_{AgrS}$ John [$_{AgrO}$ anything [$_{VP}$ (John) bought (anything)]]]]

(52) also accounts for (53b) on the assumption that its LF is (55). Being definite, *everyone* cannot be inside VP after deletion. Hence it is the foot of the chain that must delete. But this deletion places *everyone* between *Neg* and *anything*, contravening (52).

(55) I Neg believe [that [$_{AgrS}$ everyone [$_{AgrO}$ anything [$_{VP}$ (everyone) bought (anything)]]]]

(53c) has the LF (56). In this case, *many*'s being indefinite allows the copy inside VP to remain after deletion, allowing (52) to be respected.

(56) I Neg believe [that [$_{AgrS}$ (many people) [$_{AgrO}$ anything [$_{VP}$ many people bought (anything)]]]]

Evidence in support of this repackaging of Linebarger's original analysis of NPIs comes from considering embedded questions with NPIs.

(57) I don't know what anybody read

(57) is perfectly acceptable. Note, however, that it can only be given a pair–list reading. In other words, it cannot be interpreted as saying that I am ignorant of the single book read by all. If one tries to force this reading by altering the form of the WH unacceptability results.

(58)   *I don't know which single book anybody read

The pair–list version of (57) has the LF (59a), the individual reading has the LF (59b). The latter violates (52). The operator *what* intervenes between *Neg* and *anybody*. This plausibly accounts for the unacceptability of (57) on this reading (and (58)).

(59a)   I Neg know [(what) [$_{AgrS}$ anybody$_i$ [$_{AgrO}$ what (=pro$_i$ N') [$_{VP}$ (anybody) read (what)]]]]
(59b)   I Neg know [what$_i$ [$_{AgrS}$ anybody [$_{ArgO}$ (what=vbl$_i$) [$_{VP}$ (anybody) read (what)]]]]

Consider, now, one more set of data involving negation and scope. Aoun and Li (1993a: 165, ex. 65) note that scope ambiguities are eliminated in sentences with negation.

(60a)   Someone loves everyone
(60b)   Someone doesn't love everyone

They observe that *everyone* can take scope over *someone* in (60a) but not in (60b).[41] Their analysis of the restriction in terms of the MBR relies on postulating a NegP phrase with an operator in its Spec.[42] This neg operator prevents the embedded *everyone* from taking scope over the subject *someone*.[43]

(61)   [$_{AgrS}$ Someone [$_{NegP}$ Neg-Op [$_{Neg'}$ Neg [$_{TP}$ . . . [$_{VP}$ . . . everyone . . .]]]]]

The MBR prevents QR-ing *everyone* above the NegP as the postulated operator in Spec NegP would be a closer potential antecedent for *everyone*'s variable than the adjoined *everyone*.

The details of this analysis are inconsistent with the assumptions made here as it requires a QR analysis of quantifier scope. However, there is a Minimalist alternative we can adopt given the assumption that (61) is the underlying structure of a negated clause. Aoun and Li make two crucial assumptions. First, that NegPs have filled Spec positions. Second, that this position is an A'-position. The first assumption is unproblematic and can be directly adopted here. The second assumption is less clear. However, as it probably does not matter to the account outlined below what the A / A'-status of Spec NegP is, let us put the matter aside.[44]

I have argued above that quantifier scope is a function of A-chains. The unavailable scope reading in (60b) requires raising the subject *someone* from Spec VP to Spec AgrS and then deleting all copies of the chain except the one in Spec VP. However, if we assume that negated sentences have the structure in

(61) it is illicit to move from Spec VP to Spec AgrS. The reason is that the intervening filled Spec Negp will block this movement.[45] The structure prior to movement from Spec VP is (62).

(62) [$_{AgrS}$ [$_{NegP}$ Neg-Op [$_{Neg'}$ Neg [$_{TP}$ Tns [$_{AgrO}$ [$_{VP}$ someone loves everyone]]]]]]

The movement takes place prior to SPELL OUT. The intervening filled Spec NegP is a closer potential landing site than is Spec AgrS. Consequently, the movement is blocked by the MLC (Chomsky 1993, 1994).

However, if the movement is blocked, then how does Spec AgrS become filled? The only option is to base generate it there and assume that it binds a PRO form in Spec VP. The only licit structure of (60b) at LF is (63).[46]

(63) [$_{AgrS}$ Someone$_i$ [$_{NegP}$ Neg-Op [$_{Neg'}$ Neg [$_{TP}$ Tns [$_{AgrO}$ everyone [$_{VP}$ PRO$_i$ loves (everyone)]]]]]]

Interestingly, (63) does not allow *everyone* to take scope over *someone* in (63) anymore than it can in (64).

(64) Someone$_i$ hated [PRO$_i$ to kiss everyone]

The proposed structure also implies that acceptable sentential idioms should degrade in acceptability when negated. The interpretation of sentential idioms, it has long been observed, are preserved under NP movement but not control.

(65a) The cat seemed to get his tongue
(65b) The shit is likely to hit the fan
(65c) *I persuaded the cat to get his tongue
(65d) *The shit promised to hit the fan

The proposed phrase structure for negated sentences implies that sentential idioms involving negation should not support idiomatic readings as they necessarily involve binding a PRO. The contrasts below support this prediction. The examples in (66) and (67) permit the embedded clause to be idiomatically interpreted. The embedded clauses in (68) are quite degraded with the idiomatic interpretations. They are certainly less felicitous than the examples in (66) and (67), as expected if subjects in negated sentences are base generated in Spec AgrS and control a PRO in Spec VP.[47]

(66a) I heard that the cat got his tongue before his big speech
(66b) I believe that my goose is cooked
(66c) I told Bill that the shit could hit the fan after my speech
(66d) I expected the roof to fall in after my speech
(66e) I believe that birds of a feather flock together
(66f) I think that a stitch in time saves nine
(67a) I didn't hear that the cat got his tongue before his big speech

(67b)   I don't believe that my goose is cooked
(67c)   I didn't tell Bill that the shit could hit the fan after my speech
(67d)   I didn't expect the roof to fall in after my speech
(67e)   I don't believe that birds of a feather flock together
(67f)   I don't think that a stitch in time saves nine
(68a)   *I heard that the cat didn't get his tongue before his big speech
(68b)   *I believe that my goose is not cooked
(68c)   *I told Bill that the shit couldn't hit the fan after my speech
(68d)   *I expected the roof not to fall in after my speech
(68e)   *I believe that birds of a feather don't flock together
(68f)   *I think that a stitch in time doesn't save nine

In sum, the MLC plus the assumption that NegPs have obligatory (filled) Specs prevents subjects from being moved to Spec AgrS via movement. Consequently, A-chains spanning the Spec AgrS position and Spec VP cannot exist in such constructions. As subjects can only be in the scope of objects if such chains obtain, this implies that negation blocks subjects from being in the scope of objects. As idioms are licensed by movement but not control this also accounts for the contrasts in (66)–(68).[48]

These assumptions also imply that quantified objects will be interpreted as within the scope of neg.[49]

(69)   John didn't eat everything

(69) does not have the reading (70).

(70)   Everything is such that John didn't eat it

Rather, the universally quantified object is interpreted as obligatorily within the scope of negation.

(71)   It is not the case that John ate everything

This follows on the assumption that NegPs hang above TP and the scope of quantifiers is determined by their A-chains. At LF, Neg will c-command every link of the chain headed by *everything*. Consequently, objects cannot take scope over negation, as appears to be empirically the case.[50]

(72)   [$_{AgrS}$ John$_i$ [$_{NegP}$ Neg-Op [$_{Neg'}$ Neg [$_{TP}$ Tns [$_{AgrO}$ everything [$_{VP}$ PRO$_i$ eat (every-thing)]]]]]]

The current proposal has one further side benefit. It explains why NPIs are not licensed in subject positions. This was a problem for Linebarger (1987) and subsequent analyses of NPIs which assume that NPIs must be licensed at LF. Why is it that Neg cannot scope over an NPI subject at LF? We can account for this as follows. Assume that NPIs must meet a condition like (73).[51]

(73) NPIs must be asymmetrically c-commanded by a Neg at LF

Given (73), an NPI in Spec AgrS at SPELL OUT cannot be licensed at LF as it cannot come to be asymmetrically c-commanded by the Neg in any way.[52] In effect, this proposal enables us to state the licensing condition on NPIs entirely at LF, as Minimalism requires.[53,54]

6 Some Further Benefits of Eliminating QR

The above sections have argued that it is possible to handle quantifier scope phenomena without resorting to A'-operations and that it is empirically advantageous to do so. This section points out that there are also theory internal reasons for adopting the present proposal beyond the general ones mooted at the outset.

A central theme (perhaps *the* central theme) of the Minimalist program is that the only levels which exist (and therefore the only ones at which grammatical conditions can be stated) are those that interface with the modules responsible for the sound and meaning properties sentences have. The reasoning goes as follows. Observationally, it is impossible to deny that sentences are pairings of sound and meaning. Conceptually, therefore, any theory would have to postulate some function that maps sentences into sound and meaning properties. A conceptually minimal theory should postulate no more than what is absolutely required. Hence, Minimalism assumes that all conditions must be stated at LF.

Laudable as these ambitions might be, empirically, as we have seen, there are several obvious obstacles to their realization. Two particularly recalcitrant cases noted by Chomsky and Lasnik (1991) are the Subjacency Condition and parasitic gap constructions. The problem for Minimalism is that both seem best stated at a level akin to SS. In other words, empirically, both subjacency effects and the distribution of licit parasitic gaps are believed to be best treated as SS facts. Theoretically, however, Minimalism forbids SS generalizations as it denies that an SS level exists. So, one central item on the Minimalist agenda is to show (i) that these two conditions can be stated at LF and (ii) that they should be stated at LF. As Chomsky (1993) observed in discussing the BT, it is an argument in favor of a Minimalist theory on conceptual grounds if (i) can be established. The reason is that Minimalist theories are methodologically the most preferable so any empirical "tie" results in a "win" for Minimalism. If one can also show that empirical advantage accrues to a theory assuming that all conditions are at LF, so much the better. A nice feature of abandoning QR and other A'-operations at LF is that it permits the first goal to be straightforwardly realized with respect to subjacency and both goals with respect to parasitic gap effects.[55]

Consider subjacency first. As the details of the theory do not matter for the points made here, assume the earliest account of subjacency which prohibits movement across more than a single bounding node, AgrS and DP/NP being the bounding nodes (Chomsky 1973). This is not a condition statable at LF in GB-style theories for one principal reason. These theories require that WHs-*in-situ* raise at LF. Furthermore, this raising is unbounded (see chapter 3). Thus, LF phrase markers do not obey subjacency in GB-style theories so the condition cannot be stated at this level.

This is not a problem for the present theory. WH-raising has been eliminated. What this means is that LF has no A'-dependencies at LF that are not already evident at SPELL OUT. In other words, LF operations as construed here do not add to the stock of WH-chains so, as far as these are concerned, one can just as well license them via subjacency at LF as at "SS". The same is true for all other A'-operations. The present theory eliminates all A'-movement at LF. WH-raising is reanalyzed and QR has been reanalyzed. There are no other A'-operations. Thus, LF operations cannot present an obstacle to stating subjacency as an LF condition.

The same holds true for A-chains. A-movement is considerably more restricted than A'-movement. In particular, A-chain links must be closer to one another than subjacency requires. In fact, any adjacent pair of A-chain links must be in the same minimal domain given the principles that underlie movement in a Minimalist framework. Thus, even the pervasive A-movement at LF practiced here cannot lead to subjacency violations at LF that are not also otherwise prohibited by some other principles of the theory.

The conclusion for subjacency, then, is that A'-movement does not exist at LF and A-movement is irrelevant to it. Therefore, the only chains that obtain at LF that bear on subjacency are those formed prior to SPELL OUT. As these do not disappear at LF, we can state subjacency at this level with no empirical prejudice.[56]

Consider now parasitic gap constructions. The contrasts in (74) constitute the evidence that they are licensed at SS.[57]

(74a)   What$_i$ did John review rg$_i$ after [PRO reading pg$_i$]
(74b)   *Who reviewed what$_i$ after [PRO reading pg$_i$]
(74c)   This book$_i$, John reviewed rg$_i$ after [PRO reading pg$_i$]
(74d)   *John reviewed every book$_i$ after [PRO reading pg$_i$]

Assuming the standard description of parasitic gap constructions (viz. that parasitic gaps are licensed by variables, i.e. A'-bound traces), (74b, d) are problems for any theory that requires LF licensing *if LF A'-movement exists*. On a standard GB-style account, the structures of the unacceptable (74b, d) are (75a, b) at LF.

(75a)   [What$_i$ who$_j$ [t$_j$ reviewed t$_i$ after [PRO$_j$ reading t$_i$]]]
(75b)   [Every book$_i$ [John reviewed t$_i$ after [PRO reading t$_i$]]]

The problem with LF licensing of parasitic gaps is evident when one compares (74a) and (75a) and (74c) and (75b). It is hard to see how to rule out the unacceptable (74b, d) *at LF* without excluding the acceptable (74a, c) given the essential structural identity of the two pairs at this level. Hence, if one assumes that A'-movement exists at LF, some way must be found to license parasitic gap constructions at some prior level. The problem is that in a Minimalist theory no such prior level exists.

The problem of licensing parasitic gaps at LF almost disappears once A'-movement is eliminated from the grammar. I say "almost" because the issue still arises as to what the correct description of parasitic gap licensing is. We return to this below. Note for now, however, that without LF A'-operations, there is no difference between LF and "SS" with regard to A'-chains. Hence the structural differences between the good and bad sentences in (74) observable at SPELL OUT, continue to be evident at LF. Hence, it is empirically costless to transfer the licensing condition on parasitic gaps to LF and thereby meet the Minimalist requirement that all grammatical conditions be stated there.

Recall that an empirical draw methodologically favors a Minimalist theory. However, in this case, we can do better and show that the conditions on parasitic gaps cannot be stated at a level like S-structure.[58] Before seeing this it is necessary to consider how to grammatically analyze parasitic gap constructions.

There are two basic approaches to these constructions. Chomsky (1982) licenses parasitic gaps via the A'-binder of the real gap at SS. The details of how this is done are not relevant for current concerns. What is crucial is the idea that parasitic gaps are licensed iff they are A'-bound at SS. Chomsky (1986a) licenses parasitic gaps via the real gap rather than its A'-binder. This theory postulates a chain composition procedure at SS that links a 0-operator A'-chain whose tail is the parasitic gap with the real gap. The 0-operator is postulated to accommodate subjacency effects that parasitic gap constructions are subject to (see Chomsky (1986a) for details). However, the requirement that the chain of the parasitic gap compose with the real gap rather than with the WH which A'-binds it, is driven by theory internal locality conditions characteristic of the *Barriers* theory. Other options exist. One might adopt the hypothesis that PGs are formed via 0-operator movement and still hold that the ultimate antecedent of the parasitic gap is the WH in the matrix Spec CP. This amounts to the proposal that chain composition is between the 0-operator and the WH in Spec CP rather than between the 0-operator and the real gap. This hybrid position has empirical advantages and I adopt it here.[59]

Consider the following data.

(76a)   What did everyone review

(76b)   What did everyone$_i$ review rg before I$_i$ read pg

(76a) is ambiguous. It can have a pair–list reading or an individual reading. This contrasts with (76b) which only has an individual reading. In other words, it fails to have a pair–list reading. The assumptions that we made account for this fact. The structure at LF prior to deletion is (77).

(77)   [$_{CP}$ What$_j$ [$_{AgrS}$ everyone [$_{AgrO}$ what$_j$ [$_{VP}$ everyone review what$_j$] [before [0$_k$ [I read t$_k$]]]]]

The parasitic gap t_k must be licensed. If the ultimate antecedent is the A'-binder of the real gap, then the only acceptable deletions are those in (78). I represent chain composition by identifying the index k with j.

(78) [$_{CP}$ What$_j$ [$_{AgrS}$ everyone [$_{AgrO}$ (what$_j$) [$_{VP}$ (everyone) review (what$_j$)] [before [0_k=j [I read t_k=j]]]]]

Observe that this representation leads to the non-functional individual interpretation of *what*. The representation in which *what* is functionally interpreted has *what* "reconstructed" to its A-position (79). This configuration does not suffice to license the parasitic gap.

(79) [(What$_j$) [everyone [what$_j$ [(everyone) review (what$_j$)] [before [0_k=j [I read t_k=j]]]]]

In sum, given the assumption that parasitic gaps are ultimately licensed by the A'-binder of the real gap, we can derive the interpretive properties of (76). A question remains, however: why can the parasitic gap not be licensed by the real gap? A plausible answer amounts to a revamped version of the one given in Chomsky (1982). Assume that chain composition respects subjacency, i.e. the 0-operator must be subjacent to the element it links to, as in Chomsky (1987).[60] Assume, further, that subjacency requires c-command. This, in effect, adopts the symmetric definition of subjacency in Chomsky (1981) (80a), rather than the asymmetric one in Chomsky (1986a) in terms of exclusion (80b).

(80a) A is subjacent to B iff there is at most one bounding node (barrier) that dominates B but does not dominate A[61]
(80b) A is subjacent to B iff there is at most one barrier (bounding node) that includes B but not A

If we assume, last of all, that the parasitic gap cannot be c-commanded by the real gap (this is plausibly a principle C effect as Chomsky (1982) argued)[62] the only possible avenue for chain composition involves the 0-operator and the WH in Spec CP. This suffices to derive the conclusions above.[63]

Other constructions display similar effects, though the judgements are more subtle than in the contrast shown in (76). For example, superiority effects reappear in multiple *which* constructions when parasitic gap licensing is required.[64]

(81) I wonder which woman which person congratulated (*before I met)

The only licit LF for this structure requires "reconstructing" *which woman* so that it can be functionally interpreted.[65] However, this will prevent the parasitic gap from being licensed via chain composition. The "reconstructed" WH is not subjacent to 0_k as it does not c-command the adjunct. This prevents chain composition from occurring. The relevant LF phrase marker is (82).

(82) I wonder [(which woman$_j$) [which person$_i$ [[pro$_i$ woman$_j$] [(which person) congratulated (which woman)]] [before [0_k [I met t_k]]]

Another instance of the same interaction involves NPI licensing. The LF structure of (83a) is (83b).

(83a) I don't remember who anyone kissed (*before I met)
(83b) I don't remember [(who$_j$) [anyone$_i$ [[pro$_i$ person$_j$] [(anyone) congratu-lated (who)]] [before [0$_k$ [I met t$_k$]]]]

To allow the NPI *anyone* to meet the Immediate Scope Condition (52) above, *who* must reconstruct. However, to license the parasitic gap, it must remain in Spec CP. As these contradictory requirements cannot both be met, the result-ing structure is ungrammatical.[66]

To sum up. I have shown that both subjacency effects and parasitic gap constructions can be accommodated at LF in a Minimalist framework if we assume that there is no A'-movement at LF. As there is no option but to state conditions at LF in a Minimalist theory, this provides a very strong theory internal reason for eliminating QR and WH-raising rules from the grammar from a Minimalistic perspective. Furthermore, there are empirical reasons for locating the licensing of parasitic gaps at LF. We have seen that WH "recon-struction" effects interact with this process in ways that cannot be handled in a theory which treats parasitic gaps as licensed at a level prior to LF.[67] To the degree that parasitic gaps are licensed by chain composition subject to subjacency, this requires subjacency to be an LF condition as well. Thus, both empirical and theory internal reasons favor the elimination of LF A'-movement processes from universal grammar.

7 Two Residual Cases

The above has concentrated on the properties of quantified subjects and objects. In this section, I consider two other kinds of quantified expressions and sug-gest how they can be integrated into the present system. The cases of note are objects of prepositions and double object constructions. Consider them in turn.

7.1 *Prepositional Objects*

The main proposal concerning PPs involves three assumptions, each of which were adopted in earlier chapters. First, I assume that most PPs can be gener-ated as adjuncts in the sense of being adjoinable to or generable outside of the VP shell (see chapter 5). Second, I assume that objects of PPs move to Spec positions outside the PP as in (84). I assume that this structure is motivated by the Minimalist commitment to a unified theory of case in terms of Spec–head agreement (see chapter 6).

(84) [$_{Agr}$ Object$_i$ [P$_j$+Agr [$_{pp}$ t$_j$ t$_i$]]]

Third, I assume that c-command is defined in terms of lexical projections. Functional projections do not really count (see chapter 6).[68]

(85)   A c-commands B iff every lexical projection that dominates A dominates
       B

   With these three assumptions, we can handle the standard quantifier inter-actions between objects of prepositions and other quantified expressions. Consider some examples for illustration.

(86a)   Someone sang Stardust with every couple
(86b)   John sang something for every couple
(86c)   Someone left the auditorium after every aria
(86d)   John left something on every seat

The sentences in (86) have a reading in which the *every* phrase is interpreted as having wide scope. Consider the LFs of (86a, b). Given the assumptions above, these sentences can have the following LFs. Observe that the PPs are adjoined to VP.

(87a) $[_{AgrS}$ (Someone) $[_{TP}$ past $[_{AgrO}$ Stardust $[_{VP}$ $[_{VP}$ someone sang (Stardust)]
        $[_{Agr}$ every couple [with+Agr $[_{PP}$ (with) (every couple)]]]]]]]
(87b) $[_{AgrS}$ John $[_{TP}$ past $[_{AgrO}$ (something) $[_{VP}$ $[_{VP}$ John sang something] $[_{Agr}$
        everyone [for+Agr $[_{PP}$ (for) (everyone)]]]]]]]

   In these configurations, the object of the preposition has scope over expres-sions within the VP shell. Being adjoined to VP, the VP does not dominate it. Furthermore, from Spec Agr position, TP is the first lexical category to domi-nate the *every* phrase. In (87a, b) the *some* phrase is within the VP shell and so is dominated by VP.[69] This prevents it from c-commanding the *every* phrase.
   We can also reduplicate the binding and scope interactions discussed in section 3. Contrast (86c) with (88).

(88)   Someone$_i$ left the room after every one of his$_i$ arias

Whereas (86c) allows the *every* phrase within the PP to enjoy scope over the subject, this is not so in (88). *Someone* is interpreted as having wide scope here. This follows from the assumption that the adjunct is outside the VP shell and so the subject must be in Spec AgrS if it is to bind the pronoun within the prepositional object. However, when in this position, it must take scope over the *every* phrase.

(89) $[_{AgrS}$ Someone $[_{TP}$ past $[_{AgrO}$ the room $[_{VP}$ $[_{VP}$ (someone) left (the room)] $[_{Agr}$
        everyone of his arias $[_{PP}$ (after) (every one of his arias)]]]]]]]

   We can also reduplicate the neg scope facts. (90a) cannot have the *every* phrase scoping over the existential subject, in contrast with (90b).

(90a)   Someone didn't dance with everyone
(90b)   Someone danced with everyone

This, once again, follows on the assumption that subjects in negative sentences must be base generated in Spec AgrS and bind PROs in Spec VP. The structure of the PP does not matter here given that nothing takes scope over an element in Spec AgrS at LF.

(91)   [Someone$_i$ [$_{NegP}$ Op [Neg [$_{Tns}$ [$_{VP}$ [$_{VP}$ PRO$_i$ dance] with everyone]]]]]

Note that in the case of objects, it should be possible to have the object of the preposition scope over the object even in a negative sentence. The NegP does not affect movement of the object to Spec AgrO. (92a) is a well-formed LF of (92a) in which *everyone* can take scope over *something*.

(92a)   John didn't sing something for everyone
(92b)   [$_{Agrs}$ John [$_{NegP}$ Op [Neg [$_{TP}$ past [$_{AgrO}$ (something) [$_{VP}$ [$_{VP}$ PRO sang something] [$_{Agr}$ everyone [for+Agr [$_{PP}$ (for) (everyone)]]]]]]]]]

7.2   Double Object Constructions (DOCs)

DOCs have intricate quantifier scope properties. They present an interesting challenge for the current approach and I would like to touch on them here. An empirical curiosity with DOCs is that the scopes of the indirect and direct objects are fixed in English.[70]

(93a)   John assigned someone every problem
(93b)   John threw someone every football

The examples in (93) must be interpreted with *someone* having scope over the *every* phrase. This contrasts with the semantically similar sentences in (94) where this scope restriction is not evident.

(94a)   John assigned a problem to every student
(94b)   John threw a football to every student

Examples like (94) have just been discussed. The puzzle is to account for the fact that in constructions like (90) scope is reflected in the surface order of the constituents.

Before presenting a possible solution, consider some other features of these construction. First, they are problematic as regards case marking. DOCs contain two nominal expressions whose case features must be checked. In standard GB-style theories several *ad hoc* case mechanisms have been proposed to accommodate the "extra" NP. For example, prior theories proposed that the second NP is case-marked/checked by the V' rather than the V (e.g. Aoun and Li 1993a), or the indirect object is licensed by "incorporating" into the V (Aoun and Li 1989, 1993a, Larson 1988, Stowell 1981).

Second, the scope facts are more complicated than the examples in (93) indicate. The second NP cannot take scope over subjects, but the first object can.

(95a)   Someone gave everyone his report card
(95b)   Someone gave Bill everything

Third, either object can be the target of a deleted VP in an ACD construction.

(96a)   John gave everyone that I did a dollar
(96b)   John gave Frank everything that I did

Fourth, NPIs are only licensed in the first object position in multiply quantified constructions.

(97a)   John didn't give anyone every book
(97b)   *John didn't give everyone any book

Fifth, as Larson (1988) observed, NPIs in the second object can be licensed by a neg in the first object but not vice versa.

(98a)   John gave nobody anything
(98b)   *John gave anyone nothing

Sixth, it is possible to bind into the second object from the first but not vice versa.

(99a)   John showed the men each other's wives
(99b)   *John showed each other's wives the men

These data pull in somewhat different directions. The ACD facts in (96) suggest that either NP can scope out of the VP. The problem is then why can they not scope over one another. Except for the ACD data, however, the examples consistently point to the conclusion that the first object must scope over the second.

I would like to suggest that the key to a solution lies with the peculiar case facts noted above. The present approach to quantifier scope ties case tightly with scope via their common link to the structure of A-chains. The crucial question then is how case is checked in DOCs.

The theory suggests the following: (i) case checking in this instance, as in all others, is a Spec–head process; (ii) the case of both NPs must be checked by the verb that heads the DOC. If we further permit only a single AgrP between VP and TP, then the only permissible analysis will involve a structure like (100).[71]

(100) $[\ldots [_{IP} \ldots [_{AgrO} [_{NP} \ NP_1 \ [NP_2]] \ _i \ [V+AgrO \ [_{VP} \ldots V \ t_i]]]]]$

In (100) both NP_1 and NP_2 are in the checking domain of the V+AgrO as the first is adjoined to the second. This allows the V+AgrO to "see" both NPs and have both in its checking domain. This is clearly a positive result for it allows the V+AgrO to check the case of both NPs, as required in cases such as this.[72]

The reader will no doubt have noticed that the proposed structure looks quite familiar. It essentially adopts Kayne's (1984) small clause theory for DOCs. The adjunction structure for the small clause follows the analysis in Koopman and Sportiche (1991) and Stowell (1983). What is interesting is that these traditional analyses fit in well with the Minimalist machinery needed to solve the case-checking problem that DOCs present. Furthermore, this theory allows us to handle the other data points noted above given a few technical elaborations.[73]

Consider first the scope facts. NP_1 must scope over NP_2. Relative scope is a function of deletion of elements in an A-chain. The links in the A-chain in DOCs are highlighted in (101).

(101) $[\ldots [_{AgrO} [_{NP} \text{NP}_1 [\text{NP}_2]] [\text{V+AgrO} [_{VP} \ldots \text{V} [_{NP} \text{NP}_1 [\text{NP}_2]]]]]]]$

The crucial thing to observe is that the entire small clause is the link in the A-chain. Assume that deletion of A-links must be exhaustive, i.e. it is impermissible to partially delete links in deriving the LF phrase marker. This means that either the small clause in Spec AgrO deletes or the postverbal one deletes. However, whichever one deletes, the relative scope of the two NPs is the same. In other words, A-movement for case checking cannot affect the relative scope positions of these NPs because they move in tandem. Furthermore, they must move in tandem for there is no other way to check their cases. Thus, once the peculiar case properties of these constructions are addressed, the Minimalist apparatus appears to provide only one way of meeting the case-checking requirements. Further, this avenue has the pleasant property that movement cannot expand the range of potential scope relations the two constituents can have.

What of the other properties? They largely reduce to the properties of small clauses. In these small clauses NP_1 c-commands NP_2. It is adjoined to NP_2 and so is not dominated by it.[74] This means that NP_1 must be interpreted as having scope over NP_2 as the data in (93) indicate is the case.

The same structure permits the NPI licensing in (98a) but not (98b). In the former case, at LF the NPI is in the immediate scope of a neg, *nobody*. This is not so in the case of (98b).

The same story accounts for the lack of NPI licensing in (97b). At LF, NP_1 necessarily intervenes between the NPI and the Neg as it is the small clause subject. This leads to a violation of the immediate scope condition and hence unacceptability. For obvious reasons, (97a) presents no analogous difficulties.

One empirically interesting feature of this analysis is that having an indefinite between the NPI and the neg will not ameliorate the immediate scope condition violation in contrast to the cases discussed above (example (53c)). The reason is that the indefinite must lie between the neg and the NPI in DOCs. This accounts for the unacceptability of (102b).

(102a)   John didn't think that many people said anything
(102b)   *John didn't send many people anything

   The other two facts follow as well. Recall from chapter 5 that ACDs are licit
in English if the constituent with the elided VP can be moved out from under
the VP that "interprets" it. However, the analysis proposed here moves both
NPs out of the VP for case reasons. Consequently, the conditions for ACD
licensing are met. Note that we have here achieved this result without assuming that there is more than a single Agr projection, in contrast to chapter 5 and
Hornstein (1994). This is a good result, for it is quite unclear how the quantifier facts above could be duplicated were the NPs in DOCs capable of moving to different Spec Agr positions for case checking.
   The reciprocal binding data in (99) follow as well. On the assumption that
the first object asymmetrically c-commands the second, the only licit binding
configuration at LF is the one underlying (99a).
   The final datum follows from the fact that the small clause subject NP_1 is adjoined to NP_2. This adjunction permits it to have scope out of the small clause,
in contrast to NP_2. Consequently, (95a) can have the following LF structure.

(103)   [(Someone) [[everyone [his report card]] [someone gave ([everyone [his
        report card]])]]]

In this LF configuration, *everyone* c-commands *someone* and can take scope over
it. Note one more interesting fact. With this reading, *his* cannot have *someone*
as its antecedent. If *someone* is the antecedent, *someone* must have scope over
everyone. This is another instance of the scope and binding interactions discussed above. A clearer instance of this effect is provided in the contrasts in
(104). (104a) must be construed with the indefinite having wide scope, in
contrast with (104b).

(104a)   A girl$_i$ gave everyone her$_i$ picture
(104b)   A girl gave everyone$_i$ his$_i$ picture

   In sum, taken together Minimalist assumptions place rather tight requirements on an acceptable analysis of DOCs. I have suggested that this analysis
involves a small clause approach to DOCs along the lines first suggested by
Kayne (1984) and Stowell (1983). This approach, coupled with the A-chain
theory of case and quantifier scope, functions to handle all the relevant data
without recourse to QR or multiple Spec Agr positions.[75]

8   Conclusion

In this chapter, I argued for the elimination of A'-movement operations from
LF. I argued that this elimination is desirable from various perspectives.

Empirically, it allows a theory that tightly ties together quantifier scope effects with binding, ACD structures, scope of negation and more.

Theoretically, it fits nicely with Minimalist assumptions. At a pedestrian level, it parries the need for a proliferation of Q-features that a QR-based theory would otherwise need to fit comfortably with Minimalist assumptions. There is little morphological evidence for such features and within Minimalist terms this is enough to suggest they likely do not exist.

Moreover, such features would not actually get the right results. Assume that they existed. The real problem is that Specs of such Q-features, like Spec CP, would be non-L-involved. Hence these positions would be A'-positions. Much of the data above indicates that A'-chains are the wrong vehicle for the statement of quantifier scope.[76] Thus, what is wrong with QR is not simply that it involves adjunction, a problem that postulating Q-features might solve, but that it creates A'-chains, a problem Q-features cannot solve.

In fact, one might go further. The thrust of this chapter has been to show that there is a very intimate connection between A-chains, case, and quantifier scope. In particular, a quantified expression's scope potential is a function of the chain it is a part of. QNPs in English can have scopes different than their SS c-command domain because they must move for case reasons at LF. We have also seen that in the East Asian languages, NP movement in the guise of passivization allows for scope ambiguities that are otherwise unavailable. As a final illustration, consider one last instance of A-movement, the case of clause internal scrambling (CIS) in languages like Japanese.

Chapter 5 reviewed evidence that CIS in Japanese had all of the signature properties of A-movement. If relative quantifier scope piggybacks on A-chain structure (as proposed here), then we would expect CIS to function like passivization in licensing scope ambiguities that unscrambled active sentences do not support. This in fact is the case. It is well known (see Hoji 1985 for example) that in languages like Japanese two scrambled QNPs exhibit scope ambiguities despite the lack of ambiguity in the unscrambled cases. Compare the minimal pair in (105).

(105a) Dareka-ga   daremo-o   semeta
        Someone-NOM everyone-ACC blamed
(105b) Dareka-o daremo-ga semeta

(105a) exhibits the unscrambled order. The nominative subject *dareka-ga* must take scope over the accusative object *daremo-o*. (105b) shows the scrambled constituent order. Here, the clause initial scrambled object *dareka-o* can be interpreted as either within the scope of the subject *daremo-ga* or as having wide scope. The first reading of (105b) is the interesting one. It shows that CIS functions like a passive in attenuating the requirement that SS order determine relative quantifier scope in Japanese. The theory outlined above predicts that CIS should have this effect precisely because it is an instance of A-movement. The structure of (105b) prior to deletion of chain copies is (106) (only relevant structure indicated).

(106)   [$_{IP}$ Dareka-o [$_{IP}$ daremo-ga$_i$ [$_{AgrOP}$ dareka-o [$_{VP}$ PRO$_i$ semeta dareka-o]

If the highest *dareka-o* copy deletes, then the scrambled object is interpreted with scope under the subject *daremo-ga*. If it is retained, the object is interpreted as scoping over the subject. Just as in the case of passivization, A-movement impacts scope interpretation in precisely the way the theory predicts it should.

There is one last consequence of tying scope to A-chains. Elements that have no LF chains (and given the Minimalist theory outlined here this means A-chains) will have the scope that they appear to have overtly. A consequence of this is that most items must stay put. Adverbs will have the scope they have at SPELL OUT given that, so far as we know, they do not need to be case checked at LF. Neg also stays put and has the scope domain at LF that it has at SPELL OUT. And so too for most other "logical" expressions that grammarians have been far too tempted to covertly move all over the place at LF.[77]

Last of all, this chapter has argued that case theory, the BT, subjacency, parasitic gap licensing, negative polarity licensing, quantifier scope, ACD licensing, and neg scope must all be exclusively treated as due to LF conditions. No other assumption can account for the observed restraints that the requirements of each of these constructions put on the others. There is only one theory I know of that ties all these elements together and has it as a key conceptual requirement that they be satisfied exclusively at LF. That is why, if this reanalysis of QR is correct, it constitutes a powerful argument for the Minimalist program.[78]

9
Revisiting the Minimalist Program

Minimalism is the new kid on the theoretical block. As a result, the broad principles that characterize the program are less articulated than are the GB principles that have been elaborated for over a decade. The aim of chapters 4 through 8 has been to elaborate the details of the Minimalist program in ways that fit with its leading ideas and also increase its empirical reach. This journey from programmatic outlines to theoretical detail has resulted in a version of Minimalism different in various technical respects from Chomsky (1993) and very different in theoretical conception from the GB accounts of LF phenomena reviewed in chapters 2 and 3. Concretely, I have argued that the theoretical direction urged in Chomsky (1993) requires a wholesale revision of previous GB approaches to LF if consistently pursued. For example, the leading ideas in Chomsky (1993) sit ill with operations like QR or WH-raising and so, I have argued, LF is not the locus of any A'-movement operations. But without any A'-syntax to constrain, the ECP (in particular the various versions of antecedent government) loses its explanatory grip at LF. This is theoretically important. For it means that virtually all of the work on LF must be rethought given that virtually every analysis of an LF phenomenon has exploited the ECP in some form. I consider the proposals in chapters 5–8 as a first step in this direction.

In this concluding chapter, I would like to step back from the details of the analyses presented above to consider them from a more general perspective. In particular, I would like to consider (i) how the Minimalist reorientation affects what are the central research questions; (ii) how some of the distinctions required to make the details work out in the analyses above fit into an overall Minimalist picture; and (iii) what the particular analyses tell us about grammatical properties in general. Addressing these larger questions will inevitably require further articulation of the Minimalist program. As God (and the devil) is always in the details, this should grant us a better appreciation of the program's strengths and possible failings.

1 The Status of LF

The shift to a Minimalist theory brings with it an important methodological reorientation. In GB theories, the legitimacy of SS is unproblematic. The weight of argument is carried by those who think that a further LF level is required in addition to SS. In chapters 2 and 3, I reviewed the principal arguments in favor of postulating LF given GB assumptions. However one evaluates the force of these arguments, they lose much of their point in a Minimalist theory. This is not because the reasoning is unsound or the data are suspect. Rather, given a Minimalist perspective, such arguments are not necessary. The existence of LF is a given within the Minimalist framework. Hence, the burden of proof shifts to those who deny its existence. Given this theoretical starting point, the suspect level is SS, a level without theory-internal motivation within the Minimalist program.

The unavailability of SS makes the task of explaining away apparent SS effects a central item on the Minimalist research agenda. Chomsky (1993) shows how apparent SS binding effects can be handled at LF and how thus relocating the BT is empirically desirable. Other instances of this argument form are provided above. Chapter 8 argues that it is possible to relocate the subjacency condition to LF and handle parasitic gap effects there if one dispenses with LF A'-movement operations. Furthermore, this is not only possible (and so methodologically preferred given Minimalism) but it is also empirically advantageous. In fact, the argument mooted in chapter 8 can be generalized with interesting effect.

The formal observation made in chapter 8 amounts to this. If LF A'-operations are eliminated, then it is possible to state locality conditions on links in A'-chains as easily at LF as at SS.[1] However, what does the elimination of LF A'-movement mean? From a Minimalist perspective, it means that the unmarked case of movement is A-movement, i.e. movement to L-involved positions. In other words, without overt evidence to the contrary, the child assumes that all movement is A-movement. This means that A'-movement is only possible in case it is overtly signalled. In Minimalist terms, this means that it is licensed by strong morphological features which require that the movement be overt. Another way of making the same point is that all A'-movement should be driven by strong features which must be checked by SPELL OUT. Thus, I here crucially reject the possibility that A'-movement is licensed by weak features. In fact, I propose to go further. I suggest that we think of (at least some) strong features quite differently from the way they are described in Chomsky (1993).

Chomsky (1993) treats weak and strong features as fundamentally the same at LF, the only difference being that strong features come with additional phonological requirements that must be met. Thus, both strong and weak features have the same checking requirements so far as LF is concerned. But, in addition, strong features have phonological requirements that are checked before SPELL OUT. Chapter 5 noted that this way of viewing matters would imply that English verbs raise to AgrS at LF. However, LF V-raising to AgrS in English should lead to a regress problem at LF in English ACD constructions similar to the one seen in Spanish, Greek, and Japanese where the V-raising is overt. In other words, this predicts that ACDs should be prohibited in English just as they are in Spanish, contrary to fact. To accommodate this linguistic variation, chapter 5 proposed that verbs only raise as far as AgrO at

LF and that further raising is driven by morphological requirements that are not reflected universally at LF. Thus, *some* strong features are grammar specific and do not show up in the LF of every grammar. This permits overt V-raising to AgrS in Spanish before SPELL OUT without requiring it in English at LF.

With this in mind, consider the strong features that drive A'-movement. I propose that these too are strong language-specific features. This is a Minimalist way of saying that LF has no A'-movement operations. The grammatical inclusion of A'-operations requires the existence of strong features which are grammar specific. This is just to say that A'-operations are grammatically marked processes. It is very natural that grammar-specific options should coincide with morphologically strong features which make their presence felt overtly at PF. It also makes a contribution to solving some residual SS problems for Minimalism noted in Chomsky and Lasnik (1991).

To begin with, the position adopted here gives a first installment on a theory of strong features. An underspecified part of the Minimalist program is what constitutes a strong feature. The present proposal links A'-movement with strong feature checking. It ties these two grammatical properties very tightly together in that A'-movement is only possible if done before SPELL OUT. Another way of making the same point is that weak non-L-involved features do not exist. Thus, LF A'-movement is prohibited. The thrust of the discussion in chapter 8 on subjacency and parasitic gaps was to empirically and methodologically motivate this conclusion. A way to integrate this prohibition into Minimalism is by only licensing A'-movement before SPELL OUT as a by-product of strong feature checking.

This suggestion has other pleasant properties. It is an improvement over the proposals in Chomsky (1993) and Chomsky and Lasnik (1991). In the former, Chomsky proposes that +WH-features are universally strong. Chomsky and Lasnik suggest further that mood features are generally strong. However, even if correct, this fails to cover the host of other attested strong features. For example, Tanaka (1993) shows that focus (*sika*-constructions) and cleft (*koso*-) constructions in Japanese have all the marks of overt movement operations. They display the same overt movement characteristics that Watanabe (1991) and Aoun and Li (1993a) show are operative in WH-constructions. In Minimalist terms, this indicates that focus and cleft constructions in Japanese involve strong features to which operators move before SPELL OUT. However, neither focus nor clefts have much to do with mood.[2] However, both constructions are kinds of A'-movement, i.e. movement to non-L-involved specifier positions. As such, they will pattern with WH-morphemes on the present proposal.

Furthermore, the interconnection of A'-movement with strong features accounts for another SS effect observed in Chomsky and Lasnik (1991). They observe that even in languages with apparent WH-*in-situ* for questions, relative clauses have overt gaps. This can be accommodated in a Minimalist theory by stipulating that relative clauses that form open sentences via operator movement to Spec CP must move prior to SPELL OUT to satisfy a strong +PRED feature in C^0. However, given the story above, a more principled account is possible. Open sentences have the form in (1). Consequently, they *must* be formed by overt movement, i.e. via the checking of a strong feature before SPELL OUT.

(1)   ... [Op$_i$ [... vbl$_i$ ...]]

The reason for this is that LF A'-movement does not exist so the structure apparent in (1) is simply not derivable at LF. Thus, given that sentential predicates (i.e. sentences that function adjectivally) have the structure of an open sentence in which an operator A'-binds a variable then the only way of grammatically deriving this configuration at LF is to move overtly to Spec CP prior to SPELL OUT. This is just another way of saying that relative clauses have strong features in C^0 that must be checked.

Observe that this story cannot be told if we allow weak features to support A'-movement at LF. If such weak features are available, there is no way to prevent predication structures from forming at LF. However, if we assume that A'-movement is banned in the unmarked case (i.e. from LF) then we can derive the pre-SPELL OUT movement of relative clause operators from more general considerations and we need not assume that "predication must be established at S-structure" (Chomsky and Lasnik 1991). This is a good result given that this predication condition looks like another suspect SS condition that a Minimalist theory has no way of stating.[3]

2   Chains and their Properties

Minimalism recognizes (at least) three kinds of chains; X^0-chains, A-chains and A'-chains. The reanalyses above rely on this tripartite division and adopt the "reconstruction" conditions in (1) to govern the deletion of chain links at LF.

(2a)   In an X^0-chain, the head of the chain does not delete
(2b)   In an A-chain, any link can delete
(2c)   In an A'-chain, deletion is subject to the Preference Principle, i.e. all things being equal, delete contentful expressions from A'-position

These various assumptions are crucial to the results attained. (2c) is central to relocating the BT to LF, as argued in Chomsky (1993). (2a) is instrumental in accounting for the cross-linguistic availability of ACD constructions. Chapter 5 argues for a correlation between the height to which a verb overtly moves and the possibility of licensing ACDs via movement to Spec AgrO at LF. To derive this correlation, the heads of X^0-chains must be preserved under LF deletion. In other words, as regards X^0-chains, lower links are deleted and upper links retained. This derives the observed correlation as follows. If the verb moves beyond AgrO overtly, copying the XP headed by the verb into the elided VP gap results in an infinite interpretive regress (see chapter 5 for details). One more step is needed to make this account of the observed correlation fully adequate, however. We need to explain why heads are retained and tails deleted in X^0-chains.

This lacuna becomes more glaring when (2a) – the condition on deletion of links in head movement chains – is compared with (2b) – the principle for deleting A-links. Chapter 8 crucially assumes that *any* link in an A-chain can freely delete. This assumption is key to providing an account of quantifier scope in terms of A-chains.

So, given this typology of chains and the varying requirements on chain-link deletion, how are we to understand these different conditions?

Consider, first, the Preference Principle for A'-chains. Chomsky (1993) interprets this as a preference for interpreting the restrictor of a quantifier in A-position. Another way of making this point is that UG prefers the syntactic format of unrestricted quantification. Why this should be so is unclear, however.[4]

There is another way of thinking about the Preference Principle that seems more natural. There is a preference for interpreting contentful material in A-positions. This interpretation of the principle fits well with the proposed analyses in the above chapters. The thrust of these proposals is that quantifiers generally exercise their semantic powers from A-positions. Thus, by "reconstructing" to A-positions, WHs are structurally behaving like other quantifiers at LF, seeking to be interpreted in A-positions. In sum, the Preference Principle proposed in Chomsky (1993) makes sense when considered against the grammatical representation of quantification in chapter 8.[5] What is "preferred" is that WH-operators act like other quantified elements at LF, all things being equal.

Consider now the distinctive deletion requirements in head movement (X^0-) chains and (NP) A-movement chains. There are several structural differences between these two types of chains within Minimalism. The crucial one for present concerns is that head chains are formed through successive adjunctions while A-chains are formed through successive substitutions. This difference is important. Multiple adjunctions result in *several* distinct chains. Successive substitution, in contrast, serves to extend a *single* chain. Consider the details.

A verb that raises from VP to AgrS first adjoins to AgrO, the V+AgrO then raises and adjoins to T^0, finally V+AgrO+T^0 raise and adjoin to AgrS. In Minimalist terms, these adjunctions create three different chains resulting in three different (local) domains for movement. This property of head chains is crucial to the Minimalist program as it serves to define the notion of minimal movement which in turn lies at the heart of the least effort accounts of A-chain formation. The three chains formed via successive head adjunction are displayed in (3). What is crucial for present purposes is that V+AgrO+T+AgrS is not part of the same chain as V+AgrO or V. Rather each adjunction chain has only two links: (V+AgrO, V), (V+AgrO+T, V+AgrO), and (V+AgrO+T+AgrS, V+AgrO+T).

(3)

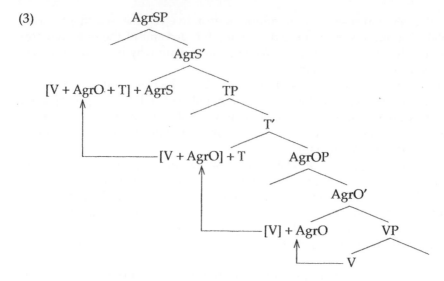

The multiple chains that result from adjunction operations contrast with the single "extended" chain that results from successive substitution. All the copies of *John* are part of the same chain in (4).

(4a)   John is likely to be arrested
(4b)   [John is likely [John to be [John [arrested John]]]]

Let us now consider how to exploit this structural difference between head chains and A-chains to derive the deletion principles in (2a) and (2b). First, recall that movement resolves into the operations of copying and deletion. Recall as well that lexical items are inserted in the course of a derivation with all their morphological features and that these features must be checked in the course of the derivation for the derivation to converge. Thus, a verb V that raises to AgrS has the structure in (5) when inserted into the derivation from the lexicon. The morphological features in (5) get checked in the course of the derivation.

(5)   [V, AgrS, T, AgrO]

Consider now what happens when a verb moves. It leaves a copy behind and this copy has all the morphological features of the element moved.[6] The full structure of a V to AgrS raising construction is (6).[7]

(6)

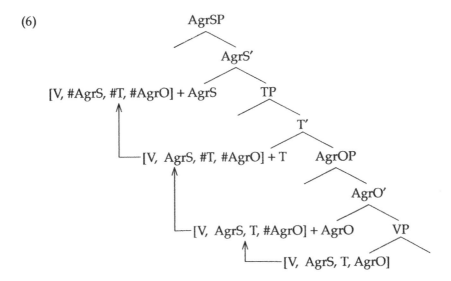

Consider now the feature properties of (6). Observe that only the topmost V is one in which all the morphological features of V have been checked. If we assume that a form with unchecked features causes the derivation to crash at the CI interface, as assumed in Chomsky (1993), then all but the top copy must delete for the derivation to converge. I will slightly refine these observations in a moment, but note that by considering the details of copying and deletion, we have essentially derived the requirement that head chains delete all copies but the head.

A slight amendment is required, however. This becomes clear when A-chains are considered. Like head chains, the elements moved are inserted with all of their morphological baggage. These features must also be checked in the course of the derivation. Assume for simplicity that only case features are relevant to the present discussion.[8] The A-chain structure of a simple transitive clause at LF after all A-movement to case positions has occurred is provided in (7).

(7) [[NP, #Nom] . . . [NP, #Acc] [[NP, Nom] V [NP, Acc]]]

If we adopt the simple approach to deletion broached in the discussion about V-chains, the structure in (7) would only converge at LF if the tails of the two A-chains were deleted. This, however, would undermine the analysis of quantifier scope in chapter 8. Let me remind the reader that the analysis of quantifier scope in terms of A-chains relies on being able to delete *any* link in a chain, not just the bottom links. In particular, it must be possible to delete the head of the Nom-chain in (7) and converge with (8).

(8) [([NP, #Nom]) . . . [NP, #Acc] [[NP, Nom] V ([NP, Acc])]]

One way to essentially keep the structures in (6) (that block ACD interpretation if the verb raises to AgrS) and allow in the required deletions in (8) (which permit an indefinite subject to be interpreted as within the scope of a universal object) I propose the All For One Principle (AFOP) (9) that exploits the adjunction versus substitution properties of head and A-chains.

(9)   *The All for One Principle*: Every link in a chain meets the morphological conditions satisfied by any link in a chain

What (9) is intended to mean is that all links within the same chain are morphologically on a par. Thus, for example, if two expressions are in the same chain and the head is in a position to check a feature, then the copy in the tail of this chain is also considered to have checked this feature. The effect of (9) as it applies to (8) is that every copy of an A-chain will be morphologically legitimate just in case every feature of the originally inserted expression has been checked somewhere. Thus, the copy of the moved *[NP, Nom]* in Spec VP has its Nom feature checked in virtue of the fact that the head of this chain has had it checked in Spec AgrS. Just as important, the effect of (9) as it applies to (6) is that only the topmost chain meets all the conditions and so the only legitimate acceptable deletions will be of links in this chain. In particular, if one deletes the upper copies and preserves the one inside AgrOP or VP the derivation crashes. Given (9), the only copies that have all of their features checked if the V has moved all the way to AgrS are the ones in AgrS and T. Note, however, that both these nodes dominate Spec AgrO and so any attempt to copy TP or AgrSP into the elided VP after deletion will result in regress. This is just the result desired.[9]

In sum, given (9) and careful consideration of the details of lexical insertion, movement, feature checking, and chain formation within a Minimalist framework, it is possible to derive the required "reconstruction" properties of A-chains and V-chains.

Before proceeding, let us stop to consider two related features of the above account. First, it treats chains rather than the links that comprise them as the domains for morphological checking. In effect, chains meet morphological requirements and their links meet them by being parts of chains that meet them. Second, the proposal relies on the assumption that features are checked in the course of the derivation. Thus, what gets copied on each successive movement is the verbal complex with whatever features have been checked on the previous move.

To see the impact of these two aspects of the argument let us consider replacing (9) with a harmony or uniformity principle that says that all the links in a chain are featurally identical and assume that # is a feature.

(10)   All links in a chain are identical

Thus, all links in a chain have the same feature matrix and the same set of checked features. (10) will not get us what we require from V-chains. The problem with (10) is that it implies that all the copies resulting from V-movement are featurally identical and so the distinction between A-movement and head movement crucial to the above story collapses. The reason is that any two adjacent chains will have one link that is a member of both chains. Thus in (11) chains (i) and (ii) have the element in T in common and the chains (ii) and (iii) have the element in AgrO in common.

(11)

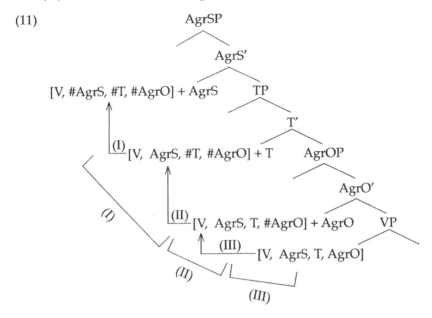

But by (10) this means that because the links in the first chain are featurally identical and those in the second chain are as well that every link in both chains has the same features. Thus, all the links in chains (i) and (ii) must be featurally identical and so too the links in (ii) and (iii). But by transitivity, this means that all the links in all the chains must be featurally identical.

The upshot of this is that either # is not a feature subject to a uniformity requirement or one must abandon (10). Either option suggests that the well-formedness conditions on V-chains must be stated derivationally for it seems that the #-property is not one transmitted across links in a chain (which can have different #-features) though it is crucial to determining the well-formedness of any link in a chain (which is licit just in case it is in a chain where some link has all the features #-ed). If this is correct, we have an argument to the effect that V-chains must be viewed as derivational objects whose grammatical properties cannot be accounted for by output conditions on them.

Furthermore, the reason for this is relatively clear. In the course of V-raising, the set of objects change though no new elements are inserted. The fact that the derivational history of an expression can change its featural structure and that these changes contribute to its well-formedness are precisely the sorts of factors that output conditions cannot handle.

Note, incidentally, that this particular derivational aspect of V-chains is not mirrored in A or A'-chains. A and A'-movement, being instances of substitution, extend chains. Thus nothing is lost by imposing a uniformity condition on these links.[10] Their properties can be stated without prejudice even if we assume that all the links are identical. This is not surprising given that substitution in fact leaves all links in a common chain. However, this should not be taken to imply that A and A'-chains can be viewed indifferently from either a derivational or representational perspective. Given how deletion operates on chains to yield the final LF object, only a derivational perspective on these chains is actually viable. This is the topic of the next section.

3   Derivational Constraints on Chains

The last section ended with a discussion of head chains and their derivational properties. What about A and A'-chains? Are the restrictions that they display a function of how they are put together, i.e. derivationally, or what they ultimately look like at LF, i.e. representationally? This sort of question has repeatedly arisen within GB theories. To date, no position has gained general acceptance though it is likely that a plurality of GBers have a representationalist bias.[11] Given Minimalist assumptions, the question can be asked anew, but this time the answer is considerably more definitive: given the sorts of chains required in previous chapters, conditions on representations, if stated as conditions on LF phrase markers, will not account for the locality effects observed. Consequently, conditions on derivations are indispensable. Let us see why.

Non-trivial A-chains at LF in both GB and Minimalist theories have two important features in common.[12] They have local links and all but one of the links are traces. In GB theories, the locality among chain links is accommodated in one of several ways. One way is to assimilate A-chain traces to anaphors and treat the locality effect as a consequence of principle A of the BT.[13] Other similar approaches reduce the locality effect to antecedent government; each trace in a chain must be antecedent governed.[14] What is similar to both approaches is that the locality among chain links reduces to local licensing requirements for traces in a chain. In other words, the ultimate licenser in both accounts is the lexical head of the chain. The buck stops there!

Consider another way of putting the same point. The above representationalist accounts rely on the fact that A-chains have a certain canonical structure in which the head is lexical and all other links are traces. This then allows the head to be the ultimate antecedent for the sequence of traces. Licensing, one could say, proceeds trace to trace until the head is reached. The head, not being a trace, needs no licensing and so it can anchor the series of licensing conditions among the traces. A graphic way of seeing this is to think of each trace as in need of a +gamma feature (as in Lasnik and Saito 1984). Each trace in the string is assigned a gamma feature if properly antecedent governed. The last trace in the chain is gamma-marked by the head, which being lexical, does not need to be antecedent governed.[15] As an element X gamma-marks a trace Y iff the former is in a government relation with the latter, the locality effects that characterize A-chains reduce to this fact.

I have stressed the role of the lexical head of a chain in licensing A-chains because it is a requirement on the viability of representationalist approaches to grammatical conditions that they have a structure more or less like the one specified above. The problem is that the proposals advanced above cannot be fitted into this format. Thus, if the proposals above are empirically adequate, something I take for granted here, it means that the locality condition on chain links cannot be representationally derived. Consider the details.

In chapter 8, we derived quantifier scope effects by assuming that any link in an A-chain can delete, all but one must delete, and that the surviving member of this chain takes scope over whatever elements it c-commands. To make this proposal adequate, I tacitly assumed (9) above, the AFOP. Thus, the surviving undeleted link assumes whatever theta role the chain possess (some link is in a theta marking position) and whatever case the chain possesses (some link is in a case position). In effect, the properties of the chain are inherited by the single undeleted link. This much is also taken to be a property of chains in GB theories. However, there is one important difference. In contrast with GB theories, traces need not be bound or c-commanded at LF by lexical antecedents. In fact, it is vital to the success of the analysis that traces need meet no licensing conditions at all save that they have been well derived (i.e. they are economical and the derivations respect the MLC), case-checked and theta-marked. The following example should help make it clear just how crucial this assumption is. Recall that the reading of (12a) in which the universal object is interpreted as taking scope over the existential subject is due to its having the representation (12b) at LF.

(12a)   Someone ate everything
(12b)   [(Someone) [everything [someone ate (everything)]]]

By convention, parentheses indicate deletion of the copy. In other words, the bracketed expressions are the functional equivalent of traces in a GB theory. For example, like traces, they are invisible to interpretation and make no semantic contribution to the interpretation of the sentence at the CI interface. Thus, (12b) is a well-formed structure in which the head of the chain is a trace. In more conventional notation, (12b) has the LF structure (13).

(13)   [t_i [everything$_j$ [someone$_i$ ate t_j]]]

In a GB theory this structure cannot be well formed as t_i cannot be bound or gamma-marked. In the above account, in contrast, there is no requirement that traces be antecedent governed or bound. The only requirement is that the chain be formed correctly; the shortest steps were taken, the morphological features were checked, no unnecessary movements were indulged in, etc. The locality conditions on chain links derive from the locality requirements on legitimate movements (e.g. they must be both economical and the shortest possible). Nothing else is required from the output except that least effort guided the derivation and all features were checked in the course of the derivation. Besides this, anything goes. In particular, these is nothing that conditions chain link deletion so that the output of this process meet a condition analogous to binding or antecedent government. In fact, as (12) shows, it is crucial to the analysis that no such requirement obtain. Thus, in the case of A-chains, the well-formedness conditions that the theory outlined in chapter 8 exploits cannot be adequately stated as structural conditions on the LF phrase marker which is the output of grammatical processes. Only derivational constraints will do.

As this point is important, let us consider an example to make it clear. A-chains meet very stringent locality conditions. Each link in a licit A-chain must be "very close" to the next. This proximity requirement on licit A-chains is stated in terms of the ECP in a GB theory through the requirement of antecedent government or Generalized Binding. For example, what makes it impossible for (14a) to have the interpretation in which *every Republican* takes scope over *someone* is that the LF phrase marker (14b) violates the ECP; in particular, the trace in the subject position of the embedded finite clause is not properly governed (nor properly bound).[16]

(14a) Someone expected (that) every Republican would win
(14b) $[_{AgrS} t_j [_{AgrO}$ every R$_i$ $[_{VP}$ someone$_j$ expected $[_{CP}$ (that) $[_{AgrS} t_i$ would win]]]]]

The problem with this approach once lowering and reconstruction are generally allowed is that (14b) violates the ECP regardless of the relation between *every R* and its trace. The relation between t_j and *someone* is already a violation of the ECP. It too is not properly governed. Moreover, this latter relationship must be counted as generally grammatical on pain of having (12b) also violate the ECP. However, (12b) with the indicated interpretation must be counted as grammatical. Thus, the ECP is simply the wrong condition once reconstruction is permitted as a grammatical mechanism. However, without the ECP, we need other locality restrictions in order to account for the data in (14).

A theory that eschews the ECP and uses least effort (e.g. some version of procrastinate) to weed out the unacceptable phrase markers does not face similar difficulties. (14b) violates least effort by raising *every R* from Spec AgrS to the matrix Spec AgrO for no apparent reason. The case has been checked in the embedded finite clause. In (12b) in contrast, raising to Spec AgrO is required if case is to be checked. This suffices to distinguish the two cases and nothing need be said about the output of the deletion processes that follow. The status of the phrase markers (14b) and (12b) can be distinguished derivationally so their final LF products need not be consulted. In other words, the ECP as a condition on representations can be dispensed with at no empirical cost. In fact, the ECP creates problems if invoked. The upshot then is that if reconstruction is a mechanism generally permitted in the grammar, then the ECP is not the right principle for stating the locality restrictions that chains manifest.[17] Rather, these conditions should be stated in terms of conditions on derivations like least effort, economy, and the MLC.[18]

The same conclusion holds for A'-chains. The account of pair–list constructions and superiority effects required that WHs in Spec CP reconstruct to A-positions they moved from.[19] For example, the LFs of (15a) and (16a) have the

LFs (15b) and (16b), the WHs "reconstructed" from Spec CP being interpreted functionally.

(15a)   What did everyone buy
(15b)   [(What) did [everyone [what [(everyone) buy (what)]]]]
(16a)   Which book did which woman buy
(16b)   [(Which book) did [which woman [which book [(which woman) buy (which book)]]]]

However, these phrase markers exhibit the same problems that the earlier A-chain structures displayed. There is a trace in Spec CP with no antecedent. This is generally illicit and the structure should be ill-formed. However, it is crucial to the analysis that (15b) and (16b) are perfectly well-formed LF phrase markers.

Once again the Minimalist theory can account for this by exploiting derivational constraints. Output conditions are neither required nor desired. Once again, trying to attain the same results by imposing structural requirements on LF phrase markers will not work.

The source of the difficulty for representational theories is not hard to discern once the examples in (13)–(16) are examined. The source of the trouble is "reconstruction." Deletion of chain links is the Minimalist mechanism for reconstruction. It is analogous to lowering rules in earlier GB theories, a species of operation that is proscribed in GB. The reason, as is now evident, is that lowering leads to massive antecedent government/binding problems; thus, their *regula non grata* status. However, given that Minimalism dispenses with the ECP, especially the antecedent government clause (and its analogues in other theories), there is no general theoretical reason why "lowering" in the guise of "reconstruction" should not be ubiquitous. The analyses above significantly exploit this difference between GB and Minimalism. If they are correct, the ECP is strongly incompatible with Minimalism. A reflex of this fact is the ineliminable derivational character of UG.

4   PF Chains

LF chains are strongly derivational. Their PF counterparts, however, closely resemble their GB ancestors. Thus, movement in overt syntax always results in the type of structure favored in GB theories; the head is lexical and the intermediate landing sites are phonologically null. In Minimalist terms, this means that all links but the head delete.[20] What accounts for the distinction between LF and PF chains? There are two possibilities. Both exploit the AFOP, albeit in slightly different ways.

The first option relies on the assumption that chains are exclusively LF objects. PF contains words, morphemes, phonemes, and other exotica but it does not contain chains. If, however, chains do not exist at PF then the AFOP will not be able to work its magic. Links in chains will not be licensable because they are chain-related to other links that have properties that they lack. In particular, the fact that some link in a chain has met a required morphological condition through movement cannot help the copy left in the launching site to meet these same conditions. Note that the AFOP cannot help matters here as it does in LF. The reason is that the AFOP is a property of chains and so cannot apply at PF where chains do not exist. In effect, without the AFOP, each chain link must stand on its own. To illustrate, consider an instance of NP movement in which a nominative subject moves from VP internal position to Spec AgrS where *Nom* case features are checked.

(17) $[_{AgrSP}$ [NP, #Nom] [. . . $[_{VP}$ [NP, Nom] . . .]]]

Observe that in (17) the NP in Spec AgrS has the *Nom* feature #-ed. At LF, the AFOP licenses the lower NP because it is part of a chain in which the feature has been checked. However, at PF, where there are not any chains, the fact that this lower NP has an unchecked *Nom* feature suffices to crash the derivation if it is not deleted. This implies that a moved element will always phonologically appear in the position of its most prominent landing site. All other copies must delete for the derivation to be well formed. This is precisely the desired result.

There is a second way of getting this conclusion. We could take the AFOP as an LF condition. This is minimally different from the first option, but it is different. The first option takes the AFOP to be part of the definition of what it is to be a chain. Chains are objects that allow the local properties of its links to indirectly license links that do not themselves have these properties. The current proposal suggests that the AFOP is not part of what it is to be a chain but simply a property of LF that holds of LF chains. As should be evident, this will derive the same results discussed above.

Of these two options, the first is clearly conceptually preferable. It is hard to understand the AFOP as an output condition that holds at LF because it itself places no conditions on chains. In this it is different from principle A of the BT, for example, which places structural constraints on well-formed LF phrase markers. The AFOP does not require chains to "look" a certain way. Rather the AFOP enables parts of chains to participate in the licensing requirements met by other parts of the same chain. It says that chains are objects that relate their links so that all equivalently meet any condition that any member meets singly. This seems less like a condition *on* chains than a part of the definition *of* chains. This makes the first option the natural choice.[21]

It is natural within the Minimalist framework to conclude that chains cannot obtain at PF. The reason is that PF, the input to the perceptual/articulatory modules, has no phrase marker properties (see Chomsky 1993: n. 19). If chains can only live in phrase markers, then chains cannot exist at PF. This conclusion suffices to derive the fact that the visible PF residue of syntactic movement must always be the head of the resultant chain formed by that movement. In other words, all links but the head must delete.

5 "Pure" Subject/Object Asymmetries

Many of the phenomena reviewed in chapters 2 and 3 have been reanalyzed in Minimalist terms. One set of data remains. These data illustrate "pure" subject/object asymmetries, asymmetries that involve operators like neg and WH but whose interpretation is not further dependent on other operators. These pure cases fall into three distinct groups and I would like to review them briefly here.

The first problematic construction is illustrated in (18).

(18a) Jean a dit que Paul a vu qui
       "Jean said that Paul saw who"
(18b) *Jean a dit que qui est venu
       "Jean said that who came"

These contrasts were first discussed in Aoun et al. (1981) where the asymmetry was attributed to the ECP (see chapter 2). In brief, it was assumed that the WH-*in-situ* moves at LF directly to the matrix Spec CP without passing through the embedded Spec CP position. This leaves a non-properly governed trace at LF in the structure underlying (18b) (in contrast to (18a)).

This account is problematic in several respects. Taken on its own terms, the explanation largely relies on an otherwise unmotivated stipulation prohibiting movement to the matrix Spec CP via the local embedded Comp position. In terms of the approach outlined above, this sort of movement should be entirely prohibited as it is an instance of LF A'-movement, i.e. movement to a non-L-involved position at LF. As argued above, there are both empirical and theoretical reasons given Minimalist assumptions to eschew this sort of movement.

A possible way around these data is to rethink their status. This is a plausible option as it appears that the data as originally reported are far less translucent than first believed. Thus, Joseph Aoun (personal communication) informs me that the contrast noted above is not very pronounced, if there at all. Support for this comes from the observation that the analogous English data have been judged differently. Thus, (19) has been deemed acceptable by some (see Lasnik and Saito 1984) and unacceptable by others (see Aoun et al. 1987).

(19)   Who said that who left

The murkiness of the data suggests that the status of the contrast in (18) is best left for the theory to decide. As the present theory renders these examples grammatical, I will assume that they are.

It should be noted that the precise analysis of the French constructions in (18) is still problematic given Minimalist assumptions. Optional WH-*in-situ* constructions are troublesome for they suggest that the matrix C^0 can optionally be marked +WH (as suggested in Aoun et al. 1981).[22] Consider the two available options. Either there is a +WH in the French WH-*in-situ* constructions or there is not. If there is, then there must be a phantom null operator in this position analogous to the overt ones discussed by Aoun and Li (1993b) and Watanabe (1991) for Chinese and Japanese respectively. There is a problem with this supposition, however. The French constructions require that the WH-*in-situ* be interpreted as having matrix scope. Thus the null WH seems restricted to matrix CP. Why this phantom +WH is prohibited from embedded clauses remains a mystery.[23]

The second option also has problems. It is standardly assumed that the WH-features of a WH-operator must be checked. This is effected by movement of the WH-operator to a +WH CP or by being bound by a +WH-expression. The problem is that the second assumption assumes that no such +WH CP or element occurs in the structure. This in turn implies that the WH-*in-situ* can be licensed in some other way. Just how licensing gets effected remains unclear.

I leave these issues unresolved and assume, perhaps incorrectly, that they can be adequately treated within a Minimalist framework.

The second group of problematic data concern neg constructions, first discussed in Kayne (1979).

(20a)   Jean n'exige que Paul a vu personne
        "Jean doesn't insist that Paul saw no one"
(20b)   *Jean n'exige que personne soit arrêtée
        "Jean doesn't insist that no one was arrested"

These sorts of contrasts have been attested in various Romance languages (see Rizzi 1982, Jaeggli 1981) so the option exercised above of impugning the data is considerably less attractive. In GB-style theories the contrast in (20) is reduced to the ECP as follows. *Personne* moves at LF to some position around the matrix neg, for concreteness say it moves to Spec NegP (see Zanuttini 1991). In analogy with WH-elements, this movement allows neg operators to check their neg features and thereby become licensed. An important ancillary assumption is that this movement proceed in one step. Passage to Spec NegP through the local Spec CP would leave the subject trace in (20b) properly governed and the contrast unaccounted for. Why movement through the local Spec CP is prohibited, however, is unclear.

Consider a possible Minimalist approach to this contrast. Assume, as above, that the neg features of a neg operator must be checked by moving to a Spec NegP position. In the examples in (20) this checking is effected at LF. Given the remarks in section 1 above, this requires that the movement not be a species of A'-movement. In other words, this requires that Spec NegP be an L-involved position.

Observe that a similar assumption is tacitly made by the ECP account: one way of prohibiting the undesired movement to Spec CP at LF in the phrase marker underlying (20b) is to treat such movement as an instance of A- to A'- to A-movement, i.e. an instance of improper movement. In short, let us adopt the assumption that Spec NegP is not an A'-position, viz. it is not a non-L-involved position.

There is additional evidence in support of this assumption. First, as is well known, in the Slavic languages Neg has case-marking properties. Elements that are normally marked accusative in affirmative clauses carry genitive marking in negated sentences. As case-marking is a standard diagnostic of an A-position, this suggests that Spec NegP has A-position properties.

Second, as noted in chapter 8, NegP has an effect on certain quantifier scope phenomena. For example, the reading in which the universal takes scope over the existential in (21a) is unavailable in (21b).

(21a)   An editor read every article
(21b)   An editor didn't read every article

This is explained in chapter 8 by assuming that *an editor* cannot move from Spec VP to Spec AgrS without violating the MLC if a NegP intervenes.[24] However, this application of the MLC requires treating Spec NegP as a potential landing site for an expression launched from Spec VP and on its way to Spec AgrS. In short, it cannot be a non-L-involved position. In other words, given the A-chain approach to quantifier scope effects in chapter 8, Spec NegP can be used to block certain movements on the assumption that it is not a non-L-involved position.[25]

Two further assumptions are required for an analysis of the contrast in (20). Let us assume (i) that preverbal subjects in Romance reside in A'-positions and (ii) that a condition on chain uniformity prohibits movement from non-L-involved to L-involved positions. Assumption (i) is proposed in Jaeggli (1981) and has recently been further defended by Barbosa (1994) (see Branigan 1992 as well). Assumption (ii) is proposed in Chomsky (1994) as a way of treating improper movement minimalistically. These two assumptions, in concert with the assumption that Spec NegP is an L-involved position, blocks the LF movement of *personne* from preverbal subject positions in the Romance languages but allows it from all others, e.g. object position or postverbal subject position. In the unacceptable (20b), the movement to Spec NegP is an instance of improper movement. The neg expression moves from a non-L-involved position to the L-involved Spec NegP. This results in a non-uniform chain and so the structure is blocked. Movement from the other positions should be acceptable (e.g. (20a)) as uniform chains will result.

Note one important feature of this analysis. It treats movement to Spec NegP as an instance of A-movement and so allows it to occur at LF given the assumptions above.[26] This contrasts with LF WH-movement, a species of movement that the present theory prohibits. There is an interesting consequence of this way of viewing things. Consider parasitic gap constructions once again. The fact that these constructions appear to be licensed at SS has been accommodated given Minimalist assumptions by banning LF WH-movement. This prohibition has the effect of not augmenting the potential A'-binders at LF and so allows parasitic gap licensing to be stated at LF, as required by a Minimalist theory (see chapter 8). In effect, then, the parasitic gap in (22) cannot be licensed at all because the only licensor, *which book*, does not ever move to a position where it can bind the parasitic gap (pg).

(22)   *Which man read which book before buying pg

The contrast between Spec CP and Spec NegP noted above implies that Negs, in contrast to WHs, should enter into parasitic gap-like phenomena at LF. The reason is that these elements can move at LF to positions from which they could license such constructions. This possibility has been amply borne out. Longobardi (1991) presents considerable evidence that LF movement can license parasitic neg constructions at LF. He points out that these multiple neg constructions pattern exactly like overt parasitic gap constructions. They obey the standard island conditions, these conditions can be circumvented by the proper insertion of a licensing item of the same sort as the parasitic one and, finally, unacceptability results if the licensing neg is too far from the licensed element. The sentences in (23) illustrate each point.[27]

(23a)   *Non fa questo lavoro per aiutare nessuno
        "He doesn't do his work in order to help anyone"
(23b)   Non fa niente per   aiutare nessuno
        Not do nothing in order to help   no one
        "He doesn't do anything in order to help anyone"
(23c)   *Non fa niente per scopire la verità indagando su nessuno
        "He doesn't do anything in order to discover the truth by investigating anyone"

What is important to observe for present purposes is that the proposal that neg licensing involves a form of L-involved movement while WH-movement is to an non-L-involved position permits the former to occur at LF while prohibits the latter from so occurring. In short, we expect that parasitic constructions should be licensable at LF if they involve neg elements but should not be licensable at LF if not already licensable at SPELL OUT if they involve WH-expressions. This is borne out in (22) and (23).

The above account of the subject/object asymmetries displayed by certain neg constructions rests on two assumptions: (i) Spec NegP is an L-involved position; (ii) movement from a non-L-involved to a L-involved position is prohibited as it is a species of improper movement. Consider another possible approach to these phenomena.

Pure subject/object asymmetries have a natural explanation in terms of the classical ECP (Chomsky 1981). Object positions are head-governed while subject positions are not. Hence, traces left in object positions are always properly head-governed while subjects never are. This sort of account is suspect within a Minimalist theory as it is stated in terms of the government relation. If, however, it were possible to find a Minimalist analogue of head government, then the asymmetry in (20) could be stated in terms of this condition.[28] Moreover, this same condition could be used to account for the third set of recalcitrant cases, viz. the fixed subject constraint effects.

(24a)   *Who did you say that t left
(24b)   *Who did you wonder whether/if t left

In most current approaches to the ECP these sorts of data are attributed to the head government part of the ECP (see Aoun et al. 1987, Rizzi 1990, Cinque 1990, Koopman and Sportiche 1986). The most efficient way to accommodate these sorts of data in a Minimalist theory would be to find an analogue of the head government condition. This restatement of the condition would have to meet two conditions. First, it would have to be stated at LF. Second, it would have to be cast exploiting X'-relations. One possible restatement of this part of the ECP is provided in (25).[29]

(25)   A trace is properly head-governed iff it is in the complement domain of some X^0 chain (at LF)

This version of the head government condition has the required Minimalist properties. I assume, furthermore, that it is no less empirically adequate than the classical version when the requisite technical adjustments are made. With (25) the data in (24) (as well as those in (20)) can be accommodated.

The aim of this section has been to point out various ways in which the pure subject/object asymmetries discussed in chapter 2 might be minimalistically accommodated. These cases seem to require theoretical resources different from those put to use in chapters 4 through 8. Perhaps this is not all that surprising. The data analyzed in these earlier chapters generally fell under the antecedent government clause of the ECP. The pure asymmetries surveyed here have generally been adduced to the head government requirement. The proposals in this section for dealing with pure subject/object asymmetries suggest that these really are phenomena with different theoretical underpinnings and will have to be so accommodated even in the context of a Minimalist theory.

6   Conclusion

The aim of this book has been to flesh out the leading ideas behind Minimalism so that they could deal with the wealth of data on LF phenomena that prior GB work has uncovered. It is clear (to me) that if Minimalism is roughly correct then the earlier GB analyses will have to be abandoned and radically rethought. Minimalism is a radical departure from the core ideas that informed GB theory. The fundamental notions, constructs, and principles are different. If the analyses above are correct, there is no place in Minimalism for the (antecedent government part of the) ECP, A'-movement, or theories based exclusively on output constraints. This is a fundamental reorientation of grammatical theory.

In addition, there is a fundamental asymmetry between PF and LF and the grammatical objects that reside at these levels. At PF, objects are visible in the positions that Move α and insertion position them. If an XP is moved to Spec AgrS by SPELL OUT then at PF it must appear in sentence initial position. Not so for LF. In fact, the only way to relate LF to PF is derivationally. Monostratal theories that try to reduce one level's basic properties to the other cannot succeed, for overt movement does not fix the positions of XPs at LF, though it does at PF. Structurally the two levels are very different and only indirectly related to one another.[30]

There are many other differences between the Minimalist program and the theoretical insights undergirding GB theory. The chapters above have touched on several of these. As noted above, Minimalism is the new theory on the block. It is clear that as Minimalist alternatives to prior GB analyses are developed more will surface. Hopefully, the proposals made here can help to clarify the fine structure of Minimalism in ways that make future work more fruitful.

Notes

Chapter 1   An Introduction

1   S-structure is analogous to (yet different from) Surface Structure. These two levels are not identical and should not be confused.
2   This organization was first proposed in Chomsky and Lasnik (1977).
3   The quantifier is restricted in that the domain it ranges over is specified. Thus, *everyone* ranges over people while *everything* ranges over objects.
4   For a recent argument to the effect that binding is not a property of phrase markers but of more abstract cognitive structures, see Jackendoff (1994).
5   This is not invariably assumed. So for example, May (1985) denies that this is the case. However, as we see below, the reasons that he gives rely on treating certain phenomena as due to the ECP. If this is incorrect, then the stronger position that LF phrase markers do disambiguate sentences can be maintained. See below.

Chapter 2   Motivating LF

1   If one thinks that interpretation is supplied by truth conditions then one must proceed via declarative propositions to give the truth conditions of interrogatives. The reason is that questions are not the sorts of things that are true or false. However, the set of appropriate answers to a question are declaratives and hence truth value vehicles. Thus, we can plausibly treat the semantics of questions within a standard semantic theory exploiting a truth definition if we concentrate on the answers that go with questions rather than the questions themselves. For a discussion of the semantics of questions see Higginbotham (1993), Higginbotham and May (1981), and Kartunnen (1977).
2   The presentation below is based on work originating in Huang (1982). Many of Huang's ideas are elaborated in Aoun et al. (1981, 1987), Kayne (1984), and Lasnik and Saito (1984).
3   Echo questions are ones typically used to secure information made .difficult to obtain by various performance factors. Consider the remark from Nancy to Maude that Bill is dancing with Sam made in a rowdy crowded auditorium. Maude, having missed the identity of the dancee, might well ask for clarification using the following echo question: "Bill is dancing with WHO." What is important is that in the French and Chinese cases noted below, we have a standard question not an echo question with the WHs *in situ*.
4   An absorbed interpretation involves treating the pair of WH-operators as if they were actually a binary operator, i.e. defined over sets of ordered pairs. For example, the answer to the question "who bought what" are ordered pairs of buyers

and things bought, e.g. John bought a car and Frank a sled. For details on the semantics, cf. Higginbotham and May (1981).

5   A governs B iff A m-commands B and no barrier intervenes between A and B. For details see Chomsky (1986a) or Haegeman (1994).

6   This version of the ECP derives from Chomsky (1981). There are several standard versions of the ECP all of which yield the desired results below. The Chomsky (1981) definition is used in the text because it is familiar but there are other adequate definitions. A definition in terms of paths is outlined in Pesetsky (1982) and is used extensively in May (1985). Other approaches to the ECP that come out essentially equivalent for current purposes include an approach in terms of Generalized Binding (Aoun 1986, Aoun et al. 1987), and Relativized Minimality (Rizzi 1990).

For discussion of the ECP in standard GB terms see Haegeman (1994). For a review of various alternative versions of the ECP see Hornstein and Weinberg (1995).

7   The status of (12a) has been contentious. In the early 1970s these sorts of sentences were judged to be quite unacceptable. Lately, they are taken to be "mere subjacency violations." The structure of (12a) violates subjacency as it involves movement of a WH-element out of a WH-island. Adopting the definition of subjacency in Chomsky (1982), (i) is ill formed as it involves moving *which car* across two bounding nodes, viz. the two IPs. Subjacency allows movement across at most one bounding node. In this case, however, *how* fills the CP "escape hatch" and forces *which car* to cross both IPs on its way to the matrix CP.

(i)   [$_{CP}$ Which car$_i$ [$_{IP}$ John wonder [$_{CP}$ how$_j$ [$_{IP}$ PRO to [fix t$_i$] t$_j$]]]]

Later reanalyses of subjacency also aim to rule out WH-island violations. The details, however, differ from the original account given in Chomsky (1973, 1982). For discussion see Haegeman (1994: chapter 10.2).

8   There are various ways of permitting the ECP to cover this case. Chomsky (1982, 1986a) does so by having the intermediate *that* block government of the subject position. Essentially, the *that* results in a barrier intervening between the antecedent WH and the trace. This suffices to block local binding. Other ways of extending the ECP have been proposed; see Aoun et al. (1981, 1987), Lasnik and Saito (1984), Pesetsky (1982), and Rizzi (1990). For present purposes any of these technical ways of blocking antecedent government suffice.

9   These data were first discussed in Aoun et al. (1981). See chapter 9 below as well.

10 The sentence is not subject to the *que* → *qui* alternation, i.e. it does not improve with "qui" in place of the Comp "que."

11 Extending the ECP to cases such as this requires the assumption that movement through Comp either does not occur at LF in these cases or that it does not suffice to license the subject gap. There are various technical ways of executing this assumption. For discussion see Aoun et al. (1981) as well as Aoun (1985), Aoun et al. (1987), and Lasnik and Saito (1984). This topic is also addressed in chapter 4.

12 The status of (20b) is contested in the literature. For example, Lasnik and Saito (1984) judge sentences with essentially the same structures to be acceptable. See chapter 9 for some discussion.

13 The details of the account do not matter much. We can make the particular proposal precise by the following definitions.

(i)   A binds B iff A c-commands and is coindexed with B
(ii) A c-commands B iff the first branching category that dominates A dominates B

Given these assumptions, then in (26b), *who*₁ fails to c-command and hence bind the subject trace.

The reason that I claim that the details are not that crucial is that this account survives alternative formulations. For some technical alternatives see Aoun et al. (1981), Lasnik and Saito (1984) for a treatment in terms of Comp indexing, and Rizzi (1990) for a similar analysis but exploiting the technology of Spec–head agreement.

14 Rudin assumes that the second WH into Comp adjoins to the right of the WH already there. The Bulgarian data are identical.

(i) Koj kakvo kupuva
     Who what   bought
     "Who bought what"

(ii) *Kakvo koj kupuva
     What   who bought

15 More precisely, there is a logical tradition that goes back to Frege and Russell that distinguishes names from quantifiers, the former being referential the latter not. For a discussion of the semantic reasons for distinguishing these two kinds of expressions, see Geach (1962).

16 This sentence remains equally unacceptable if *qui* replaces *que* in Comp.

17 For the argument to go through here and in the case in (18) we need to assume that movement through Comp is prohibited.

18 These data are discussed in Aoun and Hornstein (1985) and May (1985).

19 These sorts of examples were first discussed extensively in May (1985). He was the first to point out that the ACD construction argues powerfully for LF movement of the variety discussed here. See chapter 5 for further discussion of ACDs.

20 The problem is not one of copying *per se*. Copying is just a graphic way of illustrating the problem. A deletion approach faces analogous problems. The problem stems from a more general assumption common to most approaches to interpreting anaphoric elements; that the antecedent of an anaphor is a constituent (of similar category). Whether one actually copies the content of the antecedent VP into the gap is a technical matter.

21 These cases are discussed in Larson and May (1990) and chapter 5.

22 These types of constructions were first extensively discussed in May (1985).

23 The actual notion used is exclusion in terms of which c-command and domination are defined. The definition in terms of strong domination is easier to manipulate but it has the same effect as May's original account from which it is adapted.

24 "Free" means "not bound," i.e. not c-commanded and coindexed with its antecedent.

25 See Chomsky (1976) and Higginbotham (1980). Alternative principles have been investigated, the best known being the Bijection Principle proposed in Koopman and Sportiche (1983). For further discussion of WCO effects and possible formulations of the correct principle that underlies these effects see chapter 6.

26 These sorts of cases are discussed in Higginbotham (1980).

27 ECP issues are not relevant here. Whether the quantifier adjoins to VP or to IP is also irrelevant here.

28 Cf. Chomsky (1982) for discussion.

29 Once again, for our purposes it does not matter whether QR adjoins the quantified NP to VP or to IP. From either spot it c-commands the adjunct and so can bind a pronoun within it.

30   This was first noted in Lasnik (1976). See Hornstein and Weinberg (1990) as well. The discussion below is based on the latter paper.

31   The analysis of sloppy identity and the relevant data is from Reinhart (1983). May (1985: 68, ex. 29) observes that sloppy identity is possible in sentences with structures analogous to the unacceptable cases cited here.

(i)   Nobody from NYC rides its subways but everyone from Tokyo does

(i) supports the reading in which Tokyo residents ride the Tokyo subway. As May (1985: 163 n. 7) observes, the sloppy reading is "less favored" (to my ear, they are quite impossible) with non-action verbs. Reinhart uses sentences with such verbs. What is important for current purposes is that there appears to be a contrast distinguishing names from quantified NPs with respect to sloppy identity readings in sentences of the Reinhart variety. This suffices to make the relevant point notwithstanding May's interesting observation.

32   Recall that NPs of the form "the N," "that N" cannot be A-bound.

33   There is another interesting sentence that seems to combine two forms of elision, NP elision and VP deletion.

(i)   John's mother kissed him and Bill's did too

I assume that this too is formed by fronting the specifier to IP.

34   The definition is from Haegeman (1994: 402). More sophisticated definitions are surveyed in this book as well. For present purposes the definition in the text suffices.

35   This was proposed in Huang (1982).

36   Longobardi's point was not that subjacency held at LF but that movement obtained there. It is sufficient for his purposes that overt and covert movement parallel one another. If both respect antecedent government, the point will be made.

37   The cases involving *solo* are less clear given that association to focus is involved in these sorts of cases and these are known to involve SS intonational properties. These SS effects complicate arguments for the pure LF nature of these phenomena. The negation facts cited are cleaner in this respect.

Curiously, whatever light the neg constructions may (or may not) throw on subjacency, they support the position that neg elements move at LF. The reason is that they display effects similar to parasitic gaps. The addition of another neg phrase improves the unacceptable sentences in (87). Contrast (87b) with (i).

(i)   Non fa   niente per aiutare nessuno
     Neg does-he nothing for to-help no one
     "He does not do anything in order to help anyone"

There is an important contrast, however, with standard parasitic gap constructions. The latter fail to be licensed by LF moved expressions. (ii) contrasts with (iii) in that only in (iii) has the WH moved at SS. It appears that LF movement does not suffice to license a parasitic gap.

(ii)   *Who read what without reviewing
(iii) Which book did John read without reviewing

It is unclear what accounts for the differences in these two cases in a GB framework. Perhaps some parallelism constraint on the overt nature of the relevant variable is at stake. In a Minimalist theory, where parasitic gap conditions must be stated at LF, there is room to treat these sorts of cases in parallel. For discussion of the LF nature of parasitic gap licensing see chapters 8 and 9.

38 Cf. Fiengo et al. (1988: 82ff).
39 Pesetsky (1987), among others, argues for this position.
40 Fiengo et al. (1988) propose another way of getting the results that elude the pied piping hypothesis. They invoke a *Barriers* account to neutralize the apparent violations of island conditions at LF. It is not my concern to question this approach here. However, the aim of their positive proposal is not to present independent evidence for subjacency effects at LF so much as to show that the assumption that subjacency holds there can be maintained. In effect, Fiengo et al. aim to save the following fact; no subjacency effects are evident at LF. This, they argue, can be accommodated within a *Barriers* theory. It of course also comports with a theory that denies LF movement is subject to subjacency or that LF movement exists at all. See chapters 8 and 9.
41 Examples adapted from Bayer (1993).

Chapter 3 More on LF

1 The data extend beyond Chinese to the other East Asian languages.
   The Chinese example (3) is chosen quite carefully. It is important to have an example in which *two men* is in subject position and the universal quantifier moves from object. In Chinese this is hard to find, as "indefinites" are typically barred from subject positions. They are, however, permitted in conditionals and hence the example focused on. Cf. Aoun and Li (1989: 141, n. 1). The opposite order in which the universal takes SS scope over an indefinite does not suffice to indicate LF movement. The reason is that it is consistent even without movement that a sentence like (i) can be made true by either the value of the indefinite being the same for all values of the universal variable or changing value with that of the universal variable. Thus, the appearance of ambiguity can obtain without any structural ambiguity being present.

   (i) Everyone loves someone

2 Given the assumptions advanced in chapter 1, it is unlikely that languages could differ at LF in the way Huang proposed. How would a child come to know that LF is constrained to be isomorphic to SS in Chinese but not in English?
3 This is not a criticism of either the May (1985) or the Aoun and Li (1989) proposals. Just what interpretive properties are grammatically determined is an empirical question. This said, the loosening of the relation between syntactic form and semantic interpretation is, all things being equal, to be resisted as it weakens the potential empirical exposure of the theory.
4 X locally A'-binds Y iff X A'-binds Y and no Z is such that it A'-binds Y and X A'-binds Z.
5 Recall that a maximal projection is a barrier that prohibits the formation of licit A-chains unless its barrierhood is removed in some way. The principal way of removing barrierhood is to L-mark the VP. On the assumption that L-marking requires lexical content, then Infl cannot L-mark the VP unless the V raises to Infl to give it lexical content.
   The idea that V-raising to Infl allows the raised V to L-mark the VP and thereby

remove its barrier status is suggested in Chomsky (1986a). That V-raising obtains at LF in English is proposed in Chomsky (1991). For a review of the *Barriers* theory see Chomsky (1986a) or Haegeman (1994: chapter 10). What is crucial here, however, are not the details, but the relationship between V-raising and the ability to raise from VP internal subject position. The account presented by Aoun and Li (1989, 1993a) would be unaffected if subject raising from VP in Chinese were prohibited for some reason other than the one provided here. In Aoun and Li (1993a) they offer a different way of obtaining these same results.

6   For this lowering account to go through, we require that principle A of the BT cannot apply throughout the derivation. It must hold only at LF. The other option predicts that lowering and anaphor binding need not restrain one another. In particular, like the SP account, it predicts that there should be no dependency between anaphor binding and relative QP scope. See chapter 8 for a fuller discussion.

7   An A'-chain is comprised of traces in A'-positions that form a chain plus the case-marked trace that is interpreted as the variable.

8   Aoun (1985) argues for a version of the ECP cast in terms of Generalized Binding. For a review of this approach to the ECP see Aoun (1985), Aoun et al. (1987), and Hornstein and Weinberg (1995).

9   In the *Barriers* framework such adjunction results in a theta criterion violation.

10 Or, what comes to the same thing for present purposes, they assume that an NP in Spec IP does not move there from VP internal position. It is directly generated there. Whether, in addition, Chinese permits VP internal subjects as well is here irrelevant. Aoun and Li (1993a), in contrast to Aoun and Li (1989), do not say why this raising is prohibited, however.

11 The matrix trace is licit if it can be interpreted as a null expletive *pro*. See Aoun (1982) and May (1985) for discussion.

12 Aoun and Li (1993a) observe that the two rules resemble the proposal in Heim (1982).

13 May (1985) actually states the condition in terms of VP and claims IP is irrelevant. However, the proposal works better with the converse assumption. The counting of VP conflicts with the definition of domination provided. The quantified adjoined NP is not dominated by *every* segment of VP.

14 It need not be syntactically A'-bound. To be interpreted as a bound variable, it must be in the semantic scope of an operator. Aoun (1985, 1986) assumes that it is so bound by the WH in Comp, perhaps as a result of an operation akin to absorption as proposed by Higginbotham and May (1981).

15 See (46) below for how the ambiguity of "what did everyone say" is determined if chain scope is restricted to A'-expressions.

16 If this is true, then Q-adjunction is required to allow the object quantifier to take scope over the subject in English sentences such as (i).

(i)   A girl kissed every boy

The LF structure is (ii).

(ii)   [Every$_i$ [vbl-t$_i$ boy]]$_i$ [[a$_j$ [vbl-t$_j$ girl]]$_j$ [NP-t$_j$ kissed vbl-t$_j$]]

If only A'-elements are relevant for scope determination, then the only way for the universal quantifier to take scope over the existential is for some part of *every boy*'s A'-chain to c-command some part of *a girl*'s A'-chain. Except for the adjoined a_j, however, no part of this latter chain is plausibly in A'-position. It is not clear, however, how the A/A'-distinction applies to quantifiers and determiners. The conclusion must be, nonetheless, that it is in virtue of q_i's being c-commanded by $[every_i [vbl-t_i boy]]_i$ which permits the universal to take scope over the existential here. And this, in turn, is only possible as a result of the operation of Q-adjunction which puts the indefinite in an A'-position.

17   This hypothetical has been challenged in Lappin (1992). He suggests that ACDs are actually formed via a process of pseudo-gapping (PG). So, in (i) there is not a VP gap but only a V gap with a trace in post-gap position.

(i)   John ate everything which$_i$ Bill did [$_v$ e] t$_i$

He correctly notes that this structure does not require movement of the QNP for there is no regress involved in copying the higher verb *eat* into this position.

There are several problems with this suggestion, however (see n. 3 chapter 5). One difficulty is worth mentioning here. It is not clear that PG can actually derive sentences like the ones in (51). The reason is that PG does not easily eliminate prepositions.

(ii)   John <u>introduced Bill to</u> Sam and Harry did [e] Sheila

(ii) cannot be interpreted as (iii) with the underscored material copied into the gap.

(iii)   Harry introduced Bill to Sheila

However, in (iv) this is the sort of operation we would require.

(iv)   John introduced Bill to everyone that Sam did (introduce Bill to) t

18   For current purposes it does not matter whether QR adjoins the QNP to VP or to IP.
19   Fiengo and May (1990) develop this argument in detail. They show that defining an analogue of binding conditions in semantic terms will not work. For details see the paper and Fiengo and May (1994).
20   Fiengo and May observe instances with PRO binding. However, the judgements are extremely subtle. They start with the assumption that in (i) the elided VP can be interpreted as having the interpretation in (ii). I find this judgement questionable. The only reading I get for these is the one in (iii) in which the VP gap is interpreted as the embedded VP. See chapter 5 for further discussion of ACDs.

(i)   Bill promised John to introduce Betty to everyone that Sally did
(ii)   Bill promised John to introduce Betty to everyone that Sally promised John to introduce Betty to
(iii)   Bill promised John to introduce Betty to everyone that Sally introduced Betty to

21   These data are originally noted in Haïk (1987).
22   Observe the contrast between true quantificational antecedents and their inability to bind resumptive pronouns and definite descriptions which do so rather freely.
23   It even appears that we get a contrast with (i), which seems better than this example.

(i)   *Everyone$_i$ who Dulles wondered whether Philby suspected him$_i$

If this is correct, then subjacency may not be the source of these effects. Assume that vehicle change is obligatory and that variables in particular must be rewritten as pronouns. Then the properties of resumptive pronouns will suffice to make the relevant distinctions without assuming that subjacency is at issue.

Chapter 4   Some Minimalist Background

1   More precisely, it is the reflex of this obvious fact when coupled with the conclusion that there is a language faculty. LF and PF are grammatical levels. If there is no dedicated cognitive organ for language then there would be no linguistic levels dedicated to representing the sound and meaning properties of sentences.

2   This question was investigated most thoroughly by Williams (1986).

3   See, for example, Belletti and Rizzi (1981) and Lebeaux (1988, 1990).

4   The notions of A and A'-position are reconstructed in a Minimalist theory. For present purposes it suffices if we treat WH-movement as the paradigmatic instance of A'-movement. All else can be treated as A-movement.

5   Chomsky (1993) assumes that the deletion is required to obtain legitimate LF objects. However, the deletion process might well be driven by more theory internal considerations concerning morphological feature checking. I return to outline one such theory in chapter 9 below. For the present assume that in questions, a WH-bearing element must remain in Spec CP at LF.

6   Actually, this abstracts from the abstract case movement discussed below.

7   It is assumed that the theta criterion is defined over chains. It states that every chain must bear a theta role. This requires that at least one (and at most one) link of every A-chain be in a theta position.

8   There is a third possibility: both move. However, we can rule this out on theta theoretic grounds once again. If both reflexives move then neither copy can delete. However, this still leaves one theta role for the whole copied NP that must now be shared between two elements. This account rests on the assumption that the set of copies do *not* constitute a chain. This seems like a reasonable assumption. In effect, then, without deletion, there is no well-formed A-chain at the interface and so one of the NPs is without a theta role

9   This argument is threatened if we assume that verbs universally raise to C^0 at LF as proposed in Koopman (1994) and Watanabe (1993). After this LF raising, the raised V plus picture noun form a contiguous unit and should license an idiomatic reading, contrary to the judgements noted by Chomsky. It is worth noting, however, that these judgements are quite subtle and are not uniformly shared.

10   There are further interesting predictions. We should expect principle B and C effects to be immune to the idiomatic/non-idiomatic interpretative distinction. For discussion see Chomsky (1993: ex. 44–8).

11   In the theories referred to idiom interpretation would be at DS. If idioms are interpreted at DS and reflexives can be bound throughout the derivation it should still be possible to derive the unavailable reading. The only way to link idiomatic readings with the availability of reflexivization is to determine both at the same level. The only plausible level at which both can be determined is LF.

12   If reflexivization is executed in English via LF movement, as is standardly assumed since Chomsky (1986b), (following the suggestion in Lebeaux 1983), then there is really no alternative to having principle A apply exclusively at LF. The option of allowing the BT to apply at any level only fits well with a BT of the LGB variety in which reflexives are interpreted *in situ*. If this is correct, however, then

the reflexivization data often used to motivate allowing the BT to apply at any level cannot be so explained. In fact, only a theory of the Minimalist variety can work. However, once we need this for principle A, then it is reasonable to treat all of the BT in the same way.

13 For a recent very interesting extension of this mechanism to relative clauses and null operator constructions see Munn (1994).

14 The same considerations apply to L-marking in the *Barriers* theory as a head can L-mark what it does not theta govern. For discussion see Chomsky (1986a: 24, ex. 47).

15 To cement this conclusion observe the following. The *Barriers/Lasnik and Saito* (1984, 1992) distinction between SS gamma marking for arguments and LF gamma marking for adjuncts has no place in a Minimalist theory given the elimination of SS conditions. Thus, some of the subject/object asymmetry data that fall under the antecedent government part of the ECP cannot be incorporated into a Minimalist theory.

Lastly, with the elimination of LF movement for WHs-*in-situ* (see Chomsky 1993, and chapters 6 and 7 below), the scope of the ECP is drastically truncated even if it finds a place within the Minimalist program. Thus, even if it can be restated in Minimalist terms, the ECP will not fill the same role that it has filled in earlier GB-style theories given the elimination of LF WH-raising.

16 That is, movement prior to SPELL OUT. Chomsky (1993) endorses the GB distinction between overt syntax and covert LF operations. However, Minimalism dispenses with SS as a level. The analogue of SS in a Minimalist theory is the place in the derivation where LF and PF paths split. This point is where the operation SPELL OUT applies. It is important to appreciate that SPELL OUT is not just another name for SS. The GB version of the T-model assumes that there is a place (i.e. the level SS) such that every derivation splits at that place. The Minimalist program assumes that every derivation is such that there is a place where the derivation splits. The order of the quantifiers is key. The GB version endorses a level where, one might put it, the SPELL OUT operation applies. The Minimalist program observes that the operation applies but there is no level at which it applies.

17 As Chomsky (1993: 33) puts it: "Derivations are driven by the narrow mechanical requirement of feature-checking only, not by a 'search for intelligibility' or the like."

18 The chapters below defend the conclusion that A'-operations must be licensed by strong features. However, most of the conclusions survive if we weaken the assumption to allow some instances of WH-movement at LF. What is crucial in what follows is that the A'-movement operation of QR does not exist nor does the operation that covertly moves a WH to an already filled WH Comp position exist. For possible instances of "simple" WH-movement at LF in Japanese and Hindi, i.e. the analogue of (i) at LF, see Tsai (1994).

(i) What did John say that Bill saw

Chapter 5 Antecedent-contained Deletion

1 This chapter is a much expanded version of Hornstein (1994).

2 For present purposes it does not matter if the operation is copying or deletion under identity of structure.

3   This is extensively argued in May (1985) and Fiengo and May (1994). The premise has been challenged in Lappin (1992). He argues for assimilating ACDs to pseudo-gapping (PG) constructions such as (ia). ACDs have the structure (ib) in which only the V has been elided.

(ia)   John ate a bagel and Frank did a cracker
(ib)   John ate everything which$_i$ Bill did [$_v$ e] t$_i$

There are some problems with this suggestion, however. First, it is not clear that PG generalizes in the right way. Thus, it is very clumsy to pseudo-gap in the following cases.

(iia)   ?*John will gave this book to Bill and Frank did Sam
(iib)   ?*Frank doesn't expect to win but Bill does to lose
(iic)   ?*John might talk about Sam and Frank did Sally

The corresponding ACDs are considerably more acceptable. This is unexplained if the ACDs are species of PG structures.

(iiia)   John will give this book to everyone that Bill did
(iiib)   Frank doesn't expect everyone that Bill does to win
(iiic)   John might talk about everyone that Bill did

Second, the problem with both VP deletion and PG constructions is to explain why it is that they are bounded at all. The reason is that these operations are not part of sentence grammar and so should be completely free. It is possible for PG and VP deletion to operate into islands and across sentences.

(iva)   John saw Bill. I wonder whether Frank did (Sam)
(ivb)   John saw Bill and I heard a rumor that Frank did (Sam)
(ivc)   John kissed Mary and I met several people who said that Bill did (Sheila)

Given the freedom to so delete, the question arises why there should be any limitation on the process. A virtue of the May (1985) and Baltin (1987) accounts is that they give rationales for the boundedness in terms of avoiding regress. The Lappin account, however, does not. Pseudo-gapping never encounters a regress problem. As such, why is it that ACDs are not always acceptable? Why do they exhibit boundedness restrictions at all? What limits the scope of elision in ACD constructions? A theory that involves regress has an explanation. A PG account does not.

   Lastly, for some reason, PG is not very felicitous when it occurs inside some relative clauses.

(v)   Sally and a few others won first prize and Sam congratulated everyone who did (*first prize)

(v) is unacceptable with the reading ". . . I congratulated everyone who won first prize." However, given this, it is hard to see how it is that PG could under-write ACD constructions given that they invariably occur within relative clauses. Observe that the VP deletion version of (v) is perfectly acceptable. In short, it is unlikely that PG operates in those contexts in which ACDs occur, in contrast to VP deletion. This argues against reducing ACD constructions to PG structures.

A final point. Lappin's approach to ACDs in terms of PG is motivated by a desire to have all interpretation done at SS. Given Minimalist assumptions, this motivation becomes an encumbrance. In what follows, I assume that Lappin's very interesting proposal is incorrect. For further arguments against Lappin's proposal see Fiengo and May (1994). For a proposal similar in spirit to Lappin's see Brody (1993).

4   Adjunction to IP is not required. Adjunction to VP or any position higher than VP will do as well to circumvent the regress problem.

5   The judgements are those in Baltin (1987). As will be clear below, not all speakers find the indicated judgements and contrasts compelling.

6   A reviewer of the Hornstein (1994) paper on which this chapter is based observed that this conclusion may be too strong: . . . besides the LF operation which is literally unrepresentable because of the regress problem, there is another one that is merely ill-formed because it contains an unlicensed empty VP. In this representation everything except the unlicensed VP can be interpreted. . . ." This suggestion does not circumvent the problem noted in the text. If there is no well-formed representation at LF then there should be no determinate interpretation. Thus, the unlicensed null VP should carry no specific interpretation, contrary to fact. It might be argued, however, that what meaning there is in these cases is pragmatically driven rather than grammatically licensed. I leave this possibility aside here.

7   A similar observation is made in May (1985) and Williams (1986).

8   The same facts hold in Spanish and Italian small clauses, see chapter 8, n. 75 for further discussion of small clauses.

9   Observe that the first sentence can be augmented with the phrase "namely his mother" forcing the wide scope universal reading. This is not possible in (15b).

10   It is harder to evaluate the strength of the argument, however, at least given standard assumptions. The extraposed constituent will not be that "far" from the heads that it interacts with. In fact, it is plausible to suppose that even after extraposition, the clause and the head will be in a government configuration. Given this, it is unclear that the relevant restrictions that are generally stated in terms of government cannot be reduplicated. This said, it is clear that not leaving traces behind will complicate things, as Larson and May (1990) point out.

11   This proposal has been made independently in Roberts (1992) and Uriagereka (1988).

12   The clause boundedness of QR is addressed in chapter 8.

13   This feature of A-chains is further elaborated in chapter 8 to account for relative quantifier scope.

14   More operations may have to apply to yield a licit LF. However, what is crucial is that the regress problem is circumvented by LF A-movement.

15   I have assumed for convenience that subjects are adjoined to VP rather than generated in Spec VP. If the latter proves to be correct, then it is V'-copying that is at stake. See the discussion below and chapter 9, n. 9 for further discussion of what the copied expression is.

16   This still leaves the puzzle of why the scope facts pattern as they do. See chapter 8, n. 75 for some discussion.

17   For example, Roberts (1992) cites the following Old French example in which the embedded object has been scrambled to before the matrix verb.

(i)   Et   s'il   la   terre   ne   veult   vuidier
      And if he the land   not wants to empty

18   See Lasnik (1993) for relevant discussion of these points.

19   It is not clear why this is so or what the correct descriptive generalization is. It appears that particles such as *so, then, also, as well,* are helpful in making the VP structures felicitous. However, I have no account as to why this should be the case.

20   This was brought to my attention by Robert May (personal communication).

21   This would be the standard account for the unacceptability of the indicated binding. However, it is not clear that it comports well with a theory in which quantifiers raise and adjoin to IP and in which conjuncts have X'-structure.

22   This suggests that even in appositive relative clauses the head and the relative form an LF constituent. Otherwise raising of the head to Spec AgrO for case reasons would not license ACDs in ECM structures.

23   Schein (1993) also argues that selected manner PPs are adjuncts not arguments.

24   This discussion is predicated on the assumption that (43) is indeed deviant. For many speakers, this assumption fails to hold. For such speakers, cases such as these reduce to the problem of ACDs within non-selected adjuncts.

25   It is consistent with everything said here that the adjuncts actually hang from some AGR projection rather than VP. For concreteness, I assume that they hang from VP. For further discussion see chapter 6.

26   "AgrIO" is agreement for indirect object. It is assumed that all Agr's are featurally identical so that "O," "IO," and "S" are just written for convenience. The assumption that indirect objects move out of VP for case marking is made in Branigan (1992). For an alternative analysis of case marking in double object constructions that gets both NPs out from under the VP see chapter 8 section 6.

27   The evidence distinguishing these two options is admittedly subtle. Should the distinction turn out to be spurious little will have been lost in the particular case of prepositional indirect object constructions. These would simply be assimilated to the case of adjuncts and generated outside the VP shell. I proceed on the assumption that the data are as indicated and consider what this implies.

28   If we choose our adverbs correctly we can get apparent violations of these claims.

   (i)   John wants to sing "Stardust" more than Bill does

   (i) is genuinely ambiguous. However, this is because *more than Bill does* can be felicitously adjoined to either the higher or the lower VP. If we replace this adverbial with *as loudly as Bill does* then only a lower adjunction is semantically felicitous (one does not want something loudly in general). Moreover in this case (i) is no longer ambiguous and only has the reading (ii), not (iii).

   (ii)   John wants to sing "Stardust" more loudly than Bill sings it
   (iii)   John wants to sing "Stardust" more loudly than Bill wants to sing it

29   One other PP that appears to function like *to* PPs are benefactives. As is well known, these pairs of PPs alternate with NPs in double object constructions. From the perspective adopted here, this may not be very surprising.

   (i)   John wants to bake a pie for everyone that I do (want to bake a pie for)
   (ii)   John wanted to bake everyone that I did (want to bake a pie) a pie

30   In fact, some apparent object NPs pattern like adjuncts with respect to these tests.

   (i)   John wants to weigh as much as Bill does

(i) can only be paraphrased as (ii), not (iii).

(ii) John wants to weigh as much as Bill weighs
(iii) John wants to weigh as much as Bill wants to weigh

This follows if *as much as Bill does* is an adjunct. There is well-known evidence that the apparent NP object in (iv) is not a complement.

(iv) John weighs ten pounds

Rizzi (1991: 280ff) shows that in contrast to regular complements they result in harsh unacceptability when extracted out of WH-islands. Furthermore, in contrast to regular objects, they do not passivize.

(v) *Ten pounds is weighed by John

These three properties can be accounted for in a unified manner if we assume that the NP measure phrase in (iv) is not a complement at all but an adjunct.

31 Steve Anderson (personal communication) points out the following problem if indices are not copied. Consider (i).

(i) John gave his letter to everyone that Bill did

Assume that *his* refers to someone other than John or Bill in (i). The elided VP cannot be interpreted as anaphoric to Bill despite the fact that (ii) can be so interpreted.

(ii) John$_i$ gave his$_j$ letter to everyone that Bill$_k$ gave his$_k$ letter to

Thus, a non-anaphorically interpreted pronoun cannot become a bound pronoun under VP ellipsis. In fact, the copied pronoun must retain the interpretation of the pronoun copied, i.e. if the copied pronoun is anaphoric so is the copy, if it is deictic so is the copy.
    There is a possible way of dealing with this issue without reintroducing index copying. It requires thinking of non-anaphoric pronouns as structurally distinct from anaphoric ones. Assume that these sorts of pronouns function like deictic pronouns and that these are interpreted as contextually specified temporary names. We would then analyze (i) along the lines of (iii), with the deictic pronoun in place of *Fred*.

(iii) John gave Fred's letter to everyone that Bill did

Note that something like this is needed to analyze strict readings in any case. We might, in fact, think of the restriction in (i) as due to the same mechanism that licenses the strict reading, the only difference being that in (i) the strict reading is deictically related to the individual that the subject refers to. In effect we are reducing coreferential and deictic cataphoric uses of the pronoun to the same structure.

32 However, the evidence in favor of VP internal subjects is quite strong. We present another reason for adopting this hypothesis in chapter 8.

33 As this process of index identification simply tracks the semantic process required for interpretation, it is not an instance of treating indices as real formatives and so

is compatible with the Minimalist aversion to treating indices as true syntactic expressions.

34   It still appears to be necessary to assume that indices are not copied so that the two subjects are not coindexed. As AgrO′ dominates the VP internal subject just as AgrS′ does, the principle C problems noted above arise regardless of which constituent is copied. Thus, on either approach, we must dispense with copying indices.

35   On a more technical note, one might think that preventing V-movement to T and AgrS′ would complicate the account in Chomsky (1993: 17–19) where the necessary crossing involved in subject movement to Spec AgrS and object movement to Spec AgrO is derived. However, it is not clear that LF movement is subject to the same restrictions that overt syntactic movement is. In Chomsky (1993) the two kinds of operations are dissociated and so it is not clear that the notion of domain is even relevant for LF movement Even if it is, not raising V beyond AgrO might not be an insurmountable problem. The reason is that what is crucial to Chomsky's account is that the verb adjoin to AgrO. This is what licenses crossing in (14) (p. 17) after the object has moved to Spec AgrO. If V moves no further in English, then Obj in (16) (p. 19) will not be able to cross Subj or t_{Subj} if Spec TP is in a different minimal domain from the unmoved object. In sum, it appears that what is crucial to this derivation is that V moves to AgrO and this is all that is required for the ACD data. One last point. Failing to raise the V to AgrS does not affect case checking at LF either. Whereas it is crucial to raise V to AgrO for accusative case checking as it is the amalgam of V+Agr that checks this case, nominative case is solely a function of whether Tns is finite or not. For nominative case the specific content of the verb is irrelevant. Thus, V-raising at LF to AgrS does not affect case theory in any direct way. However, not raising V universally does imply that agreement in English is not checked the way that case is, i.e. it is not checked in a functional projection. This implies that verbal morphology in third person singular for non-raising verbs is a reflex of an operation more akin to the old affix-hopping operation than to a process like V-raising at LF. For suggestions to this effect see Lightfoot (1993), Halle and Marantz (1993), and Lasnik (1994).

36   There is independent evidence that the elided constituent is at least as large as TP, as the tense in the elided constituent is always interpreted as identical to the one in the antecedent. This is clearly not so in VP deletion or ACD configurations in English where the elided constituent is smaller than TP.

37   The same facts hold in English as well to a marginal degree.

   (i)   ?John kissed Mary and Bill, too
   (ii)   *John kissed everyone that Bill

The elided constituent in these cases is an AgrS′, or a TP. At any rate, the tense must be copied into the elision site. But if this is so, then we encounter the regress problem noted above.

   Tony Kroch notes that this implies that the *which* phrase in (iii) must be presumed to hang lower than the conjunction in (iv) despite their semantically similar roles.

   (iii)   I left the party early which Bill *(did) too
   (iv)   I left the party early and Bill (did) too

If the adjunct in (iii) hangs below TP then we expect the omission of *do* to lead to unacceptability. There is evidence that the adjunct in (iii) does indeed hang lower than the conjunct in (iv). If we VP front as in (v), the adjunct must be moved along whereas this is prohibited in (vi).

(v) I left the party early and leave the party early, which Bill did as well I should have
(vi) *I left the party early and leave the party early and Bill did as well I should have

Furthermore, it is possible for a QNP to bind into a *which* phrase but not into a conjunct.

(vii) Every boy$_i$ left the party, which he$_i$ later regretted
(viii) *Every boy$_i$ left the party and he$_i$ regretted it

This follows if the *which* phrase hangs lower than the conjunct, as suggested here.
    Note that it is reasonable to treat the *which* phrase as a modifier of the event introduced by the matrix. If the event variable is housed in TP, then we could adjoin the adjunct to AgrO" or TP and still have it govern T^0 (i.e. be in the standard modification configuration). The conjunction, in contrast, does not modify the matrix event variable. That the effect of predication as in (iii) should be semantically similar to conjunction as in (iv) is to be expected given the standard treatment of modification as conjunction.
38 I illustrate the argument, as Otani and Whitman do, using Japanese examples. They claim that the same process occurs in Chinese and Korean.
39 They cast the analysis in GB terms. They apply the rule at SS. I have translated the proposal into a Minimalist idiom.
40 I abstract away from the issue of whether the functional projections are on the right or the left.
41 Saito applies to Japanese ideas originally put forward in Mahajan (1990).
42 The present analysis essentially follows the one offered in Takahashi (1993b). There is, however, one important difference between them. Most importantly, Takahashi proposes that accusative case is inherent in Japanese. He does this to prevent movement to Spec AgrO, which, he believes, would allow the ACD interpretation in Japanese, contrary to fact. On the present analysis, treating accusative case as inherent is not required. The ACD interpretation is blocked because the verb raises higher than AgrO.
    The evidence that Takahashi cites for accusative case being inherent is not that convincing. He argues that it is only ECM verbs that argue for accusative case marking being structural in English. This is not quite correct. Rather, it is the fact that accusative case does not seem tied to any specific theta role, as inherent case purportedly is. ECM structures are just the most dramatic instance of this lack of correlation between theta role and case. To my knowledge, accusative case in Japanese is not theta-related either. In fact, if it were, it could not be optionally assigned. However, as Takahashi observes, there are constructions in which nominative and accusative case are both available without change in the thematic interpretation of the case-marked NP. (i) illustrates the alternation.

(i) John-ga nihongo-o/-ga   hanas-e-ru   (koto)
    J-NOM Japanese-ACC/NOM speak-POT-PRES (fact)
    "(The fact that) John can speak Japanese"

Moreover, it appears that Japanese has what appear to be ECM constructions.

(ii) John-ga Mary-o kasikoi to   omotteiru
      J-NOM M-ACC is-smart COMP thinks
      "John thinks Mary is smart"

To account for (ii), Takahashi suggests that it has the structure in (iii) parallel to that in (iv).

(iii) John-ga Mary$_i$-o [$_{CP}$ pro$_i$ kasikoi to] omotteiru
(iv)   John-ga Mary$_i$-o [$_{CP}$ kanojo$_i$-ga kasikoi to]   omotteiru
       J-NOM M-ACC   she-NOM   is-smart COMP thinks

This suggestion is problematic. (iv) has an interpretation in Japanese parallel to the English sentence (v).

(v)   John thinks of Mary that she is smart

(v) has the characteristic of making the embedded proposition object centered (or *de re*). To make this clearer, contrast the sentences in (vi).

(via) John thinks a woman is in the room
(vib) John thinks of a woman that she is in the room

(vib) is object centered in that it is about a particular individual. (via) is a general proposition and can be true even if there is no woman in particular that it is about. As it turns out, the Japanese analogue of (via) can express a general proposition, i.e. it need not be object centered.

(vii) John-ga A WOMAN-O kasikoi to ommotteiru

This is what we would expect if it had an ECM structure but not if it had the structure proposed by Takahashi. I conclude that Japanese does in fact have ECM constructions.

43 The scrambling data are due to Daiko Takahashi, Masanori Nakamura, and Mihoko Zushi.
44 Lasnik (1993: 43–4) claims that analogous cases are better than their unmoved counterparts. This may be correct. However, it is unclear what this implies. Lasnik observes that these cases are "rather awkward." I find them somewhat worse than this. At any rate, I take their "awkwardness" to be due to ungrammaticality. Similarly for cases such as (i), analogous to his (119).

(i)   Which person/who that I wanted to did Bill say reviewed the book

(i) cannot felicitously have the reading "Which book that I wanted to say reviewed the book did Bill say reviewed the book." This said, there may be some surface effects that the present account does not fully account for. There are surely ancillary mechanisms of interpretation beyond grammatical ones. These plausibly exploit overt word order. I ignore these in what follows.

In addition, there is one further degree of freedom that impacts the present analysis. Chomsky (1993) argues that relative clauses can be added freely in the course of a derivation. If this is correct, then one need not "reconstruct" a relative clause to its base position as there is no copy of this clause in that position. Furthermore, adjoining the relative clause after the WH has moved to Comp finesses the regress problem. As such, these cases should permit ACD readings unproblematically. What the data here indicate, as well as the Japanese data on LDS structures, is that this adjunction process has a cost and cannot be as free as Chomsky (1993) assumes. However, it may well be that speakers differ as to how high this cost is and that this accounts for the different unacceptability judgements noted.

45   Thanks to Jairo Nunes and Cristina Schmitt for the judgements.

46   The discussion of Spanish, Brazilian Portuguese, and the East Asian languages suggests that overtly raising verbs to prominent inflection positions disallows ACDs.

This suggestion introduces into Minimalism a distinction among varieties of verb raising. V-movement to AgrO, which is required universally, contrasts with the movement of verbs past AgrO. In a Minimalist theory, the difference must be driven by morphological properties. As such, the proposal rests on the viability of having language particular morphological requirements in UG. In particular, it countenances the possibility that grammars can differ in having language-specific morphological requirements that drive overt movement, i.e. are met by SPELL OUT in grammars where they obtain, and do not have covert LF counterparts in languages without this kind of overt V-movement. The present account requires that case marking be checked by movement to Spec positions but that agreement need not be checked by V-raising. It is worth observing that case marking plays a very different theoretical role from agreement. It is a necessary condition on theta visibility that a DP/NP be case-marked. This is an assumption of the Minimalist program as it was in earlier GB accounts. Agreement is not seen as playing an analogous semantic role. As such, there is room for a theoretical distinction between the two kinds of processes and room to make the claim that LF movement for case holds universally whereas V-raising for agreement is parametric.

The present proposal also requires a second assumption: V-chains do not permit LF reconstruction. This guarantees that if a verb raises past AgrO by SPELL OUT, it cannot "lower" again at LF. We return to both these assumptions in chapter 9.

47   It is interesting to note the inclusion of the *-ta* (want) affix here. It parallels the suggestion made above that English *want* is a restructuring verb. Saito (1992: n. 8) further observes that scrambling out of embedded control structures patterns like CIS rather than LDS. This also fits well with the suggestion in the text that what we get in such cases is restructuring of the biclausal sentence into a monoclausal one. Similar scrambling data obtain in Hindi as well (see Mahajan 1990).

48   The data are not crystal clear. The judgements are Takahashi's (1993b). He claims that there exists the indicated contrast.

49   This problem was brought to my attention by Steve Anderson.

Chapter 6   Linking, Binding, and Weak Cross Over

1   There are well-known problems for bijection accounts of WCO. So for example, it seems quite acceptable for quantifiers to bind pronouns in inversely linked structures, from prenominal position and from object position into adjuncts as in (i)–(iii) even though these positions do not appear to c-command the bound pronoun. We return to these sorts of cases below.

(i)   Someone from every city$_i$ hates it$_i$
(ii) Everyone's$_i$ mother kissed him$_i$
(iii) John met every senator$_i$ without recognizing him$_i$

2   He develops ideas proposed in Evans (1980). For a good exposition of the theory see Lasnik and Uriagereka (1988).
3   All theories of WCO assume that a pronoun can be interpreted as a bound variable iff it is in the scope of the quantifier that binds the variable that the variable is semantically anchored to. In particular, if a pronoun is not in the (semantic) scope of the operator that binds the variable then it cannot be interpreted as bound by that variable regardless of what other structural configurations obtain. This is a condition that holds independently of the WCO condition. I assume this restriction as well. In chapter 8, I dispense with the rule of QR. The semantic scope of a QNP is taken to be the minimal clause that it is contained in. This is similar to the position taken in Williams (1986) but stated now at LF or as part of the interpretation procedures at CI.
4   I assume that linking directly to the quantifier in A'-position is not possible. Observe that there are several independent ways of blocking this sort of linking. One might block linking to an overtly moved WH to whatever prevents English from having resumptive pronouns, for example. For non-WH QNPs one could propose that free linking (as opposed to linking under movement) can only be between NPs and that, at LF, QR (if it exists (see chapter 8)) moves a bare Q and not the whole quantified NP. If this is so, then there is no appropriate linker at LF for the pronoun except for the variable. This is essentially the view of pronominal anaphora developed in Heim (1982: chapter 2) See Chomsky (1993) and Hornstein and Weinberg (1990). Chapter 8 eliminates QR. As such the only relevant case is linking directly to an overtly moved WH. If this is out for the reasons stated above, then only linking to the "variable" position is possible.
5   If QR does not exist, then WCO will be stated as a condition between quantified phrases and pronouns. For example, it will state that pronouns cannot be bound to/linked with expressions interpreted as variables on their right. Such expressions include QNPs and some WH-traces. Thus, if one assumes that QNPs range over variables as do WH-traces then WCO is the prohibition that such expressions cannot anchor pronouns on their left. This rules out cases such as (i).

(i)   His$_i$ mother kissed everyone$_i$

In what follows, I assume that QR applies to quantified expressions to move them to A'-positions. Chapter 8 argues against this. The adjustments to the presentation required to accommodate this are obvious, so for convenience I will assume that QR holds. One can also implement this QR-less theory by adopting scope markers to indicate the scope of a QNP. If one does this, the details of the analysis will strongly resemble the approach to WCO developed in Williams (1986).
6   The cases in (20) and (22) should occasion little surprise. These are essentially English versions of the cases first discussed by Montalbetti (1984). He showed that linking could account for the intricate restrictions on the distribution of bound non-null subject pronouns in certain dialects of Spanish. As Lasnik and Uriagereka (1988) observe, there is no equally adequate account in terms of binding (the latter construed as coindexing and c-command). The acceptable English cases mimic the linking configurations that underlie Montalbetti's account.
7   The Modern Greek examples involve the clitic left dislocation construction.

8 The technical details do not matter. All that is required is that in clitic doubled constructions we have a linking between the clitic and doubled element. I have assumed that the latter is linked to the former for this comports with a valid WCO structure for the relationship. However, should the linking be reversed, the point made in the text still stands. What is required is an account for why clitic doubling constructions appear to freely violate the WCOP and a linking theory provides an answer.

9 Joseph Aoun (personal communication) pointed out that this theory predicts that in certain sloppy identity constructions, WCO effects should be alleviated as well. Compare the following examples. The proposal suggests that (ia) is better than (ib) under the sloppy reading of remnant ellipsis (see Reinhart 1983 for discussion).

(ia) His$_i$ problem with his$_i$ thesis convinced John$_i$ [PRO$_i$ to get a job] and Sam too
(ib) His$_i$ problem with his$_i$ thesis convinced John$_i$ that Sheila wouldn't graduate and Sam too

The relevant readings are provided in (ii).

(iia) . . . and Sam's problems with his thesis also convinced him to get a job
(iib) *. . . and Sam's problems with his thesis also convinced him that Sheila wouldn't graduate

I leave the evaluation of these data to the reader.

10 It is only fair to add that for many speakers none of the sentences in (26) and (29) are any good.

11 See Campbell and Martin (1989), Hermon, (1984), Hornstein and Varlokosta (1992), Stowell (1986), and Zubizarreta (1992). In fact, the theory of Belletti and Rizzi (1988) is also compatible with a linking theory using a hierarchical condition like the one in (8).

12 There is a further problem with the null epithet theory. It is not clear how Lasnik and Stowell derive the acceptability of the sentences in (26) given their *Barriers* assumptions. As noted, they tie the availability of a null epithet to the presence of a 0-operator. However, in the case of subject parasitic gaps, it is not at all clear whether there is a null operator. Given standard *Barriers* assumptions there is no place for the 0-operator to hang from. It cannot adjoin to NP as such adjunctions are prohibited. However, unless it adjoins to NP, the 0-operator cannot be 0-subjacent to the real gap. In effect, subject parasitic gaps do not fit easily with a theory that derives all such gaps from 0-operator movement. As such, it does not fit easily with the Lasnik and Stowell account of null epithets. Note that if subject parasitic gaps are not formed by movement of a 0-operator, then the null epithets theory predicts that the sentences in (26) are both unacceptable.

13 I do not discuss the Lasnik and Stowell data (1991: 706, ex. 56–58). The reason is that I do not believe it to be accurate. I am a speaker of the dialect cited and I do not find the contrast that they discuss between the two readings of the 0-operator. In short, I doubt the claim that "the distribution of WCO effects with parasitic gaps correlates precisely with the logical status of the operator that locally binds the parasitic gap (p. 706)." In any event, the data reported are murky at best and cannot bear any significant empirical weight.

14 At least if one assumes any of the standard definitions of binding and c-command. Both the Reinhart (1983) definition and the Aoun and Sportiche (1983) definitions

result in bijection violations in (20) and (22) and examples such as (31). At the end of this chapter I suggest a possible revision of the definition of c-command that revives what is essentially the bijection restriction of WCO phenomena.

15   This assumes that QR obtains and moves a Q to pre-sentential position. If QR does not exist, as suggested in chapter 8, then the relevant fact is that QNPs have scope over the immediate clauses that contain them, essentially as in Williams (1986), and the Q-marker can simply be taken as indicating the sentential scope of the quantifier, like Williams's scope indices. Observe that these indices can be treated as heuristic if one simply takes it as part of the interpretive properties of sentences that they scope over the clauses that immediately contain them.

16   For concreteness, I assume the standard Reinhart (1983) definition of c-command: A c-commands B iff the first branching category that dominates A dominates B. We return to a revision of this definition below in section 6. Observe that (37) is conceptually very close to (8), the condition proposed by Koopman and Sportiche. The main differences are (aside from being a biconditional) (i) the substitution of almost c-command for c-command and (ii) the focus on the relationship between the variable and the pronoun it anchors rather than the quantifier and the bound pronoun as in the bijection account. Below, I propose some alternatives to the standard definition of c-command that allows (8) to be maintained.

17   This does not mean to say that linearity might not be grammatically relevant (see e.g. Kayne 1993). However, it is generally seen as a supplement to more structural notions like c-command. What was curious about earlier treatments of WCO effects was that they appeared to be purely linear.

One further point. Kayne (1993) assumes that LF phrase markers are subject to linearity requirements in accord with his Linear Correspondence Axiom (LCA). Chomsky (1994) develops a version of the LCA but one that does not extend to LF phrase markers. If the linearity is not a property of LFs, the oddity of a WCOP stated in terms of leftness increases and the motivation for restating the condition in hierarchical terms increases.

18   If we assume that the variable is in Spec AgrO for case reasons, it still fails to c-command the pronoun within the subject.

19   It is well known that certain quantifiers such as *each* and *any* invoke less sharp WCO effects. It appears that this obtains in these cases as well.

(i)   At least one picture of each senator$_i$ was on his desk$_i$
(ii)   The AG's investigation of each senator$_i$ led to his$_i$ impeachment
(iii) The AG's investigation of any senator$_i$ should lead to his impeachment$_i$

(i)–(iii) seem more acceptable than the analogous cases in the text.

20   I here assume, contra Larson (1988), that the adjunct is adjoined to VP. Branigan (1992) observes that most of the arguments that Larson (1988) provides in favor of the claim that adjuncts are complements within an expanded VP shell can be equally well accommodated in a theory that has adjuncts adjoined to VPs and objects raise to Spec AgrO at LF. See chapters 5 and 8 for further reasons for adopting the position that adjuncts are adjoined to what they modify rather than the Larsonian view that they are syntactic complements within an elaborated VP shell.

21   The PP is placed within the VP here. This assumption is not required. What is required is that it hang lower than the adjunct and below Spec AgrO. This latter assumption is independently motivated by the fact that binding into the PP is possible from object position.

(i) I told John about himself

Thus, at LF, the PP hangs below Spec AgrO.

22 For simplicity I have flattened out the part of the VP shell that holds the internal arguments, as nothing depends on these details.

23 This argument has assumed the anti-c-command requirement on parasitic gap constructions. If one analyzed the restriction in terms of a 0-subjacency requirement on chain composition as in *Barriers* the argument could still go through. The question then would be whether it is possible to adjoin the adjunct high enough to have the null operator 0-subjacent to the trace in Spec AgrO but low enough to be almost c-commanded by the variable. To meet the first condition, the adjunct could be hung no lower than adjoined to VP. But this is too high given the generation of the PP inside VP.

   If we assumed that the PP could raise out of VP to some Agr position (see chapter 5), then there might be some problems if we abandoned the anti-c-command requirement. Plausibly we could still rule these structures out as the adjunct would have to be adjoined to this AgrP to be 0-subjacent to the higher Spec AgrO. But this position might still plausibly be too high for the trace in the complement of the PP to almost c-command the bound pronoun. The relevant theoretical question is whether the PP in Spec of this AgrP c-commands the adjoined adjunct. The relevant empirical question is the status of binding in cases such as (i). If (i) is acceptable, then it suggests that we require the anti-c-command requirement to make things work. If it is not we can dispense with it in favor of a 0-subjacency analysis of parasitic gaps.

(i) Everyone$_i$ from a city his$_i$ mother loves

24 See chapter 2 for details and chapter 3 for the Aoun and Li (1993a) reanalysis of these data in terms of the MBR.

25 This is true both of the May (1985) analysis and the Aoun and Li (1993a) proposal.

26 Only the bound pronoun reading yields a functional answer. If the pronoun is not bound but merely coreferential, I assume that an i-answer has been provided.

27 "?" is the interrogative operator.

28 This abstracts away from movement of objects to Spec AgrO. This additional movement leaves another copy in Spec AgrO. This requires deletion of two copies, not just one. The details, however, do not affect the main point so I ignore them here.

29 Chierchia (1991) cites some semantic reasons for preferring this approach over an ECP-style account like the one in May (1985). As noted above, Chierchia observes that the standard semantics of questions and the standard treatment of quantification together should bar quantifying into questions. Specifically, he notes that the semantic value of a question is a set of propositions. However, quantifiers do not operate on sets of propositions but on propositions simpliciter. Thus (i) is semantically uninterpretable on a flat-footed approach to the semantics of questions and quantification. At the very least, extensions to the standard accounts are called for.

(i) *Qx{ . . . x . . . }

   Moreover, Chierchia suggests that these sorts of extensions are not empirically worthwhile. One reason why not (cf. Engdahl 1985 for others) is that not all quantifiers support pair–list readings. Thus, (ii) is not ambiguous:

(ii)   What did most of the/no/few/several of the/men say

This suggests that only a subclass of quantifiers can quantify into questions and it is not clear why this should be so if the semantics of quantification and questions is extended to allow quantifying into questions quite generally. In effect, Chierchia asks why if quantification into questions is semantically natural is it restricted to only a subclass of quantifiers.

He further suggests that this question might be illuminated by thinking of things in his terms. Why, he asks, if pair–list readings are related to functional answers do all quantifiers not support them? In particular, why do (51a, c) above which permit functional answers, not support pair–list readings?

30   These data are noted in Aoun and Li (1993a). They observe that the same data obtain in Chinese.

31   Similar contrasts obtain with benefactive constructions. The double object case manifests pair–list readings while the full PP versions resist this interpretation.

(ia)   I can't recall what you made everyone for breakfast
(ib)   I can't recall what you made for everyone for breakfast
(iia)   What did you buy everyone in the office
(iib)   What did you buy for everyone in the office

32   See chapter 8 for further discussion of these quantifier scope facts.

33   It is not clear how either a May-style ECP theory or the Aoun and Li (1993a) account in terms of the MBR could deal with these data. The ECP seems irrelevant, for subjects are not involved and so subject/object asymmetries do not come into play. An MBR explanation would have to explain what is wrong with the following LF representation of (63b). For argument, I adopt the last version of the MBR stated in terms of A'-expressions alone (see chapter 3).

(i)   I know [what$_i$ [everyone$_j$ [you [$_{VP}$ t$_i$ [$_{VP}$ gave t$_i$ to t$_j$]]]]]

In this structure, the A'-elements of the WH-chain include the adjoined VP trace and the WH in Spec CP. The A'-elements of the quantifier chain only have the adjoined operator *everyone* as a member. However, *everyone* c-commands an A'-element of the WH's chain. As such it should be able to have scope over it.

Note that the adjoined trace cannot induce MBR violations. If it did, we could not account for the availability of a pair–list reading in (63a). Its LF structure is (ii). The adjoined VP trace is crucial in licensing the pair–list reading on the Aoun and Li account.

(ii)   I know [what$_i$ [everyone$_j$ you [$_{VP}$ t$_i$ [$_{VP}$ gave t$_i$ t$_j$]]]]

34   The parallel between the English and the Chinese cases suggests that subjacency is an LF condition. This is what we would expect in a Minimalist theory. For further discussion, see chapters 8 and 9.

35   The IC is very closely related to the Specificity Condition proposed in Cinque (1990) and É. Kiss (1993). All three block the movement of non-specific WHs from WH-islands for example. The suggestion in É. Kiss that the condition is actually semantic rather than syntactic anticipates the detailed proposal in Szabolcsi and Zwarts (1992–3). This latter analysis provides a lattice theoretic basis for the semantic proposal.

Szabolcsi and Zwarts only address weak islands. However, their observation extends to islands more generally. I assume, perhaps incorrectly, that it is possible to extend their analysis so that only variables that denote individuals can be left by operators when extracting out of islands in general. This would essentially prohibit all binding of WHs or their traces that do not denote individuals, e.g. *how* and *why* plus functionally interpreted WHs.

It is interesting to observe that adopting the IC comes very close to eliminating the need for antecedent government in the grammar, at least as it applies to WH-elements. The requirement that traces inside islands be interpreted as ranging over individual variables covers essentially the same ground as the stipulation that adjunct traces, e.g. *how* and *why*, must be antecedent governed. There is a possible difference, but it is a small one and it argues against the *Barriers* version of antecedent government.

The Aoun and Li (1993a) data (68) and (69) indicate that some instances of *what* and *who* must also meet the IC. In ECP terms, this means that they too must be antecedent governed. However, these expressions reside in otherwise governed positions, i.e. object positions for example. But these positions are generally exempt from the antecedent government requirement in the sense that most theories allow traces in these positions to meet the ECP in some trivial manner. These data, in other words, indicate that it is not the distribution of WH-traces *per se* that is at issue but these traces under a certain interpretation. If correct, then a purely structural account, like the *Barriers* version of the ECP and antecedent government, is less plausible than one like the IC that takes the interpretation of the trace into account. A similar point is made in Cinque (1990) and É. Kiss (1993). This does not apply to ECP-style accounts like Aoun et al. (1987), Cinque (1990), and Rizzi (1991) that recognize variable types as relevant to how the ECP applies. However, it does indicate that the distinction between arguments and adjuncts is not simply a matter of position in a phrase marker, as is tacitly assumed in *Barriers*-like theories.

The uniformity condition on chains proposed in Chomsky and Lasnik (1993) cannot accommodate the Aoun and Li data either, unless uniformity is given a more semantic gloss. Chomsky and Lasnik assume that A'-chains must be as uniform as possible. This requires deleting intermediate traces in the case of non-adjunct movement. So, for example, if *what* moves successive cyclically as in (i), the trace in Spec CP deletes to preserve as much uniformity as possible and still have a well-formed operator/variable structure.

(i) What did John say [t [Bill saw t]]

In the case of adjuncts, the chain is fully uniform without any deletion as all the links in the A'-chain are in A'-positions.

(ii) How did John say [t [Bill [fixed the car] t]]

The data above indicate that uniformity, if relevant at all, cannot be stated in terms of the syntactic position of the links of the chain.

36 In Chinese-type languages this should be extended to include the binding of a WH-*in-situ* by the Q-marker in Spec CP. See Aoun and Li (1993b) and Watanabe (1991).

37 These vary in unacceptability. I selected cases where it is generally assumed that subjacency violations are weak. The important point is that whatever their level of acceptability, none can be interpreted via a pair–list answer. A similar observation

concerning the absence of pair–list readings in these sorts of constructions can be found in Longobardi (1990).

38   Contrast this with (i):

(i)   What did everyone plan to say

(i) can have a pair–list reading.

39   Similarly for accounts cast in terms of the MBR. The extra bound expression in no way affects licit chain binding. As such, the addition of a bound pronoun should leave the possible scope interactions unaffected and a pair–list reading should remain impossible.

40   This is a personal judgement. Some who have read earlier drafts of this work have found the notion "almost c-command" attractive. That is fine with me. This section explores how this motion might be replaced and what empirical advantages might accrue to doing so.

41   For some details see Kayne (1993: section 6.3).

42   Note one further interesting fact. (8) treats cross over as a matter of the relation of the bound pronoun and the variable that is its antecedent. This contrasts with bijection-style accounts which treat WCO as essentially a problem of relating A'-binders, e.g. quantifiers, with variables and pronouns. Once WCO is treated as essentially an issue of how A-elements can be linked, the necessity for QR to feed the process recedes. Another way of putting this is as follows. If bijection-like theories are correct, then something like QR is required. This approach removes another obstacle to the elimination of QR. See chapter 8 as well.

43   Kayne (1993) observes that *every girl* c-commands *every girl's father* using a definition of c-command in terms of exclusion. Thus, *every girl's father* intervenes between *every girl* and the reflexive assuming a notion like (i).

(i)   A is closer to B than C iff A intervenes between B and C
(ii) A intervenes between B and C Iff B c-commands A and A c-commands C

44   It is unclear how the proposal that closer antecedents block more remote ones from binding will handle the ambiguity of examples such as (i).

(i)   John told Bill about himself

45   It is worth conceding that the contrast, such as it is, is not crystal clear. For me, it is sharper in the second two sentences than in the first. Moreover, it is not clear that with anaphor movement at LF (see Lebeaux 1983, Chomsky 1986b) anaphora is under c-command. More likely, the anaphor moves to an Agr position and from there it is predicated of the antecedent, much like in relative clause structures. It is plausible that the anaphor adjoins to Agr and is predicated of the NP in Spec position. Anaphora would then be another case of a Spec–head relation.

46   In a Minimalist theory, the movement to Spec DP would have to be driven by some feature-checking requirements. Perhaps the distinction between strong and weak quantifiers is of relevance here. It is not unreasonable to assume that quantifiers are differentiated along this sort of dimension. If so, perhaps this feature comes into play at LF. See Thompson (1993) for a suggestion along these lines.

There is an interesting further bit of evidence suggesting that genitive NPs do not always sit in the same position at LF.

(ia) Someone$_i$'s mother was kissing him$_i$
(ib) There was someone's mother at the door
(ic) *There was someone$_i$'s mother kissing him$_i$

We might be able to handle this contrast in the following way. Assume that to be a "definite" QNP the quantifier must be in Spec DP. Inherently definite quantifiers like *every* or *most* must raise to Spec DP. Weak quantifiers like *some* raise only if interpreted as specific (see Enç 1991). In the case of genitive weakly quantified QNPs as in (i), *someone* in (ib) is in Spec NP, while in (ia) it is in Spec DP. In effect, then, the genitive hangs higher in the DP in (ia) than it does in (ib) or (ic). Given the definition of c-command in (89) below, the genitive in (ic) does not c-command the pronoun and hence cannot be a potential linker for the pronoun. The indicated binding is therefore illicit. In (ia), in contrast, the genitive has moved to Spec DP thereby allowing the pronoun to link to it.

47 I assume that the subject is a DP with a null D^0.
48 I leave the issue of TPs open. I think that to get this approach to work in all cases requires treating TPs as lexical.
49 One issue that I leave aside here is how this proposal works if we assume that PPs can generally be adjoined to VP. This may complicate the linking issues discussed as it will affect the c-command configurations.

Chapter 7 Superiority Effects

1 The theories reviewed in chapters 2 and 3 effect this reduction in different ways. Thus, Kayne (1984) does this in terms of connectedness, Aoun et al. (1981, 1987) in terms of binding, May (1985) and Pesetsky (1982) in terms of path containment, Aoun (1986) via Generalized Binding and Lasnik and Saito (1984, 1992) in terms of antecedent government. I abstract from these all important technical details here in lumping all these proposals together as versions of the ECP.
2 This does not mean to say that analogues of the ECP might not be required. For example, the Minimal Link Condition (MLC) outlined in Chomsky (1994) has the same theoretical role as the ECP in that it prohibits certain movements and chains from being licit. However, it does this in ways different from the classic ECP. This chapter aims to continue this sort of project.
3 See Aoun et al. (1981). This algorithm is adopted in Lasnik and Saito (1984) and Aoun et al. (1987). The algorithm turns up in Rizzi (1991) as a Spec-head indexing procedure.
4 These counterexamples to superiority were first noted by Kayne (1984).
5 The problem for an ECP account already surfaces in cases such as (i).

(i) *What did John expect who to buy

The ECP is standardly taken to be evident when finite subjects are involved, unlike (i). It is possible to finesse this problem by assuming that in ECM constructions the embedded clause is actually case marked via the embedded Infl rather than through the higher verb. This is what is proposed in Hornstein and Weinberg (1986) for example. This assumption is likely incorrect, however, as there is evidence from ACD constructions that in ECM constructions the embedded subject actually raises at LF to an Spec AgrO position above the ECM verb (see chapter 5).
   Hornstein and Weinberg (1986) also propose that sentences like (5) have small

clause structure and so the apparent direct object is actually the subject of a small clause. There is some interesting evidence that supports this position. Thus, Q-float is possible here despite being generally prohibited with objects.

(ii)   John persuaded the men each to sing

In what follows, I assume that it is worth elaborating an alternative treatment of cases like (5) that need not endorse small clauses for (5) or Infl marking of accusative case in (i).

6   The MLC as stated in Chomsky (1994) is a condition on chains rather than on movement. In what follows, I remain agnostic about how to treat it. However, the discussion in chapter 9 suggests that it is more natural to treat it as a condition on derivations rather than a condition on well-formed chains. In Chomsky (1993), a version of the condition was assumed to underlie WH-island violations. These are not discussed in Chomsky (1994). I assume that the earlier intuition is correct and that such islands reduce to some version of this condition. Perhaps all islands do.

7   In specifics, however, the approach outlined here differs from the suggestion in Chomsky (1993: 26). Chomsky follows Higginbotham and May (1981) and hints of a rule of absorption that creates polyadic WH-operators. There is no concrete proposal as to how the operation "that associates two *wh*-phrases to form a generalized quantifier" works. The proposal in May (1985) cannot be adopted for it involves LF movement and restricts absorption to sigma sequences at LF after movement has applied. At any rate, the proposal elaborated above reflects the spirit if not the schematic letter of Chomsky (1993).

8   I return below to consider whether this is a reasonable assumption.

9   Assume N restricts the function by providing a range for the mapping from elements that satisfy the variable to things bought. So, the functional WH defines a function from buyers to *things* bought (in the case of "what"). This is similar to the treatment of E-type pronouns in Chierchia (1992: 159, ex. 100).
    It is tempting to relate the fact that WH-expressions can play a pronominal E-type role to their capacity to function as pronouns in relative clauses.

10   Many find this sentence somewhat more awkward than (13d). I am one of those. This is interesting for it follows on the WCO theory on the assumption that locatives are generated to the left of temporals. This is supported by the relative acceptability of the sentences in (i).

(ia)   John heard Aida there then
(ib)   ??John heard Aida then there

11   The examples in (21) and (22) are from Larson (1988).

12   Chomsky (1993) discusses two different kinds of WH-structures. One has the syntactic format of unrestricted quantification and one the format of restricted quantification. Both can be adopted here. What is crucial is that functional readings require the WH itself to be in an A-position. Should the WH remain in Spec CP an operator-variable configuration obtains. For example, in the reconstruction cases that Chomsky (1993) discusses involving picture noun phrase *which* questions, the reconstruction of the restrictor does not imply that the WH must be functionally interpreted. What determines this is the locus of the *which*. If it is in Spec CP we get an operator-variable structure. If it is reconstructed, a functional reading appears.
    The assumption that the WH is the specific locus of a functional reading is

proposed in Reinhart (1992). The present proposal makes the same assumption. Reconstruction of the WH itself is required for a functional reading.

13 Bound pronouns and functional pronouns are semantically distinct. In Chierchia (1992), it is E-type pronouns that are capable of functional interpretations. This paper has assumed that both pronouns interpreted as bound variables and those that are functionally interpreted are subject to WCO considerations. If these two types of pronouns are semantically distinct, then their formal similarity with respect to WCO speaks in favor of a "syntactic" LF treatment of such cases rather than a purely semantic execution. The reason is that they are formally analogous entities only if one abstracts away from their distinct semantic interpretations.

14 Thanks to Juan Uriagereka for discussion of these matters. Erteschik-Shir (1990, section F) makes a similar observation concerning multiple WH-questions. She discusses sentences such as (i) and makes the following observation.

(i) Who ate what
     Who wants to do what

   . . . multiple wh-questions must be interpreted restrictively i.e. they "ask" for a pairing of sets. . . . In order to ask the questions in [(i)] the set of people must be defined in context. The questions could be asked, for example in the context of a party. *Who* would then "refer" to the people at the party. The question then asks for each member of this set what s/he ate, etc. The questions do not necessitate context specification of a set of foods, . . . etc. These sets will be generated by the answers to the questions.

15 As is well known, in languages in which WH-elements must move to pre-sentential position in the syntax, d-linked WHs need not so move. Indeed, it is less felicitous to move them than to leave them in place. See Pesetsky (1987: 128).

16 I here ignore the question of whether the full WH in Spec CP is deleted or only the "restrictor." For my purposes, it does not really matter. What is important is whether the +WH feature is eliminated when checked. See below.

17 An important area of current research is to determine a way of counting derivational steps. The argument presented here is rather robust and does not rely overly much on how steps are counted. What is important in what follows is that it takes more operations to "lower" the WH in Spec CP and raise the one in Spec IP than would the derivation that leaves the WHs where they are in overt syntax. Thus, the former derivation involves two operations of "form chain" (one for each WH) and two deletion operations. The latter requires only one operation of "form chain" applying to *what* and one deletion operation, i.e. deletion of the copy *in situ*. Note that for the case at hand, we must separate chain formation from deletion otherwise we could not "reconstruct" the WH in Spec CP. Without this reconstruction, however, the intended interpretation is unavailable on the WCO account.

18 I assume that WHs-*in-situ* can be moved via QR in discussion of this case. If they cannot be moved by QR, then we have yet one more solution to the present problem that does not invoke economy. The more interesting assumption, however, is that WHs-*in-situ* like all other quantificational expressions can be moved via QR. Only a specific stipulation forbidding this, clearly theoretically undesirable, could block this possible derivation.

19 This further casts doubt on whether QR exists at all given the explicit modelling of QR on overt WH-movement. Chapter 8 argues that QR does not exist as a rule of UG.

20   Movement of a WH-operator to Spec CP after the WH-feature in Comp has been checked could be a violation of the Principle of Greed. However, this conclusion must be handled gingerly. The reason is that Greed has been variously interpreted (see, for example, Lasnik 1993). One might argue that the raising of the WH-operator at LF is required for the operator to check its own WH-features, either against a WH-feature in Spec CP or against the WH-operator in Spec CP. This would then conform to some versions of the Principle of Greed. If we assume that a WH-operator cannot check its features against those of an element in Spec CP, then the elimination of the +WH-feature on C^0 suffices to block movement to Spec CP at LF. In other words, this approach assumes that the WH-features on the *in situ* operator cannot be checked by movement at LF (or adjunction) to a Spec CP filled by a WH-expression.

21   This assumption dates back (at least) to Katz and Postal (1964: 92) and their assimilation of *which* WHs to definites and simple WHs to indefinites.

22   They must also be part of a multiple question (see n. 14). I am not sure why this latter requirement holds. One possibility is that the prohibition against quantifying into questions, which I have assumed here following Chierchia (1991), forces at least one of the WH-operators to be interpreted as a generator in a multiple interrogative to yield an interpretation. If this is so, it is not surprising that at least one of the WHs must be a generator in multiple WH-constructions.

   Note that the observation that in multiple questions the WH in Spec CP is the generator allows one to account for the unacceptability of (i) (noted by Barry Schein).

(i)   *What did everyone expect who to buy

The relevant question is why this we cannot interpret the WH in Spec CP functionally, as in (ii).

(ii)   What did everyone buy

The answer is that in multiple WH-constructions this WH must be the generator. But if so, it cannot "reconstruct" to its trace position and so a functional reading is ruled out. This, in effect, prohibits *everyone* from being the generator for the pair of WH-elements functionally interpreted. (i) is ungrammatical as it violates WCO at LF. The structure is given in (iii).

(iii)   What$_i$ [everyone expect [[pro$_i$ person] to buy t$_i$]]

   One last point. This analysis has not eliminated the need to state the requirement that WH-*in-situ* in English is only permitted if there is a WH in Spec CP to license it. WHs-*in-situ* are licensed by WHs in Spec CP, presumably under binding of the implicit pronoun. This is observed in sentences like (iv) (Audrey Li and Joseph Aoun brought these facts to my attention).

(iv)   Who said everyone bought what

(iv) must be interpreted as a general question. The embedded *what* cannot be interpreted functionally bound to *everyone*. This plausibly relates to the fact that WHs-*in-situ* must be licensed by a WH in Spec CP. One reasonable possibility is that the WH-features on the WH-*in-situ* must be checked and that these are checked under binding at LF. Note that an analogous assumption must be made in a theory in which WHs *in situ* move to Spec CP at LF. In a Minimalist theory, this movement is prompted by the requirement that the WH that moves has some features that need checking. The main difference with the present theory is that this checking is assumed to hold under binding rather than movement.

Aoun and Li (personal communication) point out that these same facts hold in Chinese. However, given Aoun and Li (1993b) and Watanabe (1991) in which the East Asian languages have been essentially reduced to English (i.e. one of the WHs *in-situ* is linked to the Q-morpheme in Spec CP moved there before SPELL OUT), the same account extends to these languages.

23 The elimination of absorption from the grammar is a natural consequence of eliminating A'-movement of WHs-*in-situ* at LF. Chomsky (1993) seems to adopt a hybrid position in which there is no LF WH-movement but there is still absorption. It is not clear how Chomsky intends to implement this proposal. The present analysis eliminates the need to do so.

For arguments that quantification into questions leads to semantic problems see Kartunnen (1977: n. 15) and Chierchia (1991).

24 The acceptability of (37) is troublesome for any theory that directly handles superiority effects in terms of a principle such as the Superiority Condition in (2).

25 Again this requires that absorption not be an option, a crucial assumption here.

26 Note that implicit in these explanations is an interpretive difference between WH-traces and unmoved WHs. In an LGB theory this sort of difference is unsurprising. In a Minimalist theory, it is more unexpected. Recall that traces are simply copies of the element moved. However, if this is so, it is unclear how traces can have properties different from those of unmoved expressions, though empirically, as indicated here, this seems to be required. Consider the problem in more detail. An unmoved WH can be functionally interpreted. In (i) the WH inside the WH-island can have a functional reading in which the pronoun is bound by the matrix WH-trace.

(ia) Who remembers who bought what
(ib) [Who$_i$ [t$_i$ remembers [who$_j$ [t$_j$ bought [pro$_j$ thing]]]]]

This contrasts with the unacceptability of functionally interpreting the trace of WH in (41) and (42).

Why should this be so? It suggests either that traces of WH-movement are not *mere* copies of what is moved or, more interestingly, that the relation between a WH and a "trace" inside an island is not a function of movement at all. This is what a strict commitment to economical movement might require, in particular adherence to a version of the MLC (see Chomsky 1994). Assume, for present purposes, that what characterizes islands is that one is always moving across a filled non-L-involved (i.e. A') Spec position. This means that all island violations are actually the result of movement that violates the MLC. In effect we are assimilating all island violations to the suggestion in Chomsky (1993) for WH-islands. Assume furthermore that movements that violate the MLC are prohibited. This entails that WHs cannot move out of islands.

What then is the nature of the relationship exemplified in sentences like (48)? One possibility is that the relationship is more akin to that of a resumptive pronoun or a 0-operator as in parasitic gap constructions (see Cinque 1990). This would fit, moreover, with the requirement that it have an individual interpretation. It would also provide a structural distinction between (i) and these examples. In fact, the "trace" is not a copy in (41) and (42) for there has been no movement from this position. An analysis along these lines was outlined in Cinque (1990) for some island effects and is currently being pursued for all islands by Baltin and Postal (1994).

Note that this sort of derivation for apparent island violations would reduced the inability of non-individual operators like *why* and *how* to violate island conditions to their inability to license null operators or null pronouns. This, in turn, can be traced to the absence of pronominal analogues of *how* and *why* (see Aoun 1985, Cinque 1990, Weinberg 1988).

One last point. Chomsky (1994) suggests that the MLC be taken as a condition on well-formedness of chains at LF. Given the "lowering" analysis for functionally interpreted WHs proposed here this interpretation is unavailable. Rather, the MLC must be taken as a condition on movement rather than the output of movement. The reason is that with "reconstruction" the A'-chains that obtain in overt syntax are eliminated after deletion of the WH in Spec CP. This sort of deletion is an option crucially required by the present analysis.

A last point if this is correct. This analysis suggests that there is no reconstruction into 0-operator structures. There is, however, apparent evidence against this proposal (see Munn 1994 for a review). This requires a reanalysis of the apparent binding data. One possible approach would be to assimilate what is going on in these constructions to the binding properties one observes in constructions such as (ii).

(ii)   John gave his paycheck to his wife. Everyone else deposited it in the bank

Here *it* can go surrogate for *his paycheck* and permits a reading in which everyone but John put his paycheck in the bank. Thus, it seems that overt pronouns can "copy" material that comes to be interpreted as a bound pronoun. This process can also "copy" reflexives.

(iiia)   John gave the picture of himself to his wife. Everyone else gave it to his best friend

(iiib)   John shaved himself slowly with a razor. Everyone else did it quickly with a machete

(iiic)   John gave a picture of himself to his wife. Everyone else gave one to his best friend

The data in (iii) suggest that both definite and indefinite pronouns can implicitly "represent" a reflexive that gets bound in a sloppy-like fashion.

Note that we get principle B like effects as well. So in (iv) the pronoun cannot be understood as coreferential to Bill or Sam.

(iv)   Bill shaved him with a machete and Sam did it with a razor

Last of all, we even seem to get principle C like effects.

(v)   Mary shaves John slowly but he does it quickly

Here *he* is not felicitously interpreted as *John*, as we would expect if principle C were at issue and the *it* went surrogate for *shave John*.

It appears, therefore, that overt pronouns act as if they involved copies of their antecedents despite there being no licit movement relation between the pronoun site and the other clause. If so, it argues that one need not reconstruct into islands to get apparent binding effects. The assumption that the null pronoun can license the binding properties in ways similar to the overt pronouns might suffice.

27 Actually, all WHs of the *who, what,* variety. The analogues of inherently d-linked WH-operators like *which book* preferably remain *in situ*.

28 For illustrative purposes, I focus on Polish from the first group and Bulgarian from the second.

29 See chapter 5 for discussion.

30 It is well known that Polish is a relatively free word order language. This too could be accounted for in terms of the sort of intraclausal scrambling typical of Japanese, another relatively free word order language.

31 Things might not be so neat, however, In the case of (63b) we are interpreting the trace of a WH functionally within a potential WH-island. I say "potential" because the WH adjoined to IP is not necessarily part of a WH-island as it is not in a Spec–head relation with a +WH-head. If the IP-adjoined WH creates an island then the problem noted arises. Recall that chapter 6 (and below in the account of B-languages) suggests that functionally interpreting a WH-trace inside an island is not generally possible. If this IP adjunction creates an island, then this approach is less preferred than the first one sketched in terms of A-scrambling. For present purposes, I put aside this reservation but see n. 33 on Hungarian for further discussion of how to characterize a WH-island.

32 See Kayne (1993) for a recent vigorous defense of this assumption.

33 Hungarian patterns essentially like English once issues of specificity are taken into account. É. Kiss (1991) provides the following contrast.

    (i) Ki milyen véleményt mondott
        Who what opinion-ACC gave
        "Who gave what opinion"
    (ii) *Milyen véleményt ki mondott

For discussion see É. Kiss (1991, 1993).

34 This is an extension of the assumption in Chomsky (1986b) that adjunction to an element prevents that element from bearing a theta role. As in *Barriers*, I assume that this holds of derived adjunctions. Note that a consequence of this is that it will severely limit adjunction. For further discussion of a similar principle see Chomsky (1994).

35 (69) suggests another possible reason for this process to be inadequate. Strictly speaking *koj* does not c-command the t-variable. Rather the whole complex WH does. On the assumption that the variable must be bound to be licit, we can rule out the deletion of *kogo* because it leads to a proper binding violation.

36 This section based on Boscovic (1993). His analysis relies on a principle rather similar to the Superiority Condition in section 1. I reanalyze the data in terms of the WCO approach to superiority effects. Boscovic presents data from both Spanish and Hebrew. The analysis presented here extends to the Hebrew data as well. For illustration, however, I stick to Spanish examples.

37 There is considerable evidence in support of this analysis. The most interesting and dramatic evidence is presented in Brandi and Cordin (1989).

38 It actually does not matter if the postverbal subject actually hangs somewhat higher, as high as AgrOP given that the movement of the object WH to Spec AgrO at LF

will allow it to c-command the inverted subject at LF. For expository convenience I assume that the inverted subject actually is adjoined to VP.

39   Thanks to Juan Uriagereka for relevant discussion and data.

40   The semantics of these constructions with multiple functional readings are discussed in Chierchia (1991: section 5). The interpretation of these questions is roughly {p: p is true & for some f,f' p= (Every x: x a buyee) (buy (f(x), x, f'(x))}.

41   This section closely follows the analysis of anti-superiority effects in S. Watanabe (1994).

42   Joseph Aoun (personal communication) observed that this further implies that paired interrogatives involving *why* and *how* should be universally odd as neither ranges over individuals and so neither should function as a generator. This, he informs me, seems to be correct. In English, for example, (i) is decidedly odd.

(ia)   *Why did Bill sing how
(ib)   *How did Bill sing why

43   For details, see Aoun and Li (1993a).

44   The WH indexed with Q in Spec CP is the variable position.

45   The acceptability of this sentence is somewhat in dispute. Huang (1982) treats it as unacceptable. Since then, Audrey Li informs me, it has been rehabilitated, some speakers judging it acceptable, others less than perfect. What is clear is that its relative acceptability contrasts with the unacceptability of (90b) and (90c).

46   Pair–list readings are unavailable in Japanese as Hoji (1985) observes. One possible reason for this is there is an SS prohibition against having WHs in the scope of quantifiers like *every* in Japanese. Thus structures like (i) are banned.

(i)   [Every . . . wh . . .]

To get a question in this sort of structure, the WH-form must be fronted to the left of the *every* phrase. This surface condition, if extended to LF, accounts for why pair–list readings are absent in Japanese given the assumption that reconstruction is required to support a functional interpretation of WH.

47   Watanabe (1994) cites Saito (1985) for the relevant data. A. Watanabe assumes that the cases are all unacceptable. However, it appears that speakers make the contrast indicated by Saito. Following S. Watanabe, I assume that Saito's original judgements are correct.

48   See Aoun et al. (1981).

49   The first assumption is proposed in Rizzi (1990).

50   I consider embedded questions under *I wonder* to control for possible echo questions. It is hard to get an echo question under this matrix verb.

51   Contrast (98a) with (i).

(ia)   I wonder which book which person read
(ib)   ?I wonder what which person saw

(ib) is less acceptable than (ia) presumably because two kinds of WHs are mixed here. However, it is still far better than (98a).

52   There is one interesting structural difference between the unacceptable examples in (102) and the more acceptable (95b). The latter has the WH-object in final position. In this position the WH seems able to bear a kind of focal stress and perhaps this contributes to improving the acceptability of the sentence.

53 The assumption must be that generating *why* in Spec CP constitutes the unmarked case. A Chinese or Japanese child will have positive data in simple "why" sentences indicating that this generalization does not hold in these languages.

54 *How* is more complex than *why* in its behavior. First, the degree of unacceptability of *how-in-situ* is far more variable than with *why*. Second, *how* covers various sorts of answers, manners and instruments to name two. Thus, (ii) are all appropriate answers to (i).

   (i)   How did Bill fix the car
(iia)   He fixed it well
(iib)   He fixed it with a wrench
(iic)   He fixed it with his usual care

It is unclear to me whether (iii) (if acceptable at all) is equally so with all these sorts of answers equally.

   (iii)   Who fixed your car how

(iii) sounds better than (iv).

   (iv)   Who fixed your car why

Furthermore, *how* appears to support pair–list readings.

   (v)   How did everyone do on the exam

(v) naturally allows a different grade to each value of *everyone*. If this is so, then *how* is rather different from *why*. I have little to say about the intricacies touched upon here.

55 Others also accept this reading. However, there are those who do not like these sorts of answers. For purposes of discussion, I assume that these answers are felicitous and that the pair–list reading is available. Should this prove to be incorrect, not much will change. We simply assume that traces of Y/N operators cannot be functionally interpreted or that they are not moved as Katz and Postal (1964) surmised and so leave no traces at all.

56 A crucial question is whether Y/N questions with quantifiers that do not have generators can yield answers analogous to (112). This is unclear. Some informants say yes, some no. I report the data as I they strike me but I am not confident they are correct.

57 There is counterevidence to this proposal, however. Consider (i). Both cases are clearly unacceptable.

(ia)   *Did John eat which sandwich
(ib)   *I wonder whether John ate which sandwich

The present theory would have led us to expect these to be on the acceptable side. They should have patterned with (111). This suggests that this extension of the foregoing analysis to Y/N questions is on the wrong track. I put this possibility aside here in order to see how far one can get pursuing the analysis. However, the reader should bear in mind these contrary data.

A last point. Should the extension in the text prove to be untenable, little else will be affected. It is consistent with the present analysis to suppose that some WHs cannot act as generators nor can they be functionally interpreted. It is plausible that the Y/N operator has both characteristics.

58 The directional assumption concerning the placement of the Y/N variable can be replaced with a hierarchical condition if we follow Katz and Postal's assumption that it hangs high up, adjoined to some prominent clausal projection. This will then fit with the structural statement of the WCO condition in chapter 6.

59 Absorption, semantically, involves the simultaneous assignment of values to the *n*-variables the operator binds rather than the recursive valuation of these variables. The recursive operation is what will lead to quantifying into questions in a way relevant to Chierchia's concerns. To drive the earlier results, this way of satisfying the restriction against quantification into questions must be stymied.

60 As Juan Uriagereka has pointed out to me, however, some Minimalist theories have an analogue of antecedent government in the MLC.

Chapter 8   Quantifier Scope

1 Chomsky (1993: 28–9) discusses the distinction between broad and narrow L-relatedness. This is to accommodate the possibility of adjunction within the Minimalist program. Recall that in chapters 6 and 7 various scrambling operations were treated in terms of adjunction to IP. Whether even this adjunction process is necessary is an open question, as Chomsky notes. However, even if it is concluded that adjunction is required for movement operations prior to SPELL OUT, we are still left with the question of whether this is required for LF operations. Assume for the sake of discussion that it is not. We could then interpret this as signifying that adjunction is a marked grammatical process requiring overt evidence for its existence. The core case of movement would then be substitution. Adjunction would be permitted, though not favored, i.e. would be a marked grammatical option.

It is also possible that the notion of broad L-relatedness should prove useful in other ways. See below for the suggestion that Spec NegP has the properties of both A and A' positions, i.e. that it is a broadly L-related position.

2 See discussion of the WH-criterion in May (1985) and Rizzi (1991). This intuition actually goes back much farther, at least to Chomsky (1973).

3 This work goes back to Chomsky (1976). It was first extensively developed in May (1977).

4 Two points. First, this does not contradict Chomsky's (1993: 37, ex. 35) analysis that A-movement is not subject to reconstruction. What Chomsky observes is that principle C effects are not forced under A-movement the way they seem to be under A'-movement. This is consistent with the claim advocated here that *any* link can delete. Second, this position is consistent with a weak *performance* generalization of the following sort: speakers prefer to delete elements lower in a chain to elements higher in a chain. In a word, heads are better than tails. This might be true (and it seems true for many speakers) and it could still be true that grammatically any link can drop. This performance principle may well be related to another grammatical fact explored here, namely that different interpretations correlate with different links surviving to the CI interface. This implies that deleting different links makes an interpretive difference. I propose (following suggestions in Diesing (1992) based on Heim (1982)) that this is so. As we shall see, the higher links

will correlate with d-linked readings. It is a pragmatically reasonable strategy to interpret one's quantifiers in a d-linked fashion if one can as it is conversationally cooperative to do so. This could underlie the performance preference noted above.

5   A lexical link is one that has not been subject to any deletion processes. In other words, every copy but one must delete.

6   This is not intended to rule out the possibility of mutual c-command. If this exists, I assume that choice of either scope option is allowable (see May 1985). However, in the cases discussed, mutual c-command does not appear to arise, even using the definition of c-command in terms of functional projections suggested in chapter 6. If this result can be generally maintained it is methodologically desirable as we can reestablish the strict relation between c-command and semantic scope dispensed with in May (1985) and Aoun and Li (1993a). In effect, we can allow LF phrase markers to once again disambiguate semantic interpretation.

7   The principle then is that a chain is interpreted as definite only if after deletion (of links) has taken place the single remaining lexical link occupies a position outside the VP shell. It would be nice to strengthen this to "if and only if," i.e. a chain is interpreted as definite iff the lexical remnant is outside the VP shell. This is what Diesing assumes in order to get the fact that ACDs are always interpreted as specific. In terms of the analysis in chapter 5, this correlation is expected iff specifically interpreted DP/NPs are outside the VP shell. Recall, to avoid the regress problem the expression containing the null VP must raise out of the VP shell to Spec AgrO (at least). Given Diesing's principle, this requires that it carry a specific or definite interpretation (thanks to Ellen Thompson for discussion on this point).
    If this is correct, certain data in Laka (1993) from Basque become empirically relevant to the present proposals. Laka observes that all indefinites must raise outside the VP shell in Basque for case-marking reasons. However, some of these can be interpreted as non-specific. If this is so, then the only way to save Diesing's generalization in light of Laka's observations concerning Basque is to allow the sort of A-chain reconstruction proposed in the text. In other words, Diesing's principle in conjunction with Laka's analysis constitutes independent evidence for the deletion process proposed in (1).

8   For my purposes, "definites" include expressions headed by *the* and the strong quantifiers, e.g. *each*, *every*, *most*. Indefinites outside the VP shell are interpreted as specifics if one accepts the strong version of Diesing's proposal discussed in n. 7.

9   Some quantifiers (almost) always seem to require wide scope readings. *Each* is the paradigmatic instance of this. Its scope properties seem largely unrelated to its syntactic positions. Thus, it can take wide scope even when in the subject position of a finite embedded question. If scope for *each* were determined by QR it would violate several conditions, including the ECP.

(i)   Someone wondered whether each man would win

I assume that *each*'s scope properties are independent of QR or QR substitutes. In discussing scope facts I concentrate on *every/some* interactions.

10   Irrelevant structure pertaining to X^0-movement has been omitted.

11   An NP in parentheses signifies deletion. A deleted NP is the analogue of a trace in GB-style theories.

12   The present account does not treat (i) as structurally ambiguous.

(i)   Everyone kissed someone

At LF, *everyone* must take scope over *someone*. The two interpretations generally associated with (i) can be traced to the fact that it is true in two distinct models; if everyone kissed someone different or if all kissed the same person. Thus, the ambiguity of (i), on the present theory, is more correctly thought of as vagueness. The models compatible with the structure are vague as to how many kisses there are.

Paul Pietroski (personal communication) noted that it is reasonable to treat this as a case of vagueness given the following line of reasoning. Consider a model with 100 men and 50 women. Then consider the interpretation of (ii).

(ii) Every man kissed a woman

This is true if all 100 men kissed the same woman, or if every two men kissed a different woman. Thus, each woman is kissed by two men. Of course there are a bunch of models in between that satisfy this sentence. Thus, one woman is kissed by three men and all the others by two but one is left unkissed. Do we really want to say that this means the sentence is three ways ambiguous? Or more exactly, *at least* three ways ambiguous? This seems incorrect. But why then distinguish only the two extreme cases noted? Rather, the sentence is vague or indeterminate as to how men and women are related.

Note that this does not work in the case of (iii).

(iii) Someone kissed everyone

For whereas some/every order implies every/some order the converse does not hold. Hence the two interpretations are disjoint rather than vague.

13   There are other options. An interesting question is whether opacity is represented in LF structures. If it were, we would predict that if *someone* were in the scope of *every class* then it would necessarily be interpreted as within the scope of *seems*. This sort of prediction is very hard to test and it is not clear that opacity effects are actually represented at LF. One reason for thinking that it is not is that it is possible to interpret the indefinite in (i) transparently as easily as one can (ii) but the embedded indefinite in (i) cannot c-command the matrix verb at any level.

(i)   It seems that someone ate the petunias (namely Fred)
(ii) Someone seems to have eaten the petunias (namely Fred)

See Hornstein (1984, 1987) for discussion.

14   These data were accounted for in a Generalized Binding framework in Aoun and Hornstein (1985). Note, incidentally, that this contrast requires that raising not be analyzed as a lexical process. It is crucial that movement be involved as it is movement that leaves copies that in turn enter into possible scope relations. The same observation holds for passives and the scope opportunities that they afford in languages like Chinese (see section 4 below).

15   Recall that this same assumption was exploited in chapter 5 to handle certain ACD cases.

16   Generalized Binding achieves this result via its theory of A'-anaphors. Most other accounts simply stipulate the fact that quantifiers are scopally restricted to the clauses that contain them (see Chomsky 1975a). This account allows us to dispense with A'-anaphors without *ad hoc* stipulations.

17   This property of natural language quantifiers was observed in Chomsky (1975a) and May (1977).

18 These cases were first discussed by Higginbotham (1980).

19 The *every* phrase being definite must be outside the VP shell after deletion given the Mapping Principle. Hence, this is the only option available given the interpretation.

20 Indices are employed to indicate binding. Linking would also suffice but it is typographically more cumbersome.

21 I assume that the object of the preposition raises to a Spec Agr position to permit the pronoun binding, as in chapter 6.

22 Earlier QR-based theories did not easily derive this correlation either. Higginbotham (1980) traces it to a WCO violation stated as a condition on derivations. He assumes that the syntactic format of QR is that of restricted quantification and that in moving the *every* phrase above someone to derive the correct quantifier scope representations, the pronoun ends up to the left of *someone*'s variable. This violates WCO. However, it is unlikely that this is the correct account given the ability to "violate" WCO in case of overt WH-movement. One can handle these cases in terms of reconstructing the restrictor of the WH but then the account of (14) should allow this same reconstruction and so be acceptable.

(i)   Which of his$_i$ poems did every poet recite

Note, incidentally, that there is little reason to think that the classical theory of QR should move the Q+restrictor at LF. There are empirical problems with this assumption (see Hornstein and Weinberg 1990 for some discussion). The Aoun and Li (1993a) theory also requires A'-movement and runs into similar difficulties.

23 The argument here is simply a restatement in Minimalist terms of the observation that quantifier lowering is blocked by binding requirements. Chomsky and Lasnik (1991) argue that quantifier lowering cannot exist because of the following data.

(i)   Everyone didn't leave
(ii) Everyone seems not to have left

They argue that (i) can have *everyone* in the scope of neg. This contrasts with (ii) where this is not possible. However, if lowering were available we would expect the latter to allow the same sort of interpretation. There is an empirical flaw with this argument, however. Consider (iii).

(iiia) John would prefer for everyone not to leave
(iiib) John wanted very much for everyone not to leave

These sentences do not allow neg to scope over *everyone* either. But if these do not allow this, we expect (ii) not to allow it either. Thus, even if lowering is permitted the ambiguity Chomsky and Lasnik point to is not expected.
   See below for further discussion of neg/quantifier scope effects.

24 This is assumed, for example, by standard theories of parasitic gaps. See Chomsky (1982) and discussion below.

25 The strong version of Diesing's principle states that an expression is interpreted as definite/specific iff it is outside the VP shell. If this is correct, then we expect that (ib) is the phrase marker that obtains at LF if *someone* is interpreted as specific in (ia).

(ia) Everybody bought a book yesterday
(ib) [Everybody [a book [(everybody) bought (a book)] yesterday]]

If this is correct, then we expect that binding into an adjunct should affect the interpretation of sentences such as (i). In particular, the indefinite should be interpreted specifically when binding occurs. The interpretation of (ii) suggests that this is correct.

(ii) Everybody bought a book$_i$ yesterday after *The Times* reviewed it$_i$

(ii) seems to favor the reading in which there is a single book purchased, a reading analogous to (iii).

(iii) Everybody bought a certain book after *The Times* reviewed it

A specific interpretation of an indefinite favors the reading in which one book is at issue. This is not required, however (see Liu 1990, Enc 1991). Interestingly, to the degree that a singular interpretation is required in cases such as (iii), it is favored in cases such as (ii). This suggests that the strong version of Diesing's principle holds.

26 Given the definitions in Chomsky (1993), it appears that Minimalism repudiates the Larsonian treatment of adjuncts as syntactic complements. A Larsonian treatment would require that adjuncts be subject to the principles of the cycle, in particular the Extension Condition. This condition essentially requires that derivations not disturb established X'-relations. Given the definitions in Chomsky (1993) and some recent proposals concerning X'-theory in Chomsky (1994), the only place that adjuncts can legitimately go is adjoined to the maximal projection. In short, the old structural distinction between adjuncts and complements is redeemed and placed at the center of the theory.

   If this is correct, then the data cited here become that much more interesting as they crucially rely on a non-Larsonian structural distinction between adjuncts and complements, a distinction that lies at the center of X'-theory and, thereby, at the center of the Minimalist program. For a very lucid discussion of the connections between X'-theory, the cycle, extension, adjuncts, and complements see Uriagereka (1994).

27 Recall that indices are not "real" and are not actually copied. Rather, the trace requires and antecedent at LF and *Bill* can serve as its antecedent. The indices are copied here for convenience. See chapter 5 for a more careful discussion.

28 This is so both in the May (1985) analysis and the Aoun and Li (1993a) theory.

29 Observe too that this account hinges on subjects being generated VP internally in English. In addition, it provides another piece of evidence against assimilating ACD structures to pseudo-gapping constructions as in Lappin (1992).

30 I assume that passives first move through Spec AgrO. Nothing hangs on this assumption. I further assume that the *bei* ("by") phrase in Chinese is adjoined to VP. It does not affect the account should it be higher than this in the tree.

31 I assume that here that *bei* does not obstruct the c-command domain of the subject. This is to treat it as simply a case marker. If it is better analyzed as a preposition, then *subject* in prepositional object position moves to a higher Spec Agr position as in chapter 6. For further discussion of quantified phrases within PPs see section 7.

32 See section 8 for a brief discussion of CIS and its effect on relative quantifier scope.

33 Once again, I assume that in nominal expressions, quantified determiners move to Spec DP at LF allowing them to c-command outside the NP that initially contains them. See chapter 6 for discussion.

34 To derive the standard WCO effects in cases such as (i), it is necessary to assume that NPs with nominal determiners are definite and so must be in Spec AgrS at LF after deletion. This is a natural assumption given the standard assimilation of these phrases to definite descriptions (see Neale 1990).

(i) His$_i$ mother kissed everyone$_i$

35 This analysis of WCO should allow reflexives not c-commanded by their antecedents at SPELL OUT (i.e. SS) to nonetheless be bound. The data on anaphora are subtle and this is not the place to go into the intricacies of the process. However, apparent instances of this sort of process do obtain. Consider the following data.

(i)   An aging portrait of himself kept Dorian Gray looking young
(ii)   In the haunted house, pictures of each other chased the men around the room
(iii) Compromising pictures of himself forced John out of the presidential race

In each of these sentences a reflexive is inside an indefinite NP that c-commands the reflexive's antecedent. These can be analyzed along the lines of the WCO data discussed in the text. However, these data should be treated gingerly given the well-known difficulties that surround picture NP data.
What of the unacceptability of non-picture NP cases?

(iv) *Himself saw John
(v)   Each other kissed the men

The unacceptability of these data follows on the assumption that reciprocals and reflexives (like pronouns in general) are definite. This would force them to be out of the VP shell and in Spec AgrS after deletion. But this would then make them incapable of having c-commanding antecedents.
Howard Lasnik (personal communication) has pointed out one further problem: how to rule out (vi).

(via) *Themselves seem to the men to be on display
(vib) *Each other seem to the men to be on display

Why is it not possible to reconstruct the reflexive or reciprocal to the embedded matrix subject position and thereby allow binding to be licit? Note that binding from the *to* phrase into a picture NP with a reciprocal is fine.

(vii) It seemed to the men that pictures of each other were on display

I have no very good answer at present. The fact seems to be that a bare (in contrast to one embedded within another NP) reciprocal or reflexive cannot be interpreted lower than its overt position. One possibility is that for some reason reciprocals and reflexives cannot carry nominative case. If this were so, then (vi) could be ruled out independently of binding considerations. This has been proposed on the basis of certain Icelandic data in Maling (1984). However, this sort of stipulated morphological gap is theoretically unattractive.
This note is not intended as an analysis of reflexives. The topic is larger than can be adequately dealt with here. However, these observations hopefully suggest that

they do not necessarily render the approach developed in the text empirically untenable.

36 Similar data are noted in Boscovic (1993).

37 The acceptability of (i) (noted in Hornstein and Weinberg 1990) follows on the assumption that *whose* is a generator.

(i) What did whose friend say to Bill

This seems to be a reasonable assumption given that the sentence is felicitous on the presupposition that all the sayers-to-Bill were friends-of-someone.

38 This analysis implies that examples the (i) cited in Boscovic (1993) are ill-formed, contrary to his judgement.

(i) What did friends of who insist that Peter wanted

The reason is that the variable of the generator *what* must be lower than the functionally interpreted *who*. It is unclear, however, whether (i) is significantly worse than the examples in the text.

39 I define "intervene" in terms of c-command. Thus, A intervenes between B and C iff B c-commands A and A c-commands C.

40 It is important for (52) to be applicable that opaque verbs such as *believe* do not count as "logical" or scope-bearing expressions nor do names. Indeed it would appear that for (52) to be empirically adequate, definite descriptions should not be treated as "logical" in the sense required. Definite descriptions appear to function differently from universal quantifiers like *every*. Consider cases like (i). *Give a damn* and *a red cent* are NPIs. Observe the contrasts in acceptability.

(i) I don't think that
    (a) *everyone gave a damn about the outcome
    (b) *each man paid a red cent . . .
    (c) John gave a damn . . .
    (d) the judge paid a red cent . . .
    (e) many people give a damn about Bosnia

The definite description in (id) patterns differently from the other "universal" expressions in (ia) and (ib). This suggests that definite descriptions are grammatically more akin to names than quantifiers, at least as far as (52) is concerned.

Similar observations hold for generic NPs. These too permit the licensing of NPIs, in contrast to strong universal quantifiers like *every* and *each*.

(ii) I don't think that
    (a) whales ever eat caribou
    (b) whales give a damn about us
    (c) *each whale ate anything
    (d) *every whale ever eats caribou

This suggests that Diesing's (1992) treatment of these as involving a generic operator binding the bare plural in Spec AgrS is incorrect. The operators involved in these cases are syntactically inert and do not block NPI licensing.

A last point. The same holds for generics with the form in (iii).

(iii) I don't think that
    (a) the whale ever eats caribou
    (b) the whale eats any plankton before the age of three

41   The data are somewhat subtle in my opinion. For current purposes, I assume that the data are as Aoun and Li report them to be.

42   The details of this sort of analysis are worked out in Zanuttini (1991).

43   I modify the structure to fit with the phrase structure assumptions adopted in Chomsky (1993).

44   I say "probably" for there is room within a Minimalist theory for a "relativized" version of closest potential landing site. This is likely to be required independently to allow WH-movement to "ignore" intermediate Spec positions on its way to Spec CP, e.g. in the case of WH-movement from object position or the case of Comp to Comp movement. This said, it is unclear whether Spec NegP should be considered an A-position, an A'-position, or perhaps both. In Minimalist terms, the issue is whether Spec NegP is narrowly L-related, broadly L-related or non-L-related.

     There is some evidence that it is at least narrowly L-related. In the Slavic languages, for example, negation affects case marking. DP/NPs that in active sentences are marked accusative, in negative sentences come to bear genitive case. Case marking is a standard diagnostic for A-positions and narrow L-relatedness. This suggests that Spec NegP is an L-related position and so an A-position. If it is indeed an A-position, then the problem of relativization can be ignored. However, chapter 7, n. 26 suggested that NegPs also block WH-movement. If this is so, then it suggests that Spec NegP is also acting like an A'-position. Theoretically, it is possible that it has properties of both A and A'-positions, i.e. that it is a broadly L-related position. As the analysis presented here can proceed without settling this important issue, I leave it aside. However, the data in chapter 7 and the data here strongly suggest that Spec NegP has both A and A'-properties and so that it is broadly L-related. Note, incidentally, that if it is indeed of this ilk, then the intimate connection between negs and verbs is theoretically very natural. For current purposes, I assume that relativization is unnecessary and that Spec NegP is filled.

45   The logic of this account suggests that in languages with overt object shift, subjects are base generated in Spec AgrS and linked to a PRO in Spec VP.

46   I assume that this is a PRO rather than a pro, as the binding established is obligatory. Note that this assumption parallels the one made for Chinese by Aoun and Li (1993a). A parallel structure is proposed for English individual level predicates in Diesing as well. If this is correct, it suggests that the licensing of PRO is somewhat more complicated than suggested in Chomsky and Lasnik (1991). It would appear that null case or whatever licenses this null category can be assigned in Spec VP. Not much would be lost, however, if pro rather than PRO were in Spec VP.

47   It appears that similar idiom facts hold in Modern Greek.

   (i) Kilise o tetzeris ke vrike to kapaki tou
       Rolled the kettle   and found the top   his
       "Somebody found his match"
   (ii) *Den kilise o tetzeris ke vrike to kapaki tou
       Not rolled the kettle   and found the top   his
       "Somebody didn't find his match"

48   Chomsky (1993) requires idioms to reconstruct back into the VP shell at LF. The problem with negated sentences, then, is that this reconstruction is impossible

given the negated clause's control structure. Observe, incidentally, that the present discussion treats the MLC as a condition on convergence rather than economy. I believe it is possible to recast the present analysis assuming the MLC is an economy condition. However, as this would take the discussion too far afield, I leave this for another occasion.

49 This fact was first noted in Jackendoff (1977). The problems for a QR approach to quantifier scope and scope of negation are discussed in Hornstein (1984). It is important that *everything* in (69) not be read with focal stress.

50 The definition of c-command provided in chapter 6 allows us to distinguish the object from the subject case on the assumption adopted there that TP is a lexical projection and that c-command is defined in terms of lexical projections.

51 See Linebarger (1987) for the standard version of this proposal.

52 Note that by eschewing A'-movement at LF, we eliminate the possibility of adjoining Neg to some higher projection via the LF movement of Neg.

53 Things are more complicated, however. There are languages in which NPIs can be licensed from this position. Furthermore, in English, sentences like (i) are standardly taken as capable of having scope under negation.

(i) Everyone didn't come on time

Consider the second problem first. The proposal in chapter 6 for redefining c-command in terms of lexical categories would allow NegP to c-command Spec AgrS in (63). The converse is also true. If we assume that c-command is sufficient for scope, then NegP should be able to scope over the subject in (i). If we assume this, however, then we will require that NPIs can only be licensed if they are *asymmetrically* c-commanded at LF, at least in the unmarked case. Note that if this is correct, then the variation noted with respect to NPIs cross-linguistically can also be accommodated. In some languages, NPIs need only be c-commanded, not asymmetrically c-commanded as in English.

There is a more interesting option for handling this variation, however. It is possible that negation involves different kinds of NegPs (or even no NegPs) across languages. Zanuttini (1991) explores this possibility in detail. As "reconstruction" at LF is intimately tied to the structure of NegPs on this analysis, it is possible that different types of NegPs would have different consequences for movement. Thus, in some languages, subject NPIs might be allowed because they can reconstruct to Spec VP positions. This is not the place to pursue these speculations.

54 Lasnik and Saito (1992) argue that A-lowering must be generally prohibited. Given the analysis outlined here, this conclusion must be resisted. Their argument is as follows. Consider the data in (i).

(ia) It is unlikely that anyone will address the rally
(ib) *Anyone is unlikely to address the rally
(ic) *?Someone is unlikely to address the rally

Their point is that if reconstruction under A-movement were possible then we should expect that the NPI *anyone* in (ib) should be acceptable and the reading in which *someone* has scope under the negative predicate *unlikely* should be fine as well. The relevant non-existent LFs are provided in (ii).

(iia) [ec_i is unlikely [that [anyone$_i$ to address the rally]]]
(iib) [ec_i is unlikely [that [someone$_i$ to address the rally]]]

One conclusion consistent with Minimalism is that lowering does not take place in A-chains and that reconstruction is limited to A'-chains. This is a conclusion that the present analysis must resist. In this case, this is not too difficult.

The argument relies on the assumption that in these sentences, *anyone* and *someone* have raised from embedded Spec AgrS. However, if we assume that analysis of these constructions in Laka (1990) and Progovac (1988) then the embedded CP has a Neg-like properties. In particular, these sorts of verbs select embedded Negs in CP which in turn license the NPIs. If this is correct, then the MLC blocks movement across the selected neg. However, once movement is blocked there is no possible reconstruction and the data Lasnik and Saito (1992) note are directly accounted for. The structure of (ib), for example, is (iii). The embedded NegP prevents movement across it. Only a control relationship is permitted.

(iii)   Anyone is unlikely [$_{CP}$ [$_{NegP}$ 0 [Neg]] [that [PRO to . . .

Without movement, however, lowering is not an option. Hence *anyone* can never become asymmetrically c-commanded by Neg and so cannot get licensed.

55   This was brought to my attention by Cristina Schmitt who in turn attributed the observation to Alan Munn.

56   In the practice adopted here, links become invisible to the interpretive apparatus at the CI interface but they do not disappear. One could interpret bracketed constituents as traces. The bracketing is just a convenience. Bracketed material has been deleted and so it functionally identical to a trace in GB-style theories.

57   "rg" is the real gap and "pg" the parasitic gap.

58   Haïk (1987) and Fiengo and May (1990, 1994) provide evidence that subjacency and parasitic gap conditions hold in ACD gaps. Thus the phrase marker obtained after ellipsis interpretation seems subject to the sorts of locality effects typical of overt movement. They correctly conclude that these conditions must then apply at LF. This conclusion is clearly compatible with the suggestions made in the text. Longobardi (1991) provides evidence that negation can also participate in parasitic gap-like licensing structures. This suggests that this licensing is accomplished at LF. This too is compatible with the conclusions drawn here. In effect, by relocating subjacency and parasitic gaps to LF via the elimination of A'-movement at LF, it is possible to accommodate the LF data that have been analyzed in these terms. Furthermore, Diesing's analysis of the definiteness effect as an instance of subjacency also points to the conclusion that subjacency must be an LF principle.

59   This sort of theory was proposed in Aoun and Clark (1985) set in a Generalized Binding theory and Weinberg (1988) set within a subjacency-based theory. The approach in Browning (1987) postulates a strong binding condition on the 0-operator. This serves to "identify" it at SS. The idea seems to assimilate it to other 0-operator constructions such as purposives with PROs in Spec CP.

(i)   John bought a book$_i$ [PRO$_i$ [PRO to read t$_i$]]

The data provided below are inconsistent with this theory.

60   One way of interpreting this condition is to assimilate the 0-operator to PRO and allow it to function as an intermediate link in an "extended" A'-chain. The Subjacency Condition then states that lexical gaps must be subjacent to antecedents. The parasitic gap, which is phonologically null, meets this requirement through the PRO which acts as a bridge to the WH in Spec CP. See Weinberg (1988).

61   It is irrelevant for present purposes how the inventory of bounding nodes is determined. What is relevant is that subjacency be defined in terms of domination so that subjacency will imply c-command.

62   This is preserved in Browning (1987) as well as Aoun and Clark (1985) and Weinberg (1988).

63   A strong binding condition like the one proposed in Browning (1987) also suffices so long as strong binding is under c-command, the real gap does not c-command the parasitic gap (or, thereby, the 0-operator that the parasitic gap is linked to), and WH-operators can be strong binders. The only strong binder will then be the WH in Spec CP. This proposal and the one in Aoun and Clark (1985) are essentially identical as regards current concerns.

64   These data are more subtle than the ones above. However, the judgement strikes me as correct. I would like to thank Barry Schein for seconding this opinion.

65   Recall that interpreting the WH is Spec AgrS functionally leads to a WCO violation. See chapter 7 for details.

66   The theory of parasitic gap constructions adopted here comes close to yielding the ideal advocated in Chomsky (1982) for such a theory. All that one needs to say is that parasitic gaps must be licensed via chain composition and that this composition is subject to subjacency. The rest follows essentially the lines of Chomsky (1982), supplemented with a parallelism constraint on variables of the type advocated in Safir (1985).

67   The account above crucially relies on assuming that pair–list readings and superiority effects are not due to WH-raising and absorption. If "reconstruction" were not forced in (76), (81), and (83), we would have had no way of deriving the influence that parasitic gaps had on these constructions. These considerations support the conclusion in chapters 6 and 7.

68   As in chapter 6, I assume that TP is lexical rather than functional. For present purposes, the functional projections are all AgrPs and DPs.

69   I assume that subjects are in Spec VP. Should they be adjoined to VP, this would still allow the prepositional object to c-command the VP internal subject. The converse would also hold, however. This would then require allowing either QP to scope over the other. This would suffice to get the scope facts here. However, I will continue to assume that the subject is VP internal rather than adjoined.

70   This was noted and discussed in Aoun and Li (1989) and (1993a).

71   The single AgrP assumption is contrary to the proposal made in chapter 5 and Hornstein (1994). This other proposal is also incompatible with the treatment of sentences like (i) in Chomsky (1994: 32–3).

(ia)   John reads often to the children
(ib)   *John reads often books

The proposal presented below is compatible with Chomsky's suggestion as it does not require moving indirect objects to an extra Agr. See below for further discussion.

72   In many languages the case possibilities for the pair of NPs is rather intricate and verb dependent. For some illustration see Ottósson (1993) for Icelandic, a particularly challenging case. These verb-dependent case-marking intricacies support the view that the case-checking mechanism must be verb sensitive, as assumed here.

73   Aoun and Li (1993a: 29ff) provide the only other analysis that I am familiar with of these data. They develop a modified Larsonian analysis of DOCs. The primary assumption is that (i) has the SS (ii).

(i) John gave someone every book

(ii) John [$_{V'}$ [$_V$ give someone] $_j$ [$_{VP}$ every problem$_i$ [$_{V'}$ t$_j$ t$_i$]]]

As (ii) indicates, they assume that in these constructions *someone* incorporates into the verb for reasons of case and then moves with the verb into which it has incorporated to a higher level of the VP shell. At LF, they assume that the incorporated NP then excorporates and adjoins to some non-X^0-projection to get scope. The nearest non-head projection is the higher *V'* in (ii). From this position, *someone* blocks the movement of *every problem* to a higher adjoined position via the MBR.

This analysis has several problematic aspects. Both the incorporation and subsequent excorporation are problematic. This is something that clitics may perhaps do but XPs have not been seen to do this. Moreover, it is not clear why *someone* must move at all to get a scope assignment. Aoun and Li must be assuming that the incorporated position is a theta position so that Q-adjunction cannot take place *in situ*. However, this is unlikely to be the case. If *someone* has incorporated into the verb, then it has moved from another position. Presumably this other position is its theta position. But then the incorporation site is a non-theta position. Note that this is a problem, for it would permit *someone* to gain scope without moving at all. Q-adjunction can take place *in situ* if the NP is in a non-theta position. But if it need not move, *every problem* can adjoin to the higher *V'* above it and take scope over it. Thus, it is crucial that *someone* be in a *derived* theta position after incorporation. This is not a natural assumption.

There are other difficulties. Incorporation by XPs into X^{0}s is generally considered undesirable. Chomsky (1994), for example, bars this in overt syntax. Here it is crucial. Further, it is unclear why *someone* can incorporate into the verb but not then adjoin to it for reasons of scope.

This, to repeat, is the only analysis that I am aware of that tries to account for the scope facts noted in the text. The special purpose nature of the technical devices necessary to make the account adequate suggest that there is something amiss with Aoun and Li's account.

74 This may not be a trivial assumption. I have assumed above that c-command is in terms of domination. We can ask whether NP$_2$ is dominated by the small clause. If it is, then there is no problem. But this seems to suggest that NP$_2$ dominates itself in this case, that domination is reflexive. Now, in cases of adjunction it is true that every segment of NP$_2$ dominates the contents of the head of the small clause, i.e. NP$_2$. However, it is not clear that we wish to allow domination to be reflexive in general. I will put these worries aside here and assume that in small clauses of this type, NP$_1$ asymmetrically c-commands NP$_2$.

75 Not all small clauses are of the DOC variety. The most typical instances are those in *consider* complements. These plausibly do not involve marking of the second NP for case as this NP is predicative rather than an argument (see Safir 1987). Given this consider the fact about (i) discussed in chapter 5 once again.

(ia) Someone considers every congressman a fool

(ib) Someone considers every congressman to be a fool

I noted in chapter 5 that whereas (ib) can be interpreted with the subject in the scope of the *every* phrase, this was not possible in (ia). The interpretation of (ib) is what we expect given that in these small clauses *every congressman* moves to the matrix Spec AgrO position to get case-marked and so can take scope over a "reconstructed" subject.

(ii)   [(Someone) [every congressman [someone [considers [(every congressman) a
       fool]]]]]]

The problem is why this is forbidden in (ia). It must be that "reconstruction" of the
matrix subject is forbidden in this case. The question is why.

One possible answer comes from considering the licensing of predicates. Assume that like all other expressions, they too must be licensed. Assume, furthermore, that they are licensed by the functional categories that typically go with
predicates, i.e. AgrPs, TPs. Then in small clauses, we would have to license
predicates. How do we do this in cases like (ia)? The problem is that these are very
"bare" small clauses, with virtually no layers of functional structure. These contrast, for example, with naked infinitives which plausibly have more functional
structure (for discussion of this and how the stage/individual level distinction is
reflected in layers of functional structure see Schmitt 1993). Assume then that
predicates must be licensed by incorporating into functional heads, AgrO for concreteness. Then the predicate in a *consider* complement cannot be licensed by a
functional head, i.e. by adjoining to AgrO, but must be licensed in some other way
(note that as Schmitt's theories would require, in these small clauses, the predicate
must be stage level). Assume that the way it gets licensed is by incorporating into
the matrix verb *consider*. This analysis has been proposed in Stowell (1991) and is
a modern update of the analysis in Chomsky (1975b). Thus at LF, prior to deletion
we have the structure in (iii).

(iii)   [Someone [every congressman [[a fool+considers] +AgrO [someone [a
        fool+considers] [every congressman a fool]]]]]]

The small clause predicate *a fool* has incorporated into *considers* which then raises
and adjoins to AgrO. *Every congressman* raises to Spec AgrO for case checking and
someone raises to Spec AgrS for similar reasons. If *someone* could not reconstruct to
Spec VP, the data noted above would follow. Let us assume that the fact that *a fool*
incorporates into the predicate somehow prevents the reconstruction. I have no
idea why this should be so at the moment. It would yield the correct result, however. Note that it would also lead us to expect that (ib) should be acceptable with
the *every/some* scope as the predicate can be licensed within the embedded clause,
i.e. without incorporating into the higher predicate. I leave it as an exercise for the
reader to come up with a reason why predicate incorporation prevents reconstruction. Observe, by the way, that it must be the "reconstruction" of the matrix indefinite which is blocked rather than the raising of the embedded *every* phrase or its
required reconstruction. The reason is that these sorts of small clauses permit
acceptable ACDs, as noted in chapter 5.

Note, incidentally, that the present worries do not speak in favor of a QR-like account. QR-based accounts are also without a principled account for the contrasts
in (i).

76   At least for languages like English in which quantifier scope is determined in
covert syntax. This chapter has argued that QR is not the correct mechanism for
determining quantifier scope if this determined at LF. However, it leaves open the
question of whether every language determines quantifier scope in the same way.
For example, it is possible that in some languages quantifier scope piggybacks on
A'-chains rather than A-chains as in English. Hungarian might be such a language.
NPs in Hungarian overtly move to A'-positions (topic and focus) from which they
apparently exercise their quantificational powers. If this is correct, then it would

appear that quantification in Hungarian is not determined via A-chains. Nothing proposed in this chapter precludes this possibility.

Chapter 9 discusses one way of treating A'-movement within Minimalism. Basically, it requires that all A'-movement be overt. If one adopts the Chomsky (1993) treatment of WH-chains and extends it to A'-chains in general it comes close to implying that for quantifiers in A'-positions at SPELL OUT the scope you see is the scope you get. However, this conclusion should be treated as very tentative. The issues of Hungarian interact with issues of how to treat topics and focus. These issues, however, are not well understood.

77 One consequence of this analysis is that the fact that QNPs are second-order operators is not grammatically represented. Recall that QR and WH-raising syntactically reflected the fact that quantifiers take properties as arguments by syntactically having them take scope over open sentences. This is no longer true in the present analysis. The relative quantifier facts are grammatically represented but this feature of quantifiers is not. Frege's approach to quantification had a similar property. In this it contrasted with the Tarskian analysis of quantification. The details of quantifier interpretation in this theory will closely resemble the proposal advanced in Williams (1986) where SS quantifier interpretation was urged.

78 Thanks to Joseph Aoun and Jean-Roger Vergnaud for helping me clarify this point.

Chapter 9 Revisiting the Minimalist Program

1 If one ignores parasitic gap constructions, it is possible to treat subjacency as a condition on derivations. The main obstacle to this in earlier theories was the apparent LF A'-movement operations that were able to extract constituents out of islands with no apparent grammatical consequence. On the assumption that these operations are instances of "Move α", subjacency cannot be treated as a condition on rule application. The additional problem that parasitic gaps provide is that chain composition is not reducible to movement. As such, if parasitic gap licensing is stated in terms of subjacency, then the principle must be seen as applying to the output of derivations rather than to derivations themselves. Other options exist. If, for example, the 0-operator were licensed via an identification condition subject to a locality requirement of the kind suggested in Aoun and Clark (1985) or Browning (1987) then subjacency could be treated as simply a condition on derivations, much as Chomsky (1993) treats the cycle. This would be theoretically neater for it would eliminate any need for chains *per se* to meet any well-formedness conditions (see below for further discussion). I am personally partial to this conclusion. The important point, however, is that this approach to subjacency is only viable once we eliminate LF A'-operations, as urged above.

2 The same remarks apply to topicalization in English. Note that Chomsky (1993: 32) extends the strong feature to focus and topic constructions.

3 It is often taken to be a drawback of the Minimalist program that it relies on the weak/strong feature distinction. However, this distinction, whatever its evident incompleteness, is no less motivated than is the GB distinction between SS and LF operations. Thus, in GB theories there is seldom a reason why some operations or condition are relegated to SS versus LF. Therefore, it is not a problem for Minimalism *per se* that it has only the impressionistic distinction between weak and strong features to rely on in accounting for the difference between overt and covert movement. This said, it would be nice to shore up the dichotomy. The proposal in the text does this by hooking this distinction up with a second one, the

difference between A and A'-movement which itself is linked to the difference between L and non-L-involved positions. By tying these various theoretical strands together, the theory decreases the wiggle room available, at least such is the hope.

4   There is some reason to think that quantifiers in natural language are always restricted (semantically). See Barwise and Cooper (1981), Higginbotham and May (1981), and Keenan and Stavi (1986) for discussion.

5   A plausible account of what takes place in the preferred case is that English LF comes to resemble Chinese SS. There is a WH in CP that binds into the reconstructed WH. The latter then functions as a variable. Without this sort of A'-binding from CP the reconstructed WH is interpreted functionally. The interpretive differences discussed in chapters 6 through 8 then reduce to the semantic function of the "reconstructed" WH. See Aoun and Li (1993a) and Watanabe (1991) for details of WH-movement in Chinese and Japanese.

6   This fact was pointed out to me by Jairo Nunes. He exploits this property of Minimalist derivations in a slightly different way in Nunes (1994).

7   I have indicated the fact that a feature has been checked by putting a "#" next to it.

8   As will become evident below, it does not really matter how many features get checked so long as only a single chain eventuates from the movement.

9   This result crucially assumes that there is a T-node between AgrO and AgrS. It also assumes that verb-movement languages without ACDs move the V at least as high as AgrS. It is not clear whether the results noted here could be sustained without these assumptions. Some recent work in Chomsky (1994) suggests that they might be even without the assumption that an intermediate T-node exists.

  Chomsky (1994) proposes that X'-levels are grammatically invisible. If so, an elision site must be an XP projection. In particular, it cannot be an X'. Chapter 5 considered the possibility that what gets copied into the gap is an AgrO' in English. If Chomsky (1994) is correct, this is not an option. It must be VP that is the copied expression. However, this means that in English it is the *head* of the V-chain spanning AgrO and V that is deleted, leaving the copy inside the VP. This VP now has specific content and if copied into the elision site will yield a fully determinate proposition.

  If this is correct, then to have a licit ACD structure there must be a V-chain spanning at least as far as the "D-structure" V-position. However, if V-movement is via adjunction, even without TPs, this will be impossible. The topmost chain will span AgrS and AgrO and the second chain will span AgrO and V. This latter chain will not have all its features checked and the XPs dominating the links of the top chain will dominate the elision site inside the ACD relative clause inside Spec AgrO. Thus, there is no way to avoid regress and also have a morphologically well-formed verb at LF. In sum, if the line of reasoning in Chomsky (1994) is correct about the grammatical invisibility of X's, we can derive the facts noted in the text without recourse to TP projections.

10   These observations are analogous to the observations in Chomsky and Lasnik (1991) concerning the derivational character of the Head Movement Constraint.

11   For a current attempt to defend a representationalist thesis see Brody (1993). Brody outlines what he calls a radical Minimalist thesis in which, in effect, a monostratal theory is presented in which SS is the only level. Empirically, the thesis would have trouble handling the data in chapters 5 through 8. The data Brody presents in chapter 2 in favor of his thesis can be accommodated within the present theory now that subjacency is statable at LF.

12   "Non-trivial A-chains" are ones with more than a single link.

13 See Chomsky (1981) for an elaboration of this sort of theory.

14 See Chomsky 1986b and Rizzi (1991: chapter 1) for example.

15 The same story exists in a Generalized Binding framework. Just replace "antecedent governed" with "X-bound." In this case, the locality is a reflex of principle
A and domains rather than some computation over barriers. The details are
irrelevant.

16 Observe we are assuming that the analysis in chapter 8 is correct and seeing how
the ECP comports with it. This is not the standard GB analysis of these facts.

17 There is a brasher way of making this point. The reason that the ECP is problematic if reconstruction abounds is that chains have no canonical configuration save
the fact that the links are local. In GB theories, chains are objects whose heads are
canonically lexical and whose feet are canonically traces. If these two features are
abandoned then chains have no standard form and so cannot support principles
like the ECP that traded on these canonical features of chains.

18 The latter seems to be treated in Chomsky (1994) as a condition on representations.
If the reasoning here is correct, then it should be treated as a condition on derivations instead. See chapters 7 and 8 for more discussion.

19 Also, they cannot be bound by the WH-operator in Spec CP. The distinction between functionally interpreted WHs and quantificational ones revolves around
whether the WH in A-position is A'-bound from Spec CP or not.

20 This abstracts away from clitic doubling which plausibly involves allowing more
than one phonological copy. See Nunes (1994) for discussion. The current presentation is heavily indebted to this work.

21 Nunes (1994) argues that copies must be deleted (at PF) so that phrase markers can
get linearized by a version of Kayne's (1993) Linear Correspondence Axiom (LCA)
at SPELL OUT. He shows that without this deletion linearization cannot take
place. Chomsky (1994) proposes that the LCA is part of the SPELL OUT process.
It is consistent with Nunes' analysis that the output of the SPELL OUT procedure
no longer contain chains. Thus deletion could still be forced by the LCA. From this
perspective, the LCA converts a phrase marker with hierarchical phrase marker
structure to an object with linear non-phrase-marker structure. This is the way
Kayne (1993) conceives the LCA. Chomsky (1993) clearly takes PF to be distinct
from LF in not being a phrase marker. This, for example, is why conditions like
head government cannot apply at PF. If chains are only defined within phrase
markers, then the output of linearization, the operation that produces PF, cannot
contain chains. If this is correct, then the first option forwarded above gets us the
right results.

22 The reason that the +WH must be optionally inserted is that its presence requires
movement while its absence forbids it given the standard assumption that the
+WH-feature is universally strong (Chomsky 1993).

23 As Aoun et al. observe, this +WH-operator is prohibited in the C^0 of optional
+WH-verbs like *savoir* ("know"). Thus, (i) is unambiguous. The *qui in situ* only
has wide scope.

(i) Jean ne sait pas que Paul a vu qui
   Jean not know   that Paul saw who
   "Who doesn't Jean know that Paul saw"

24 Recall that following Aoun and Li (1993a), I assumed that the Spec NegP is filled
by an operator which blocks passage through the Spec NegP. Other assumptions
would serve as nicely. For example, it would suffice if Spec NegP were restricted

to negative expressions. This makes sense if one pursues the analogy with +WH CPs. The neg feature in Neg^0 must be checked by having a negative operator in Spec NegP. Operators like *someone* and *everyone* do not carry this feature. Thus, movement via Spec NegP will prohibit this feature from being checked and the derivation will crash. However, if this position is a potential landing site for these NPs, as it would be if it is non-L-involved, then bypassing this position violates the MLC. For current purposes, either of these approaches suffices to get the desired distinctions.

25   Another kind of support for this assumption is the observation that NegPs and tensed Vs enjoy one another's company. This makes sense if neg is L-involved in much the same way that Tense is.

26   It is worth being a bit more careful here. I have proposed treating Spec NegP as L-involved. This should not be read as identical to being an A-position. As noted in chapters 6 and 7, Spec NegP has A'-qualities as well. As noted, this confluence of A and A'-characteristics can be accommodated by treating Spec NegP as broadly L-involved rather than narrowly L-involved. This means that improper movement prohibits chains with links in non-L-involved and broadly or narrowly L-involved positions. The prohibition advocated above against A'-movement at LF is more accurately seen as a prohibition against movement to non-L-involved positions at LF.

27   For detailed discussion see Longobardi (1991). These cases are also discussed extensively in Brody (1993).

28   More exactly, it seems that the head government condition is not part of a disjunctive ECP but is a condition in its own right. Furthermore, in a Minimalist theory, it must apply at LF. This means that the evidence that it applies only to overt movement must be reanalyzed (see Aoun et al. 1987 and Hornstein and Lightfoot 1991 for the data; see Lightfoot and Hornstein forthcoming for an analysis). Note that it reallocated to LF, the head government condition could extend to the asymmetries in (20) and could also handle some data (note in Rizzi 1990) which pointed to the conclusion that head government was required at LF.

29   These remarks rely on a Minimalist reanalysis of head government explored in Lightfoot and Hornstein (forthcoming).

30   In terms of Chomsky (1994), they are related by being computed from the same array.

Bibliography

Aoun, J.: 1982, "On the Logical Nature of the Binding Principles: Quantifier Lowering, Double Raising of 'There' and the Notion Empty Element," *Proceedings of NELS*, GLSA, University of Massachusetts, Amherst, 16–35.

Aoun, J.: 1985, *A Grammar of Anaphora*, MIT Press, Cambridge, Mass.

Aoun, J.: 1986, *Generalized Binding*, Foris, Dordrecht.

Aoun, J. and R. Clark: 1985, "On Non-overt Operators," *Southern California Occasional Papers in Linguistics*, USC, 17–36.

Aoun, J. and N. Hornstein: 1985, "Quantifier Types," *Linguistic Inquiry*, 16, 623–37.

Aoun, J., N. Hornstein, D. Lightfoot, and A. Weinberg: 1987, "Two Types of Locality," *Linguistic Inquiry*, 18, 537–77.

Aoun, J., N. Hornstein, and D. Sportiche: 1981, "Some Aspects of Wide Scope Quantification," *Journal of Linguistic Research*, 1, 69–95.

Aoun, J. and A. Li: 1989, "Constituency and Scope," *Linguistic Inquiry*, 20, 141–72.

Aoun, J. and A. Li: 1993a, *Syntax of Scope*, MIT Press, Cambridge, Mass.

Aoun, J. and A. Li: 1993b, "WH-elements in Situ: Syntax or LF," *Linguistic Inquiry*, 24, 199–238.

Aoun, J. and D. Sportiche: 1983, "On the Formal Theory of Government," *The Linguistic Review*, 2, 211–36.

Baker, M.: 1988, *Incorporation*, University of Chicago Press, Chicago.

Baltin, M.: 1987, "Do Antecedent Contained Deletions Exist," *Linguistic Inquiry*, 18, 579–95.

Baltin, M. and P. Postal: 1994, "Extraction from Selective Islands," MS, NYU.

Barbosa, P.: 1994, "A New Look at the Null Subject Parameter," talk delivered at the University of Maryland.

Barwise, J. and R. Cooper: 1981, "Generalized Quantifiers and Natural Language," *Linguistics and Philosophy*, 4, 159–219.

Bayer, J.: 1993, "Elliptical Conjunctions and Subjacency at LF," talk presented at the University of Maryland, September 1993.

Belletti, A. and L. Rizzi: 1981, "The Syntax of *ne*: Some Theoretical Implications," *The Linguistic Review*, 1, 117–55.

Belletti, A. and L. Rizzi: 1988, "Psych Verbs and Theta Theory," *Natural Language and Linguistic Theory*, 6, 291–352.

Boscovic, Z.: 1993, "On Certain Violations of the Superiority Condition, AgrO, and Economy of Derivation," MS, University of Connecticut.

Brandi, L. and P. Cordin: 1989, "Two Italian Dialects and the Null Subject Parameter," in O. Jaeggli and K. Safir (eds) *The Null Subject Parameter*, Kluwer, Dordrecht.

Branigan, P.: 1992, "Subjects and Complementizers," Ph.D. dissertation, MIT, Cambridge, Mass.

Brody, M.: 1993, "Lexico-logical Form – a Radically Minimalist Theory," MS, University of London.

Browning, M.: 1987, "Null Operator Constructions," Ph.D. dissertation, MIT, Cambridge, Mass.

Burzio, L.: 1986, *Italian Syntax*, Kluwer, Dordrecht.

Campbell, R. and J. Martin: 1989, "Sensation Predicates and the Syntax of Stativity," in E.J. Fee and K. Hunt (eds) *Proceedings of WCCFL 8*, Stanford, 44–55.

Chierchia, G.: 1991, "Functional WH and Weak Crossover," in D. Bates (ed.) *Proceedings of WCCFL 10*, Stanford, 75–90.

Chierchia, G.: 1992, "Anaphora and Dynamic Binding," *Linguistics and Philosophy*, 15, 111–83.

Chomsky, N.: 1965, *Aspects of the Theory of Syntax*, MIT Press, Cambridge, Mass.

Chomsky, N.: 1973, "Conditions on Transformations," reprinted in Chomsky 1977, *Essays on Form and Interpretation*, North-Holland, New York.

Chomsky, N.: 1975a, "Questions of Form and Interpretation," in Chomsky 1977, *Essays on Form and Interpretation*, North-Holland, New York.

Chomsky, N.: 1975b, *The Logical Structure of Linguistic Theory*, Plenum, New York.

Chomsky, N.: 1976, "Conditions on Rules of Grammar," in Chomsky 1977, *Essays on Form and Interpretation*, North-Holland, New York.

Chomsky, N.: 1977, *Essays on Form and Interpretation*, North-Holland, New York.

Chomsky, N.: 1981, *Lectures on Government and Binding*, Foris, Dordrecht.

Chomsky, N.: 1982, *Some Concepts and Consequences of the Theory of Government and Binding*, MIT Press, Cambridge, Mass.

Chomsky, N.: 1986a, *Barriers*, MIT Press, Cambridge, Mass.

Chomsky, N.: 1986b, *Knowledge of Language*, Praeger, New York.

Chomsky, N.: 1991, "Some Notes on the Economy of Derivation," in R. Freidin (ed.) *Principles and Parameters in Comparative Grammar*, MIT Press, Cambridge, Mass.

Chomsky, N.: 1993, "A Minimalist Program for Linguistic Theory," in K. Hale and S.J. Keyser eds *The View from Building 20*, MIT Press, Cambridge, Mass.

Chomsky, N.: 1994, "Bare Phrase Structure," MIT *Occasional Papers in Linguistics*, 5, MIT, Cambridge, Mass.

Chomsky, N. and H. Lasnik: 1977, "Filters and Control," *Linguistic Inquiry*, 8, 425–505.

Chomsky, N. and H. Lasnik: 1993, "Principles and Parameters Theory," in J. Jacobs, A. von Stechow, W. Sternefled, and T. Vennemann (eds) *Syntax: An International Handbook of Contemporary Research*, Walter de Gruyter, Berlin.

Cinque, G.: 1990, *Types of A′-Dependencies*, MIT Press, Cambridge, Mass.

Cooper, R.: 1983, *Quantification and Syntactic Theory*, Reidel, Dordrecht.

Diesing, M.: 1992, *Indefinites*, MIT Press, Cambridge, Mass.

Enç, M.: 1991, "The Semantics of Specificity," *Linguistic Inquiry*, 22, 4–25.

Engdahl, E.: 1985, *Constituent Questions*, Reidel, Dordrecht.

Erteschik-Shir, N.: 1990, "What's What," MS, Ben Gurion University.

Evans, G.: 1980, "Pronouns," *Linguistic Inquiry*, 11, 337–62.

Fiengo, R., J. Huang, H. Lasnik, and T. Reinhart: 1988, "The Syntax of WH-In-Situ," *Proceedings WCCFL 7*, Stanford, 81–98.

Fiengo, R. and R. May: 1990, "Anaphora and Ellipsis," MS, UC Irvine and CUNY.

Fiengo, R. and R. May: 1994, *Indices and Identity*, MIT Press, Cambridge, Mass.

Fisher, C., G. Hall, S. Rakowitz, and L. Gleitman: 1994, "When it is Better to Receive than to Give," *Lingua*, 92, vols 1–4.

Freidin, R. ed.: 1991, *Principles and Parameters in Comparative Grammar*, MIT Press, Cambridge, Mass.

Geach, P.: 1962, *Reference and Generality*, Cornell University Press, Ithaca.

Haegeman, L.: 1994, *Introduction to Government and Binding Theory*, Blackwell, Oxford.

Haïk, I.: 1987, "Bound VPs that Need to Be," *Linguistics and Philosophy*, 10, 503–30.

Hale, K. and S.J. Keyser eds: 1993, *The View from Building 20*, MIT Press, Cambridge, Mass.

Halle, M. and A. Marantz: 1993, "Distributed Morphology and the Pieces of Inflection," in K. Hale and S.J. Keyser (eds) *The View from Building 20*, MIT Press, Cambridge.

Heim, I.: 1982, "The Semantics of Definite and Indefinite Noun Phrases," Ph.D. dissertation, University of Massachussetts, Amherst.

Hendrick, R. and M. Rochemont: 1982, "Complementation, Multiple WH and echo questions," MS, University of North Carolina and University of California (Irvine).

Hermon, G.: 1984, *Syntactic Modularity*, Foris, Dordrecht.

Higginbotham, J.: 1980, "Pronouns and Bound Variables," *Linguistic Inquiry*, 11, 679–708.

Higginbotham, J.: 1983, "Logical Form, Binding and Nominals," *Linguistic Inquiry*, 14, 395–420.

Higginbotham, J.: 1985, "On Semantics," *Linguistic Inquiry*, 16, 547–93.

Higginbotham, J.: 1993, "Interrogatives," in K. Hale and S.J. Keyser (eds) *The View from Building 20*, MIT Press, Cambridge.

Higginbotham, J. and R. May: 1981, "Questions, Quantifiers and Crossing," *The Linguistic Review*, 1, 41–80.

Hoji, H.: 1985, *"Logical Form Constraints and Configurational Structures in Japanese,"* Ph.D. dissertation, University of Massachussetts, Amherst.

Hornstein, N.: 1984, *Logic as Grammar*, MIT Press, Cambridge, Mass.

Hornstein, N.: 1987, "Levels of Meaning," in J. Garfield ed. *Modularity in Knowledge Representation and Natural Language Understanding*, MIT Press, Cambridge, Mass.

Hornstein, N.: 1994, "An Argument for Minimalism: the Case of Antecedent Contained Deletion," *Linguistic Inquiry*, 25, 455–80.

Hornstein, N. and D.W. Lightfoot: 1991, "On the Nature of Lexical Government," in R. Freidin (ed.) *Principles and Parameters in Comparative Grammar*, MIT Press, Cambridge.

Hornstein, N. and S. Varlokosta: 1992, "Psych Verbs and Bound Pronouns in Modern Greek," *Proceedings of WCCFL 11*, Stanford, 277–88.

Hornstein, N. and A. Weinberg: 1986, "Superiority and Generalized Binding," *Proceedings of NELS 17*, GLSA, University of Massachusetts, Amherst, 311–26.

Hornstein, N. and A. Weinberg: 1990, "The Necessity of LF," *The Linguistic Review*, 7, 129–67.

Hornstein, N. and A. Weinberg: 1995, "The Empty Category Principle," in G. Webelhuth (ed.) *Government and Binding Theory and the Minimalist Program*, Blackwell, Oxford.

Huang, J.: 1982, "Logical Relations in Chinese and the Theory of Grammar," Ph.D. dissertation, MIT, Cambridge, Mass.

Huang, J. and R. May eds: 1991, *Logical Structure and Linguistic Structure*, Kluwer, Dordrecht.

Jackendoff, R.: 1972, *Semantic Interpretation in Generative Grammar*, MIT Press, Cambridge, Mass.

Jackendoff, R.: 1977, *X' Syntax: A Study of Phrase Structure*, MIT Press, Cambridge, Mass.

Jackendoff, R.: 1994, "Lexical Insertion in a Post-Minimalist Theory of Grammar," MS, Brandeis University.

Jaeggli, O.: 1981, *Topics in Romance Syntax*, Foris, Dordrecht.

Kartunnen, L.: 1977, "The Syntax and Semantics of Questions," *Linguistics and Philosophy*, 1, 3–44.

Kasher, A.: 1991, *The Chomskyan Turn*, Blackwell, Oxford.

Katz, J. and P. Postal: 1964, *An Integrated Theory of Linguistic Description*, MIT Press, Cambridge, Mass.

Kayne, R.: 1979, "Two Notes on the NIC," printed as chapter 2 in Kayne 1984, *Connectedness and Binary Branching*, Foris, Dordrecht.

Kayne, R.: 1981, "ECP Extensions," *Linguistic Inquiry*, 12, 93–133.

Kayne, R.: 1984, *Connectedness and Binary Branching*, Foris, Dordrecht.

Kayne, R.: 1993, "The Antisymmetry of Syntax," MS, CUNY.

Keenan, E. and J. Stavi: 1986, "A Semantic Characterization of Natural Language Determiners," *Linguistics and Philosophy*, 9, 253–326.

É. Kiss, K.: 1991, "WH-movement and Specificity," MS, Linguistic Institute of the Hungarian Academy of Sciences, Budapest.

É. Kiss, K.: 1993, "Wh-movement and Specificity," *Natural Language and Linguistic Theory*, 11, 85–120.

Koopman, H.: 1994, "Licensing Heads," in D. Lightfoot and N. Hornstein (eds) *Verb Movement*, Cambridge University Press, Cambridge.

Koopman, H. and D. Sportiche: 1983, "Variables and the Bijection Principle," *The Linguistic Review*, 2, 139–60.

Koopman, H. and D. Sportiche: 1986, "A Note on Long Extraction in Vata and the ECP," *Natural Language and Linguistic Theory*, 4, 357–74.

Koopman, H. and D. Sportiche: 1991, "The Position of Subjects," *Lingua*, 85, 211–59.

Laka, I.: 1990, "Negation in Syntax," Ph.D. dissertation, MIT, Cambridge, Mass.

Laka, I.: 1993, "Unergatives that assign Ergative, Unaccusatives that Assign Accusative," *MIT Working Papers in Linguistics*, vol. 18, Cambridge, Mass.

Lappin, S.: 1992, *The Syntactic Basis of Ellipsis Resolution*, IBM Research Report RC 18177, Yorktown Heights.

Larson, R.: 1988, "On the Double Object Construction," *Linguistic Inquiry*, 19, 335–91.

Larson, R. and R. May: 1990, "Antecedent Containment or Vacuous Movement: Reply to Baltin," *Linguistic Inquiry*, 21, 103–22.

Lasnik, H.: 1976, "Remarks on Coreference," *Linguistic Analysis*, 2, 1–22.

Lasnik, H.: 1993, "Lectures on Minimalist Syntax," Univ. of Connecticut Working Papers in Linguistics, Storrs.

Lasnik, H.: 1994, "Weakness and Greed: a Consideration of Some Minimalist Concepts", paper delivered at University of Maryland, College Park, 12 May.

Lasnik, H. and M. Saito: 1984, "On the Nature of Proper Government," *Linguistic Inquiry*, 15, 235–89.

Lasnik, H. and M. Saito: 1992, *Move α*, MIT Press, Cambridge, Mass.

Lasnik, H. and T. Stowell: 1991, "Weakest Crossover," *Linguistic Inquiry*, 22, 687–720.

Lasnik, H. and J. Uriagereka: 1988, *A Course in GB Syntax*, MIT Press, Cambridge, Mass.

Lebeaux, D.: 1983, "A Distributional Difference between Reciprocals and Reflexives," *Linguistic Inquiry*, 14, 723–30.

Lebeaux, D.: 1988, "Language Acquisition and the Form of Grammar," Ph.D. dissertation, University of Massachusetts, Amherst.

Lebeaux, D.: 1990, "Relative Clauses, Licensing, and the Nature of Derivation," *Proceedings of NELS 20*, GLSA, University of Massachusetts, Amherst, 318–32.

Lightfoot, D.: 1993, "Why UG Needs a Learning Theory: Triggering Verb Movement," in C. Jones ed. *Historical Linguistics: Problems and Perspectives*, Longman.

Lightfoot, D. and N. Hornstein: 1994, *Verb Movement*, Cambridge University Press, Cambridge.

Lightfoot, D.W. and N. Hornstein: forthcoming, "Head Government in a Minimalist Theory."

Linebarger, M.: 1980, "The Grammar of Negative Polarity," Ph.D. dissertation, MIT, Cambridge, Mass.

Linebarger, M.: 1987, "Negative Polarity and Grammatical Representation," *Linguistics and Philosophy*, 10, 325–87.

Longobardi, G.: 1990, "Extraction from NP and the Proper Notion of Head Government," chapter 2 in A. Giorgi and G. Longobardi, *The Syntax of Noun Phrases*, Cambridge University Press.

Liu, Feng-hsi: 1990, "Scope Dependency in English and Chinese," Ph.D. dissertation, UCLA, Los Angeles.

Longobardi, G.: 1991, "In Defense of the Correspondence Hypothesis: Island Effects and Parasitic Gap Constructions in Logical Form," in J. Huang and R. May eds *Logical Structure and Linguistic Structure*, Kluwer, Dordrecht.

Mahajan, A.: 1990, "The A/A' Distinction and Movement Theory," Doctoral dissertation, MIT, Cambridge, Mass.

Maling, J.: 1984, "Non-clause-bounded Reflexives in Modern Icelandic," *Linguistics and Philosophy*, 7, 211–41.

May, R.: 1977, "The Grammar of Quantification," Ph.D. dissertation, MIT, Cambridge, Mass.

May, R.: 1985, *Logical Form*, MIT Press, Cambridge, Mass.

Montalbetti, M.: 1984, "After Binding," Ph.D. dissertation, MIT, Cambridge, Mass.

Munn, A.: 1993, "Topics in the Syntax and Semantics of Coordinate Structures," Ph.D. dissertation, University of Maryland, College Park.

Munn, A.: 1994, "A Minimalist Account of Reconstruction Asymmetries," *Proceedings of NELS 24*, GLSA, University of Massachusetts, Amherst, 397–410.

Neale, S.: 1990, *Descriptions*, MIT Press, Cambridge, Mass.

Nishigauchi, T.: 1990, *Quantification in the Theory of Grammar*, Reidel, Dordrecht.

Nunes, J.: 1994, "Linearization of Non-trivial Chains at PF," MS, University of Maryland, College Park.

Otani, K. and J. Whitman: 1991, "V-raising and VP-ellipsis," *Linguistic Inquiry*, 22, 345–58.

Ottósson, K.: 1993, "Double Object Small Clauses and Reanalysis in Icelandic Passives," *Proceedings of WCCFL 11*, Stanford, 371–87.

Pesetsky, D.: 1982, "Paths and Categories," Ph.D. dissertation, MIT, Cambridge, Mass.

Pesetsky, D.: 1987, "WH-in-situ: Movement and Unselective Binding," in E. Reuland and A. ter Meulen (eds) *The Representation of (In)definiteness*, MIT Press, Cambridge, Mass.

Pollock, J-Y.: 1989, "Verb Movement, Universal Grammar and the Structure of IP," *Linguistic Inquiry*, 20, 365–424.

Progovac, L.: 1988, "A Binding Approach to Polarity Sensitivity," Ph.D. dissertation, USC, Los Angeles.

Reinhart, T.: 1983, *Anaphora and Semantic Interpretation*, Croom Helm, London.

Reinhart, T.: 1991, "Non-quantificational LF," in A. Kasher (ed.) *The Chomskyan Turn*, Blackwell, Oxford.

Reinhart, T.: 1992, "Interpreting WH-in-situ," MS, University of Tel-Aviv.

Rizzi, L.: 1982, *Issues in Italian Syntax*, Foris, Dordrecht.

Rizzi, L.: 1990, *Relativized Minimality*, MIT Press, Cambridge, Mass.

Rizzi, L: 1991, "On the Status of Referential Indices," in A. Kasher (ed.) *The Chomskyan Turn*, Blackwell, Oxford.

Roberts, I.: 1992, "Restructuring and Clitic Movement," MS, University of Wales, Bangor.

Ross, J.R.: 1967, "Constraints on Variables in Syntax," Ph.D. dissertation, MIT, Cambridge, Mass.

Rudin, C.: 1988, "On Multiple Questions and Multiple WH Fronting," *Natural Language and Linguistic Theory*, 6, 445–501.

Safir, K.: 1985, *Syntactic Chains*, Cambridge University Press, Cambridge.

Safir, K.: 1987, "What Explains the Definiteness Effect?" in E. Reuland and A. ter Meulen (eds) *The Representation of (In)definiteness*, MIT Press, Cambridge, Mass.

Sag, I.: 1976, "Deletion and Logical Form," Ph.D. dissertation, MIT, Cambridge, Mass.

Saito, M.: 1985, "Some Asymmetries in Japanese and their Theoretical Implications," Ph.D. dissertation, MIT, Cambridge, Mass.

Saito, M.: 1992, "Long Distance Scrambling in Japanese," *Journal of East Asian Linguistics*, 1, 69–118.

Schein, B.: 1993, *Plurals and Events*, MIT Press, Cambridge, Mass.

Schmitt, C.: 1993, "Aspectual Selection and Composition: the Case of *Ser* and *Estar*," MS, University of Maryland, College Park.

Shlonsky, U.: 1987, "Null and Displaced Subjects," Ph.D. dissertation, MIT, Cambridge, Mass.

Stowell, T.: 1981, "The Origins of Phrase Structure," Ph.D. dissertation, MIT, Cambridge, Mass.

Stowell, T.: 1983, "Subjects across Categories," *The Linguistic Review*, 2, 285–312.

Stowell, T.: 1986, "Psych-Movement in the Mapping from D-structure to Logical Form," *GLOW* Abstract.

Stowell, T.: 1991, "Small Clause Restructuring," in R. Freidin (ed.) *Principles and Parameters in Comparative Grammar*, MIT Press, Cambridge, Mass.

Szabolcsi, A. and F. Zwarts: 1992–3, "Weak Islands and an Algebraic Semantics for Scope Taking," *Natural Language Semantics*, 1, 235–84.

Tada, H.: 1992, "Nominative Objects in Japanese," MS, MIT, Cambridge, Mass.

Tanaka, H.: 1993, "Invisible Movement in *Sika-Nai* and the Linear Crossing Constraint," MS, McGill University, Montreal.

Takahashi, D.: 1993a, "Movement of Wh-phrases in Japanese," *Natural Language and Linguistic Theory*, 11, 655–78.

Takahashi, D.: 1993b, "On Antecedent Contained Deletion," MS, University of Connecticut, Storrs.

Thompson, E.: 1993, "The Emergence of the Definite Determiner in the History of English, MS, University of Maryland, College Park.

Tsai, W.T.D.: 1994, "On Economizing A-Bar Dependencies," Ph.D. dissertation, MIT, Cambridge, Mass.

Uriagereka, J.: 1988, "On Government," Ph.D. dissertation, University of Connecticut, Storrs.

Uriagereka, J.: 1994, "Rhyme and Reason," MS, University of Maryland, College Park.

Watanabe, A.: 1991, "Wh-in-situ, Subjacency and Chain Formation," MS, MIT, Cambridge, Mass.

Watanabe, A.: 1993, "AGR-based Case Theory and its Interaction with the A-Bar System," Ph.D. dissertation, MIT, Cambridge, Mass.

Watanabe, S.: 1994, "(Anti-)Superiority as Weak Crossover," MS, USC, Los Angeles.

Webelhuth, G.: 1989, "Syntactic Saturation Phenomena and the Modern Germanic Languages, Ph.D. dissertation, University of Massachusetts, Amherst.

Webelhuth, G. (ed.) 1995, *Government and Binding Theory and the Minimalist Program*, Blackwell, Oxford.

Weinberg, A.: 1988, "Locality Principles in Syntax and Parsing," Ph.D. dissertation, MIT, Cambridge, Mass.

Williams, E.: 1986, "The Reassignment of the Functions of LF," *Linguistic Inquiry*, 17, 265–99.

Zanuttini, R.: 1991, "Syntactic Properties of Sentential Negation," Ph.D. dissertation, University of Pennsylvania, Philadelphia.

Zubizarreta, M.L.: 1992, "The Lexical Encoding of Scope Relations among Arguments," *Syntax and Semantics*, 26, 211–58.

Index

Printed and bound by CPI Group (UK) Ltd, Croydon, CR0 4YY

16/04/2023

03210786-0001